LONDON'S BEST SHOPS

timeout.com

Published by

Time Out Guides Limited
Universal House
251 Tottenham Court Road
London W1T 7AB
Tel +44 (0)20 7813 3000
Fax +44 (0)20 7813 6001
email guides@timeout.com
www.timeout.com

Editorial

Editors Dan Jones, Sarah Guy
Researchers Danielle-Louise Watt, William Crow, Matthew Bremner
Proofreader Ros Sales
Indexer Holly Pick

Editorial Director Sarah Guy
Management Accountant Margaret Wright

Design

Senior Designer Kei Ishimaru
Designer Darryl Bell
Guides Commercial Senior Designer Jason Tansley

Picture Desk

Picture Editor Jael Marschner
Picture Researchers Ben Rowe, Oliver Puglisi

Advertising

Sales Director St John Betteridge
Account Managers Deborah Maclaren, Bobbie Kelsall-Freeman
@ The Media Sales House

Marketing

Group Commercial Art Director Anthony Huggins
Head of Circulation Dan Collins

Production

Group Production Manager Brendan McKeown
Production Controller Katie Mulhern-Bhudia

Time Out Group

Chairman & Founder Tony Elliott
Chief Executive Officer Aksel Van der Wal
Editor-in-Chief Tim Arthur
Group Financial Director Paul Rakkar
UK Chief Commercial Officer David Pepper
Time Out International Ltd MD Cathy Runciman
Group IT Director Simon Chappell
Group Marketing Director Carolyn Sims

Sections in the Guide were written by: Dan Jones (One-Stop, Fashion), Christina Stewart (Skincare & Cosmetics), Sophie Lanning (Perfumeries & Herbalists), Clare Considine (Furniture & Homewares, Vintage Furniture & Homewares, Books, Records & CDs, Musical Insutments, Pets, Drink), Ronnie Haydon-Jones (Gardens & Flowers, Crafts, Hobbies & Parties, Babies & Children), Derek Adams (Electronics & Photography), Matthew Bremner (Sport), Emma McWhinney (Food), Joshua Minopoli (Streetwise).

The Editors would like to thank Yessi Bello Perez, Anna Norman.

Maps London Underground map supplied by Transport for London.

Photography pages 9 (top), 33, 44, 46 (bottom), 199 (bottom), 202 Ed Marshall; pages 13, 32, 57, 98, 196, 197, 210 (right and bottom), 224 (left), 227, 230, 231, 253, 255 Rob Greig; pages 21, 194 Andrew Brackenbury; pages 25, 26, 120, 262, 265 Ben Rowe; pages 28, 29 Alys Tomlinson; pages 30/31, 61, 134, 158, 164, 165, 178, 189, 191, 195, 199 (top), 200, 203 (bottom), 205, 208, 209, 223, 247 Ming Tang-Evans; pages 37, 137 Elisabeth Blanchet; pages 42, 94, 144, 163, 180, 188, 210 (left), 222, 224 (right), 250 Britta Jaschinski; pages 46 (top), 136, 204, 213 (top and left) Michelle Grant; page 47 Jess Orchard; pages 48/49 Celia Topping; page 54 Chris Tubbs; page 73 (top) Debbie Bragg; pages 73 (bottom), 74, 75 Melvyn Vincent; pages 90, 91 Jean Goldsmith; page 93 Michael Franke; page 97 (left) Nic Shonfeld; page 110 Rosie Parsons; page 113 Tom Leighton; pages 116, 117, 192 Scott Wishart; page 135 Richard Booth; page 140 Dennis Gilbert/VIEW; page 179 Gemma Day; page 146 Andrew Porter; pages 154, 155 Nick Harvey; page 198 Josh Kearns; page 203 (top) Iwan Essery; page 213 (bottom right) Nick Ballon; page 215 Louise Hayward-Schiefer; page 218 Gemma Day; page 220 Heloise Bergman; page 233 Tyson Sadlo; page 245 Rogan Macdonald; page 252 Oliver Knight; page 263 Christina Theisen; page 266 Tricia De Courcy Ling; page 267 Shara Henderson.

The following images were provided by the featured establishment: pages 9, 11 (middle and bottom), 12, 20, 22, 24, 27, 34, 35, 36, 39, 40, 41, 56, 59, 60, 62, 63, 67, 68, 70, 71, 77, 78, 81, 82, 83, 84, 85, 86, 88, 97 (right), 101, 103, 104, 106, 107, 108, 109, 111, 112, 115, 118, 119, 122, 123, 125, 126, 127, 128, 129, 130, 141, 143, 145, 147, 153, 157, 160, 161, 166, 168, 170, 171, 172, 174, 175, 176, 185, 186, 206, 207, 217, 232, 234, 235, 238, 242, 243, 244, 246, 249, 254, 256, 258.

Printer Wyndeham Group.
Time Out Group uses paper products that are environmentally friendly, from well managed forests and mills that use certified (PEFC) Chain of Custody pulp in their production.

ISBN 978-1-905042-76-0
ISSN 17526167-02

Distribution by Comag Specialist (01895 433 800).
For further distribution details, see www.timeout.com.

Introduction

With its grand department stores, avant-garde boutiques, vibrant markets, glamorous designer flagships and classic book, record and accessories shops, London will always be one of the world's most exciting cities for shopping. Its size and diversity can, however, make it an overwhelming – not to mention exhausting – place in which to flex the plastic. To save you pounding the busy streets in search of the often quite hidden gems, our knowledgeable team of shopping experts has narrowed the huge number of London shops down to around 500 of the very best – places that aren't just marketplaces, but which engage customers through lovely interiors, exemplary service, original products and a personal atmosphere.

Independent shops exemplify this experience-led spirit better than the large chain stores (the best of which aren't far behind, however), which is why we've chosen to include so many of them in this guide. From old favourites such as John Sandoe bookshop in Chelsea, to newcomers such as interiors outlet Folklore in Islington, London's indie shops are getting better and better, despite some sad recession-induced closures.

Our **Shop Talk** interviews illuminate what it's like to own an independent shop in London, and show that, despite unstable economic conditions, things are looking fairly positive for the city's dedicated shopkeepers. Opening a small business is always going to pose a degree of financial risk, but the fact that so many enterprising folk are still prepared to take that risk is testament to their faith that a sizeable number of city dwellers and visitors will be there to support them. And, as we discuss in the feature on pages 9-13, this support appears to be increasing, with the growth of an experience-fused shopping scene led by the capital's concept stores and pop-up shops.

Our **Streetwise** features flag up shopping streets containing a high number of these places, and which are therefore some of the most enjoyable places in which to shop. They also highlight the chasm that has formed between the high street and the indie boutiques.

London has long been associated with cutting-edge fashion and design, but these scenes have become especially active of late, spawning a plethora of avant-garde boutiques. Like the food industry, the clothing sector has been under the eco spotlight over the past few years, and, consequently, a more eco-minded brand of consumerism has been developing. The number of shops led by ethical and green principles is still in a minority, but shops such as Unpackaged – now moved to bigger premises in Hackney – gives us hope.

One good way to shop more ethically, of course, is to buy second-hand, and London's vintage and thrift shops are looking stronger than ever. Blitz, London's first vintage department store, opened just off Brick Lane in 2011, and that whole area is a good hunting ground for pre-loved fashion and homewares. Soho's Berwick Street is also something of a vintage hotspot, and there are smaller second-hand clothes boutiques now peppered around the city. We also list the best of the capital's many charity shops – Pimlico is a good spot to start looking for buried treasures.

There may have been a tightening of belts over the past few years due to the economic doom and gloom, but, partly as a consequence of this, many of us have become more discerning about where we shop. This guide will help you get to the heart of the city's exciting consumer culture and discover its myriad of lovely stores. Happy shopping!

About the Guide

This guide to London's shops isn't meant to be completely comprehensive; instead, we have tried to select what we believe are the very best of the capital's shops. If you feel we've missed somewhere exceptional, or included a place that's gone downhill, please email us at guides@timeout.com.

Opening hours

Although many of the shops listed in this guide keep regular store hours, others are small concerns run from private addresses or workshops that have erratic opening hours, or are open by appointment only. In such cases, the times given are a guide as to when to phone, not when to visit.

The opening times were correct at the time of going to press, but if you're going out of your way to visit a particular shop, always phone first to check (especially as stores are constantly launching and closing down in London). Many outlets extend their opening times in summer to benefit from tourist traffic and in the run-up to Christmas. Some are closed on bank holidays or have reduced opening times.

Credit cards and abbreviations

Most shops featured in this book accept all of the major credit cards; if they don't accept plastic, we have indicated this in the listings. Some larger shops and department stores accept euros as well as sterling. For shops in this guide that sell clothes and/or fashion accessories, we have indicated whether they sell menswear and/or womenswear with the letters **M** and **W**, respectively. Childrenswear is represented by a **C**.

Prices

Any prices listed in this guide were accurate at the time of writing, but are subject to change.

Mail order and online

Many of the shops listed have online ordering services; visit their websites for details.

Branches

We have included details for shops' London branches after the listings and in the A-Z Index. For shops with branches throughout the city, please see the phone directory or the shop's website for the location of your nearest. Note that branches may have different opening hours from the reviewed shop, so it is advisable to call to check times before visiting.

FILLING THE TOWN WITH ARTISTS

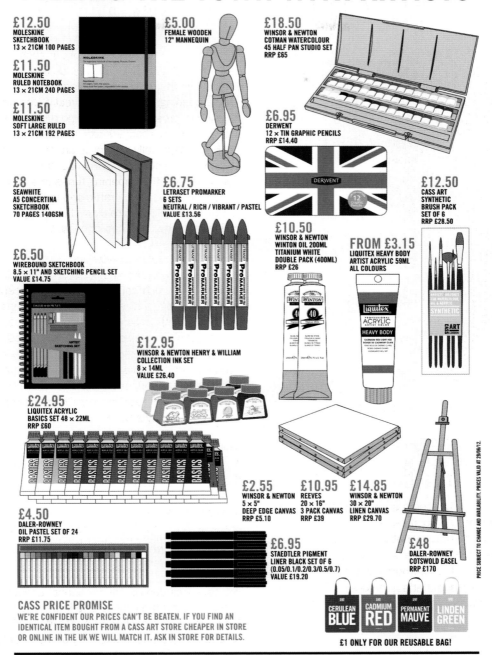

£12.50
MOLESKINE
SKETCHBOOK
13 × 21CM 100 PAGES

£11.50
MOLESKINE
RULED NOTEBOOK
13 × 21CM 240 PAGES

£11.50
MOLESKINE
SOFT LARGE RULED
13 × 21CM 192 PAGES

£8
SEAWHITE
A5 CONCERTINA
SKETCHBOOK
70 PAGES 140GSM

£6.50
WIREBOUND SKETCHBOOK
8.5 × 11" AND SKETCHING PENCIL SET
VALUE £14.75

£24.95
LIQUITEX ACRYLIC
BASICS SET 48 × 22ML
RRP £60

£4.50
DALER-ROWNEY
OIL PASTEL SET OF 24
RRP £11.75

£5.00
FEMALE WOODEN
12" MANNEQUIN

£6.75
LETRASET PROMARKER
6 SETS
NEUTRAL / RICH / VIBRANT / PASTEL
VALUE £13.56

£12.95
WINSOR & NEWTON HENRY & WILLIAM
COLLECTION INK SET
8 × 14ML
VALUE £26.40

£18.50
WINSOR & NEWTON
COTMAN WATERCOLOUR
45 HALF PAN STUDIO SET
RRP £65

£6.95
DERWENT
12 × TIN GRAPHIC PENCILS
RRP £14.40

£10.50
WINSOR & NEWTON
WINTON OIL 200ML
TITANIUM WHITE
DOUBLE PACK (400ML)
RRP £26

FROM £3.15
LIQUITEX HEAVY BODY
ARTIST ACRYLIC 59ML
ALL COLOURS

£12.50
CASS ART
SYNTHETIC
BRUSH PACK
SET OF 6
RRP £28.50

£2.55
WINSOR & NEWTON
5 × 5"
DEEP EDGE CANVAS
RRP £5.10

£10.95
REEVES
20 × 16"
3 PACK CANVAS
RRP £39

£14.85
WINSOR & NEWTON
30 × 20"
LINEN CANVAS
RRP £29.70

£6.95
STAEDTLER PIGMENT
LINER BLACK SET OF 6
(0.05/0.1/0.2/0.3/0.5/0.7)
VALUE £19.20

£48
DALER-ROWNEY
COTSWOLD EASEL
RRP £170

PRICE SUBJECT TO CHANGE AND AVAILABILITY. PRICES VALID AT 29/06/12.

CASS PRICE PROMISE
WE'RE CONFIDENT OUR PRICES CAN'T BE BEATEN. IF YOU FIND AN IDENTICAL ITEM BOUGHT FROM A CASS ART STORE CHEAPER IN STORE OR ONLINE IN THE UK WE WILL MATCH IT. ASK IN STORE FOR DETAILS.

CERULEAN BLUE / CADMIUM RED / PERMANENT MAUVE / LINDEN GREEN

£1 ONLY FOR OUR REUSABLE BAG!

FLAGSHIP STORE: 66–67 COLEBROOKE ROW ISLINGTON N1
13 CHARING CROSS ROAD WC2 (NEXT TO THE NATIONAL GALLERY), 58–62 HEATH STREET HAMPSTEAD NW3,
24 BERWICK ST SOHO W1, 220 KENSINGTON HIGH ST W8. ALL STORES OPEN 7 DAYS

CASS ART LONDON
WWW.CASSART.CO.UK

Contents

ST MARTIN'S COURTYARD
COVENT GARDEN

Covent Garden's Newest Shopping and Dining Destination

Westfield Stratford City

London's Shopping Evolution

The retail landscape changes to deal with lean times. By **Dan Jones**.

When this guide was last published, in 2011, Londoners were in the throes of tea parties and vintage bunting, cupcakes and retro fashion fairs, in a reimagining of thrifty wartime culture. We would battle the recession with strong cups of tea and sewing circles, jumble sales and Victoria sponges – turning our backs on the flashiness of luxury retail that seemed suddenly at odds with austerity Britain. At best, it meant the empowerment of indie designers and entrepreneurs who found themselves setting up stalls, mini-markets, and pop-up shops. At worst, throwaway fashion brands seemed to flourish, and the adopted World War II slogan of 'Keep calm and carry on' appeared on just about everything, from dog bowls to G-strings.

The financial crisis continues to be felt, cutting through any feel-good Olympic effect, and both independent stores and established chains continue to close – but there are openings too, and in 2012 many of them have been high-end. It seems London shopping has polarised; the capital's shoppers are thriftier than ever, but it seems they will occasionally invest in aspirational brands, too. This leaves the middle ground squeezed out by luxury fashion on the one hand and budget labels on the other. What's more, shopping in London's latest stores is less about the purchase and more and more about the experiences (reactive robotics and giant iPads on legs included).

In September 2012, budget retailer **Primark** opened its second London flagship close to Tottenham Court Road tube station, bookending Oxford Street with two gigantic stores. The brand has its critics, namely those who oppose the idea

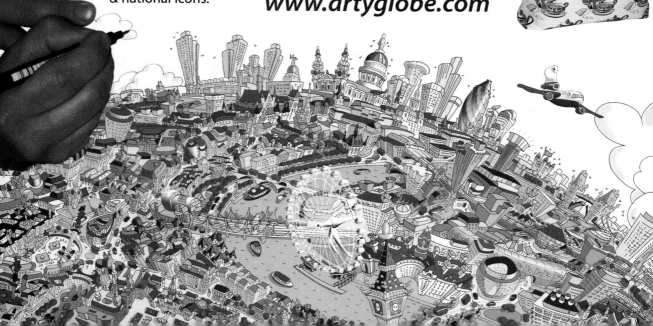

of throwaway fashion. But for every hater out on the street, there are 20 fans in the stores, fighting over floral-print leggings and knicker shorts – and the brand is more popular than ever. Still, after a tricky few years in the press (including a child labour accusation – proven false), there is something defiant about Primark opening an 82,000 square foot store on London's most popular shopping street. And what a grown-up store it is: four vast storeys of men's, women's and kids' clothing and accessories, plus homewares. And what an interior it is – a slick sci-fi blast of dark grey, with black brick walls and chrome fittings, neon signage and overwhelmingly huge and bright LED video screens – it's the *Blade Runner* of flagships.

At the other end of the scale, size-wise, is another new tech-focused shop, Nike FuelStation. It's a tiny concept store at Shoreditch's brilliant **Boxpark** mall – a five-year pop-up built from shipping containers – that has an interior that tracks your movements, projecting them on to a giant screen. But both Nike FuelStation and Primark are bettered by McQ, the **Alexander McQueen** diffusion brand that has docked on Mayfair's Dover Street. Step into the Georgian townhouse, and you'll be greeted by a large white digital table – rather like a giant iPad. From here you can project catwalk images and videos on to the wall using small viewing boxes – it's weirdly addictive. Downstairs, past the Brutalism-inspired concrete walls and thick red carpets, there are 'gesture-control' digital mirrors where you can photograph yourself – and then email the results – posing in looks from the collection. **Burberry**'s Regent Street flagship was 2012's biggest and most impressive shop opening, with its digital rainstorms and garments that activate video content behind changing room mirrors (something of a shock when you're shoehorning yourself into a pair of too-skinny skinny jeans).

The point of all these high-tech add-ons, of course, is to get people into the stores; and if all this knob twiddling and button pressing makes for an inclusive experience, and brings the shopper one step closer to the till, so much the better. And if you're peddling £18,000 croc leather totes, you're going to need all the bells and whistles you can muster.

Away from this unreal world, there are London shops that rely for allure on their own creative concepts, idiosyncratic stock, and great service – and they're often just a block or so back from London's most iconic streets. Bond Street, for instance, is bettered for creativity by its neighbours Dover Street and Mount Street – the former housing APC, Vanessa Bruno and Dover

Primark

Burberry

Street Market, the latter, Balenciaga, Marc Jacobs, Rick Owens and Ralph Lauren's RRL. A few steps from Oxford Street, Soho retail flourishes with the recent opening of cult skate brand **Supreme** and a re-opening of sneaker boutique **Foot Patrol**. In the east, famous Brick Lane is second to neighbouring **Redchurch Street** with its Aubin & Wills, APC, Sunspel and Aesop stores, with the MHL by Margaret Howell shop just around the corner.

The east, particularly Dalston, continues to be particularly fashion-led, with any number of new openings, both vintage-focused – **Beyond Retro**, **Pelicans & Parrots**, the **Princess May Car Boot Sale** and an impressive new branch of **Traid** (106-108 Kingsland High Street, E8 2NS, 7923 4475) – and otherwise. It's in Hackney that we've seen the revival of some almost-extinct street markets (**Broadway Market** gets bigger all the time, and **Chatsworth Road**, further east in E5, has proved itself too); also exciting is the sucess of **Brixton Village**, south of the river.

At the other end of the scale, London's large-scale developments continue to thrive, and the biggest is **Westfield Stratford City**. The £1.45 billion retail site snakes through the London Olympic Park, with 300 retail units – the cornerstones of which are gigantic versions of John Lewis, Marks & Spencer and Waitrose – 70 restaurants, bars and cafés, and a 17-screen digital cinema. The mega-mall flourished before and during the Olympics, but its long-term legacy remains to be seen. Subtle change is also under way in Covent Garden. Many Londoners have an affection for the historic neighbourhood, but most have tended to give it a wide berth, thanks to the mishmash of retailers dedicated to the tourist pound. But under the watchful eye of Covent Garden brand manager Bev Churchill, one-time marketing director at Selfridges, the Piazza and surrounding streets have slowly begun to evolve. So far, it's been an interesting overhaul that includes Ralph Lauren's Rugby brand, one of the world's largest **Apple** stores, NYC-cult store and label **Opening Ceremony** and a pop-up from Chanel. The scheme has its critics, but – so far – Covent Garden has changed for the better.

As the recession continues to add pressure to London's shopping landscape, there's a certain pleasure in witnessing the tenacity of the capital's shopkeepers, from fledgling stallholders to mega-brands managers. Shopping events are on the increase – particularly pop-ups – and there's ambition to be seen in both big and small developments.

Supreme

BE DELIGHTED
by YOUR CITY

Your City Break doesn't have to cost the earth

Trees for Cities

Reduce the impact of your flight by donating to Trees for Cities

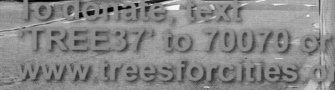

To donate, text 'TREE37' to 70070 or visit www.treesforcities.org

Trees for Cities, Prince Consort Lodge, Kennington Park, Kennington Park Place, London SE11 4AS
Tel. +44 (0)20 7587 1320; Charity registration 1032154

One-Stop

One-Stop

These days, department stores aren't just rather dull places to buy all your essentials under one roof: those listed in this guide contain top-notch eateries, cutting-edge fashion, fabulous beauty halls, indulgent spas, covetable homewares, and an entire market town's worth of mini-shop concessions, with a roster of pop-up concessions now also part of the parcel. While London has always been famous for its department stores, we didn't know just how much better they could be until **Selfridges** (*see p24*) upped the ante by bringing in niche labels, exciting interior design and regular in-store events. And the store continues to innovate. Even the more classic stalwarts, **John Lewis** (*see p22*), **Liberty** (*see p23*) and **Fortnum & Mason** (*see p21*), have submitted to the winds of change, with major nip and tucks in recent times that have ushered in swanky food halls and fabulous beauty counters.

The city's markets have enjoyed revived popularity in recent times – as evidenced by the continual crowds at the evolution of both **Borough Market** (*see p42*) and **Broadway Market** (*see p46*) into places to be seen on a sunny Saturday. Bermondsey's **Maltby Street** (*see p48*) is also emerging as a Saturday morning foodie spot, after several ex-Borough Market traders set up stalls there in late 2010.

Markets are an asset to any local economy as they draw consumers to the shops that surround them.

Mayfair's royal arcades are often overlooked by residents, but they have more to offer than the quaint looks the tourists love. These genteel proto-shopping centres have been back in the spotlight since the daddy of them all, **Burlington Arcade** (*see p30*), was restored to its Regency glory. Meanwhile, Brixton's Granville Arcade has been given a new lease of life as **Brixton Village** (*see p29*), housing a delightful selection of down-to-earth vintage fashion and home accessories boutiques, alongside retro-inspired and exotic food spots.

Shopping centres, meanwhile, are getting bigger and bigger, and are symbolic of the chasm that has developed within London's shopping scene; at the opposite end of the scale to the mall shoppers – who were treated to the opening of **Westfield Stratford City** (*see p27*) in summer 2011 – are those who are embracing London's increasingly experience-led shopping culture, frequenting the increasingly popular concept stores such as **Dover Street Market** (*see p36*), **Darkroom** (*see p35*) and **Wolf & Badger** (*see p41*) and lifestyle boutiques, which offer a range of covetable products under one, normally very stylish, roof.

Fortnum & Mason

Department Stores

Fortnum & Mason

181 Piccadilly, W1A 1ER (7734 8040, www.fortnum andmason.com). Green Park or Piccadilly Circus tube. **Open** 10am-9pm Mon-Sat; 11.30am-7pm Sun.

The results of a £24 million, two-year revamp – revealed in 2007 (300 years after the store's opening in 1707) – are still stunning: F&M retains all that was marvellous about its Georgian past while changing just enough to position itself as a 21st-century shopping experience. A sweeping spiral staircase soars through the four-storey building, while light floods down from a central glass dome. The iconic F&M eau de nil blue and gold colour scheme with flashes of rose pink abounds on both the store design and the packaging of the fabulous ground-floor treats (chocolates, biscuits, teas and preserves). The first floor is for homewares: china and glassware as well as finishing touches such as silver scoops for stilton, eau de nil linen and cashmere hot-water bottles; there are regular cooking sessions too. The second floor is home to beauty rooms, fashion accessories, jewellery and a perfumery, while the third floor has menswear, luggage and writing accessories, along with an excellent wrapping service. The five restaurants, all redesigned by David Collins, are equally impressive, with the ice-cream parlour a welcome addition. The food hall in the basement has a huge range of fresh and dried produce, as well as top-notch wines from all over the world. In March 2012 Fortnum's reworked St James's restaurant was relaunched as the Diamond Jubilee Tea Salon. Look out, too, for craft exhibitions, literary lunches and gallery collaborations. Fortnum & Mason is fabulously redolent of a time when luxury meant the highest degree of comfort rather than ostentation and remains a treat for all who venture through its oak doors – and for those who don't: Fortnum's will drop off your lunch sandwiches, via delivery men in tails, to any local address.

Harrods

87-135 Brompton Road, SW1X 7XL (7730 1234, www.harrods.com). Knightsbridge tube. **Open** 10am-8pm Mon-Sat; noon-6pm Sun (browsing from 11.30am).

It's sublime, it's ridiculous, and no trip to London would really be complete without a visit to this hugely impressive department store. Previous owner Mohammed Al-Fayed left a big gold mark on the place – from the blinging Egyptian escalators to the Dodi and Diana memorial. But there's also lots of high fashion, a legendary fairground food hall – and an absolutely delightful pet department that sells a range of live furry friends as well as spa services including 'pawdicures' and pet-friendly profiteroles. The store that boasts of selling everything works hard to inject its image with ever more style: always strong on fashion, Harrods offers women a 10,000sq ft Designer Studio with a host of British designer launches, as well as swimwear, Designer Plus (for the larger lady), a wedding dress boutique and a Denim Lounge packed with coveted jeans lines. Menswear on the ground and lower ground floors provides a gentlemen's club atmosphere where tailoring, fragrance, a cigar shop and a huge shoe salon are joined by the instore Tom Ford boutique. In September 2012 the Luxury and Designer Accessories rooms opened, doubling Harrod's accessory offering to 40,000sq ft, with mini big brand boutiques from Chanel and Gucci to the world's first Tom Ford Accessories boutique and an Elliot Rhodes 'belt bar.' The excellent sports section, with equipment and clothing for a vast range of sporting occasions, now also has dedicated Nike and Adidas areas. Much more than just a tourist attraction.

Harvey Nichols

109-125 Knightsbridge, SW1X 7RJ (7235 5000, www.harveynichols.com). Knightsbridge tube. **Open** *Store* 10am-8pm Mon-Sat; noon-6pm Sun (browsing from 11.30am). *Café* 8am-11pm Mon-Sat; 11am-6pm Sun. *Restaurant* noon-11pm, Mon-Sat; noon-5pm Sun.

Harvey Nichols

Harvey Nichols is one of the most glamorous fashion destinations in town. While it lacks in the quirkiness of Liberty and the sheer size of Selfridges, it makes up for it in its airy interior and dependable modernity. You'll find a worthy clutch of unique brands over its eight floors of beauty, fashion, food and home. In beauty, there's skin-firming Rodial and La Prairie, with Acqua di Parma for men, as well as beauty services that include Beyond MediSpa, with a team of doctors and medical 'aestheticians', and the Daniel Hersheson hair salon. Fashion, on the first and fourth floors, showcases emerging British talent (Peter Pilotto, Mary Katrantzou), new brands (Lulu & Co) and old favourites Donna Karan and Marc Jacobs. A Sneaker Wall displays hi-tops and plimsolls by Christian Louboutin and others, and then there's the denim phenomenon… everyone from Lanvin to D&G. The fine foodmarket on the fifth floor boasts over 600 exclusive products in Harvey Nichols' smart black and silver livery, along with accessories and kitchen products such as the wonderfully whimsical Blaue Blume china. Those with a taste for luxury can adjourn to the stylish bar, while hunger pangs can be sated by Wagamama, Yo! Sushi or the fab Fifth Floor restaurant and café. HN's newest additions include impressive World of Burberry and revamped DKNY spaces.

John Lewis

300 Oxford Street, W1A 1EX (7629 7711, www.johnlewis.co.uk). Bond Street or Oxford Circus tube. **Open** 9.30am-8pm Mon-Wed, Fri; 9.30am-9pm Thur; 9.30am-7pm Sat; noon-6pm Sun (browsing from 11.30am).

With a sensible ratio of quality to price for all its products, John Lewis retains its rightful crown as the retail world's safe pair of hands. Arguably the strongest selling point is the lower ground-floor cookware and white goods section, where an excellent range of kitchen staples is backed up by exemplary customer service. Well-

Harrods. See p21.

informed staff will guide you to the right product for your purse, delivery is usually smooth and the after-care service, should you need it, admirable. The food hall from Waitrose has speciality food galore, a walk-in cheese room and a plethora of check-out staff to keep the queues moving swiftly. The relaunched ground-floor beauty hall – almost always packed – stocks niche lines such as This Works and Bliss, alongside stalwarts like Benefit, MAC and Clarins. There's also an Elemis spa pod for express facials and Lancome and Guerlain treatment rooms. Under the auspices of the buying & brand director, Peter Ruis, fashion at John Lewis is becoming more directional, with labels such as Day Birger et Mikkelsen being added together with exclusive ranges such as Somerset by Alice Temperley (the store's fastest selling collection ever, at the time of writing) and men's designer Joe Casely-Hayford for John Lewis. The clutch of respectable classics is also still strong, with Coast, Jaeger and Fenn Wright Manson among them. Other strengths include technology, home furnishings, crafts, schoolwear, and the new childrenswear floor, offering a Nintendo entertainment area and a dedicated Lego hall.

Branches Wood Street, Kingston upon Thames, Surrey KT1 1TE (8547 3000); Brent Cross Shopping Centre, NW4 3FL (8202 6535); **Peter Jones** Sloane Square, SW1W 8EL (7730 3434); Westfield Stratford, Montifichet Road, E20 1EL (8532 3500).

Liberty

Regent Street, W1B 5AH (7734 1234, www.liberty.co.uk). Oxford Circus tube.
Open 10am-8pm Mon-Sat; noon-6pm Sun.
London's mock Tudor masterpiece, Liberty is an experience to savour; artful and arresting window displays, exciting new collections, exclusive collaborations and luxe labels help to create a very special atmosphere. The wood-panelled interior (the shop has been open since 1875) provides the perfect backdrop for such high-end fashion labels as Vivienne Westwood and Alexander McQueen, with a long-standing emphasis on British designers, including Richard Nicoll, Jonathan Saunders, Antipodium and Christopher Kane. Menswear lines – in the huge basement level men's department – come from APC, Norse Projects, YMC and Spencer Hart, with the latter providing made-to-measure tailoring exclusive to

Best for...

Food treats
Harrods (*see p21*); **Harvey Nichols** (*see p21*); **Selfridges** (*see p24*); **Fortnum & Mason** (*see p21*).

Creative concepts and special events
Selfridges (*see p24*).

Directional fashion
Liberty (*see left*); **Selfridges** (*see p24*); **Harvey Nichols** (*see p21*).

Homewares
John Lewis (*see left*).

Luggage
Harrods (*see p21*); **Selfridges** (*see p24*); **John Lewis** (*see left*)

Gifts
Liberty (*see left*); **Harrods** (*see p21*); **Fortnum & Mason** (*see p21*)

High Street brands and on-trend concessions
Selfridges (*see p24*).

Footwear – from flats to flatforms
Selfridges (*see p24*); **Harrods** (*see p21*).

ONE-STOP

Liberty. The array of beautiful and original jewellery includes pieces by Jordan Askill, Eddie Borgo and Alex Monroe, while the new accessories salon – a sun-lit space leading on to Kingly Street – stocks Liberty's edit of it-bags, with brands pointing towards the heavyweights, such as Mulberry and Chloé. And despite being fashion forward, Liberty still respects its dressmaking heritage with an extensive range of cottons in the third-floor haberdashery department, with Liberty furnishing fabrics and curtain-making up on fourth. Stationery also pays court to the traditional (alongside the modern), with beautiful Liberty of London notebooks, address books and photo albums embossed with the art nouveau Ianthe print. Interiors are equally impressive with regular exhibitions showcasing new and classic furniture designs on the fourth floor, alongside a dazzling permanent collection of 20th-century classics such as Charles and Ray Eames's famous armchair. Meanwhile, a well-edited collection of homeware includes ethereal and romantic Astier de Villatte ceramics and beautiful silk and Egyptian cotton bedlinen. The ground-floor beauty hall includes Le Labo and Byredo fragrances, and in February 2012 a group of beauty treatment rooms opened, overlooking Carnaby Street. In the basement, the Margaret Dabbs Sole Spa continues to work its magic on shoppers' feet.

Selfridges

400 Oxford Street, W1A 1AB (0800 123 400, www.selfridges.com). Bond Street or Marble Arch tube.
Open 9.30am-11pm Mon-Sat; 11.30am-6pm Sun.
Selfridges – one of *Time Out*'s favourite department stores – celebrated its centenary in 2009. With its plethora of concession boutiques, store-wide themed events, the world's largest shoe department, loopy pop-up shops and collections from the hottest new brands, it's as dynamic as a department store can be, and a first port of call for stylish one-stop shopping. The store changes regularly and 2012 saw a host of big improvements, with the beauty hall tripling in size to 5,000sq ft (with a focus on the experiential – make-overs, manicures, blow-drying – the works), new men's fashion and children's spaces, and the reopening of the roof café, under the auspices of Daylesford. The basement is chock-full of hip home accessories and stylish but practical kitchen equipment (think Alessi and the UK's largest Le Creuset concession), while on the ground floor the Wonder Room – 19,000sq ft of luxury brands – goes from strength to strength. There's plenty of new draws in the ground floor food hall, too. Too many shoppers bypass these delights as they make a bee-line for Selfridges's excellent fashion floors. With a winning combination of new talent, hip and edgy labels, high street labels (including new H&M and Topshop concessions, the latter focusing on designer collaborations) and luxury high-end brands, the store stays ahead of the pack, while covering all styles and budgets. There's also a huge selection of jeans and the extensive Shoe Galleries (Level 2) – the best and biggest footwear collection in the UK. Menswear is also superb, and the store's 3rd Central initiative – located, funnily enough, in the centre of the third floor – is where you'll find the hippest brands of the day, with an ever-evolving mix of contemporary labels. Meanwhile, regularly changing pop-ups and special events make an actual visit to Selfridges (as opposed to shopping online) essential.

Liberty. See p23.

Shopping Centres & Arcades

Shopping centres

The past few years have seen increasing competition among London's shopping centres, with the completion of the huge **Westfield Stratford City** in September 2011, and the opening of **One New Change**, a Jean-Nouvel designed mall near St Paul's, in late 2010. **Boxpark**, opened in late 2011, is a quirky take on the shopping mall concept.

Brunswick

Hunter Street, Bernard Street & Marchmont Street, WC1N 1BS (7833 6066, www.brunswick.co.uk). Russell Square tube or King's Cross tube/rail. **Open** varies; check website for opening hours of individual shops.

Conceived as an experimental retail and social housing complex in the 1960s, the Brunswick was neglected throughout the 1980s and '90s. In 2006, however, the Grade II-listed centre was given a much-needed £24 million facelift by an architectural partnership that included the building's original designer, Patrick Hodgkinson. The concrete-heavy complex has retained its 1960s character but it is now brighter, whiter and considerably more popular. The retail outlets are largely of the high street chain variety (there's French Connection, Hobbs, Joy, Space NK, Hobbs, Oasis), but on a summer evening the central walkway buzzes with shoppers and diners (at Apostrophe, Carluccio's, Giraffe and Strada, among other eateries) creating a lively continental vibe. And the crowning glory is still here – the arthouse Renoir cinema.

Boxpark

2-4 Bethnal Green Road, E1 6GY (7033 2899, www.boxpark.co.uk). Shoreditch High Street rail or Liverpool Street tube/rail. **Open** 11am-7pm Mon-Wed, Sat; 11am-8pm Thur; 11am-5pm Sun.

Refitted shipping containers plonked artfully underneath the elevated Shoreditch High Street Overground station make up this contemporary shopping and eating mall. Installed in late 2011, Boxpark was founded by Boxfresh entrepreneur Roger Wade who, along with developers Hammerson and Ballymore, created this symbol of a new kind of Shoreditch. Big brands of the hyper-cool variety inhabit the miniature spaces – you'll find Dockers, Evisu and Nike. Book publishers Phaidon and Scandinavian interiors peddlers Marimekko offer great gift-buying options. Food and drink outfits come courtesy of the likes of Bukowski burgers and Vietnamese street food joint Hop-Namo. If the sun is out, take to the first-floor outdoor seating to dine overlooking the area's urban sprawl.

Brunswick

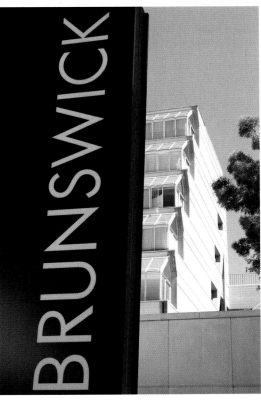

ONE-STOP

Kingly Court

Cardinal Place

Victoria Street, SW1E 5JH (www.cardinalplace.co.uk).
Victoria tube/rail or bus 11, 24, 148, 211, 507.
Open varies; check website for opening hours
of individual shops.
This slickly impressive glass and metal building on the
corner of Victoria Street and Bressenden Place opened
in 2004, bringing a much-needed burst of new life to
what was a rather bleak part of Westminster as far as
shopping was concerned. You'll find Topshop,
L'Occitane, Zara, North Face and Hawes & Curtis, and
there's a good range of eateries. The space also houses
the sleekly designed 3,000sq ft SW1 Gallery
(www.sw1gallery.co.uk). And if you want to exercise –
or exorcise – your soul after an excess of consumption,
cross the road and duck into the darkly mysterious interior of Westminster Cathedral.

Covent Garden Market

Between King Street & Henrietta Street, WC2E 8RF
(0870 780 5001, www.coventgardenlondonuk.com).
Covent Garden or Charing Cross tube/rail. **Open**
10am-7pm Mon-Wed, Sun; 10am-8pm Thur-Sat;
Apple Market varies; *East Colonnade Market* 10am-
7pm daily; *Jubilee Market* 9.30am-6pm Mon-Fri; 9am-
6pm Sat, Sun.

Although something of a London institution, for years
Covent Garden Market was too commercial and generally
too crowded to provide a particularly characterful retail
experience. However, the area – underpinned by its
impressive colonnaded 19th-century building and
piazza – has been ruthlessly re-edited in recent times into
an upscale neighbourhood with posh shops and eateries,
delighting the tourists and even luring back Londoners.
Overseen by brand director Bev Churchill (onetime marketing director at Selfridges), the tat shops are gone and
big new brands have taken root, including some interesting pop-ups that have included NYC store Opening
Ceremony. The change of fortune is nowhere more obvious than the appearance of a rather refined Ladurée café
and shop, once the site of a pasty shop.

Kingly Court

Carnaby Street, opposite Broadwick Street, W1B 5PW
(7333 8118, www.carnaby.co.uk). Oxford Circus tube.
Open 10am-7pm Mon-Sat; noon-6pm Sun.
Kingly Court has helped London's Carnaby Street to
reclaim its 1960s reputation as the heart of swinging
London (well, at least a vein of it, anyway), although the
shopping centre itself is often a bit short of footfall. The
three-tiered complex boasts an interesting mix of chains,
independents, vintage and gift shops. The café-filled

courtyard generates the most bustle, attracting custom to ground-level outfits. Shops include vintage store Fur Coat No Knickers, Traffic People (masterful prints and girl designs as well as menswear), Carry Me Home (baby gear and childrenswear) and Mnini (vintage-style gifts). Crafts get a look in at All the Fun of the Fair (knitting supplies). There are also outposts of Triyoga and Walk-In Backrub and highly recommended retro barber and hair salon It's Something Hells.

One New Change

New Change Road, EC4M 9AF (7002 8900, www.onenewchange.com). St Paul's or Mansion House tube or Bank tube/DLR. **Open** varies; check website for opening hours of individual shops.
This new development, a short stroll away from St Paul's Cathedral, is a sprawling shopping mall designed by Jean Nouvel, featuring a warren of high street retailers, office buildings and restaurants. Known as the 'stealth building' – some say it resembles a stealth bomber – the glass structure itself has been controversial, but there's no denying that it offers fantastic views. Unsurprisingly, it's popular with nearby City workers on their lunchbreak or here for a stress-busting post-work spending spree. Highlights from the shops here include Banana Republic, Topshop and Topman, Kurt Geiger, the North Face, Swatch, the Foyles 'booktique', a Strip waxing bar, bakery/patisserie Bea's of Bloomsbury and monthly lunchtime food markets. Eateries are strong, with the Jamie Oliver-Adam Perry Lang collaboration Barbecoa one of the most renowned restaurants. Gordon Ramsay's Bread Street Kitchen opened in September 2011.

Westfield London

Ariel Way, W12 7SL (3371 2300, www.westfield. com/london). Shepherd's Bush tube. **Open** 10am-10pm Mon-Fri; 9am-10pm Sat; noon-6pm Sun; check website for opening hours of individual shops.
Occupying 46 acres and covering nine different postcodes, Westfield London took the crown of Europe's largest shopping centre when it opened in autumn 2008. The impressive site, which was where the 1908 Olympics were held, cost around £1.6 billion to build, and houses some 265 shops. Popular labels that have never had stand-alone stores in the UK, such as Hollister, have shops here; you'll also find luxury fashion houses, including Louis Vuitton and Burberry. Highlights from the boutique-like labels include Maje, Donna Ida and Whistles.

Westfield Stratford City

Great Eastern Road, E20 (8221 7300, www. westfield.com/stratfordcity). Stratford tube/rail/

ONE-STOP

Westfield Stratford City

DLR. **Open** 10am-9pm Mon-Fri; 9am-9pm Sat; noon-6pm Sun; check website for opening hours of individual shops.

The 'city within a city', Westfield's £1.45 billion retail behemoth snakes through the Olympic site, with 300 retail units – the cornerstones of which are gigantic versions of High Street brands John Lewis, Marks & Spencer and Waitrose – 70 restaurants, bars and cafés, and a 17-screen digital cinema. There's no denying that it's a mega-mall, but Westfield Stratford City has attempted to be led a little by its east London neighbours, looking to the creative hubs of Shoreditch and Hoxton (rather than further east to Romford and Billericay). Projects such as Studio East – an industry panel that includes Roland Mouret, Tracey Emin, Tom Dixon and Erin O'Connor – have given opportunities to young British creatives, awarding them roles to create uniforms, lighting systems, public art and environmental projects for the Westfield Stratford City site.

Whiteleys

151 Queensway, W2 4YN (7229 8844, www. whiteleys.com). Bayswater or Queensway tube.
Open 10am-8pm Mon-Sat; noon-6pm Sun; check website for opening hours of individual shops.
London's first official department store was considered the height of luxury when it was opened in 1911 (the original Whiteleys department store in Westbourne Grove burned down in 1897). Today's largely mainstream tenants are at odds with the refined Edwardian structure – its marble floors, huge glass atrium and impressive La Scala staircase mean the place sometimes gets used in film shoots (it features in both *Love Actually* and *Closer*). The mainly mid-range high street shops include Zara, French Connection, Muji and H&M. A more unique shopping experience is available, however, at the Victory Vintage retro clothes shop. There's also an eight-screen Odeon cinema and a branch of the upmarket bowling chain All Star Lanes.

Arcades

The capital's five royal arcades are a throwback to the gentility of the 19th-century shopping experience, with many of the shops holding royal warrants for decades. By way of contrast **Portobello Green** gives retail space to emerging designers and quirky one-offs, while **Brixton Village** (formerly Granville Arcade) is great for vintage clothes, knick-knacks and exotic food.

Brixton Village

Corner of Coldharbour Lane and Brixton Station Road, SW9 8PR (7274 2990, www.spacemakers. org.uk/brixton). Brixton tube/rail. **Open** varies; check website for opening hours of individual shops.
Once almost forgotten, Granville Arcade has found a new lease of life. It opened in 1937, with a smart art deco façade that proclaimed it 'London's Largest Emporium'. Under a glazed roof, its airy avenues teemed with grocer's and specialist retailers. In the 1960s, it became a Caribbean market, and a flagship for the fruit and veg newly available from the West Indies. But as Brixton's main market expanded, business began to dip. By the mid 1990s many of the arcade's units were unoccupied, and its old avenues were falling into a dilapidated state.

In 2009, Lambeth Council called in Spacemakers, an agency specialising in the regeneration of urban spaces, which launched a competition whereby local entrepreneurs, food suppliers and creatives could apply for a unit; the best bids would be rewarded with a free three-month lease. Spacemakers then awarded the best initiatives a place on site and renamed the arcade Brixton Village, in line with its eclectic, locally minded new contents – from bijoux bakeries and vintage boutiques to international eateries and fledgling fashion labels.

Brixton Village is now open all week, drawing a cosmopolitan cross-section of visitors. Head there around lunchtime, and you'll be treated to a voyage round the

Brixton Village

TEN
More shopping centres & arcades

Bentall Centre
Wood Street, Kingston-upon-Thames, Surrey, KT1 1TP (8541 5066, www.the bentallcentre-shopping.com). Kingston rail. **Open** 9.30am-6pm Mon-Wed, Fri; 9.30am-9pm Thur; 9am-6pm Sat; 11am-5pm Sun.
Home to 85 high street brands – from H&M to Hollister – this centre links into Kingston's popular Bentall's department store on every level.

Brent Cross Shopping Centre
Prince Charles Drive, NW4 3FP (8457 3997, www.brentcross.co.uk). Brent Cross tube of Hendon Central tube. **Open** 10am-8pm Mon-Fri; 9am-8pm Sat; noon-6pm Sun.
The UK's first enclosed modern shopping centre – Brent Cross has lured in some high profile stores like Fenwick and Whistles in amongst the Clinton Cards and Claire's Accessories.

Canary Wharf Shopping Centres
Canada Place, Cabot Place & Jubilee Place, E14 5EW (7477 1477, www.my canarywharf.com). Canary Wharf tube/DLR. **Open** 9am-7pm Mon-Wed; 9am-8pm Thur, Fri; noon-6pm Sat, Sun.
Upper-end stores that suit the financial crowd (Church's shoes, Alfred Dunhill, Hackett, the White Company), plus mid-range fashion chains, fill this centre's three main malls.

Centre Court Shopping Centre
4 Queens Road, SW19 8YA (8944 8323, www.centrecourtshopping.co.uk). Wimbledon tube/rail. **Open** 9.30am-7pm Mon-Wed, Fri; 9.30am-8pm Thur; 9am-6pm Sat; 11am-5pm Sun.
The usual high street chains abound, including Accessorize, H&M, River Island Gap, Topman – and an Ann Summers.

Duke of York Square
King's Road, between Sloane Square & Cheltenham Terrace, SW3 4LY (www.dukeofyorksquare.com). Sloane Square tube. **Open** varies.

world in 80 paces. Bookended by cheap and cheerful cafés from Venezuela and Jamaica, international food vendors representing every continent on the globe pepper the arcade's avenues. For the unashamed bourgeoisie, there are numerous places to break artisan bread. All of this may ring a few bells for those Londoners who remember the chaotic variety and noise of Spitalfields Sunday Market before it was redeveloped in 2005. The comparison also rings true for the arcade's independent retail offerings.

Burlington Arcade
Burlington Arcade, between Piccadilly & Burlington Gardens, W1 (7630 1411, www.burlington-arcade.co.uk). Green Park or Piccadilly Circus tube. **Open** 10am-7pm Mon-Fri; 9am-6.30pm Sat; 11am-5pm Sun.
Built in 1819 by Lord Cavendish, to provide 'industrious females' with employment, and to stop people throwing oyster shells into the garden of Burlington House, Burlington Arcade is the grandest arcade in London.

Burlington Arcade

With its 'whale mouth' entrance and soft globe lights, you can dive from the flurry of Piccadilly into a far more genteel shopping experience. Decorum is guarded by the ever-present beadles who, to this day, prevent shoppers from whistling, running and 'making merry loudly'; you've been warned. Step into Ladurée's golden grotto for one of its rainbow-hued macaroons before idling past the arcade's sparkling row of jewellers. Smart luggage in Globe-Trotter caught our eye, as did the handcrafted leather and silver accessories in Thomas Lyte. Luxury goods abound in the form of watches from David Duggan, pens from Pen Friend, shoes from Jimmy Choo and custom-made gloves from Sermoneta Gloves. The arcade was purchased for £104 million in 2011 and new owners Meyer Bergman have been developing the site. Visit the quintessentially English fragrance house, Penhaligon's, for old-fashioned scents like Bluebell, Violetta and the rather bracing Extract of Limes. Burlington Arcade also houses a proper shoe shine boy working with waxes and creams for just £4. Suits you guv'nor!

This magnificently made-over military barracks houses upper-end high street and designer stores Whistles, Agnes b, Space NK, Mary Quant and Joseph, plus posh food emporium Partridges and a Gelateria Valerie.

N1 Islington
21 Park Street, N1 OPS (7359 2674, www.n1islington.com). Angel tube.
Open varies.
High street fashion stalwarts Oasis, H&M and French Connection dominate. N1 Islington also houses Tinderbox café, music venue the O2 Academy and a Vue cinema in this unremarkable but practical complex.

Princes Arcade
38 Jermyn Street, SW1Y 6DN (www.princesarcade.co.uk). Green Park tube. **Open** 8am-7pm Mon-Sat; 10am-5pm Sun.
It's the smallest and perhaps least grand of Piccadilly's arcades, but Princes is well worth a visit – not least as it houses a Prestat chocolatier.

Royal Opera Arcade
Between Charles II Street & Pall Mall, SW1Y 4UY (7839 2440, www.royaloperaarcade.com). Piccadilly Circus tube. **Open** varies.
The Royal Opera is the oldest of London's covered arcades. It was designed by John Nash and houses an eclectic collection of rather eccentric shops.

St Martin's Courtyard
Between Long Acre & Upper St. Martin's Lane, WC2 (www.stmartinscourtyard. co.uk). Covent Garden tube. **Open** varies.
This new-ish enclave is Covent Garden without the stress. It houses a smattering of quality brands, from Twenty8Twelve to COS and Joules, a branch of Jamie's Italian, Bill's and – on Long Acre – the UK's Jack Wills flagship.

Thomas Neals
29-41 Earlham Street, WC2H 9LD (7240 4741, www.sevendials.co.uk). Covent Garden tube. **Open** varies.
Small complex housing Brit heritage brands (Fred Perry, Baracuta) and a few youth-oriented ones.

ONE-STOP

Piccadilly Arcade

*Between Piccadilly & Jermyn Street, SW1Y
6NH (7647 3000, www.piccadilly-arcade.com).
Green Park or Piccadilly Circus tube.* **Open**
varies; check website for opening hours of
individual shops.

Just across the road from Burlington Arcade, running
from Piccadilly to Jermyn Street, you will find Piccadilly
Arcade. Smaller than Burlington but with just as impressive a lineage, this arcade is well worth a visit. Squeezed
into the cusp of the arcade is the beautiful mirrored space
of Santa Maria Novella. Established by Dominican

Royal Arcade

monks in Florence in 1612, this perfumery is sacred in
perfume circles. Try Opoponax which was created as a
preventative from witchcraft. Further reverence is
required in Iconastas, the hallowed home to Russian fine
art and antiques, specialising in Orthodox icons. For mil-
itaria and royal memorabilia stop off at the Armoury of
St James, where you will find model soldiers, orders of
chivalry and antiques. Gents, if wedding season is upon
you then why not swagger through the nuptial proceedings in one of Favourbrook's sumptuous waistcoats and
bow ties. It's worth checking out the shoes in Jeffery West
which, with its skull-bedecked shop and gothic influ-
ences, is something of a renegade presence in the otherwise austere arcade.

Portobello Green Arcade

*281 Portobello Road, under the Westway, W10
5TZ (8960 2277, www.portobellodesigners.com).
Ladbroke Grove or Westbourne Park tube.*
Open varies; check website for opening hours
of individual shops.

Our fashionable arcade pick has to be Portobello Green
Arcade. Here, new and established designers are showcased minutes away from the rowdy markets of
Portobello Road. Loved by John Galliano and Jerry Hall,
Zarvis London is a pampering shop with a difference –
all the ingredients for its products are derived from
plants grown in England; the range is especially suitable
for sensitive skins. Also check out Preen, the hip, minimalist fashion label for women and men, which counts
Kate Moss among its followers. Accessorise your look
with some fabulous jewellery from Sarah Bunting, who
specialises in silver, platinum and gold contemporary
jewellery, inspired by organic forms. Then make like a
pre-war pin-up and slip into something slinky at What
Katie Did, which makes beautiful, vintage-style lingerie.
Gents in search of sharp tailoring should make a beeline
for Adam of London, selling 1960s-inspired ready-to-
wear suits, shirts and ties.

Royal Arcade

*28 Old Bond Street, W1S 4BT (www.mayfair.
org.uk/shopping/royal-arcade). Green Park tube.*
Open 10am-6pm Mon-Sat.

The Royal Arcade retains its old-fashioned charm while
ringing the changes with the presence of some more
contemporary names. It's one of London's most visually
stunning arcades, yet you are far less likely to find your
average tourist here so the pace is relaxed and you can
meander at your leisure. Enjoy mouthwatering chocolates at Charbonnel et Walker (chocolatier to the Queen)
and peruse rare lithographs in the William West Gallery.
Get your fashion fix at the Paul Smith accessory shop,
and find a scent to suit your mood at the original shop
of upscale perfumier Ormonde Jayne. The arcade also
holds opticians EB Meyrowitz, selling high-end, newly
hip frames and sunglasses. How's that for London style?

Anthropologie

Lifestyle Boutiques & Concept Stores

The term 'concept store' has now infiltrated the collective consciousness of London shoppers; defined as shops selling a range of items from desirable brands aimed at discerning and aspirational shoppers, they provide a shopping 'experience' rather than just a marketplace.

The lines between a concept store, a lifestyle boutique and a good gift shop are thin, and sometimes just a question of self-labelling by the shop. What all of the places listed below have in common is their covetable items for sale that span a wide range of categories – from cult homewares and retro stationery to original jewellery and stylish clothes; they all make excellent browsing grounds for gifts.

Anthropologie

158 Regent Street, W1B 5SW (7529 9800, www.anthropologie.co.uk). Piccadilly Circus tube. **Open** 10am-7pm Mon-Wed, Fri, Sat; 10am-8pm Thur; noon-6pm Sun. **Sells** W.

Anthropologie, the romantically inclined elder sister to Urban Outfitters, opened the doors of its first European store in autumn 2009, so those who stocked up during New York shopping sprees could access the US brand's signature classics closer to home. The store's large-scale window displays and installations, and a light-filled atrium with a jaw-dropping 1,500sq ft living wall of 11,000 plants, help to challenge London gloominess, while stock is of a feminine bent, with delicate necklaces adorned with puppies and birds, soft knit cardies, craft-edged homewares and blouses with ruffles and bows. London designers have collaborated with the label to produce exclusive pieces for the store; but it's the vintage-inspired range of homewares that has really filled a hole

Dover Street Market. See p36.

in the London market. As well as the store in the old Antiquarius building in Chelsea, there's also a concession in Selfridges.

Branch 131-141 King's Road, SW3 4PW (7349 3110).

Cath Kidston

28-32 Shelton Street, WC2H 9JE (7836 4803, www.cathkidston.co.uk). Covent Garden tube.
Open 10am-8pm Mon-Sat; noon-6pm Sun.
There are numerous ways to embrace the nostalgic Cath Kidston lifestyle, with her retro floral/cherry/stripey/dotty prints covering everything from washbags to tableware, via plimsolls, laptop cases, key rings, coats, scarves and more. The Covent Garden store is always bustling with shoppers in search of gift items and traditional English accessories. Oilcloth accessories are in abundance, used for glasses and phone cases, ticket holders and the well-designed cosmetics cases and washbags, which come in a wide variety of sizes. Bedspreads, cushions, blankets and eiderdowns, umbrellas, chinaware and a wide range of bags and luggage are also for sale, and there's a range of kidswear and accessories to boot, including kids' lunchboxes, bath sets, teddybears and cute babygrows.

Branches throughout the city.

Couverture & the Garbstore

188 Kensington Park Road, W11 2ES (7229 2178, www.couvertureandthegarbstore.com). Ladbroke Grove tube. **Open** 10am-6pm Mon-Sat; (Dec only) noon-5pm Sun.
Husband-and-wife team Emily Dyson and Ian Paley opened Couverture & the Garbstore in March 2008; Emily's Couverture shop was previously housed in Chelsea, while the Garbstore was a wholesale operation with a cult international fanbase. Couverture, upstairs, stocks clothes, accessories and jewellery, a large selection of choice kids' items (including eco-label Oeuf), homewares, furniture and the odd vintage knick-knack. Both shops stock exclusive label collaborations. Garbstore, on the lower level, is the first stand-alone shop stocking Paley's vintage-inspired label for men. The shop also stocks Japanese designers such as Ikou Tschuss, Colenimo and Mina Perhonen and cult New York labels such as Ace & Jig, Rachel Comey Jeffrey Monteiro and A Détacher.

Darkroom

52 Lamb's Conduit Street, WC1N 3LL (7831 7244, www.darkroomlondon.com). Holborn or Russell Square tube. **Open** 11am-7pm Mon-Fri; 11am-6pm Sat; noon-5pm Sun.
Darkroom is not somewhere you go to develop 35mm film. It is in fact a concept store that opened at the start of 2010, adding further credence to Lamb's Conduit Street's claim to being one of London's most intriguing shopping destinations. The shop is quite literally dark (the walls and

Darkroom. See p35.

lampshades are black), creating a blank canvas for the carefully chosen selection of unisex fashion, accessories and interiors items on sale. Designer items include Fleet Ilya and H by Harris bags, DMK glassware and Solomia ceramics. The space doubles up as a gallery, with displays intermingling with a range of sculptural jewellery by Elke Kramer, Eddie Borgo and Scott Wilson. Each piece begs the question – do I wear it or hang it on the wall? An own-brand product line, featuring prints, cushions, tote bags and more, was recently introduced, and has reportedly been very popular.

Dover Street Market

17-18 Dover Street, W1S 4LT (7518 0680, www.doverstreetmarket.com). Green Park tube. **Open** 11am-6.30pm Mon-Wed; 11am-7pm Thur-Sat; noon-5pm Sun. **Sells** M, W.

Comme des Garçons designer Rei Kawakubo's ground-breaking six-storey space combines the edgy energy of London's indoor markets – concrete floors, tills housed in corrugated-iron shacks, Portaloo dressing rooms – with rarefied labels. All 14 of the Comme collections are here, alongside lines such as Lanvin, Erdem and Alaïa and new London designer Simone Rocha. Dover Street's biannual Tachiagari event sees the store close while designers make changes to their concessions, ensuring the space is constantly evolving. There's a Hussein Chalayan area with exclusive pieces, and an area devoted to Celine, plus an Idea Books concession in the basement stocking wonderfully rare, vintage mags and photo books. Once you've taken it all in, have a sit-down in the Rose Bakery on the top floor.

Family Tree

53 Exmouth Market, EC1R 4QL (7278 1084, www.familytreeshop.co.uk). Angel tube or bus 19, 38, 341. **Open** 11am-6pm Mon-Sat.

A little gem on Exmouth Market, Family Tree offers a carefully chosen selection of designer-made gifts, home-wares and accessories sourced from all around the globe. Owner Takako Copeland makes sure the shop's wares have an eco slant, with plenty of Fairtrade and organic cotton represented in the stock; but the main draw is her delicate lamps, made from Japanese rice paper. A diminutive version costs around £59. A few pretty pieces point to Copeland's past as a jeweller – like the rice paper patterns of birds and butterflies encased in resin.

Ganesha

3-4 Gabriel's Wharf, 56 Upper Ground, SE1 9PP (7928 3444, www.ganesha.co.uk). Waterloo tube/rail. **Open** 11.30am-7pm daily

Jo Lawbuary and Purnendu Roy source goods from local co-operatives and small-scale producers in India, Bangladesh and beyond, to ensure every item in their store is fairly traded. There's a good selection of

Shop Talk Chuko and Juliet, co-owners of Pelicans & Parrots

Tell us about your shop
Our stock comes from all over the world. Our furniture and objects are a mixture of new and vintage and come from different antiques fairs and markets across the UK and EU. Many of our newer pieces are from the US, independent designers in the UK, and other areas of Europe. All our clothes are vintage and about 80 per cent are sourced in Italy. The only premise we have for stocking an item is that we both love it.

What is special about it?
The special thing about our shop is that it is truly a lifestyle shop. You can leave with anything from a contemporary sofa to a '90s Versace Betty Boo dress to a Cameroon feathered Bamileke hat, which doubles up as an eye-catching wall hanging.

Who are your customers?
People who like unique and unusual things. They are as varied as the objects we sell. We're lucky to be surrounded by a healthy mix of locals who have lived here for decades and creatives who have migrated from Shoreditch. We have also noticed that in the last year people from other parts of London will make the trip to Dalston to shop. As Dalston goes global, we've seen a lot of Japanese and French tourists find their way to us.

What are your favourite shops in London?
One of favourite shops in London is Kilim in Dalston – it's stacked high with everything from traditional Nigerian robes, to intricate cowrie shell jewellery and kitsch religious iconography. We also love Juniors, which is on a residential back street in Stoke Newington. Without question it serves the best 'home-cooked' Caribbean food to be found for miles. Ozlem, opposite Pelicans & Parrots Black, is always good for a Turkish chai.

What's the best thing about owning shops?
The best thing about owning the shops is the myriad characters you meet. Especially being based in Dalston, you get to meet some great people. It's also very rewarding to be able to find something completely out of context, perhaps at an antiques fair, and bring it back to the shop and breathe new life into it.

ONE-STOP

Fairtrade and recycled homewares (organic bedlinen, embroidered cushions from Bangladesh, laptop bags made from cement sacking, disposable leaf plates made from sali leaves from forests in India), as well as wall-hangings and accessories, including attractive silk scarves, camel-wool hats, baby alpaca gloves, and a range of bags made from cotton and leather. Ganesha also offers a wedding list service.
Branch 38 King Street, WC2E 8JT (7240 8068).

LN-CC

18-24 Shacklewell Lane, E8 2EZ (3174 0726, www.ln-cc.com). Dalston Kingsland rail. **Open** by appointment only.
It's not often that you have to book an appointment for the privilege of entering a shop, but then LN-CC is no ordinary boutique. The jaw-dropping interior, which is somewhere between a crafty art installation and a futuristic tree house, is located underneath a drab office block, which you enter via a very ordinary side door. Inside, the avant-garde designer stock is creatively merchandised and separated into themed zones by art director Gary Card. Big price-tag brands include Rick Owens, Maison Martin Margiela and Dries Van Noten. There's also a record and bookstore, a backroom disco space, and – in the past – rumours of an in-house tattooist. Perhaps LN-CC's genuine uniqueness is explained by its prowess online – you could argue that LN-CC is really an online retailer (it has a huge fanbase in New York), and the E8 site is a showroom for London shoppers who want more of a tangible experience. But that would probably be too simple an explanation for what is London's most wonderfully loopy store.

Luna & Curious

24-26 Calvert Avenue, E2 7JP (3222 0034, www.luna andcurious.com). Shoreditch High Street rail. **Open** 11am-7pm Mon-Sat; 10am-6pm Sun. **Sells** M, W.
The stock here is put together by a collective of young artisans. Look out for the quintessentially English teacups and ceramics from Polly George and welovekaoru, as well as the fabulous hand-stitched creatures – artworks in their own right – by Finch, and jewellery by Rheanna Lingham, who uses ceramics, feathers and old embroidery to make necklaces, earrings and headbands. Prices are surprisingly reasonable for products so lovingly put together. Thankfully, the Luna & Curious empire isn't limited to one store – there's a small boutique inside the Sanderson Hotel (50 Berners Street, W1T 3NG). The Calvert Avenue store doubles as a gallery and is often used for art events and pop-up concessions.

Marimekko

16-17 St Christopher's Place, W1U 1NT (7486 6454, www.marimekko.com). Bond Street tube. **Open** 10am-6.30pm Mon-Wed, Fri, Sat; 10am-7pm Thur; noon-5pm Sun. **Sells** M, W, C.

Finnish textile firm Marimekko is famous for the bold, brightly coloured floral prints that it has been producing since 1951. Dozens of new designs are produced every year, and these are used to create wall-hangings, bags, cushions, crockery, tea pots, duvet covers, aprons, scarves and umbrellas. A clothing range for women, men and children means that the prints are now also available on tunics, dresses, shirts, T-shirts and babygrows. The company has been expanding internationally in recent years, and has a second London store at the Boxpark mall (www.boxpark.co.uk) in Shoreditch.

Muji

37-78 Long Acre, WC2E 9JT (7379 0820, www.muji.co.uk). Covent Garden or Leicester Square tube. **Open** 10am-8pm daily. **Sells** M, W.
The Japanese concept store has long been a favourite of style-conscious Londoners when it comes to practical, affordable and aesthetically pleasing goods for the office, home or wardrobe. Stock runs the gamut from useful gadgets (umbrellas, alarm clocks) and stationery (a huge range of pens, notebooks, photo albums) to pleasingly plain bedroom furniture, storage units and furnishings. While you can't help feeling that prices for some of the plastic storage drawers are a little steep, the collection of vanity cases, hair grips and travel pots for creams and lotions is unbeatable in terms of usefulness. Bedlinen – in understated colours – is reasonably priced, as are the durable laptop bags. The kitchenware range is of good quality and particularly strong on glasses and tableware, while the clothing range (which includes underwear) is worth a look if you're not after anything wildly exciting.
Branches throughout the city.

Oliver Bonas

137 Northcote Road, SW11 6PX (7223 5223, www.oliverbonas.com). Clapham Junction rail. **Open** 10am-6.30pm Mon-Wed, Fri; 10am-7.30pm Thur; 10am-6pm Sat; 11am-5pm Sun.
With branches across London, as well as its original location in SW11, Oliver Bonas's target clientele is crystal clear. Twenty- and thirtysomething media mums flock here for safely stylish clothing from the likes of Emily & Fin, Vero Moda and Trollied Dolly, affordable jewellery, and bodycare products of the Korres ilk, as well as a good range of gifty type items such as cookbooks, Keel's diaries, arty birthday cards and attractive kitchenware. The chain is also an unsurprisingly good bet for 'new baby' presents.
Branches throughout the city.

Opening Ceremony

35 King Street, WC2E 8JG (7836 4978, www.openingceremony.us). Leicester Square tube. **Open** 11am-8pm Mon-Sat; noon-6pm Sun. **Sells** M, W.

Shop at Bluebird. See p40.

Opened in October 2012, Opening Ceremony is a long-awaited addition to London's concept store landscape. And boy does it put the 'concept' into concept store. Each year the international brand has a featured country, showcasing exciting new designers from its flag of choice. It is also big on collaborations, past mens- and womenswear collections coming from team-ups with the likes of actress Chloe Sevigny, artist Pablo Bronstein and sportswear giants Adidas. Founders Carol Lim and Humberto Leon are heavily influenced by the art world, so expect exhibitions and installations in-store. There's also a small Claire de Rouen bookshop concession for the latest in fashion and photography books. Clothing and accessories options tend to be influenced by Japanese styles, with lots of colour and quirky design. You'll find everything from Rodarte to Jeremy Scott in this 7,500sq ft shrine to off-the-wall and irreverent fashion.

Pelicans & Parrots

40 Stoke Newington Road, N16 7XJ (3215 2083, www.pelicansandparrots.com). Dalston Kingsland rail. **Open** noon-8pm Mon-Sat; noon-7pm Sun.
When Ochuko Ojiri and Juliet Da Silva opened their vintage fashion and homes emporium in August 2010, it was a tiny outpost on a somewhat forgotten stretch of road. Now it's the go-to for stylists, with its mix of contemporary and vintage furniture and bric-à-brac, its stellar range of mounted animal skulls, and its classic tailored and trend-led vintage clothes, all artfully arranged. The owners take their inspiration from curiosities from the 17th century, but most of the pieces defy categorisation. So you might find anything from a beautiful full-feathered black and red headdress from the Notting Hill Carnival to a pair of late 1980s high-waisted ski pants. All very Dalston, but very intriguing too. Pelicans & Parrots Black (81 Stoke Newington Road, N16 8AD) is Ochuko and Juliet's delightful – and slightly more upscale – sister store with a focus on rare interior design. *See p37* **Shop Talk**.

Shop at Bluebird

350 King's Road, SW3 5UU (7351 3873, www.theshopatbluebird.com). Sloane Square tube. **Open** 10am-7pm Mon-Sat; noon-6pm Sun. **Sells** M, W.
In an airy art deco garage on the King's Road you'll find this chic lifestyle boutique. Owners John and Belle Robinson (the people behind womenswear chain Jigsaw) may cite European concept stores such as Colette in Paris as inspiration, but there's none of the froideur associated with such temples to avant-garde design. On display in the 10,000sq ft space is a broad selection of designer clothing, shoes, accessories, books, music and the odd piece of furniture. The shop also boasts a spa offering shoppers the chance to unwind with a variety of treatments. There's a slew of hard-to-find niche skincare brands, including New

Wolf & Badger

York's C.O. Bigelow and Malin+Goetz. Fashion is wide-ranging; London-based designers Casely-Hayford and Chinti & Parker are to be found, as is Acne and Balenciaga. Cool denim brands also feature heavily.

Smug
13 Camden Passage, N1 8EA (7354 0253, www.ifeelsmug.com). Angel tube. **Open** 11am-6pm Wed, Fri, Sat; noon-7pm Thur; noon-5pm Sun.
Graphic designer Lizzie Evans has decked out this lovely lifestyle boutique with all her favourite things; the result is a space that's a labour of love as well as a canny commercial move. With its well-edited selection of home accessories, such as owl ceramic candlesticks and gorgeous teacups and saucers, as well as vintage homewares such as Welsh blankets and 1950s and '60s furniture (of the Formica and Maid Server ilk), you can see why she might be proud of it. Pixie make-up, rainbow kitchen accessories, homemade brooches, old-fashioned notebooks, retro and knitted toys, stylish watches and clocks, colourful cushions and a range of tea towels and men's T-shirts emblazoned with cool graphic prints are further draws, and various Smug exclusives are available.

Space EC1
25 Exmouth Market, EC1R 4QL (7837 1344). Angel tube or Farringdon tube/rail or bus 19, 38, 341. **Open** 10.30am-6pm Mon-Fri; 11am-6pm Sat.

This kitsch independent gift shop does novelty with humour and class, and is a good bet for quick-fix presents with heart. You'll find a cache of top-notch cards, quirky and gifty items, such as origami kits, notebooks, tea cosies, knitted hot-water bottle covers, soft toys, and kitchenware. Tasteful wrapping paper, and a range of coffee-table, gift- and cookbooks rounds off Space EC1's well-chosen selection.

Wolf & Badger
46 Ledbury Road, W11 2AB (7229 5698, www.wolfandbadger.com). Notting Hill Gate or Westbourne Park tube. **Open** 11am-6.30pm Mon-Wed; 11am-7pm Thur-Sat; noon-5pm Sun.
To the uninformed eye, this boutique on W11's millionaire mile looks like any other ruthlessly expensive joint. But don't dismiss it as a first wives' club just yet. It's actually a glittering collective of emerging designers, who rent units within the bright space, and who span fashion, accessories, jewellery and homewares. So you might find patterned scarves by Scottish designer Helen Ruth; unique contemporary fine bone china and ceramics from We Love Kaoru, Phoebe Richardson and Jimbob Art; hand-blown glass pendant lights from Curiousa & Curiousa; and womens- and menswear from a range of experimental international designers. Take a look at the website to get an idea of the wide choice – up tp 70 designers at any one time.
Branch 32 Dover Street, W1S 4NE (3627 3191).

Borough Market

Markets

The city's neighbourhood markets are still the lifeblood of London shopping, but relatively few remain the domain of salt-of-the-earth Cockney costermongers. Instead, you'll find fashion kids showing off their new vintage sunglasses over a soy latte and a bag of heirloom tomatoes – particularly the case with the now hyped to the max **Broadway Market**.

London's most famous markets are still going strong: despite ongoing major redevelopment, **Camden Market**, **Portobello Road Market** and **Borough Market** remain key tourist attractions – so only visit if you can stomach the crowds and get there as early as possible. The last named market is, however, being challenged by former Borough Market traders who have set up camp under the railway arches on nearby **Maltby Street** in Bermondsey.

For antiques' markets and arcades, *see p169*.

Central

Bermondsey Square Antiques Market

Corner of Bermondsey Street & Long Lane, SE1 (www.bermondseysquare.co.uk/antiques. html). Borough tube or London Bridge tube/rail. **Open** 5am-1pm Fri.

Following the redevelopment of Bermondsey Square, the ancient antiques' market – which started in 1855 in north London – continues in an expanded space that now accommodates 200 stalls. Traditionally good for china and silver as well as furniture and glassware (with items from Georgian, Victorian and Edwardian times), there are now also food, fashion and craft stalls. Browsing here is like going through Fagin's gang's loot, and, indeed, the market is famous for being the spot where, back in the day, thieves could sell their goods with impunity. It's half car boot sale, half chic Parisian fleamarket. Insider tip: get there early. Lunchtime arrivals will be disappointed to find grouchy antique sellers (well, they did start work in the dark) packing up.

Borough Market

Southwark Street, SE1 1TL (7407 1002, www.boroughmarket.org.uk). London Bridge tube/rail. **Open** 11am-5pm Thur; noon-6pm Fri; 8am-5pm Sat.

The food hound's favourite market is also London's oldest – dating back to the 13th century. It's also the busiest, occupying a sprawling site near London Bridge. Gourmet goodies run the gamut, from fresh loaves from Flour Station to chorizo and rocket rolls from Spanish specialist Brindisa, plus rare-breed meats, fish and game, fruit and veg, cakes and all manner of preserves, oils and teas; head out hungry to take advantage of the numerous free samples. Seasonal tasting days and festivals run throughout the year and opening hours extend in the run-up to Christmas. The market is now also open on Thursdays, when it tends to be quieter than on always-mobbed Saturdays. Work is under way on a rail viaduct above the space, despite a campaign against it, but a plan for the market to expand into the adjacent Jubilee Market area means that the space shouldn't be lost (even if some Grade II-listed structures are). The new area will be reserved for 'raw food' specialists. Note that several former Borough Market traders, including Fern Verrow, have now set up under the railway arches in Bermondsey's Maltby Street, which is now a hive of laid-back activity on Saturday mornings (see p48).

Cabbages & Frocks

St Marylebone Parish Church Grounds, Marylebone High Street, W1U 5BA (7794 1636, www.cabbages andfrocks.co.uk). Baker Street tube. **Open** 11am-5pm Sat.

Held in the attractive cobbled yard of St Marylebone parish church, this market was started by food-loving fashionista Angela Cash. The Saturday crowd is drawn to a host of fashion retailers as well as mouthwatering grub. You can choose to take your goods home or eat them on the spot. There's a range of retro and vintage clothing, plus work from independent designers and craftspeople. Look out for special events (dog day, children's workshops, music performances) that are held throughout the year.

Camden Markets

Camden Market *192-200 Camden High Street, junction with Buck Street, NW1 (www.camden markets.org). Camden Town tube.* **Open** 10am-5.30pm Thur-Sun.
Camden Lock Market *Camden Lock Place, off Chalk Farm Road, NW1 (7485 7963, www. camdenlockmarket.com). Camden Town tube.* **Open** 10am-6pm daily.
Electric Ballroom *184 Camden High Street, NW1 (7485 9006, www.electricballroom.co.uk). Camden Town tube.* **Open** 10am-5pm Sat, Sun.
Stables Market *off Chalk Farm Road, opposite junction with Hartland Road, NW1 (7485 5511, www.stablesmarket.com). Camden Town tube.* **Open** 10am-6pm daily.

With around 700 shops and stalls, Camden's collection of markets offers a smörgåsbord of street culture. Weekends are by far the busiest time to visit, although some stalls are open all week. Camden Market is the place for neon sunglasses and pseudo-witty slogan garments. Almost next door is the Electric Ballroom, which sells vinyl and CDs at weekends and is also a music venue. Inverness Street market opposite sells similar garb to Camden Market, as well as a diminishing supply of fruit and veg. North, next to the railway bridge, is Camden Lock, with numerous stalls selling crafts, home furnishings, jewellery, toys and gifts; West Yard has some tasty food stalls. Camden Lock Village, which runs along the towpath, opened after major fire damage in 2009. North along Chalk Farm Road is the Stables Market, noted for its new and vintage fashion.

FIVE

More central markets

Berwick Street Market

Berwick Street, Rupert Street, W1. Oxford Circus tube. **Open** 9am-5pm Mon-Sat.
This upbeat, busy street market has a mix of traditional fruit and veg traders and posh lunchtime food sellers, a florist and the Nutman – a trader who has wonderful nuts.

Leather Lane

Leather Lane, between Greville Street & Clerkenwell Road, EC4 (www.leather lanemarket.co.uk). Chancery Lane tube. **Open** 9am-2.30pm Mon-Fri.
Excellent lunchtime market selling cut-price clothing, cheap towels, plus flowers, fruit and veg.

Lower Marsh

Lower Marsh, from Westminster Bridge Road to Baylis Road, SE1 (7926 2530, www.lower-marsh.co.uk). Lambeth North tube. **Open** 8am-6pm Mon, Tue, Thur, Sat; 10am-3pm Wed; 8am-7pm Fri.
A street market since Victorian times; there's some quality veg, women's clothes, jewellery and vintage shops.

Petticoat Lane Market

Middlesex Street, Goulston Street, New Goulston Street, Toynbee Street, Wentworth Street, Bell Lane, Cobb Street, Leyden Street, Strype Street, E1 (7364 1717). Aldgate or Aldgate East tube. **Open** 8am-4pm Mon-Fri (Goulston Street, Toynbee Street & Wentworth Street only); 9am-2pm Sun.
Streets of discounted homewares and clothing – lots of tat but good for a bargain.

Whitecross Street Food Market

Whitecross Street, EC1 (7527 1761, www.whitecrossstreet.co.uk). Barbican tube. **Open** 11am-3pm Thur, Fri.
Now a twice-weekly affair (with some stalls open Monday to Friday); the Latin American street food stalls are excellent.

ONE-STOP

Camden Markets. See p43.

Portobello Road Market

Portobello Road, W10 & W11 (www.portobello road.co.uk). Ladbroke Grove, Notting Hill Gate or Westbourne Park tube. **Open** *General* 8am-6pm Mon-Wed; 9am-1pm Thur; 7am-7pm Fri, Sat. *Antiques* 6am-4pm Sat.

Portobello is actually several markets stretched out up one long strip of road: antiques start at the Notting Hill Gate end; further up are food stalls, and emerging designer and vintage clothes are found under the Westway flyover and along the walkway to Ladbroke Grove. A visit here is as much about soaking up the vibe as it is about shopping. Saturdays are manically busy so head out early, especially if you're serious about buying antiques. Friday is less hectic and one of the best days for sourcing clothes from up-and-coming fashion designers. Best of all are the fantastic shops lining the surrounding streets; escape the crowds with a browse round Ledbury Road's boutiques.

Spitalfields Market

Commercial Street, between Lamb Street & Brushfield Street, E1 (7247 8556, www.visitspitalfields.com). Liverpool Street tube/rail or Shoreditch High Street rail. **Open** *General* 10am-5pm Mon-Fri; 11am-5pm Sat; 9am-5pm Sun. See website for details of the many one-off markets held throughout the month.

Redevelopment has seen this East End stalwart combine the refurbished 1887 covered market with a modern shopping precinct. Around the edge, enthusiastic stallholders sell grub from just about every corner of the world. Sunday is busiest; browsing options include creations by up-and-coming designers, vintage clobber, crafts, jewellery, books and sheepskin rugs. A record market is held twice a month. There's a vintage clothes market on the first Saturday of the month, designers and pop-up vintage stalls on the third Saturday of the month, and books, art and prints on the last Saturday of the month. There's also a new fine food market held three times a week in Crispin Place with over 20 traders, many of whom can also be found at Borough Market.

Sunday (Up)Market

91 Brick Lane, The Old Truman Brewery (entrances on Brick Lane & Hanbury Street), E1 6QL (7770 6028, www.sundayupmarket.co.uk). Shoreditch High Street rail. **Open** 10am-5pm Sun.

Another good reason to head out east on Sundays (and very easily combined with a trip to nearby Spitalfields (*see above*) or Brick Lane (*see p46*), the Old Truman Brewery's buzzy (Up)Market boasts some 140 stalls toting edgy fashion from young designers (many fresh from fashion college), vintage gear, gifts, art and crafts, and well-priced jewellery. Food stalls offer everything from dainty, pastel-coloured cupcakes to rich Ethiopian coffee, Japanese yakisoba, tapas and dim sum (a few of the

SIX
More local markets

Brixton Market

Electric Avenue, Pope's Road, Brixton Station Road, SW9 (7926 2530, www.brixtonmarket.net). Brixton tube/rail. **Open** 8am-6pm Mon, Tue, Thur-Sat; 8am-3pm Wed.

Fruit and veg, halal meats, fish, fabrics, household goods, reggae music and wigs.

Chatsworth Road Market

Chatsworth Road, E5 (www.chatsworthroade5.co.uk). Homerton rail. **Open** 11am-4pm Sun.

Posh food and knick-knacks, vintage clothing and a few traders from Broadway Market can all be spotted here.

Northcote Road Market

Northcote Road, SW11. Clapham Junction tube/rail. **Open** 9am-5pm Mon-Sat. *Antiques* 10am-6pm Mon-Sat; noon-5pm Sun.

Fruit and veg, flowers, ceramics, vintage clothes, plus the antiques arcade (no.155A, 7228 6850).

Ridley Road Market

Ridley Road, off Kingsland High Street, E8 (www.ridleyroad.co.uk). Dalston Kingsland tube. **Open** 9am-5pm Mon-Fri; 9am-5.30pm Sat.

Fruit and veg, fish and meat, plus cheap clothes, bric-a-brac and fabrics from Africa and India.

Southall Market

The Cattle Market, High Street, opposite North Road, Southall, Middx UB1 3DG. Southall rail. **Open** *General* 9am-3pm Sat. *Furniture* 4am-1pm Fri.

A cross between a trad market and a trip to India: fresh produce, spices and fabric.

Walthamstow Market

Walthamstow High Street, E17 (8496 3000, www.walthamstowmarket.com). Walthamstow Queen's Road rail. **Open** 8am-5pm Tue-Sat.

Fruit and veg stalls, Asian and Caribbean products, fabrics and flowers, plus the new Saturdays at St James Street (8am-5pm – selling street food to antiques).

ONE-STOP

vendors have lounging areas for customers too). There's a more relaxed vibe here than at Spitalfields and prices tend to be lower.

Local

For **Brixton Village**, *see p29.*

Brick Lane Market

Brick Lane (north of railway bridge), Cygnet Street, Sclater Street, E1; Bacon Street, Cheshire Street, E2 (7364 1717). Aldgate East tube or Shoreditch High Street rail. **Open** 9am-5pm Sun.
Tools, household goods and fruit and veg sold by the bowl are among the offerings at this busy East End market. Also worth a look are the fascinating makeshift stalls set up on blankets at the side of the road – dodgy old videos, broken dolls, CD players and dubiously acquired bicycles abound. After you've browsed the Sunday (Up)Market (*see p45*), nip into the Backyard Market (on the right just past Dray Walk) for more than 100 stalls selling vintage clothes, accessories, jewellery, antiques, collectibles, food and bric-a-brac of all kinds.

Broadway Market

Broadway Market, E8 4PH (www.broadway market.co.uk). London Fields rail or 236, 394 bus. **Open** 9am-5pm Sat.
If it's Saturday, then it must be Hackney's Broadway Market, at least as far as east London's fashionably attired food-lovers are concerned. Many of them congregate on the market, picking up fresh fruit and veg, artisan cheeses, rare-breed meat and luscious cakes, and indulging in top-notch snacking options from an array of hot-food stalls. There are also stalls selling vintage and new designer threads, old *Vogue* patterns, buttons, Ladybird books, flowers and hand-knits. The shops, restaurants and pubs that line the street are worth browsing through as well – in particular Black Truffle, Hub, Fabrications, the Broadway Bookshop and Artwords. Nearby Netil Market (11-25 Westgate Street, E8, www.netilmarket.tumblr.com), at the top of Broadway Market, is worth a visit too. Also open on Saturdays (11am-6pm), it offers vintage clothing, handmade jewellery, artworks and prints, as well as food.

Columbia Road Market

Columbia Road, E2 (7364 1717, www.columbia road.info). Hoxton or Shoreditch High Street rail. **Open** 8am-2pm Sun.
One of London's most visually appealing markets, Columbia Road overflows with buckets full of beautiful flowers. There are bulbs, herbs, shrubs and bedding plants too. Alongside the market you'll find a host of independent galleries and shops selling pottery, perfume, vintage clothes, hats (two shops), children's clothes and the like. Turn up as things start to wind down at around

Brick Lane Market

The Best Car boot sales

Battersea
*Battersea Park School, Battersea Park Road,
SW11 5AP.* **Open** 11.30am-5pm Sun.
Not the cheapest around, but with bargains of
the high-end and vintage variety for late risers,
what's not to love?

Capital Car Boot Sale
*Pimlico Academy (Chichester Street entrance),
SW1V 3AT (www.capitalcarboot.com).* **Open**
12.30-4pm Sun.
Faye Marriott's chichi car boot attracts a youthful
crowd. Not everything's a designer find (though
we've heard rumours of Mulberry and Isabel
Marant), but with over 100 sellers on good
days, you're bound to find a pre-loved to love.

Holloway
*Holloway Road, opposite Odeon Cinema, N7
6LJ.* **Open** 8am-4pm Sat; 10am-2.30pm Sun.
With the odd fashion gem, funky bric-a-brac and
a good spread of second-hand DVDs, this car
boot sale is worth a rummage. Prices are very
reasonable – we picked up a pair of tan Chelsea
boots for £8.

Nags Head
*22 Seven Sisters Road, N7 6AG (7607 3527,
www.nagsheadmarket.co.uk).* **Open** 7.30am-
3.30pm daily.
The Nags Head sells everything from decorative
Victorian knife sets and stamp collections to
(mostly) working toasters, DVDs and remote
controls. A no-frills, rough-around-the-edges
retail experience; arrive early for the bargains.

Princess May
*Princess May School, Princess May Road,
N16 8DF (www.thelondoncarbootco.co.uk).*
Open 9am-3pm Sat; 9am-2pm Sun.
The bright young things of Stokie and Dalston
gather here to rummage among the junk (half
a bottle of foot lotion? or some plate hangers
anyone?). Clothes and costume jewellery are
here too. In summer, you can punctuate bargain-
hunting with bangers from the barbecue.

St Augustine's
*St Augustine's School, Kilburn Park Road,
NW6 5SN (www.thelondoncarbootco.com).*
Open 10.30am-3pm Sat.
Like any car boot sale worth its second-hand
salt, it packs all kinds of bric-a-brac, from old
tins to TVs. If you want to poke around the
goods before 11am, you'll need to pay a £3
'early bird' fee.

St Mary's
*St Mary's Church of England Primary School,
Quex Road, NW6 4PG (www.thelondoncarboot
co.com).* **Open** 10am-3pm Sat.
A mecca for would-be interior designers and DIY
lovers: think quirky home furnishings, retro light
fittings, vintage vinyls and textiles. Run by the
same company as St Augustine's, it also charges
bargain hunters for early entry.

Shepperton
*New Road, Shepperton, Surrey TW17 0QQ
(www.sheppertoncarboot.co.uk).* **Open** 8.30am-
late afternoon Sat.
Shepperton's all about cheap and cheerful;
you'd be hard put to find a car boot in London
with a friendlier atmosphere. With its attentive,
knowledgeable stall holders, it's a great
starter-sale for car boot newbies, as well as
for seasoned booters willing to travel for their
second-hand bargains.

Wimbledon
Wimbledon Stadium, Plough Lane, SW17 0BL.
Open 10.30am-2pm Wed; 6.30am-1.30pm Sat;
7am-1.30pm Sun.
Still one of London's best boot sales, selling
everything from vintage and jewellery to books,
furniture and toys. With over 2,000 stalls to
browse, bring a big bag and expect to fill it.

ONE-STOP

2pm for the best bargains, or as early as humanly possible if you want to guarantee yourself the pick of the crop. There are also a number of decent places to have coffee and cake or a full-blown Sunday lunch.

Greenwich Market

Off College Approach, SE10 (8269 5096, www. greenwichmarket.net). Greenwich rail or Cutty Sark DLR. **Open** *Antiques & collectibles* 10.30am-5.30pm Tue, Thur, Fri. *Arts, crafts & food* 10.30am-5.30pm Wed, Sat, Sun.

There are plenty of stalls selling bric-a-brac, second-hand clothes, ethnic ornaments, CDs, crafts and jewellery galore at Greenwich Market at weekends. On Tuesdays, Thursdays and Fridays, the market takes a different turn with an excellent antiques and collectibles market. Thursday is the best day for unearthing unusual finds and provides a selection of stalls dealing in antique jewellery, vintage clothes, old books, music and collectibles.

Maltby Street Market

Druid Street, Maltby Street and Dockley Road, SE1 (www.maltbystreet.com). Bermondsey tube or London Bridge tube/rail. **Open** 9am-2pm Sat.

If you're struggling to find Maltby Street Market, simply follow the trail of St John Bakery's brown paper bags that litter the street (take your rubbish with you, people). Many come here for their legendary custard doughnuts alone, but there's a great deal more to this new foodie alternative to the nearby Borough Market. Lurking unassumingly beneath railway arches you'll find everything from artisan ice-cream peddlers to dinky wine bars. For piles of fluffy pancakes, there's Bea's Diner; you'll find seasonal meals teamed with fine wines at 40 Maltby Street; and the UK's best cheeses are all on display at Neal's Yard Dairy. There are stalls running the length of Ropewalk – a small street that links Maltby Street to Millstream Road. Come early to avoid disappointment; once the treats are gone, they're gone.

Shepherd's Bush Market

East side of railway viaduct, between Uxbridge Road & Goldhawk Road, W12 (8749 3042, www.shepherds bushmarket.co.uk). Goldhawk Road or Shepherd's Bush tube. **Open** 9am-6pm Mon-Sat.

While Shepherd's Bush Market is just a hop and a skip away from Europe's largest urban shopping centre at Westfield, it's a world apart in every other sense. At this gritty, multicultural market you'll find a fantastic range of ethnic foodstuffs (Indian, Caribbean, African and Polish). Stalls selling fragrant spices, yams, coconuts, cassava, okra, falafel, mangoes and some of the freshest fish in the capital line the strip between Uxbridge and Goldhawk Roads. You'll also see vivid print fabrics, goatskin rugs, saris, home furnishings, electronic equipment, CDs and DVDs.

Maltby Street Market

ONE-STOP

Fashion

Bags packed, milk cancelled, house raised on stilts.

You've packed the suntan lotion, the snorkel set, the stay-pressed shirts. Just one more thing left to do – your bit for climate change. In some of the world's poorest countries, changing weather patterns are destroying lives.

You can help people to deal with the extreme effects of climate change. Raising houses in flood-prone regions is just one life-saving solution.

**Climate change costs lives.
Give £5 and let's sort it *Here & Now***

www.oxfam.org.uk/climate-change

Be Humankind Ⓧ Oxfam

Fashion

London remains one of the world's top destinations for clothes shopping, catering for all styles and budgets; designer fiends, directional fashionistas, as well as those with more traditional sartorial tastes, all have a host of top-notch independents in which to flex the plastic, on top of the excellent fashion sections of London's department stores. For, despite the homogenisation of the high street over the past decade or so, London's independent fashion shops are flourishing, with boutique-dominated shopping streets – such as **Lamb's Conduit** and **Redchurch Street** – well-trodden destinations for style-savvy consumers who want a more personal shopping experience.

This experience-led trend has been propelled by the city's concept stores and pop-up shops and concessions. As the realms of shopping, eating and entertainment have merged into each other, stores such as **Dover Street Market** (*see p36*), **Other/shop** (*see p58*) and Shoreditch menswear shop **Present** (*see p62*) have become hip hangouts for the city's fashionistas, with the latter example housing an in-house espresso bar. There has been an increasing number of shops catering for menswear in recent years too; boutiques such as **Folk**, **Goodhood** and **Hub** (for all *see p55*) are as well versed in current menswear labels as they are women's.

Those with wallets thick enough to buy them a designer wardrobe also have much to celebrate; the opening of the first London store for Parisian designer **Vanessa Bruno** (*see p86*) in 2011 means yet another high-profile designer flagship in the city. Many retro designer pieces can also be picked up from the city's vintage shops, which have been getting better and better over the past couple of years. Both **Vintage Showroom** (*see p100*) and **Lucy in Disguise** (*see p96*) have good pickings for mid-range to high-end budgets; for cheaper, flea-market-style garb, head to the huge Brick Lane and Dalston branches of **Beyond Retro** (*see p91*), which also put on regular events.

For a traditional London experience, head to the capital's accessories boutiques; shops such as umbrella specialist **James Smith & Sons** (*see p130*) and **Bates the Hatter** (*see p123*) have been features of the city's shopping scene for well over a century, complemented by comparative newcomers, such as **Ally Capellino** (*see p122*).

In London, high street shops still have much to compete with, meaning that the chains are forced to stay on their toes; the flagships of **Urban Outfitters** (*see p76*) and **Topshop** (*see p75*) are much more than your average high street shops, stocking lots of directional labels to compliment their own lines.

Boutiques &
Indie Labels

Men & women

Aubin & Wills

64-66 Redchurch Street, E2 7DP (3487 0066, www.aubinandwills.com). Shoreditch High Street rail. **Open** 11am-7pm Mon-Sat; 11am-5pm Sun.

Brit brand Aubin & Wills opened this ambitious boutique, 45-seat cinema and gallery in Redchurch Street in June 2010, and in doing so signalled new times ahead for the formerly rough-edged, now fashion-forward street. The 7,500sq ft space houses its men's and women's lines in a sort of grown-up collegiate style reminiscent of Aubin's teen labelmate Jack Wills. Among the womenswear, the casual shirts, dresses and blazers are some of the strong points, all made from high-quality fabrics and utilising simple, stylish lines. For men, the peacoats, knitwear and boxer shorts are notable. The accessories include some very covetable items (hankies, hats, scarves, laptop bags, belts), and the brand also sells a growing range of home-wares (mainly cushions and lovely wool rugs). Upstairs is the Aubin Gallery, originally overseen by Brit artist and curator Stuart Semple, but now under new management. In the basement is the flashy Aubin Cinema – a collabo-ration with neighbour Shoreditch House.

Branches 12 Floral Street, WC2E 9DH (7240 4024); 188 Westbourne Grove, W11 2RH (7243 5830); 26 Marylebone High Street, W1U 4PJ (7486 8873).

Browns

23-27 South Molton Street, W1K 5RD (7514 0000, www.brownsfashion.com). Bond Street tube. **Open** 10am-6.30pm Mon-Wed, Fri, Sat; 10am-7pm Thur.

For the ultimate fashion fix look no further than Joan Burstein's venerable store, which celebrated its 40th anniversary in 2010. Among the 100-odd designers jostling for attention at its five interconnecting shops are fashion heavyweights Kenzo, Dries Van Noten, Maison Martin Margiela and Roksanda Ilincic. Burstein (aka Mrs B) has always championed the next big things from the fashion elite, so you'll also find Carven and fine jeweller Duffy, and shop exclusives are common. The women's shoe salon, meanwhile, showcases fabulous footwear from Lanvin and Christian Louboutin. The two-floor menswear section brings together an unri-valled collection of high-end designer gear, from Acne to Kolor. Across the road, Browns Focus caters for a younger crowd, with more accessibly priced labels, such as Simone Rocha, Alexander Wang and Rodarte, as well as shoes by Nicholas Kirkwood and denim from Orjan Andersson. No.24 now also houses in-house boutique Shop 24, selling what it calls 'the staple items you can't live without': Breton tops, cotton T-shirts and everyday items. The idea is that you can come here for all your

Aubin & Wills

FASHION

wardrobe essentials, albeit luxurious ones. Up at no.50, the sale shop, Browns Labels for Less, is loaded with leftovers from the previous season.
Branches Browns Focus 38-39 South Molton Street, W1K 5RL (7514 0000); **Browns Labels for Less** 50 South Molton Street, W1K 5RD (7514 0000); **Browns Bride** 11-12 Hinde Street, W1U 3BE (7514 0056); 6C Sloane Street, SW1X 9LE (7514 0040); **Vera Wang at Browns** 59 Brook Street, W1K 4HS (7514 0000).

Diverse

294 Upper Street, N1 2TU (7359 8877, www.diverse clothing.com). Angel tube. **Open** 10.30am-6.30pm Mon-Wed, Fri, Sat; 10.30am-7pm Thur; 11.30am-5.30pm Sun.
Islington stalwart Diverse does a fine job of keeping N1's style queens in fashion-forward mode. Despite the cool clobber, chic layout and striking window displays, this is the sort of place where you can rock up in jeans and scuzzy Converse and not feel uncomfortable trying on next season's Carven or Acne. And while you're there, you might as well give those MIH jeans a try, and maybe a little something by Vanessa Bruno Athé, and those Sessun shoes are looking good, come to think of it. You get the picture. This is a well-edited collection of incredibly desirable garments, plus some original jewellery, accessories and shoes thrown in for good measure. There's plenty for the more feminine or classic dresser too, such as tasteful labels By Malene Birger, and stalwart boutique brands such as Vivienne Westwood Anglomania and Marc by Marc Jacobs. There are also J Brand jeans, bags by Sophie Hulme and jewellery by Maison Martin Margiela. Universal Works, PS by Paul Smith, French shoe brand Veja and Grenson make up the small but well-formed men's selection.

Folk

49 & 53 Lamb's Conduit Street, WC1N 3NG (menswear 7404 6458, womenswear 8616 4191, www.folkclothing.com). Holborn tube.
Open 11am-7pm Mon-Sat; noon-5pm Sun.
Folk was born in 2001 and is the label of choice for guys who once dressed like skaters, then progressed to labels like Silas and are now after more quality, more respectability and less branding. The silhouette and the fabrics are comfortable but hip and slightly dishevelled – in an upscale rather than grungey way (think stripes, quality knits and casual jackets in bold colours). Head to no.49 for own-label pieces including Folk's line of footwear, which has a hand-crafted feel. The women's store at no.53 has developed into a confident boutique stocking Folk's own womenswear as well as Acne, Dutch label Humanoid and Parisian brand Sessùn. Bags from Ally Capellino and skincare from Aesop are also stocked here, with a men's barber's popping up occasionally in the basement. Additional menswear stores

can be found in east London's Old Truman Brewery and Mayfair's Shepherd Market, and there are concessions in Selfridges and Liberty.
Branches 11 Dray Walk, E1 6QL (7375 2844); 12-14 Shepherd Street, W1J 7JF (7495 6197).

Goodhood

41 Coronet Street, N1 6HD (7729 3600, www.goodhoodstore.com). Old Street tube/rail.
Open 11am-6.30pm Mon-Sat; noon-5pm Sun.
Stock for this brilliant boutique-like store is selected by streetwear obsessives/owners Kyle and Jo, with items weighted towards Japanese, Australian, cult US and Danish independent labels. Hot picks from the well-edited selection include shirts and tops for men from Norse Projects, and supremely covetable pieces for both men and women from Perks & Mini, Antipodium, Wood Wood, Opening Ceremony, Pendleton and more. To celebrate its fifth birthday, Goodhood expanded into more retail space in September 2012, initially housing special collaborations and one-offs. The perfect place to find for gifts for hard-to-please boyfriends and girlfriends.

Hub

49 & 88 Stoke Newington Church Street, N16 0AR (7254 4494, www.hubshop.co.uk). Bus 73, 393, 476.
Open 10.30am-6pm Mon-Sat; 11am-5pm Sun.
Hub stocks a well-edited selection of covetable mid-range designer labels, with fashion-forward brands such as Acne and YMC much in evidence. Spot a brace of young media mums in a Stokey café and chances are they'll have picked up their skinny jeans or Veja leather totes here. No.49 houses the womenswear; as well as the labels mentioned above, there are pieces by Something Else, jewellery by Janine Barraclough, denim by Nudie and AG Jeans, plus everyday knits, stylish tops and dresses with a quirky edge by co-owner Beth Graham. Over the road at no.88, Hub Men (refurbished in October 2012) sells Won Hundred, Our Legacy and grooming products from Portland General Store, as well as meaty backpacks by Herschel and a selection of items from Vanishing Elephant, Barbour and more. The newer Broadway Market boutique sometimes stocks slightly edgier items, in line with the locale, from the same labels.
Branch 2a Ada Street, E8 4QU (7923 9354).

HUH

56 Stoke Newington Road, N16 7XB (7246 8239, www.huhmagazine.co.uk). Dalston Kingsland rail.
Open noon-7pm Tue-Sat; noon-6pm Sun.
Online hip culture mag *HUH* launched its first store in late 2011, selling a selection of its favourite sartorial items, plus caffeine treats from the now-requisite slick and shiny coffee machine. The selection is reliably good: Armor-Lux striped tops, Herschel satchels and

Goodhood. See p55.

Carhartt chinos for the boys, and Swedish Hasbeens clogs, Cheap Monday skinnies and WeSc jumpsuits for the girls. There are also Happy Socks and an impressive selection of the latest trendy magazines. It might be an obvious formula, but at this end of east London it's hard to find anything except vintage retailers or pound shops to spend your fashion budget on. Take a listen to the store playlist too – it's been co-complied by *HUH* magazine readers.

JW Beeton

48-50 Ledbury Road, W11 2AJ (7229 8874, www.jw beeton.co.uk). Westbourne Park or Notting Hill Gate tube. **Open** 10am-6pm Mon-Sat; noon-5pm Sun.
JW Beeton is one of the longest-established boutiques in this now-crowded patch of west London. Keen to cater for all sorts of budgets, owner Debbie Potts buys small quantities of European and international labels (for men, women and children) and sells them at non-extravagant prices. Recent labels stocked include Fake London, Olive & Orange, Saltwater, Des Petits Hauts, Bella Jones and Roberto Collina.

Kokon To Zai

86 Golborne Road, W10 5PS (8960 3736, www.kokontozai.co.uk). Ladbroke Grove tube.
Open 10am-6pm Mon-Sat.
Kokon To Zai specialises in the avant-garde, weird and wonderful. The buyers are adept at picking up young designers from the nearby London College of Fashion and Central Saint Martins, so you'll often see new names here first. The selection is constantly changing. Ever present, however, is Marjan Pejoski, who made Björk's famous swan dress. For offbeat streetwear, look no further than the house label KTZ, which excels in T-shirts and sweats with bold prints (from £40). The flagship store also has a range of homewares and curiosities that are well worth checking out.
Branch 57 Greek Street, W1D 3DX (7434 1316).

Lewis Leathers

3-5 Whitfield Street, W1T 2SA (7636 4314, www.lewisleathers.com). Goodge Street tube.
Open 11am-6pm Mon-Sat.
With Kate Moss parading around in its tough-ass boots and every rocker worth their salt (the Clash, the Ramones, Iggy Pop) having worn its biker jackets, Lewis Leathers is a true Brit heritage brand. Reopening in January 2010 a stone's throw away from its old Great Portland Street site (which it occupied from 1892 until 1993), this icon of bikerwear cool is back with a fashion vengeance. Despite its cult Tokyo following and one-time collaboration with Comme des Garçons, Lewis has left high-tech wizardry at the door at this made-to-measure shop selling 15 classic vintage designs from the 1960s and '70s. It's not cheap – the top-selling Roadmaster jacket is £735 – but if it ain't broke…

Lewis Leathers

FASHION

Matches

60-64 Ledbury Road, W11 2AJ (7221 0255, www.matchesfashion.com). Notting Hill Gate or Westbourne Park tube. **Open** *10am-6pm Mon-Sat; noon-6pm Sun.*

The pick of the crop of assorted international designers is on show at this well-established west London boutique. Get yourself kitted out in high-end labels, the likes of Bottega Veneta, Burberry Prorsum, Stella McCartney, Chloé, Dolce & Gabbana, Lanvin, Balenciaga, Alexander McQueen and Marc Jacobs. Across the road at Matches Spy there's more casual gear to be had, such as Acne, Heidi Klein, Theory and J Brand. A good bet for fashion exclusives, the shop is aimed at moneyed women and men who have an eye for luxury.

Branches Matches Spy 85 Ledbury Road, W11 2AJ (7221 7334); 87 Marlebone High Street, W1U 4QU (7487 5400); 34 Wimbledon High Street, SW19 5BY (8947 8707); 13 Hill Street, Richmond, TW9 1SX (8332 9733).

no-one

1 Kingsland Road, E2 8AA (7613 5314, www.no-one.co.uk). Old Street tube/rail. **Open** *11am-7pm Mon-Wed, Fri, Sat; 11am-8pm Thur; noon-6pm Sun.*

On the style-setting axis between Old Street and Kingsland Road, this indie boutique, café and bar is a favourite of Shoreditch locals. Part of the Jaguarshoes collective (named after the group's popular bar, opposite), no-one's buyers are brilliant at spotting cool new labels, and were the first to champion Swedish denim label Cheap Monday in Britain, which it continues to sell alongside denim by Lee. The stock ranges from the latest Won Hundred and House of Dagmar pieces to T-shirt prints by local tattooist Liam Sparkes, jewellery from Noemi Klein and leather goods by Veja. Look out for Black Eyewear sunglasses, knitted accessories, badges, wittily branded toiletries and cult magazines and books.

Other/shop

21 Kingly Street, W1B 5QA (7734 6846, www.other-shop.com). Oxford Circus tube. **Open** *10.30am-6.30pm Mon-Fri; noon-5pm Sat.*

The Other/shop opened in the summer of 2012, but founders Matthew Murphy and Kirk Beattie have more than a decade's experience in running another successful indie boutique – b Store. Other occupies the same site as its (now defunct) predecessor, sells similar stock, even a continuation of the excellent b Clothing brand – now called Other – that the store had become famous for. The re-brand is part of a wholly new outlook, and the store interior feels open, airy and slightly whimsical. Natural wood, spider plants, and a sun-lit basement stock Other's edit of brands such as Peter Jensen, Our Legacy, Sophie Hulme, Opening Ceremony, and MM6 by Maison Martin Margiela. The store often houses installations and exhibitions by artists, and also stocks a range of fashion and photography mags and coffee-table books.

Preen

5 Portobello Green, 281 Portobello Road, W10 5TZ (8968 1542, www.preen.eu). Ladbroke Grove tube. **Open** *10am-6pm Thur-Sat.*

Tucked quite literally under the Westway overpass, Preen – the Brit label from Justin Thornton and Thea Bregazzi – brings imaginative takes to traditional silhouettes; it's all about not trying too hard. Collections are characterised by urban, minimalist shapes and tame colour palettes cut with splashes of bombastic colour, such as cobalt blue, to stunning effect. Highlights include typical Preen cocoon-shaped jackets, billowy shirt-dresses, skirts with belts, and tailored trousers. It was one of the first labels to produce a capsule collection for Topshop. Look out for a great range of bags and shoes, plus an accessories range.

Start

42-44 Rivington Street, EC2A 3BN (7729 3334, www.start-london.com). Old Street or Liverpool Street tube/rail. **Open** *10.30am-6.30pm Mon-Wed, Fri; 10.30am-7pm Thur; 11am-6pm Sat; 1-5pm Sun.*

Philip Start (founder of Woodhouse) and his wife Brix (former guitarist for punk rock band the Fall, and style expert on *Gok's Fashion Fix*) own these his 'n' hers shops, which were instrumental in kick-starting the Shoreditch fashion boutique scene. In the women's store you'll find well-known brands such as Acne and Sonia by Sonia Rykiel, alongside up-and-coming labels like Richard Nicoll and pieces by Helmut Lang, Emma Cook and Rick Owens. There's also a hugely covetable range of accessories, such as sunglasses by Thierry Lasry, Mulberry bags and a selection of cashmere. A small but attractive range of footwear comes from the likes of Martin Margiela and Acne. Across the road at the men's store, enjoy browsing rails of A.P.C., Acne, Woolrich and Maison Martin Margiela, with fragrances from Comme des Garçons. A third store on Rivington Street houses the Mr Start label, with suits, ties, shirts and a made-to-measure service (prices for the latter start at £750).

Branches (menswear) 59 Rivington Street, EC2A 3QQ (7739 3636); **Mr Start** 40 Rivington Street, EC2A 3LX (7729 6272).

Sunspel

7 Redchurch Street, E2 7DJ (7739 9729, www.sunspel.com). Shoredich High Street rail. **Open** *11am-7pm Mon-Sat; noon-6pm Sun.*

It may look like a trendy Redchurch Street newcomer, but Sunspel is actually a classic British label, which has been producing quality menswear for over 150 years. It

Other/shop

even claims to have introduced boxer shorts to the UK, back in 1947. This small corner space with a lovely pale-blue shopfront is the brand's first retail outlet, showcasing the range of quality men's underwear, T-shirts, Merino wool base-layers, knitwear and polo shirts, as well as the new, smaller range of womenswear, consisting of similarly pared-down styles, and sometimes featuring Liberty prints. Clothes are wonderfully long-lasting – with all garments still hand-sewn in the original warehouse in Nottinghamshire – and the company's aesthetics timeless.
Branch 4 Old Compton Street, W1D 4TU (7734 4491).

YMC

11 Poland Street, W1F 8QA (7494 1619, www.you mustcreate.com). Oxford Circus or Tottenham Court Road tube. **Open** 11am-7pm Mon-Sat.

The flagship of the London label that made us go weak at the wallets for impeccably designed, high-quality yet affordable staples. YMC (You Must Create) is the place to head for simple vest tops, T-shirts and shirts, stylish macs and duffle coats, tasteful knits and chino-style trousers for men and women. The focus of the brand is wardrobe longevity rather than high fashion, but items are nevertheless extremely covetable, with recent collections having a more designed feel. The shop itself is a lovely space, with a bike displayed in the window, stuffed animals in glass cases, and beautifully arranged clothes (including

a little vintage section) and shoes. Steve Mono and Frost River bags are also stocked, and a small selection of jewellery, along with Baxter of California toiletries for men.
Branch 23 Hanbury Street, E1 6QR (3432 3010).

Men

Albam

Old Spitalfields Market, 111a Commercial Street, E1 6BG (7247 6254, www.albamclothing.com). Liverpool Street tube/rail. **Open** 11am-7pm Mon-Sat; 11am-6pm Sun.

Late in 2007, Alastair Rae and James Shaw's excellent menswear line, Albam, jumped off the internet and into its first store on Beak Street. The label's refined yet rather manly aesthetic soon won it a loyal fanbase, dressing well-heeled gents, fashion editors and regular guys who appreciate no-nonsense style. With a focus on classic, high-quality design with a subtle retro edge (Steve McQueen has been cited as inspiration), the store is the label's unofficial clubhouse: airy and minimal, but unselfconsciously warm and friendly. Bestsellers such as the classic T-shirt (£30) and chinos (from £59) periodically sell out, having popped up in style mags and Saturday supplements the week before.
Branches 23 Beak Street, W1F 9RS (3157 7000); 286 Upper Street, N1 2TZ (7288 0835); 39 Monmouth Street, WC2H 9DD (7240 9391).

Start

Sunspel. See p58.

Anthem

Calvert Avenue, E2 7JP (7033 0054, www.anthem store.co.uk). Shoreditch High Street rail. **Open** 11am-7pm Tue-Fri; 11am-6.30pm Sat; 10am-4pm Sun.

Simon Spiteri, Liberty's former head of menswear, has brought some of the department store's quaint, creaky aesthetic to the East End with Anthem, his friendly men's indie clothing store with business partner Jeremy Baron. Natural wood, chipped brick walls and odd ephemera abound, but the moneyed shoppers will be drawn in by Spiteri and Baron's clever edit of brands, including Comme des Garçons Homme Plus (of which Anthem is London's only independent stockist), Club Monaco, Campbell Cole, Italian 1960s brand Barina Venezia, Brit brand Oliver Spencer and wonderfully obscure Japanese labels like Kaptital and scarves from the Hill-side. Smaller items – gifts, accessories, fragrances, stationery and flea market knick-knacks – are also on sale, with purchases packaged up in Fair Isle wrapping paper.

Article

96 Kingsland Road, E2 8DP (no phone, www.urbanexcess.com). Hoxton or Shoreditch High Street rail. **Open** 11.30am-7.30pm Mon-Sat; 12.30-6pm Sun.

Article is a further welcome addition to east London's ever-growing menswear market. Tucked in among the area's wealth of Vietnamese restaurants, it is the brainchild of Phil Stace, the man behind streetwear and contemporary clothing online retailer Urban Excess. In many ways, this store is a shop window for the website, with the same labels and design aesthetic. The range of special-edition Pointer sneakers, cycle-friendly Sandqvist Swedish backpacks (£99-£150) and cheap skinny jeans from Dr. Denim is the perfect fit for the local demographic, while streetier T-shirts from Obey and Puma collaboration trainers keep the kids dancing through the door. It doesn't hurt that the massive shop window leaves the store brightly lit, and the neatly merchandised stock on clear display to the passing footfall. Products are constantly re-stocked and updated; at the time of writing, some Saucony re-issue trainers were due in the next drop.

Hideout

7 Upper James Street, W1F 9DH (7437 4929, www.hideoutstore.com). Oxford Circus or Piccadilly Circus tube. **Open** 11am-7pm Mon-Fri; 11am-6.30pm Sat; noon-5pm Sun.

This small but central streetwear store has a New York feel to it – unsurprising as much of the stock comes from the Big Apple and Japan. There are also cool labels from London and further afield, popular with the city's skater contingent – such as Norse Projects, Palace, Neighborhood, Stussy, Carhartt, Supreme and Original Fake. All the streetwear staples are in attendance – hoodies, polos, sneakers and caps – and the quality and design of the garments are a definite cut above, with labels like Head Porter that can justify their slightly above-average pricing. One for those into exclusives and rare releases.

Interstate

17 Endell Street, WC2H 9BJ (7836 0421). Covent Garden tube. **Open** 11am-6.45pm Mon-Fri; 11am-6.30pm Sat; noon-6pm Sun.

Interstate was a central London staple for denim, polos and overcoats long before the likes of Urban Outfitters muscled in on the scene, and it's still as popular as ever. Denim and workwear are the focus, and it's packed with a decent range of sizes and well-chosen brands. There's a stack of tees and polos but its real appeal lies in its selection of workwear by Carhartt, Woolrich and Penfield, or as a place to pick up a sturdy pair of jeans from Japan's Edwin or Sweden's Nudie. Staff are helpful, if a little hawk-eyed, but overall the place is laid-back and unpretentious compared with some of its competitors.

Present

140 Shoreditch High Street, E1 6JE (7033 0500, www.present-london.com). Shoreditch High Street rail. **Open** 10am-7pm Mon-Fri; 11am-6.30pm Sat; 11am-5pm Sun.

Shoreditch men's boutique Present works to a clever ethic: rare labels and accessories from around the globe, cool collaborations – and coffee – all in a bright, contemporary space. Especially pick-uppable is the Japanese outerwear. There's also a good range of coats and jackets from Penfield, Nigel Cabourn and Heritage Research; Levi's jeans; backpacks from William Fox & Sons; toiletries from Aesop; shoes from F Troupe; brightly coloured socks from Duchamp; and good-quality lambswool scarves and gloves (as well as shirts, jumpers, jackets and shoes) from the eponymous, good-value house label. A selection of cool books, magazines, accessories and gadgets are also sold, while the Prufrock espresso bar sells top-quality single origin coffee – for those who want to fully appreciate their cup of joe. A very Shoreditch boutique for boys.

Sefton

196 Upper Street, N1 1RQ (7226 7076, www.seftonfashion.com). Highbury & Islington tube/rail. **Open** 10am-6.30pm Mon-Wed; 10am-7pm Thur, Fri; 10am-6.30pm Sat; noon-6pm Sun.

One of Islington's best-established boutiques, Sefton, the brainchild of Ben Elsdale, first opened its Upper Street doors back in 1999. The concept was to showcase the very best of British and international clothing design, and the store still sells a large variety of coveted menswear items from fashion-forward brands such as Acne, Moncler, Comme des Garçons, Edwin, Calabrese

and Sunspel, among others. Accessories are a particular strong point, while for relaxed everyday designerwear, Sefton's own label is very popular.

Supreme

2-3 Peter Street, W1F 0AA (7437 0493, www.supremenewyork.com). Oxford Circus tube.
Open 11am-7pm Mon-Sat; noon-6pm Sun.
Europe's first Supreme store opened in September 2011, to much excitement among London's skaters and streetwear obsessives (several of whom camped outside the store the night before it opened). The New York brand's products – previously only sold in London in nearby the Hideout and Dover Street Market – have retained their super-cool status since Supreme's 1994 debut through the hard work of a small team operating with a simple formula: great own-brand clothing, boards and accessories, a minimal approach to marketing and, crucially, skateboarding as a driving force. The stand-alone black-fronted Soho shop stocks, like its counterparts in the US and Japan, the entire collection of Supreme clothing, footwear and boards, as well as all the special releases. Expect to find an array of simple, wearable gear – tailored camo pieces without army-surplus bulk, unexpected animal patterns, barely branded basics, paisley on athletic fleecewear, collaborative projects with the likes of Levi's, and its trademark five-panel hats. The min-imalist split-level interior feels more like a gallery than a shop, with parquet floors, white walls, black-and-white prints and comic-style 3D artworks by Mark Gonzales.

Women

Aimé

32 Ledbury Road, W11 2AB (7221 7070, www.aimelondon.com). Notting Hill Gate tube.
Open 10am-6.30pm Mon-Sat.
Shoppers searching for a touch of Gallic chic on London's streets should make Aimé – the offspring of French-Cambodian sisters Val and Vanda Heng-Vong – their first port of call. Inside you'll find the crème de la crème of French designers, with labels like APC, Isabel Marant and Forte Forte. Bath products and seductive home accessories by Rice, including a range of scented candles, are equally attractive. Next door, Petit Aimé stocks a range of clothes for babies and children.
Branch Petit Aimé 34 Ledbury Road, W11 2AB (7221 3123).

Austique

330 King's Road, SW3 5UR (7376 4555, www. austique.co.uk). Sloane Square tube then 11, 22 bus. **Open** 10.30am-7pm Mon-Sat; noon-5pm Sun.

Anthem. See p61.

London's Best Charity Shops

With vintage shopping now out-pricing the high street, charity shopping is one of the few ways left to stock up your wardrobe on a budget. If you have a light wallet but a good eye and an explorer's spirit, hardcore rummaging can reap just rewards. Return visits can prove fruitful, but if you're really lucky you might just chance upon a Chanel blazer or Versace blouse on your first visit.

It's always a good idea to head to charity shops in affluent areas, where ladies who lunch wouldn't be seen dead dropping off anything less than than a bin bag full of Harvey Nics purchases. Try out West Hampstead's West End Lane (where you'll find Scope, Oxfam and Cancer Research), Chelsea and Pimlico for some of the best.

All Aboard West Hampstead

224 West End Lane, NW6 1UU (7794 3404, www.allaboardshops.com). West Hampstead tube/rail. **Open** 10am-6pm Mon-Fri; 10am-4pm Sun.

There are plenty of granny cast-offs to root through here – and believe us, you'll need to root. Apparel is in plentiful supply, and while reasonably organised, the stock is not as ruthlessly edited as that of more commercial-minded charity shops. It's just as well, as the volume means you're likely to turf up some real vintage finds – and cheap ones at that. All Aboard is a chain of stores raising funds for a selection of Jewish charities.

Barnado's Brixton

414 Brixton Road, SW9 7AY (7274 4165, www.barnardos.org.uk). Brixton tube/rail. **Open** 9am-5pm Mon-Sat; 10am-5pm Sun

A vast and lively charity shop with an exciting, unpredictable mix of clothes and accessories, stocking all kinds of high street brands, and with designer bargains going for no more than £50.

British Heart Foundation Balham

184 Balham High Road, SW12 9BW (8675 5401, www.bhf.org.uk). Balham tube/rail. **Open** 10am-6pm Mon-Sat; 11am-5pm Sun

This clean (it reeks of Mr Sheen) and brightly lit branch sells a good selection of high street and mid-range brands at very good prices. The shoes and jeans are well worth a look here. They're all sold alongside a range of new, cheaply priced accessories, including necklaces and earrings.

British Red Cross Chelsea

69-71 Old Church Street, SW3 5BS (7376 7300, www.redcross.org.uk). South Kensington tube. **Open** 10am-6pm Mon-Sat.

This expansive store is arguably Chelsea's most popular and well-known charity shop. It shares a street with the only Manolo Blahnik outpost in London and it's where Chelsea residents like to off-load last season's wardrobe. The store suitably bills itself as a designer charity shop, packing its rails with pieces by Vivienne Westwood, Jaeger, Max Mara and the like. Items are priced according to their original value, so while you might well find a steal, the price tags aren't quite as low as those in less savvy charity shops. Classic blazers, grown-up shift dresses and workwear shirts and skirts are staples and you'll often find a strong selection of bags and shoes.

British Red Cross Victoria

85 Ebury Street, SW1W 9QU (7730 2235, www.redcross.org.uk). Victoria tube/rail. **Open** 10am-5.30pm Mon-Sat.

Located a few minutes' walk from Victoria station in a salubrious street, this branch of the British Red Cross – always stuffed with expensive labels – has a comically conservative vibe. Navy blazers? Check. Padded Barbour-style jackets? Yep. Big, old, opulent ballgowns, no doubt bought for that charity auction circa 1985 in plentiful supply. Men are well catered for here too, with a fine selection of quality suits along the back wall by labels such as Hugo Boss, Crombie and Reiss.

Cancer Research UK

Marylebone High Street, W1U 4PQ (7487 4986, www.cancerresearchuk.org). Baker Street or Bond Street tube. **Open** 10am-6pm Mon-Wed; 10am-7pm Thur-Sat; noon-6pm Sun.

One street back from the chain stores and bustle of Oxford Street is this two-floor thrifty oasis of calm. On our last visit we found a red-and-navy wool military jacket, rails of men's suits and a great pair of 1970s silver platforms. It's a favourite with students from the nearby London College of Fashion and employees from *Vogue*, so if you want to bag the designer bargains, you'll need to visit regularly.

FASHION

Fara Kids

40 Tachbrook Street, SW1V 2JS (7630 7730, www.faracharityshops.org). Pimlico tube. **Open** 9.30am-5.30pm daily.
Pimlico, a real destination for charity shops, is home to three Fara stores – including Retromania – and they're close enough to do all of them in one sweep. This childrenswear shop offers an excellent selection of quality stock, which makes sense when you consider that children are likely to outgrow their wardrobes more quickly than they wear them out. Each item here looks about as good as new, with trusted labels like John Lewis, Marks & Spencer and Mini Boden spoiling thrifty mums for choice. From baby to eight years, there's plenty for both boys and girls as well as lots of toys, books, prams and a few decent cots.

Retromania

6 Upper Tachbrook Street, SW1V 1SH (7630 7406, www.faracharityshops.org). Pimlico tube. **Open** 10am-6pm daily
Retromania is the antithesis of shabby shopping, with all of the wow labels and fashion-forward merchandising of a savvy designer vintage store. Despite glam appearances, the store is actually part of the Fara charity retail group which spends its profits on orphaned and abandoned Romanian children. Fara has several London branches, but Retromania is where all of the really good fashion is directed; our recent visit turned up more Chanel than you could shake a 2.55 at, plus pieces by Marc Jacobs, Alexander McQueen, Pierre Cardin, Anna Sui and many more. Celebrities don't just pick up designer labels here, they drop them off too – Laurence Olivier once donated his 1920s-'40s jazz record collection to the store.

Salvation Army Oxford Circus

9 Princes Street, W1B 2LQ (7495 3958, www.salvationarmy.org). Oxford Circus tube. **Open** 10am-6pm Mon-Sat.
It's worth noting that this long-established store sits just a few stiletto clops from Vogue House, and takes receipt of some very fashionable cast-offs. The store takes up two floors with a variety of clothing, shoes, and accessories, with regular appearances from a range of high street brands from Oasis, Zara and Warehouse to Hobbs, East and MaxMara. On our visit, the branch had an incredible selection of branded shoes that looked as if they'd been worn just twice, including labels such as Carvela and Kurt Geiger for £18 a pop. The menswear section offers various suits from £30, and shirts, jeans and jumpers such as a barely worn Ted Baker number for £12.

Terrence Higgins Trust Shop

19 Churton Street, SW1V 2LY (7233 8736, www.tht.org.uk). Pimlico tube. **Open** 10am-6pm Mon-Sat; noon-4pm Sun.
With its Shirley Bassey soundtrack and dedicated gay section, this charmingly eccentric charity shop was termed 'the Harvey Nichols of charity shops' by comedian and regular shopper Alan Carr. Happily, the prices are somewhat more purse-friendly than the Knightsbridge department store. There are lots of cheap jeans (from £8) hanging neatly next to bargain cotton shirts and rock T-shirts, as well as more opulent designer creations, donated regularly by top brands including Hackett, Nicole Farhi and Ralph Lauren. We spotted a floor-length woollen camel Givenchy coat and a divine Yves Saint Laurent peacoat.

Traid

61 Westbourne Grove, W2 4UA (7221 2421, www.traid.org.uk). Notting Hill Gate tube. **Open** 10am-6pm Mon-Sat; 11am-5pm Sun.
Unlike some charity shops in the area, where all you find is tatty high street cast-offs, Traid (which stands for Textile Recycling for Aid and International Development) has a huge mix of good vintage, high street and designer. While rummaging, we found a woman's wool Aquascutum coat. There's also a fine range of accessories for both men and women.

Trinity Hospice

33 Kensington Church Street, W8 4LL (7376 1098, www.trinityhospice.org.uk). High Street Kensington tube. **Open** 10.30am-6pm Mon-Sat; 10am-4pm Sun.
Renowned for its smart ladies' clothing and accessories, this is a great charity shop where you're bound to unearth designer pieces. There's always a top selection of handbags and shoes, often including Prada evening shoes and DKNY bags.

FASHION

Opened by sisters Katie Cancin and Lindy Lopes, Austique displays a super-feminine collection of clothes, lingerie and accessories in a light, two-floor space. Unsurprisingly, given the name, there's a strong Antipodean influence, with designs from the likes of Camilla & Marc and a sexy range of swimwear from Zimmermann. But labels are sourced from all over the world, taking in pieces by upmarket designers such as Madeleine Thompson. The shop also stocks its own label, Austique, offering an assortment of silk dresses, pyjamas and pretty ballet shoes. There's a lovely selection of jewellery from the likes of Alex Monroe, and bags from Wilbur & Gussie and Rebecca Minkoff – all in keeping with the girly feel of the clothes. Upstairs you'll find everything for the boudoir including a great range of knickers, negligees and camisoles. Essie nail polish is also stocked.

Cochinechine
74 Heath Street, NW3 1DN (7435 9377, www.cochinechine.com). Hampstead tube.
Open 10am-6pm Mon-Sat; noon-6pm Sun.
Eftychia Georgilis's airy and feminine boutique brings an interesting selection of designer labels to Hampstead. Spread over two floors are hip, wearable clothes from boutique favourites Anna Sui, McQ, Sonia by Sonia Rykiel, Carven, Acne and Peter Jensen. Accessories include Jennifer Behr headbands and a range of Eddie Borgo jewellery as well as Comme des Garçons leather goods. There's a good selection of shoes by Maloles, Opening Ceremony and Penelope Chilvers. Customer service and a welcoming vibe are high priorities here.

Iris
97 Northcote Road, SW11 6PL (7924 1836, www.irisfashion.co.uk). Clapham Junction tube/rail.
Open 10am-6pm Mon-Sat; 11am-5pm Sun.
The first Iris – the ultimate media mum neighbourhood boutique – opened in 2005 in Queen's Park; since then, owners Annie Pollet and Sarah Claassen have opened two more stores – this one on Battersea's Northcote Road, and another one more recently on Chiswick High Road – turning the brand into a mini-chain of feminine frocks. As well as stylish womenswear from a good mix of classic boutique labels, such as APC, Etoile Isabel Marant and J Brand. Pollet and Claassen's friendly approach to their customer base of stylish young mums (there are toy boxes provided to keep the tots occupied, for instance) helps to create a stress-free shopping experience.
Branches 73 Salisbury Road, NW6 6NJ (7372 1777); 129 Chiswick High Road, W4 2ED (8742 3811).

KJ's Laundry
74 Marylebone Lane, W1U 2PW (7486 7855, www.kjslaundry.com). Bond Street tube.
Open 10am-7pm Mon-Wed, Fri, Sat; 10am-8pm Thur; 11am-5pm Sun.
Owners Jane Ellis and Kate Allden stock a mix of lesser-known designers in their super chic and spacious Marylebone store, including Samatha Sung, Iro, Vanessa Bruno Athé and Eternal Child. Look out for Leathers by Doma and Mackage coats, as well as day to evening dresses from Rebecca Taylor. Hidden behind the over-hyped high street, this attitude-free boutique has lines you won't see all over town (as well as a few established boutique names such as YMC and Sessùn), and by manning the shop floor themselves, the owners can adapt their buying according to demand. It is a business model that seems to be working – a second KJ's Laundry opened in Chelsea in September 2012.
Branch 149 King's Road, SW3 5TX (7486 7855).

Labour of Love
193 Upper Street, N1 1RQ (no phone, www.labour-of-love.co.uk). Angel tube or Highbury & Islington tube/rail. **Open** 11am-6pm Tue-Sun.
This Islington gem stocks a range of colourful clothing for those who want something a little bit different. The shop stocks individual pieces by the likes of Peter Jensen (renowned for his witty prints) and Eley Kishimoto (for stylish footwear), hand-picked by owner Francesca Forcolini. Forcolini's own Labour of Love label goes from strength to strength. Expect to find playful yet wearable clothes at reasonable prices for the level of quality: key pieces include trenches, and leather and suede gloves, as well as the label's popular jazz shoes in a great range of eye-popping colours. It's also a great place to browse for gifts; look out for original jewellery by Momocreatura and hats from Hilary Grant. The place to go for pieces that combine high style with longevity.

Press
3 Erskine Road, NW3 3AJ (7449 0081, www.pressprimrosehill.com). Chalk Farm tube.
Open 9.30am-6pm Mon-Fri; 9.45am-6.15pm Sat; noon-6pm Sun.
Before opening her boutique in 2004, Melanie Press had solid retail credentials as former creative director of Whistles. The ultimate Primrose Hill chick's closet, Press sells a good mix of trendy designer labels from its shabby chic space, such as APC, Current Elliott, Humanoid and Anglomania by Vivienne Westwood, alongside a select range of vintage pieces. The shop also stocks an impressive range of denim, including cult jeans label J Brand.

Relax Garden
40 Kingsland Road, E2 8DA (7033 1881, www.relaxgarden.com). Old Street tube/rail.
Open noon-7pm Mon-Wed; noon-8pm Thur, Fri; noon-6pm Sat, Sun.

FASHION

KJ's Laundry

This tiny Kingsland Road boutique aims to bring lesser-known independent labels from abroad to the UK and is a good bet for original garb at Topshop prices. Look out for LA-based GLAM, jersey knitwear by Italian label Northland and a wide selection of Japanese labels and, new in 2012, Color People. The shop's own label, Relax Garden, designed by owner Eriko Nagata, offers reasonably priced, simple, feminine designs in silk and jersey. There's also a good selection of well-priced accessories and shoes, and pretty jewellery by London-based label Mille & Me. The shop is a good stop-off for cute hair clips, hairbands, vintage-style plastic earrings and patterned tights.

Sixty 6

4 Blenheim Terrace, NW8 0EB (7372 6100). St John's Wood or Maida Vale tube. **Open** noon-6.30pm Tue-Sat.

The owner of this lovely St John's Wood boutique, former antiques dealer Jane Collins, has a knack for choosing clothes that are eye-catching and feminine without being showy; many items are distinguished by interesting trimmings or embellishments. A tempting mix of designers is in evidence, including Anne Louise Roswald, David Meister, Samantha Sung and there are beautiful dresses from La Petite S. There's a mid-range line-up too, with Malene Birger and Just In Case pieces displayed in combinations you might not have thought of putting together yourself. The shop also has the widest range of tops and dresses by Velvet we've seen in the capital, including unusual styles. Look out for the large variety of cashmere, knitwear and scarves by Magaschoni and Crumpet as well as a great selection of vintage earrings.

Village Bicycle

79-81 Ledbury Road, W11 2AG (7313 9031, www.imavillagebicycle.com). Notting Hill Gate or Westbourne Park tube. **Open** 10am-6pm Mon-Wed, Fri, Sat; 10am-7pm Thur; noon-5pm Sun.

When you hear the words 'socialite-owned-boutique' and 'Ledbury Road' you can be forgiven for imagining a Trinny and Susannah-endorsed affair. The Village Bicycle, opened by 'fashion entrepreneur' Willa Keswick (with fashion royalty Tallulah Harlech on styling duty) in June 2011, is actually nothing of the sort, despite rubbing shoulders with the likes of Diane Von Furstenburg and Brora cashmere on a very sedate street indeed. There's plenty to surprise and delight even the edgiest of shoppers. Labels like Lulu & Co, Alice McCall and Surface to Air abound, with a small selection of menswear from Eleven Paris. Staff are relaxed, cool and friendly, and happy for you to lounge on the *Beetlejuice*-style sofas, reading coffee-table books and eating penny sweets. Hey – Shoreditch called – they want their shop back!

Village Bicycle

Streetwise **Redchurch Street, E2**

Formerly edgy Redchurch Street is now London's most fashion-forward road.

Not so long ago, Redchurch Street was a rough-edged cut-through between Shoreditch High Street and Brick Lane. In recent years it has undergone a dramatic transformation, and now finds itself at the centre of the hipster East End, surrounded by Bethnal Green Road, Shoreditch High Street, Calvert Avenue and Club Row.

Turn into Redchurch Street from Shoreditch High Street and you'll see an outpost of Australian skincare brand **Aesop** (no.5, 7613 3793) in a typically pared-down store where you can try out the paraben-free products. French fashion label **APC** (*see p79*) is next door at no.5a, bringing some understated Parisian chic to the street. Lovely back-to-basics fashion is also available at the boutique at no.7: **Sunspel** (*see p58*). This classic British menswear-maker specialises in quality underwear, T-shirts and polo shirts.

For goods that are equally English, but edible rather than sartorial, head to **Albion** (www.albioncaff.co.uk), the café-shop that's part of Terence Conran's Boundary Project (www.theboundary.co.uk), on the corner of Redchurch and Boundary streets. You'll find a wealth of home-grown brands in the shop, from HP Sauce to Neal's Yard. The buzz surrounding Redchurch Street was intensified by the hullabaloo that greeted Boundary and nearby members' club **Shoreditch House** on Ebor Street, which houses an open-to-all branch of the Cowshed spa (7749 4531). A little further up Boundary Street, womenswear boutique **11 Boundary** (no.11, 7033 0310, www.11boundary.com) stocks labels such as Wildfox and Day Birger et Mikkelsen.

Further up Redchurch Street, there are more exciting shops. **Hostem** (nos.41-43, 7739 9733,

www.hostem.co.uk) is a darkly lit menswear shop with a well-edited selection from the likes of Adam Kimmel, Ann Demuelemeester and rare brands such as Mastermind Japan. Decadent **Maison Trois Garçons** (no.45, 07879 640858, www.lestroisgarcons.com) deals in interiors. No.63 houses one of the street's trendiest stores (and that's saying something here); **Zone7Style** (www.zone7style.blogspot.com) specialises in cult 1980s and '90s gear (think brightly coloured Versace, Moschino and Chipie numbers, focusing on menswear), and has a fabulous range of high-end retro sunglasses. Next door is the **Painted Lady** (no.65, 7729 2154, www.thepaintedladylondon.com), a cute hair salon and nail bar, offering vintage-style up-dos and great-value manicures.

Three of the highest-profile shops on the street are capacious British concept store **Aubin & Wills** (no.64; *see p54*), where you can buy men's, women's and homewares lines in a sort of grown-up collegiate style, as well as catching a film in the small luxury cinema or some art in the gallery; the homespun homewares shop **Labour & Wait** (no.85; *see p161*; and, at no.73a, a branch of fashionable women's footwear brand **Tracey Neuls** (*see p120*). One street north, on Old Nichol Street, is Margaret Howell's **MHL store** (no.19, 7033 9494), with it's wonderfully neat-freak interior of folded jumpers and tees.

After this style overload, you may need some light refreshment. For a quick caffeine hit at one of the street's new-wave spots, try the **Allpress Espresso** (no.58, 7749 1780) roastery and café.

FASHION

High Street

Abercrombie & Fitch

7 Burlington Gardens, W1S 3ES (0844 412 5750, www.uk.abercrombie.com). Oxford Circus or Piccadilly Circus tube. **Open** 10am-8pm Mon-Sat; noon-6pm Sun. **Sells** M, W.

This is a case of having to be seen to be believed. The US clothing brand's 2007 arrival horrified the neighbours. The way not to impress the Savile Row set that it's now geographically a part of: with banging tunes and a male model standing in the doorway at all times. Indeed, with its dimmed lighting and weird scent, the place feels more like a bizarre, posh club than a shop. Despite this, or maybe because of it, A&F's logo-heavy sweaters, jeans and polos (to be worn with collars turned up, of course) are mighty popular with the Sloane Square set. Oddly, you may have to queue to get in.

All Saints

57-59 Long Acre, WC2E 9JL (7836 0801, www.allsaints.co.uk). Covent Garden tube. **Open** 9am-8pm Mon-Sat; noon-6pm Sun. **Sells** M, W.

With its distressed denim, leather and glitzy sequinned asymmetric dresses, All Saints provides edgy glamour with a dose of knowingly trashy bling. Inside the store, the exposed brickwork and pumping music create a warehouse-like feel that has made it a hit with the twentysomething market. On offer is a blend of indie band inspired shirts, boots, and embellished vest tops and dresses. The selection of jeans is probably the brand's high point, along with the statement shoes and edgy women's accessories. Boys are well looked after with a good selection of slim-fitting shirts, skinny jeans and offbeat T-shirts.

Branches throughout the city.

American Apparel

3-4 Carnaby Street, W1F 9PB (7734 4477, www.americanapparel.net). Oxford Circus tube. **Open** 10am-8pm Mon-Wed, Fri, Sat; 10am-9pm Thur; noon-6pm Sun. **Sells** M, W, C.

Since it opened its first shop in London some seven years ago, ethically minded US-import American Apparel has expanded at breakneck speed. The colourful, kinky 1980s-inspired garb (leggings, figure-hugging jersey and lace dresses, spandex leotards, skinny jeans, tracksuit bottoms, cheerleader-style knee-highs, parkas, and a large range of tops) seemed to capture the spirit of recent times – at least as far as twentysomethings were concerned – with simple cuts, comfortable materials and semi-affordable prices. The company first conquered with well-fitting cotton tees, then the nigh-on-perfect hoody that became the

COS. See p72.

uniform of the East End trendy, and, more recently with its nudge nudge, wink wink retro briefs. **Branches** throughout the city.

Banana Republic

224 Regent Street, W1B 3BR (7758 3550, www. bananarepublic.eu). Oxford Circus tube. **Open** 10am-8pm Mon-Wed, Fri; 10am-9pm Thur; 9am-8pm Sat; noon-6pm Sun. **Sells** M, W.
The 17,000sq ft store on Regent Street covers two vast floors and feels like a posh hotel lobby, with its chandeliers, spiral staircases and plush chairs. The stock is equally elegant, encompassing a selection of refined clothes and accessories. For women, there is a good selection of wardrobe staples and workwear, as well as chic eveningwear in the form of ruffled shirts and fitted shift dresses. The ground-floor collection has more than a nod to Burberry with its creamy trenches and gathered blouses, while upstairs are more youthful numbers, like silk printed smock dresses, tees and embellished tops. Pieces are often highly tactile, with lots of cashmere and satin. The modern city gent will also feel at home here, with a choice of casual chinos, sweaters and smart shirts in the basement. Back on the ground, the impressive array of moderately priced jewellery is well worth a gander, as is the collection of shoes. Styles here may not be hot off the runway, but it's a good bet for timeless style. **Branches** throughout the city.

Best for...

Vintage inspired design – all the style, none of the weird smell
Oasis (*see p73*); **American Apparel** (*see p70*).

Style that will last – confidently classic designs with staying power
Banana Republic (*see above*); **French Connection** (*see p72*); **Uniqlo** (*see p75*); **Whistles** (*see p76*); **COS** (*see p72*).

Menswear – the best men's brands in town
Topman (*see p74*); **Reiss** (*see p74*); **Banana Republic** (*see above*).

Big designer collaborations – from fashion heavyweights to LFW newcomers
Topshop (*see p75*); **H&M** (*see p73*); **Whistles** (*see p76*).

Being on trend – the stores that lead the way
Topshop (*see p75*); **H&M** (*see p73*); **Oasis** (*see p73*).

Fashion First Aid

Menders

British Invisible Mending Service
32 Thayer Street, W1U 2QT (7487 4292, www.invisible-mending.co.uk). Bond Street tube.
Also known as BIMS, craftsmen here are able to repair small holes in a garment by taking fibres from a hidden section and using it to weave over the damaged area. Saville Row tailors send moth-eaten suits here for repair.

Franco Santoro
26 Kingly Street, W1B 5QD (7437 8440). Oxford Street tube.
The main denim retailers in the area send jeans to the alterations veteran Franco Santoro to be taken up for their special customers. He painstakingly takes the original thread out of jeans and re-uses to avoid a mismatching thread colour.

Tosca & Daughters
85 Sloane Street, SW1 (7730 1400). Sloane Square tube.
These traditionally trained tailors are experts in refurbishing and altering clothes made from delicate fabrics such as chiffon and silk.

Cobblers

Broadway Shoe Repairs
2 Bank Chambers, Tooting High Street, SW17 0SU (8682 0618). Tooting Broadway tube.
This no-frills local offers great value on-the-spot repairs. From £5.35 for a re-heel to £49.50 for complete stitched leather resoling.

City Cobbler
215 City Road, EC1V 1JN (7251 8658). Old Street tube/rail.
All fixing needs are catered for – from resoling shoes to handbag repairs – at this friendly City cobbler. From £7.95 for stilletto reheeling.

Classic Shoe Repair
23-25 Brecknock Road, N7 0BL (7485 5275, www.classicshoerepairs.com). Caledonian Road tube.
Manolo Blahnik, no less, gets his shoes fixed at this long-established Islington repair shop. From £7.95 for a re-heel to £48 for a Christian Louboutin red resole.

Fifth Avenue
41 Goodge Street, W1T 2PY (7636 6705, www.fifthavenueshoerepairs.com). Goodge Street tube.
No job is too big or too small for these traditional bag and shoe repairers. From £7.95 for a reheel to £52 for a stitched leather resole.

Kelpis
761 Fulham Road, SW6 5UU (7736 3856). Parsons Green tube.
A favourite with fashion designers, this traditional cobbler provides solid shoe and bag repairs and alterations. From £12 for re-heeling.

COS
222 Regent Street, W1B 5BD (7478 0400, www. cosstores.com). Oxford Circus tube. **Open** 10am-9pm Mon-Fri; 10am-8pm Sat; noon-6pm Sun. **Sells** M, W.
H&M created a buzz when it opened this flagship store in 2007, and the brand has gone from strength to strength, offering Scandinavian-led affordable fashion. For those who have grown tired of fighting their way through a frenzy of teenagers at the sale rails, COS (which stands for Collection of Style) is the antithesis to H&M's throwaway trend-led fashion – and is championed by style bloggers and fashion editors alike. The slick, well laid-out store houses an impressive range of simple, classic separates and coats, jackets and eveningwear in good-quality fabrics and both neutral and vibrant colours. Recent collections have focused on simple shift dresses, classic narrow leg suits for men, and loose-fitting T-shirts and puffy skirts for women. Prices start at around £50 for a dress and £69 for jackets; men's suits average between £200 and £250. The store also boasts some cute retro underwear, good accessories (such as leather clutch bags and pared-down jewellery) and quality leather belts. **Branches** throughout the city.

French Connection
396 Oxford Street, W1C 1JX (7629 7766, www.frenchconnection.com). Bond Street tube.
Open 10am-9pm Mon-Fri; 10am-8pm Sat; noon-6pm Sun. **Sells** M, W.
Now considered an old-timer on the list of high street brands, French Connection has worked hard over the past couple of years to free itself from the shackles of its FCUK identity – and it appears to have succeeded. Designs are a mix of mature and on-trend, with unfussy separates and outerwear in a range of good-quality

fabrics and in bright but rarely garish colours and patterns; the look manages to be very distinctively 'French Connection', even though it's not that obviously different from the rest of the high street. Dresses and eveningwear in sequinned and glittery fabrics, and simple cotton shift dresses are among the most popular offerings for women. The classic T-shirts and knitwear remain firm favourites, and its good selection of denim jeans and cotton workwear trousers complement every wardrobe.
Branches throughout the city.

H&M

261-271 Regent Street, W1B 2ES (7493 4004, www.hm.com). Oxford Circus tube. **Open** 10am-9pm Mon-Sat; noon-6pm Sun. **Sells** M, W.
H&M, for those who have been living under a rock, has been one of the high street frontrunners for catwalk-inspired, affordable (but low-quality) clothing. The low-priced retailer that opened its first store in Västerås, Sweden back in 1947 is now a multinational with over 2,000 stores worldwide. The brand partly made its name through attracting superdesigners such as Karl Lagerfeld, Marni and Versace – as well as, um, Madonna and Kylie – to create in-house diffusion lines. Recent innovations have included an organic, affordable skincare range as well as a nice lingerie line. The shop is a good bet for on-trend jackets and T-shirts, stylish accessories, beachwear and budget staples.
Branches throughout the city.

Jigsaw

21 Long Acre, WC2E 9LD (7240 3855, www.jigsaw-online.com). Covent Garden or Leicester Square tube or Charing Cross tube/rail. **Open** 10am-8pm Mon-Sat; noon-6pm Sun. **Sells** W, C.
With its classic lines, simply cut separates and luxurious fabrics, Jigsaw feels every inch the grown-up of high street fashion; and after keeping something of a low profile in the early noughties, it's now back on the radars of the capital's style-conscious thirtysomethings. While designs seem to vary little from season to season, there's the occasional on-trend surprise, with jackets and dresses a strong point. But Jigsaw is really more about the quality of the materials rather than the edginess of the cuts – with tweed, merino wool, cashmere and silky cottons often appearing, in earthy, tasteful tones. Accessories are a highlight, with a good range of sunglasses, belts, scarves and soft leather bags, shoes and boots.
Branches throughout the city.

Oasis

12-14 Argyll Street, W1F 7NT (7434 1799, www.oasis-stores.com). Oxford Circus tube. **Open** 10am-8pm Mon-Wed, Fri, Sat; 10am-9pm Thur; 10am-6pm Sun. **Sells** W.
Well-made, often vintage-inspired clothes for young women. Over the past few seasons, Oasis has been

Topman. See p74.

particularly strong on shift and tea-style summer dresses, pretty blouses, leather biker jackets, khaki parkas and playsuits, as well as being a good bet for glamorous eveningwear for fashion-conscious twentysomethings. Oasis also does a good line in cheap spangly jewellery, patterned tights, silky lingerie, leather bags, printed neckscarves, and other accessories. It's also worth checking out its affordable workwear, such as suit jackets, tube skirts and court shoes. Impressive. **Branches** throughout the city.

Reiss

Kent House, 14-17 Market Place, W1H 7AJ (7637 9112, www.reiss.co.uk). Oxford Circus tube. **Open** 10am-7pm Mon-Sat; noon-6pm Sun. **Sells** M, W.

Bridging a cavernous gap between high street and high-end fashion, Reiss is the place to shop if you like your clothing well made and safely stylish. With its mix of tailored suits and separates, and after-dark and special-occasion dresses, it's not hard to figure out why this shop is popular. The layout of the shop is clean, uncluttered and well organised, with staff readily available to offer advice. Overall, the look is smart, with menswear offering heavyweight dark denim, crisp shirts with epaulettes and chunky knits in neutral colours. For women, there are flirty shift dresses with exquisite details and ruching in the finest of fabrics. The brand's 1971 Reiss collection is a highlight, while its no-refunds policy is a definite low point. **Branches** throughout the city.

Topman

214 Oxford Street, W1W 8LG (0844 848 7487, www.topman.com). Oxford Circus tube. **Open** 9am-9pm Mon-Wed, Sat; 9am-10pm Thur, Fri; 11am-9pm Sun. **Sells** M.

Topman is as on-trend as the high street gets for guys. And while it's true that on a Saturday this flagship, occupying the top two floors of the Topshop Topman building, resembles something of a teenage Hades – crowds and queues – everyone here knows that they're on to a good thing. Well-cut jeans and chinos for all shapes and sizes are dirt cheap and bang on trend, with everything from photo-print T-shirts and bombers to leather jackets and patterned shirts. The top floor houses Topman's smarter wear, branded concessions, in house label Topman LTD and capsule collections by young designers. Next to a branch of barbershop Sharpe's is a personal shopping suite designed by Lee Broome, featuring consultation rooms, Xbox 360s, an exhibition space and pop-up food events. Topman

opened a boutique-style shop – Topman General Store (98 Commercial Street, E1 6LZ, 7377 2671) in Spitalfields in October 2011 and another in April 2012 in Covent Garden (36-38 Earlham Street, WC2H 9LA, 7240 1971). **Branches** throughout the city.

Topshop

214 Oxford Street, W1W 8LG (0844 124 1144, www.topshop.com). Oxford Circus tube. **Open** 9am-9pm Mon-Wed; 9am-10pm Thur, Fri; 9am-9pm Sat; 11am-9pm Sun. **Sells** W.

London's teenage girls (and their parents) are no stranger to Topshop. The biggest, bossiest, pushiest member of Philip Green's Arcadia group, the brand has been the queen of the British high street for the past decade, and walking into the busy Oxford Street flagship, it's easy to see why. A simple, stark layout, but with every surface crammed full of gear, the place is buzzing with fashion-forward teens and twentysomethings. Spanning three floors, the store boasts huge accessories collections, and has in-house concessions for Office and Miss Selfridge. Keen to reinforce its hipster credentials with links to London Fashion Week, Topshop also champions the cause of the young British designer and often holds events and collaborations with high-profile industry figures, such as blogger Susie Bubble and fashion editor

Katie Shillingford. It appointed one-time *Vogue* fashion director Kate Phelan as its creative director in 2011. The huge range on offer covers a multitude of styles, with often poor-quality fabrics the flipside of the brand's on-trend styles. The flagship also has personal shoppers, a blow dry bar, Wah Nails manicures, Bleach hair design, waxing, eye-brow threading, a café – even a tattoo concession with the addition of Metalmorphosis. A fun, if frenzied, shopping experience. If you lack the stamina to fight your way through the throng, then try the less stressful Brompton Road 'boutique branch', which opened in summer 2010; or, better still, use Topshop To Go, where a selection of clothing is brought to your home or office. **Branches** throughout the city.

Uniqlo

311 Oxford Street, W1C 2HP (7290 7701, www.uniqlo.co.uk). Oxford Circus tube. **Open** 10am-9pm Mon-Sat; noon-6pm Sun (browsing from 11.30am). **Sells** M, W.

Uniqlo ferociously attempted to rebrand in 2007, with celeb envoys like Chloë Sevigny, a Terry Richardson advertising campaign and the opening of two new stores on Oxford Street. However, whether Uniqlo is more than simply a Japanese Gap is a case for debate; useful staples – such as the HEATTECH thermal

Topshop

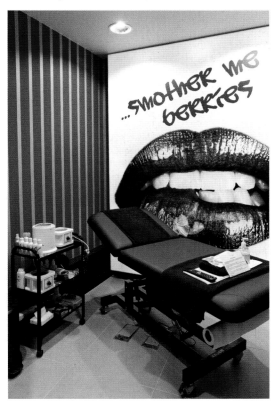

FASHION

Streetwise
Earlham Street, WC2

On the edge of Covent Garden and close to Soho is Earlham Street, with its mix of music, fashion, vintage and art shops. At the Cambridge Circus end sits **Fopp** (no.1; *see p194*), selling an impressive collection of books, bargain DVDs (including a very good arthouse collection) and music spread over three floors. For the more particular shopper is **Orc's Nest** at no.6 (7329 4254), which caters for all manner of geekery: otherworldly plastic miniatures, comics, magazines and trading cards for role playing are plentiful here. The **Dover Bookshop** (no.18, 7836 2111) has illustrated books stacked high, while arts specialist **Magma Books** (no.8; *see p190*) is a must-visit for magazine junkies, with a collection that runs from international glossies to fanzines. Sister store **Magma Products** (a few doors down) sells an eclectic mix of stationary, ornaments, tea towels and other curios.

Fashion-wise, **Urban Outfitters** (no.42-56, 7759 6390) offers both modern streetwear, from labels such as Shore Leave, Cheap Monday and Libertine-Libertine, and well sourced vintage collections. Continuing on the retro theme, the **Vintage Showroom** (*see p97 and p100*), at no.14, is a wonderful menswear store, stocking quality brands such as Pendelton and Barbour, as well as lots of Americana and more specialist items (heavy duty ex-Soviet army surplus and sailor's smocks, for example). **Carhartt** (no .17, 7836 1551) is worth a visit; its recent collaboration with A.P.C. has made its well-made and functional work wear a more familiar sight on London's streets. If you're more a lover of old school hip-hop chic, then a visit to the **Adidas Originals Store** at no. 9 (7379 4042) is a treat – despite the expense.

For a splash of colour amid the grey urban terrain, check out florists the **Wild Bunch** (7497 1200). Staff here will artfully arrange a bouquet for you in minutes.

underwear for men and women, the well-cut jeans, graphic T-shirts, smart shirts, and cut-price cashmere and merino wool jumpers and cardigans – are the brand's strong point. However, look beyond these items, and it becomes apparent that many of the styles here are rather unremarkable, although the occasional vintage-inspired top or well-cut mac may surprise. **Branches** throughout the city.

Urban Outfitters
200 Oxford Street, W1D 1NU (7907 0800, www.urbanoutfitters.co.uk). Oxford Circus tube. **Open** 10am-8pm Mon-Wed, Fri, Sat; 10am-9pm Thur; 10am-8pm Sat; noon-6pm Sun. **Sells** M, W.
Urban Outfitters is vintage shopping for people who don't like vintage shopping; the brand may hail from America but its London stores have strong traces of Cool Britannia. You'll find homewares, accessories and clothes for every occasion; step into the Oxford Street store and be greeted by an overwhelming mix of casualwear, coffee-table books and kitschy pieces for gifts, such as floral picture frames, retro lip balm and plastic cameras from Lomography and Holga. Menswear is in the basement, with the first and second floors dedicated to womenswear, covering a wide range of styles, from vintage and bohemian to classic, and with lots of pieces from in-house concessions Kimchi Blue and Silence + Noise. There's also a good selection of jeans and denim (including popular Swedish brand Cheap Monday). Prices climb as you go upstairs to the second floor, where ultra-stylish labels such as Something Else, Whyred, APC Madras, Sessùn, Vanessa Bruno Athé and Vivienne Westwood are all stocked. If prices are above your budget, keep an eye out for the sales periods when real bargains can be had.
Branches 42-56 Earlham Street, WC2H 9LJ (7759 6390); 36-38 Kensington High Street, W8 4PF (7761 1001).

Whistles
12-14 St Christopher's Place, W1U 1NH (7487 4484, www.whistles.co.uk). Bond Street tube. **Open** 10am-7pm Mon-Wed, Fri; 10am-8pm Thur; 10am-6.30pm Sat; noon-6pm Sun. **Sells** W.
With Jane Shepherdson at the helm for the past few years, Whistles has become the queen of the high street, turning out high-quality, on-trend, feminine yet practical styles. With its floaty fabrics, vintage-inspired shapes and eclectic mix of separates, the overall feel is a sort of urban Bohemia. Prices are higher than the usual high street outlet but, with an emphasis on materials and finishing, these well-made pieces should last a lifetime. Staple items include blouses in soft fabrics, loose knits, drop-waist gathered skirts and pencil skirts. Prices start from around £85 for knitwear and dresses and £165 for coats.
Branches throughout the city.

Whistles

Alexander McQueen

International Designer

Mayfair's **Old Bond Street**, **New Bond Street**, **Dover Street** and Chelsea's **Sloane Street** are key streets to familiarise yourself with if you're a fan of high-end designer garb. **Mount Street** has more recently established itself as another spot for high spenders.

Men & women

Acne Studio
13 Dover Street, W1S 4LN (7629 9374, www.acne-studios.com). Green Park tube. **Open** 10am-7pm Mon-Sat; noon-5pm Sun.
When it was established in 1997, Acne was less a fashion brand, more a high-concept collective. Four friends sat around in a posh Stockholm new-build, thinking about product design and sharing a single motivating idea: the Ambition to Create Novel Expressions (Acne, get it?). Since then it's produced all manner of intelligent – and expensive – things. Advertising campaigns and commercials, a pretty decent magazine called *Acne Paper*, a book and shirt collection, *Snowdon Blue*, commemorating the iconic photographer, branding for other fashion labels, films (including a project with Ridley Scott), odd-shaped luxury furniture that looks like an optical illusion and all sorts of digital cleverness. Not least, a simple, sophisticated fashion brand that has found its way into the wardrobes of fashion editors and stylists the world over. Its shop on Dover Street, Mayfair, the brand's first stand-alone store in the UK, represents the coming together of Acne's many parts, and it looks just as clean, clipped and conceptual as you would imagine. A one-time gallery, it's a skinny, four-storey affair, wedged in between two Georgian townhouses. Men's and women's clothing collections hang on the ground floor. Up on the first, giant lumps of amethyst populate a miniature roof garden viewed through a picture window, leading on to more clothing, with the brand's wonderfully wonky furniture to lounge around on. On the top floor is the brand's bread and butter: women's shoes and a complete denim collection, plus a small outside area in among the chimney pots. There's also an Acne womenswear concession in Harrods.

Alexander McQueen
4-5 Old Bond Street, W1S 4PD (7355 0088, www.alexandermcqueen.com). Green Park tube. **Open** 10am-6pm Mon-Wed, Fri, Sat; 10am-7pm Thur.
The late Alexander McQueen's only UK store is a contemporary space with curved lines and soft lighting. The ground floor is dedicated to womenswear and accessories, which spill into the lower-ground floor, where you'll also find some wickedly sharp men's tailoring, outrageously

Sales & events

Browns Labels for Less
50 South Molton Street W1K 5RD (7514 0056) Bond Street tube. **Open** 10am-6.30pm Mon-Wed, Fri, Sat; 10am-7pm Thur.
The Browns group's outlet store carrying men's and women's designer brands at permanently discounted prices.

Burberry Factory Shop
29-31 Chatham Place, E9 6LP (8328 4287). Hackney Central rail. **Open** 9am-7pm Mon-Sat; 11am-5pm Sun.
This glittering warehouse-sized space showcases seconds and excess stock reduced by 50% or more. Classic men's macs can be had for around £199 or less.

Designer Sales UK
www.designersalesuk.com
This sample sale pops up throughout the year and often features big-name bargains from Vivienne Westwood and Maison Martin Margiela, to Viktor & Rolf and Marc Jacobs, starting at just £15. Expect a smattering of handbags, shoes, accessories and vintage pieces as well.

Designer Warehouse Sale
5-6 Islington Studios, Thane Villas, N7 7NU (www.designerwarehousesales.com).
The Designer Warehouse Sale is now well over 25 years old, and still selling discount designer goods like they're going out of fashion. Twelve times a year, the three-day womenswear event sells labels like Celine, Dior and Calvin Klein at bargain prices for the eagle-eyed.

London Accessory Sale
www.londonaccessorysale.co.uk
Expect big names from this multi-brand sale, such as Marc Jacobs, Missoni and Helmut Lang. It's a members-only event catering to label junkies of both sexes (visit the website for free membership).

London Fashion Weekend
Somerset House, the Strand, WC2R 1LA (www.londonfashionweekend.co.uk).
The tail end of the bi-annual London Fashion Week brings with it a wave of fashion excitement in the form of London Fashion Weekend, where we mere mortals have the chance to dip our toes in the fashion pool at Somerset House. By the time you depart you'll be too hot to trot with your steals from the Weekend Boutique's various pop-up stores that, in the past, have featured Antipodium, Aubin & Wills, Twenty8Twelve, Finsk and more (all up to 70% off).

dapper footwear and manbags. The bags for women are equally delectable. Since McQueen's death in 2010, the collections have been designed by his former right-hand woman, Sarah Burton, now the label's creative director. She achieved acclaim in her own right by designing Kate Middleton's dress, which has taken the brand into a more glamorous arena. Fans of the label on a tighter budget should seek out the diffusion line, McQ, which packs a gutsy McQueen punch at more pocket-friendly prices.

APC
5 Redchurch Street, E2 7DJ (7729 7727, www.apc.fr). Shoreditch High Street rail. **Open** 11am-7pm Mon-Fri; 10am-7pm Sat; noon-5pm Sun.
Jean Touitou's understated Parisian label APC (Atelier de Production et de Creation) is the latest addition to the ever-trendy Redchurch Street. Touitou's hip, European style has been attracting discerning dressers since the late 1980s and this albeit tiny store (the second in London) should please a flock of men in search of a pair of APC's near cult-famous jeans. If you're new to the brand, seek out its well-cut basics for both sexes and enjoy its simple, effortless design – some-thing the French seem eternally adept at. There's certainly precious little pomp or flash in the prettily minimalist collection currently in store.
Branch 35A Dover Street, W1S 4NQ (7409 0121).

Burberry Regent Street
121 Regent Street, W1B 4TB (7806 8904, www.burberry.com). Piccadilly Circus tube.
Open 10am-9pm Mon-Sat; noon-6pm Sun.
After two years of restoration, Burberry's future-focused flagship opened on Regent Street in September 2012, melding together the building's near-200 years of history with all the bells and whistles of hyper-modern retailing. Built in 1820 for the Prince Regent, no.121 has hosted galleries, a cinema, stables and a radio broadcaster over the years, but the luxury brand is perhaps the most ambi-tious of its inhabitants – dedicated to making a visit to the building an immersive, memorable experience full of clever audiovisual tricks and reactive technology. Alongside the iPad wielding shop assistants is Radio Frequency Identification Technology that Burberry has woven into certain garments, triggering films and sounds relevant to the product – you might try on a

FASHION

TEN
Global Designer Flagships

Agnes b
35-36 Floral Street, WC2E 9DJ (7379 1992, www.agnesb.com). Covent Garden tube. **Open** 10.30am-6.30pm Mon-Sat; noon-6pm Sun. **Sells** M, W.
The quest for the perfect Breton T-shirt will end here, where refined and understated classics by this French label lie in wait.

Chanel
167-170 Sloane Street, SW1X 9QF (7235 6631, www.chanel.com). Knightsbridge tube. **Open** 10am-6pm Mon-Sat. **Sells** W.
For that quilted 2.55 handbag or timeless tweed twin set, the Maison's London flagship is the ultimate luxury stop-off.

Chloe
152-153 Sloane Street, SW1X 9BX (7823 5348, www.chloe.com). Sloane Square tube. **Open** 10am-6pm Mon, Tue, Thur-Sat; 10am-7pm Wed. **Sells** W.
Feminine allure does not get much more powerful than at Chloe, with the label's cool-whimsy designs and desirable shoes – find it all at its glossy London store.

Diane von Furstenberg
25 Bruton Street, W1J 6QH (7499 0886, www.dvf.com). Bond Street tube. **Open** 10am-6pm Mon-Wed, Fri, Sat; 10am-7pm Thur; noon-6pm Sun. **Sells** W.
Style mavens should pencil a visit to this store into their shopping schedule to find the perfect DVF print dress.

Gucci
18 Sloane Street, SW1X 9NE (7235 6707, www.gucci.com). Knightsbridge tube. **Open** 10am-6pm Mon, Tue, Thur-Sat; 10am-7pm Wed. **Sells** M, W, C.
Italy's flashiest export is hard to miss at its Knightsbridge location thanks to sheer opulence and extravagance. The store stocks the latest season's must-have bags and shoes.

trench coat, say, and suddenly mirrors become video screens showing shots of the same product on the runway, or special video content. Digital signage and nearly 500 speakers and 100 screens pump out sudden (digital) rain showers. Of course, the real focus is the stock itself and Burberry's impressive stable of women's, men's, children's and accessories collections are all here, including a bespoke trench coat service and some in-store exclusives. An emphasis on natural light (via an atrium created from the building's original cinema auditorium), herringbone parquet, inviting lounge areas and a programme of events and acoustic musical performances take the edge off the store's sci-fi pretensions, creating an inviting, world class flagship.
Branches throughout the city.

Jaeger
200-206 Regent Street, W1B 5BN (7979 1100, www.jaeger.co.uk). Oxford Circus tube. **Open** 10am-8pm Mon-Fri; 10am-7pm Sat; noon-6pm Sun.
Founded over 125 years ago, Jaeger was once synonymous with middle England; today it's a byword for classic British chic, and Jaeger's womenswear, menswear and accessories lines are covetable once again. Coats and tailoring in classic fabrics, such as herringbone tweed and plaid, and luxurious knitwear (wool, angora, cashmere and camelhair) are central to the brand's collections. And while most of the clothes have a chic but serious look, with chocolate, terracotta, navy and grey dominating, brighter colours have nevertheless made more of an appearance in recent collections. A hipper Jaeger London diffusion label has also given the brand a boost, but on the whole, Jaeger has had a tricky time of late (reporting a loss of revenue in 2011). Its accessories range, including belts, purses and jewellery, contains some very covetable items that are surprisingly affordable.
Branches throughout the city.

John Smedley
24 Brook Street, W1K 5DG (7495 2222, www.johnsmedley.com). Bond Street tube. **Open** 10am-6pm Mon-Wed, Fri, Sat; 10am-7pm Thur; noon-5pm Sun.
This cult British knitwear label has been around in some form or other since 1784 – and the brand still manufactures its high-quality garments in its original Lea Mills factory in Derbyshire. Initially an underwear specialist, John Smedley is now a brand associated with fine-knit merino wool sweaters and tops for both men and women; and despite its proud heritage, the label manages to retain a contemporary look with colourful yet muted hues and flattering cuts. The relaxed and stylish flagship shop has been open since 2000, receiving a redesign in 2009 to reflect the company's Derbyshire roots with limestone flooring and green tones. As well as ethically sourced New Zealand merino wool, extra-fine jersey is now used for some garments. A Brit classic.

Burberry. See p79.

Joseph

*16 Sloane Street, SW1 9LQ (7235 1991,
www.joseph.co.uk). Knightsbridge tube.*
Open 10am-6.30pm Mon-Sat noon-6pm Sun.
Joseph Ettedgui started his eponymous label in 1983,
creating a collection of simple, masculine-influenced
womenswear, and gaining an instant popularity on which
he built an impressive legacy – boutiques and concessions
across London and Paris, and outposts in Japan and
Russia. Ettedgui passed away in 2010 but creative director
Louise Trotter (ex-Jigsaw fashion director) is now at the
helm and seems to have set about refreshing the brand.
Alongside the in-house label, Joseph stocks a mix of
British and international design, from Alexander
McQueen to Balmain and Thakoon. The 13 London stores
(plus concessions in Harvey Nichols and Selfridges) are all
contemporary spaces for pared-down, timeless fashion.
Branches throughout the city.

Margaret Howell

*34 Wigmore Street, W1U 2RS (7009 9009,
www.margarethowell.co.uk). Bond Street tube.*
Open 10am-6pm Mon-Wed, Fri, Sat; 10am-7pm
Thur; noon-5pm Sun.
The thing that makes Howell's wonderfully wearable
clothes so contemporary is her old-fashioned attitude to
quality. She believes in making things well, in the UK and
with the finest of fabrics (Harris tweed, Irish linen). These
principles combine with her elegant designs to make for

Louis Vuitton

*17-20 New Bond Street, W1S 2RB (3214
9200, www.louisvuitton.com). Bond Street
tube.* **Open** 10am-7pm Mon-Sat; noon-6pm
Sun. **Sells**, M, W.
Saturn-esque spheres orbit above fine art
and jewellery at this flagship, with
constellations of monogrammed bags
making it fashion's own Big Bang.

Marc Jacobs

*24-25 Mount Street, W1K 2RR (7399
1690, www.marcjacobs.com). Bond Street
or Green Park tube.* **Open** 11am-7pm Mon-
Sat; noon-6pm Sun. **Sells** M, W.
Marc Jacobs' playful designs have won over
legions of fans, making his boutique an
unmissable pit stop for designer shoppers.

Miu Miu

*150 New Bond Street, W1S 2TU (7409
0900, www.miumiu.com). Bond Street or
Oxford Circus tube.* **Open** 10am-6pm Mon-
Wed, Fri, Sat; 10am-7pm Thur; noon-5pm
Sun. **Sells** W.
The brand's eye-popping designs fit right
into their lavish surroundings on London's
prime shopping street.

Prada

*16-18 Old Bond Street, W1X 3DA (7647
5000, www.prada.com). Green Park tube.*
Open 10am-6pm Mon-Wed, Fri, Sat; 10am-
7pm Thur; noon-5pm Sun. **Sells** M, W.
Newly renovated, this flagship strikes a
chord with designer-hungry punters looking
for sophistication with quirk.

Sonia Rykiel

*27-29 Brook Street, W1K 4HE (7493
5255, www.soniarykiel.com). Bond Street
tube.* **Open** 10am-6.30pm Mon-Wed, Fri,
Sat; 10am-7pm Thur. **Sells** W, C.
Kooky, characterful designs inhabit this
store, attracting customers with a fervour
for something punky.

FASHION

Louis Vuitton Maison. See p81.

some of the best 'simple' clothes for sale in London. Her pared-down approach means prices seem steep, but unlike cheap, throwaway fashion these are clothes to cherish, and which will seem to improve with time. Her shops are also worth a visit for anyone interested in 20th-century British design – she offers both vintage and reissued homeware classics by Ercol, Anglepoise, Robert Welch and others. As well as the branches listed below, there is a Margaret Howell concession in Liberty.

Branches 111 Fulham Road, SW3 6RL (7591 2255); 2-8 Duke Street, Richmond, TW9 1HP (8948 5005).

Paul Smith

Westbourne House, 120 & 122 Kensington Park Road, W11 2EP (7727 3553, www.paulsmith.co.uk). Notting Hill Gate tube. **Open** 10am-6pm Mon-Fri; 10am-6.30pm Sat; noon-5pm Sun.

Paul Smith's Notting Hill shop is branded a 'shop in a house'; customers step through its doors into a world of eccentricity. There are clothes for men, women and children, plus accessories, homewares and the odd piece of furniture, over four floors. The place is dotted with Sir Paul's collection of art and other objects, giving insight into the vision behind his quirky-classic tailoring. Womenswear has moved away somewhat from its silhouette-enhancing garments towards a more androgynous aesthetic. Masculine jackets are cut in Prince of Wales checks, pinstripes and flannels. Menswear has traditionally been a rich collection of tartans, checks and colourful stripes, with recent seasons being influenced by classic workwear, with a modern, elegant twist. The brand is still strong on accessories, with a standalone Paul Smith Accessories store on Marylebone High Street.

Branches throughout the city.

Men

Bosideng

28 South Molton Street, W1K 5RF (7290 3170, www.bosidenglondon.com). Bond Street tube. **Open** 10am-8pm Mon-Sat; noon-6pm Sun.

Set over three floors and converted from the rather less upmarket Hog in the Pound pub on South Molton Street, Bosideng's first overseas flagship store and honorary European headquarters is looking as plush as its 500-piece collection (the £30 million renovation includes a £10,000 origami sculpture). This menswear label is Asia's largest manufacturer of down apparel, and has – jetting straight in from China, where it has a whopping 10,000 outlets in China alone. Every item in the collection is sourced from the UK and Europe (apart from the down, every feather of which is a by-product) and rendered in up-market fabrics: pure cashmere cardies, wool-blend tweed blazers and Egyptian-cotton tops all go to form the label's rather sophisticated look. The space itself is ultra-glossy and airy. Sportswear and daywear is housed

Bosideng

Mulberry

on the lower and ground floors; tailoring is on the first floor. While you're up there take a peek through the binoculars to get a bird's-eye view of Oxford Street.

Nigel Hall

15 Floral Street, WC2H 9DS (7836 7922, www.nigelhallmenswear.co.uk). Covent Garden or Leicester Square tube. **Open** 10am-7pm Mon-Sat; 11am-5pm Sun.

Nigel Hall, with its no-nonsense sense of style, is fast becoming a staple. Clean, simple garments, like the classic overcoats, have a Riviera elegance, but Hall also gives them a fashionable edge. Knitwear (such as the ever-popular lambswool blazers) is modern, straightforward and wearable, in a range of unfussy pastel hues. Trousers and jackets are gently fitted and appeal to those of a retro-preppy persuasion. But the clincher is the winning combination of affordable prices and high quality; the details are particularly impressive – stitching, hems and collars are every bit as sophisticated as grander brands that cost three times as much. The clothes are arranged by colour in the airy store and the staff are smart and obliging. Concessions in Selfridges and Harvey Nichols.

Branches 18 Floral Street, WC2E 9DH (7379 3600); 106A Upper Street, N1 1QN (7704 3173); 75-77 Brushfield Street, E1 6AA (7377 0317); 42-44 Broadwick Street, W1F 7AE (7494 1999).

Women

Hoss Intropia

213 Regent Street, W1B 4NF (7287 3569, www.hossintropia.com). Oxford Circus tube. **Open** 10am-8pm Mon-Sat; noon-6pm Sun.

This flagship proved so successful that the Spanish label opened a second shop in Sloane Square in autumn 2007, and a third in Covent Garden in spring 2010. Expect clothing characterised by unusual fabrics, contrasting prints and vibrant colours. As well as useful basics, collections boast fantastic dresses: look out for short and sassy sequined mini-dresses, full-length silk gowns, smocks and knitted dresses. Attention to detail is paramount, hence the use of hand embroidery, sequins, stones and beading. Prices vary considerably – a simple dress or trousers can be had for £100, but more elaborate pieces are over £300. The accessories range has expanded significantly.

Branches 27A Sloane Square, SW1W 8AB (7259 9072); 124 Long Acre, WC2E 9PE (7240 4900).

Kate Spade New York

2 Symons Street, SW3 2TJ (7259 0645, www.kate spade.com). Sloane Square tube. **Open** 10am-7pm Mon-Sat; 11am-5pm Sun.

American fashion label Kate Spade New York opened two London stores in 2011; this one on Symons Street, a small paved area on the side of Peter Jones, is fast becoming a

Orla Kiely's individual mismatching colour combos made her a name in the fashion world, and graphic prints and layered textures adorn the Covent Garden flagship. The Dublin-born designer has been called a 'quiet force' in the industry but her designs speak loud and clear, from original laminate totes and purses to leather bags. It may have been accessories that shot Kiely to fame, but her womenswear is attracting an increasing following. Stripy jackets, tops and flowery dresses are inspired by the 1960s and '70s. The quality of the fabrics is top notch and garments are temptingly tactile, but they're not cheap. This flagship store also stocks a selection of the label's increasingly established homewares line.
Branch 207 King's Road, SW3 5ED (7351 2644).

Paul & Joe
134 Sloane Street, SW1X 9AX (7824 8844, www.paulandjoe.com). Sloane Square tube.
Open 10am-6.30pm Mon-Sat.
French designer Sophie Albou's Paul & Joe is a seductive space with interiors that resemble a princess's boudoir and match the romantic, elegant and forward-thinking pieces for sale. Think classic French tailoring with a contemporary edge: structured jackets, wide-leg trousers, fringe and lace detailing, alongside impressive party dresses, all in flamboyant prints and feminine fabrics. A nod to the 1970s has been evident in recent collections, with a range of maxi skirts and flared trousers, and a wealth of floral prints. And there's a make-up range to match. Albou named her brand after her two sons and aimed to introduce variety to the menswear market (gents should visit the Floral Street branch). This is prêt-à-porter at its best, so invest to possess timeless pieces. Also worth a peek is Paul & Joe Sister, a more casual range featuring mini-dresses.
Branch Paul & Joe Homme 33 Floral Street, WC2E 9DJ (7836 3388).

Stella McCartney
30 Bruton Street, W1J 6QR (7518 3100, www.stella mccartney.com). Bond Street or Green Park tube.
Open 10am-7pm Mon-Sat.
It's been more than seven years since Stella McCartney launched her label, and, with every collection stronger than the last, even her original doubters have become converts. Her easy-to-wear, luxe but sporty look has enduring appeal and is a hit with young Hollywood, off-duty supermodels and fashionistas with cash to flash. Sweater dresses, swing coats, poetic blouses, broderie anglaise dresses and platform boots have all featured heavily in collections, and are destined to work their way into many fashion-conscious wardrobes. Joining the main line, fragrance, skincare and sportswear collaboration with Adidas (worn by Team GB at the 2012 Olympics), is an expanded accessories line, as well as a lingerie line. McCartney's views on animal rights are well known, so her bags, belts and shoes are made in

major hangout. On launch night in September 2011, two yellow NYC cabs parked up; inside, guests admired the signature colourful clothing and accessories. The taxis aren't a permanent fixture; the covetable merchandise, however – think crocodile embossed handbags, cashmere sweaters, ruffled blouses, as well as baby gear and homewares – is.
Branch 1-4 Langley Court, WC2E 9JY (7836 3988).

Mulberry
50 New Bond Street, W1S 1BJ (7491 3900, www. mulberry.com). Bond Street tube. **Open** 10am-7pm Mon-Sat; 11am-6pm Sun.
Having established its credentials as a bona fide fashion brand in recent years – in particular for its leather 'it' bags – Mulberry has been working hard to maintain the momentum, and succeeding. Creative director Emma Hill's first collection featured Bayswater clutches, soft leather canvas Taylor totes, and leather jackets. Meanwhile, classic handbags such as the Bayswater and Elkington are reinvented in new finishes, colours and materials. The latest must-have bag, the Del Rey, is named after indie-pop singer Lana Del Rey, who's long been a fan of the brand.
Branches throughout the city.

Orla Kiely
31-33 Monmouth Street, WC2H 9DD (7240 4022, www.orlakiely.com). Covent Garden tube. **Open** 10am-6.30pm Mon-Sat; noon-5pm Sun.

cruelty-free fabrics such as satin, velvet, nylon and canvas. Stella McCartney is also available from Harvey Nichols and Selfridges.

Vanessa Bruno

1A Grafton Street, W1S 4EB (7499 7838, www.vanessabruno.com). Green Park tube. **Open** 10.30am-6.30pm Mon-Sat.
Vanessa Bruno sold originally in Harvey Nichols and boutiques nationwide, but the capital was more than ready for the 200sq ft of dedicated Bruno boudoir that opened in October 2010. The move into London was an obvious one for Bruno, who has long admired the city and its residents. The boutique sits very comfortably in Mayfair, just a few strides from Acne, APC and fashion lover's paradise Dover Street Market, and houses the main collection and the Athé diffusion line in characteristically low-key style. Like that of her Parisian contemporary Isabel Marant, Vanessa Bruno's brand has grown by word of mouth rather than an aggressive marketing campaign or retail presence. The clothes are gorgeous knits, wafty printed dresses and well-cut blazers, all worn with clumpy boots, and investment coats with cosy hoods; what Bruno describes as 'vêtements faciles pour filles difficiles' ('easy clothes for difficult girls'). So roll up your Breton sleeves and give it a nonchalant look.

Vivienne Westwood

44 Conduit Street, W1S 2YL (7439 1109, www.viviennewestwood.com). Oxford Circus or Piccadilly Circus tube. **Open** 10am-6pm Mon-Wed, Fri, Sat; 10am-7pm Thur; noon-5pm Sun.
Vivienne Westwood is part of British fashion history, with over 30 years in the business and a damehood to her credit. Perhaps still best known for pioneering the punk look, she's since become one of Britain's most revered designers. Her pieces are recognisable for their voluminous quantities of fabric (frequently in her trademark tartan), and of course those signature corsets. The Conduit Street flagship houses the women's Gold Label main line and the two diffusion ranges – Red Label and the more casual Anglomania. The original World's End premises carries a smaller selection of clothing and the full range of accessories, as well as special-edition pieces, which are exclusive to the store. The small Davies Street salon stocks only the Gold Label and accessories, and provides a couture and bridal service. There are also Vivienne Westwood concessions in Harrods, Liberty, Harvey Nichols and Selfridges department stores.
Branches 6 Davies Street, W1K 3DN (7629 3757); World's End, 430 King's Road, SW10 0LJ (7352 6551); (Men's) 18 Conduit Street, W1S 2XN.

Vivienne Westwood

Streetwise **Mount Street, W1**

The traditional Mayfair enclave has become a byword for upmarket but hip brands.

Significant swaths of W1 have always been known for their rather stuffy atmosphere. Mount Street, with its dignified Victorian terracotta façades and by-appointment-only art galleries, still harbours a Mayfair elite; consider, for example, traditional vendors such as master butcher **Allens of Mayfair** (no.117, *see p243*), cigar shop **Sautter** (no.106, 7499 4866, www.sauttercigars.com), with its dusty collection of antique crocodile-skin cigar cases, and **Purdey** (7499 1801, www.purdey.com), the traditional gunsmith that has stood aloof just around the corner at 57-58 South Audley Street since 1882.

But it's the mix of avant garde international fashion and accessory brands that now excites. Towards the east end of the street, by the Connaught Hotel, sits the **Balenciaga** flagship (no.12, 7317 4400), its super-chic clothing set against a glowing sci-fi interior. The lovely **Mount Street Printers & Stationers** (*see p219*) is nearby.

Across the road, gentlemen's tailor **Rubinacci** (no.96, 7499 2299) sits near the **Mount Street Galleries** (no.94, 7493 1613, www.mountstreet galleries.com), one of several fine art and antiques dealers in the area – a group that includes **Adrian Alan** (7495 2324, www.adrian alan.com) at 66-67 South Audley Street. The latter holds court with upmarket china and homewares store **Thomas Goode & Co** (no.19, 7499 2823, www.thomasgoode.com) and the serene **Spa Illuminata** (no.63, 7499 7777, www.spa illuminata.com). At no.64 South Audley Street, the pared-down interior of **Rick Owens**' shop (7493 7145, www.rickowens.eu) is the perfect place to show off his cult, goth-edged designs.

But it's back on Mount Street where the new lease of life is most in evidence, where **Marc Jacobs**' first UK boutique (nos.24-25, 7399 1690) was one of the first of the superbrands to appear. Ralph Lauren's new **RRL** store (no.16, 7953 4120) is a dark curiosity shop housing antique clothing and Ralph Lauren's premium, vintage-inspired collection. Another red-hot name is revered shoe designer **Christian Louboutin** (no.17, 7491 0033), whose eye-catching storefront displays are often the talk of the street. Cult Australian skincare brand **Aesop** (no.91; *see p134*) and the best highlights in town at **Jo Hansford**'s salon (no.19, 7495 7774, www.johansford.com) are also here.

High-end fashion brands may have opened up on this previously sleepy stretch, but it's the absence of brash, ultra-luxe fashion houses such as Louis Vuitton and Gucci that has given Mount Street its real cachet. The idea behind the renaissance was to source the best of everything – but not necessarily the most expensive or best known. The conspicuous absence of some of the biggest brands means there's no chance of this becoming another Bond Street – at least for now.

Other shops on or around the Mount Street include **Lanvin** (no.128, 7491 1839), bridal and cocktail dress shop **Jenny Packham** (3a Carlos Place; *see p107*), and men's shoe store **Harry's of London** (59 South Audley Street, 7409 7988).

When the luxury gets too much, take time out in Mount Street Gardens, which snakes behind the south side of the street.

FASHION

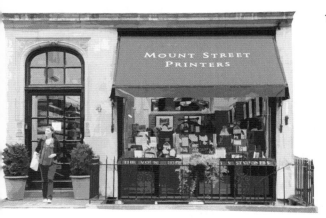

Tailoring & Bespoke

Mayfair's **Savile Row** is famous the world over, having been synonymous with bespoke tailoring since the 1800s. However, what the term 'bespoke' actually means has been the subject of controversy in recent years, with many of the street's old-school tailors arguing that newcomers have been using the term to offer tailoring services that were not actually bespoke, but simply 'made-to-measure'. Determined to preserve their centuries-old technique, the high houses of Mayfair tailoring formed the **Savile Row Bespoke Association** (www.savilerowbespoke.com) in 2004, drawing up a list of standards by which to distinguish themselves as the real deal.

Initial outgoings for made-to-measure will always be cheaper. However, if you're after a suit that will exactly fit your proportions and physique, which will last for decades, be easily adjustable with age, and which will be a real expression of your tastes and personality, then you might choose to enlist the services of an expert bespoke tailor, who trains for years before being let loose on the luxurious fabrics of your choosing.

Suits

Chris Kerr

31 Berwick Street, W1F 8RJ, 7437 3727, www.chris kerr.com). Oxford Circus or Tottenham Court Road tube. **Open** 9am-5.30pm Mon-Fri; 9am-1pm Sat. While the majority of the finest suit-makers are still on Savile Row, there is one London tailor who offers Mayfair sophistication on a Soho budget: Chris Kerr, who learnt the trade from his father, legendary 1960s tailor Eddie Kerr. Located in the heart of Soho, the purple façade of his shop is a stylish stand-out amid a row of curry houses, hair salons and bustling sidewalk cafés. Inside, the vibe is more artist's studio than shop, and everyone from Johnny Depp and Liam Neeson to Michael Caine and Vic Reeves has stepped inside. But despite the star-studded clientele, Kerr tells us that the shop's mission remains simple: to make pure bespoke suits for the man on the street. £1,500 'is expensive enough,' he says. It's thus the ideal place to commission your first bespoke suit.

FASHION

Gieves & Hawkes

Dege & Skinner

10 Savile Row, W1S 3PF (7287 2941, www.dege-skinner.co.uk). Piccadilly Circus tube. **Open** 9.15am-5.15pm Mon-Fri; 9.15am-12.30pm Sat.

This Savile Row stalwart has built a formidable reputation as a bespoke tailor and highland dressmaker, but also commands great respect for its military uniforms and shirt-making services. With three royal warrants to its name, it's a sure bet for top-notch service and, according to owner William Skinner, it makes 'the best uniforms in London'. Prices for a Dege & Skinner bespoke two-piece start at £3,300, with shirts from £210 (prices include VAT); master shirt-maker Robert Whitaker cuts with a skill that's hard to match, even on Savile Row. Equally impressive is the selection of dressing gowns.

Gieves & Hawkes

1 Savile Row, W1S 3JR (7434 2001, www.gievesand hawkes.com). Piccadilly Circus tube. **Open** 10am-7pm Mon-Fri; 10am-6pm Sat; noon-5pm Sun.

Gieves & Hawkes isn't just about fine tailoring; it's also a history lesson for anyone interested in the development of men's clothes. Despite having held royal warrants without interruption for 200 years (the Queen, the Duke of Edinburgh and Prince Charles are all customers), the company continues to innovate. It offers three services: the beautiful ready-to-wear collection starts at £800, while its made-to-measure service starts a little higher, at £1,000; handmade bespoke is the premier service – it's a long procedure (we're talking months), but you'll eventually take home a luxury handmade garment made to your exact measurements and requirements.

Henry Poole & Co

15 Savile Row, W1S 3PJ (7734 5985, www.henry poole.com). Piccadilly Circus tube. **Open** 9am-5.15pm Mon-Fri.

Henry Poole & Co was established in 1806, and founded Savile Row. Since then, it has served royalty and historical notables, from Napoleon III and Emperor Haile Selassie to 'Buffalo' Bill Cody, Winston Churchill, and has provided the livery of Queen Elizabeth II. History buffs can examine King George II's household livery on display in the store. All suits here are 'pure bespoke', with two-piece suits from £2,960 and three-pieces from £3,260 (prices exclude VAT).

SuitSupply

9 Vigo Street, W1S 3HH (7851 2961, www.suit supply.com). Piccadilly Circus tube. **Open** 10am-8pm Mon-Fri; 10am-7pm Sat; noon-6pm Sun.

If you aren't yet ready to invest in a bespoke suit, then quality ready-to-wear and tailored suits are available at Dutch-owned SuitSupply, which opened in 2010, around the corner from Savile Row. You won't get the personal attention of a truly bespoke tailor, but the company's tailoring session is still comprehensive – customers are measured by a 35-point system, and then details are sent to Italy, where a tailor creates your suit in 100% Italian fabric, posting it back to the UK in six to eight weeks. Alterations can then be made in store. And with prices starting at just £499 (or from £259 for a ready-to-wear suit), it's a fraction of the price of a Savile Row number.

Shirts & accessories

African Waistcoat Company

33 Islington Green, N1 8DU (7704 9698, www.africanwaistcoatcompany.com). Angel tube. **Open** 10am-6pm Wed, Sat; noon-6pm Sun.

For a snazzy contrast to a classic English look, head to Camden Passage to check out the colourful garments made by the African Waistcoat Company. Here, Calum Robertson marries African and Savile Row traditions, producing dazzling waistcoats made from West African cottons and silks known as *aso oke*, which means high-status or 'up country' cloth in Yoruba. Patterns range from centuries-old Yoruba patterns to contemporary designs. Robertson makes regular trips to Nigeria to add to a range that takes in over 30 dazzling designs. As well as the peacockish waistcoats (starting at around £150), the shop offers a selection of traditional robes, scarves and beads.

Alexander Boyd

54 Artillery Lane, E1 7LS (7377 8755, www.alexanderboyd.co.uk). Liverpool Street tube/rail. **Open** 8am-6.30pm Mon-Fri.

Whether you go for fully bespoke, off-the-peg, or somewhere in between, you'll need a decent shirt to complete the look. As well as offering expert tailoring (master cutter Clive Phythian trained at Gieves & Hawkes), Alexander Boyd, over in Spitalfields, can measure you up and make you a beautiful handmade tailored shirt to order (prices start at £175). Even the shop's off-the-peg shirts are made in the finest cotton in a factory in Kent; ties are handmade from silk woven in Suffolk.

Drakes

3 Clifford Street, W1S 2LF (7734 2367, www.drakes-london.com). Oxford Circus tube. **Open** 10am-6pm Mon-Wed, Fri; 10am-7pm Thur; 11am-6pm Sat.

If you're the kind of gentleman who knows his Cagney 'kerchief knot from his Astaire, and his ostrich skin from his stingray, you're likely to have made acquaintance with luxury accessories label Drakes. The company's first store opened just off Savile Row in June 2011, and is packed with knits, shirts, shoes, socks and formalwear alongside its core products – luxury scarves and silk ties, all handmade in England. The brand was set up in 1978. Now the UK's largest independent tie-maker, Drakes makes everything at its premises in Clerkenwell. The ties are cut by hand and 18 separate checks ensure only perfect products leave the workshop.

FASHION

Vintage & Second-hand

East London's **Pattern Market** (Kingsland Road, E8 4DG, noon-6pm Tue-Sun), a collective of individual vendors tucked away on the corner of Kingsland Road and Dunston Road, is a hotspot for vintage threads; each seller peddles something different, with the clothes tending toward the eccentric side of vintage, with outrageous pieces from the 1980s and '90s as well as colourful numbers from further back. Soho's **Berwick Street**, previously known for fruit and veg, has also recently become something of a vintage clothing destination, with a plethora of new openings in the past couple of years, including branches of **Absolute Vintage** and **Bang Bang**. Every third Saturday of the month in **Brixton Village**, dozens of stallholders bring an eclectic mix of home furnishings, dresses, menswear, jewellery and collectable goods to the vintage market held here.

Absolute Vintage
15 Hanbury Street, E1 6QR (7247 3883, www.absolutevintage.co.uk). Shoreditch High Street rail. **Open** 11am-7pm daily. **Sells** M, W.
The range here will make you giddy: there are over 1,000 pairs of shoes, arranged in size, colour and era, from 1940s suede courts through to 1980s white high-heels.

Men can find brown country brogues or lizard-skin pimp numbers. Stock is priced to sell and you can kit yourself out for £50. There are day dresses, of mixed vintage and arranged by colour, cotton maxis, slinky '70s disco dresses and '80s posh frocks. A matching clutch bag won't be a problem; they are stacked in their hundreds. Around the corner, sister store Blondie (Unit 2, 114-118 Commercial Street, 7247 0050, www.blondievintage.co.uk) has a more boutiquey atmosphere and an edited selection, ideal for those who don't want to trawl through the rails. **Branch** 79 Berwick Street, W1F 8TL (7434 1544).

Annie's Vintage Clothes
12 Camden Passage, N1 8ED (7359 0796, www.anniesvintageclothing.co.uk). Angel tube.
Open 11am-6pm daily. **Sells** W, C.
Annie Moss's shop was the obvious choice for providing dresses for the 1980s *Brideshead Revisited* TV series. Knockout flapper dresses are the speciality. Everything is sheer, floaty and ethereal. The paler dresses are currently popular with brides, and are good value compared to modern off-the-peg frocks. For a more traditional choice, there's a rail of wedding dresses from the Victorian period and slinkier bias cut numbers from the 1930s. Most day dresses date from the 1930s and '40s, but you'll also find later vintage, too, such as 1950s appliqué skirts. There is a good selection of accessories (for men, too) – delicate fans, parasols, hats, 1920s shoes, swimwear and even baby clothes.

Beyond Retro

Bang Bang

21 Goodge Street, W1T 2PJ (7631 4191). Goodge Street tube. **Open** 10am-6.30pm Mon-Fri; 11am-6pm Sat. **Sells** W.

It's all down to luck and timing at this lunch-break browser's fave. More dress agency than vintage shop, top-end labels such as Dries Van Noten and Moschino hang alongside mediocre high street pieces. Sharp eyes are rewarded: in the past a well-priced Ossie Clark gown has been spotted in the mix. Nearly new shoes sport labels such as Gina, Costume National and Miu Miu, and there are usually plenty for larger feet too. The turnover of stock is fast, so it's worth popping in regularly. There's also a sister store on Berwick Street (no.9), with similar vintage womenswear on the ground floor and menswear in the basement (accessed by a separate staircase to the right of the main store).
Branch 9 Berwick Street, W1F 0PJ (7494 2042).

The Beehive

320-322 Creek Road SE10 9SW (8858 1964). Greenwich Cutty Sark rail. **Open** 10.30am-6pm Mon-Fri; 10.30am-6.30pm Sat-Sun. **Sells** W.

With its leopard-skin ceiling, racks of vinyl and rails of retro fashion, the Beehive is a colourful Greenwich must-see. The Beehive is the umbrella name for Retrobates Vintage and the record shop next door. Crimplene enthusiast and store owner Deborah loves the '60s , but gears her buying towards the local student population, whose idea of vintage is the era in which they were born. Rails are lined with high-waisted Levi's jean shorts at £20 a pair, Peter Pan-collared cardigans at £15 and quilted patterned jackets at £35. There is even a trunk full of shirts, scarves and other accessories where each item is £5, for those that are still waiting for their student loan to come through.

Beyond Retro

110-112 Cheshire Street, E2 6EJ (7729 9001, www.beyondretro.com). Shoreditch High Street rail. **Open** 10am-7pm Mon-Wed, Fri, Sat; 10am-8pm Thur; 11.30am-6pm Sun. **Sells** M, W.

This East End institution has a loyal following of fancy-dress seekers, hard-up students and offbeat musicians. The vast former warehouse is crammed with around 10,000 items of stock, helpfully arranged by colour and, if you have the time and patience, you can literally dress yourself from top to toe: there are vintage corsets and suspender belts, silk slips and net petticoats, Polynesian-print maxi dresses, frou-frou prom dresses, vintage kimonos, lace and satin wedding dresses and lots more. For men, there are sharp '70s suits, trilbies, and a vast array of T-shirts and denim. Not everything is in great nick, but it's ideal if you're after an instant wear-once look. Following on from the store's success, a new East End flagship opened in Dalston in September 2011, in the 10,000sq ft Simpson House, previously a manufacturing warehouse for men's clothing for British tailoring brand Daks.

Sales & shopping events

Clerkenwell Vintage Fashion Fair

The Old Finsbury Town Hall, Rosebery Avenue, EC1R 4RP (www.clerkenwellvintagefashion fair.co.uk).

With 50 top dealers trading in quality apparel from the 1800s to 1980s, including some designer bits from Dior, YSL and Biba, you can recreate your own vintage version of what you see on the catwalk. The organisers often throw a bespoke alteration service into the mix, with personal shoppers, fashion illustrators, live acts and a tearoom also boosting your shopping experience.

Frock Me!

www.frockmevintagefashion.com. Venues vary.

A one-day event to get the vintage devotees among you rattling your change. Frock Me! is a one day shopping event, selling authentic garments from the 1920s right through to the 1980s. The occasion promises thrifty bargains with prices starting at just £1, and generally not exceeding £20. Cakes, cream teas and sandwiches are served too.

North London Vintage Market

northlondonvintagemarket.blogspot.co.uk. St Mary's Parish Hall, Cranley Gardens/Park Road, N10.

Ali Winstanley and Lucy Welsh are veterans of the vintage fashion world, having manned a stall at Spitalfields Antique Market since 2009. This ongoing stint has left the girls with an extensive network of traders from which to pick for North London Vintage, a small market with a stellar stall line-up, focusing mainly on items for the home. Look out for quirky pieces such as tea sets from the 1930s, coat hooks from the '50s and printed curtains from the '60s. Kitchen finds aside, there is also vintage clothing on sale for those who can't live without a retro fashion fix – items range from brooches and petticoats to tea dresses and handbags.

The Vintage Event

The Balham Bowls Club, 7-9 Ramsden Road, SW12 8QX (www.thevintageevent.com).

This event keeps vintage-loving south Londoners smiling. The fair brings together pre-loved fashion, accessories, tea sets, gifts and homewares from the 1920s to the '80s. There's also live music, a vintage beauty parlour hosted by Lashes 'n' Curls and a Mother's Ruin gin and tearoom for cheeky (or innocent) refreshment.

Vintage Kilo Sale

www.judysvintagefair.co.uk/kilo

This event is a regular on the *Time Out* shopping pages, and it offers a rare chance to get truly bargain vintage. The concept is simple – fill your baskets with thrift, and when you've got to a kilo's worth, you can take it home for a mere £15. Your kilo can be made up from men's and women's vintage pieces – and there are three tonnes of stock to choose from, with finds from the 1970s onwards.

Branches 58-59 Great Marlborough Street, W1F 7JY (7434 1406); Simpson House, 92-100 Stoke Newington Road, N16 7XB (7613 3636).

Blackout II

51 Endell Street WC2H 9AJ (7240 5006, www.blackout2.com). Tottenham Court Road tube. **Open** 11am-7pm Mon-Fri; 11.30am-6.30pm Sat. **Sells** M, W.

Blackout II was peddling vintage threads long before it became fashionable. For some 25 years, the Covent Garden store has specialised in antique apparel (largely dresses from the 1920s and '30s) as well as more wearable men's and women's clothing and accessories from the '40s through to the '80s. The duplex store is heaving with stock, and you'll need a great deal of rummager's enthusiasm to prise through the stuffed rails, but incredibly knowledgeable staff, together with signs on rails indicating era, make the shopping experience a smidge easier. An ideal place to go if you're after a specific item from a specific decade.

Blitz

55-59 Hanbury Street, E1 5JP (7377 0730, www.blitzlondon.co.uk). Liverpool Street tube/rail or Shoreditch High Street rail. **Open** 11am-7pm Mon-Wed, Sun; 11am-8pm Thur-Sat. **Sells** M, W, C.

London's first vintage department store opened in August 2011, just off Brick Lane. Blitz is the brainchild of various established vintage dealers and sells clothing for men and women from every decade and designer (Vivienne Westwood, Biba, Ossie Clark, Alexander McQueen), as well as luggage and homewares. The five-room warehouse space covers 9,000sq ft and boasts more stock than any other vintage store in London to date. Books, records, luggage, sunglasses and trinkets complete the mix; in addition, an on-site café serves coffee from a converted vintage Fiat car.

FASHION

Blitz

FASHION

Butler & Wilson

189 Fulham Road, SW3 6JN (7352 3045, www.butlerandwilson.co.uk). South Kensington tube. **Open** 10am-6.30pm Mon-Wed, Fri, Sat; 10am-7pm Thur; noon-6pm Sun. **Sells** W.

The costume jewellery range, for which the brand is famous, is at ground level, along with original pieces by Stanley Hugler. But to the left of the jewellery showroom, a gated stairway leads to vintage heaven. Up here, rails of beaded dresses that once shimmied to the charleston are ready to party once more. You'll also find feminine Edwardian white lace dresses, bought by brides-to-be. And if you've ever fancied delivering the line 'I'll just slip into something more comfortable', then one of the exotic silk kimonos should do the job. There are later vintage surprises here too. Collectable 1950s novelty bags are another Butler & Wilson strength.

Branch 20 South Molton Street, W1K 5QY (7409 2955).

Cafe Vintage

88 Mountgrove Road, N5 2LT (07903 875750, www.cafevintage.co.uk). Finsbury Park tube/rail. **Open** 8.30am-5.30pm Tue-Fri; 9am-5pm Sat; 10am-4pm Sun. **Sells** W, M.

Tucked away on the largely residential Mountgrove Road, Cafe Vintage joins a petite parade of independent shops. Sisters Aysha Sparks and Nadia Allman head up the bijou boutique-café crossover and offer a distinctly nostalgic nod to 1940s Britain. The charming café (featuring homemade, retro-influenced cakes and artisan breads) leads to a small backroom rammed with personally selected, washed and ironed vintage. The wartime era is well represented here, but '80s and '90s outfits, shoes and accessories also feature and, though the space is small, a good scour is usually well rewarded. If you have spare threads yourself, Cafe Vintage also runs a competitive consignment service, with 50% of the sale price going back to the seller.

Lucy In Disguise. See p96.

Camden Thrift Shop

51 Chalk Farm Road, NW1 8AN (no phone). Chalk Farm tube. **Open** 1-6.30pm daily. **Sells** W, M.
Clothing and accessories are piled up on every surface of this long, narrow shop in Chalk Farm Road, but don't be put off by the madcap merchandising. While this store is lacking a little in presentation, the varied stock and helpful owner more than compensate. She'll ask what you're looking for and pull out several items for you to try on – a rare service in vintage shops. We were tempted by an immaculate '60s A-line pure wool dress for £25, as well as a '70s coat suit at £30. The quality of some items is a bit hit and miss, but, with bags at £10-£20 and tops starting at £10, prices are reasonable for the area.

Cloud Cuckoo Land

6 Charlton Place, Camden Passage, N1 8AJ (7354 3141). Angel tube. **Open** 11am-5.30pm Tue, Thur-Sat; 9.30am-5.30pm Wed. **Sells** W.
This fun little shop has a great selection of very wearable dresses from the 1930s to 1970s. Stock is feminine and quirky: elegant 1930s full-length silk slips, '40s crêpe cocktail gowns and '50s circle skirts. There are often some good '70s labels here too, such as John Varon, Bus Stop and Janice Wainwright, or perhaps a superb 1960s Susan Small black satin duster coat, beautifully lined. At the back of the shop you'll find accessories, coats and jackets, plus a good selection of wraps, scarves, shawls and '50s novelty bags. The cheerful owner is happy to make suggestions if you're after a particular vintage look.

Crazy Man Crazy

18A Church Road SE19 2ET (8653 6548, www.crazymancrazylondon.co.uk). Crystal Palace rail. **Open** 10am-6pm Thur-Sun. **Sells** M.
One of the very few menswear-only vintage shops in London, Crazy Man Crazy is worth the trek from Crystal Palace station. Owner Paul Davies is about to celebrate two years of trading, and stocks American-style clothing from the 1940s-'50s. Although small in size, the store is cleverly laid out by style, and is stylishly propped with a gigantic white double bass and a retro radio playing '50s rock and roll. The shop provides the vintage clothing of choice for numerous rockabilly bands, and stocks a great variety of leather and bomber jackets priced at £65-£225, and a neat selection of jeans hung on mini meat hooks for £25 to £130.

Deborah Woolf Vintage

28 Church Street, NW8 8EP (7767 437732, www.deborahwoolf.com). Marylebone tube/rail. **Open** 10.30am-6pm Tue-Sat. **Sells** M, W, C.
Deborah Woolf offers a fantastic mix of clothing and accessories from luxury brands through to high street. As well as a passion for Eastern European folk garments, Deborah also has an amazing collection of 1950s-'70s costume jewellery and precious pieces by top designers. The

shop itself is organised and easy to browse, as Deborah keeps her overflowing archive (which you can visit by appointment) across the road at Alfies Antiques Market. Prices start at £60 for dresses, but the quality of each piece ensures that paying £260 for early '80s Yves Saint Laurent is entirely reasonable. There's also a small selection of menswear, including ties and cufflinks.

Dolly Diamond

51 Pembridge Road, W11 3HG (7792 2479, www.dollydiamond.com). Notting Hill Gate tube.

Open 10.30am-6.30pm Mon-Fri; 9.30am-6.30pm Sat; noon-6pm Sun. **Sells** M ,W.

One minute you're in the 21st century, then you step through the door into the 1940s. The shop has a delightfully old-fashioned feel, with its neat displays and vintage bra mannequins. The stock doesn't disappoint, whether it's a glam 1940s grosgrain gown or a cute burlesque hat. There are men's clothes too, with 1940s dinner jackets and shirts. At the back of the store you'll find a rail of vintage bridalwear, which takes in accessories and headdresses.

Pint-sized vintage shops

Some of London's most fruitful vintage hunts take place in small arcades and undercover markets.

Leftovers

Unit 71, Fourth Avenue, Brixton Village, SW9 8PR (0011 1918, www.leftoverslondon.com). Brixton tube/rail. **Open** 11am-5.30pm Tue, Wed, Fri, Sat; 11am-10pm Thur; noon-4pm Sun. **Sells** W.

This pocket-sized shop is stocked by Gallic owner Margot Waggoner with sweet sailorette dresses and bleached cotton petticoats. If you're a bit crafty, you can buy a sweet little lace collar from here and sew it on to a plain dress to make it your own. There are also lots of collectable items that look as if they've been taken from a 1950s Parisian larder: cute rusty tins and vintage bits and bobs that would make perfect gifts for the kind of people who never throw anything away.

Persiflage

Alfies Antique Market, 13-25 Church Street, NW8 8DT (7723 6066, www.alfiesantiques.com). Marylebone tube/rail. **Open** 10am-6pm Tue-Sat. **Sells** W.

A cosy vintage shop on the second floor of Alfies Antiques Market, owned by Gwyneth Trefor-Jones, who is also responsible for much-loved Essex Road boutique Past Caring. Persiflage has been going for an amazing 25 years and is frequented by fashion students, stylists and even, apparently, Whoopi Goldberg. The shop features a wide variety of pieces from the 1920s right through to the '80s, as well as Victorian items, with prices ranging from £30 to £200. If you're into restoring or recreating vintage clothing, then you'll love Persiflage's second-hand lace, buttons, beads and sequins, as well as sewing patterns and books on how to become an expert dressmaker.

Velvet Atelier

Alfies Antique Market, 13-25 Church Street NW8 8DT (7093 147 263, www.velvetatelier.com). Marylebone tube/rail. **Open** 10am-6pm Tue-Sat. **Sells** W.

Owners Anna and Mike recently moved from the second floor to the ground floor of Alfies Antique Market, giving them a street-facing shopfront. Velvet Atelier is already a favourite with the *Downton Abbey* wardrobe department and designers such as Nicole Fahri because of pieces such as a 1920s flapper dress or a '50s creation by Marilyn Monroe's designer Ceil Chapman. Pieces can also be rented for 20% of their cost, a great option for brides-to-be who only need one day in white. If you're after something a little more contemporary, the shop also stocks a carefully chosen selection of '80s and '90s pieces from the likes of Moschino, Vivienne Westwood, Oscar de la Renta and Alexander McQueen.

Vintage Planet

Unit D-23, Stables Market, NW1 8AH (07526 734951). Camden Town or Chalk Farm tube. **Open** noon-6.30pm Mon-Wed; 11am-7pm Thur, Fri; 10.30am-7pm Sat, Sun. **Sells** W.

Hunters of 1970s and '80s treasures could graze for hours among the rails of this stall, which meanders across three sections of the Horse Tunnels in Camden Stables Market. There's a huge selection of denim, with flares starting at £10; branded skinny jeans are slightly more (Levi's, £25; Diesel, £35). You can pick up retro extras such as a Polaroid camera for £55, and even a pair of '70s roller skates for £45. An '80s designer rail included a Céline velvet jacket (£160) and a YSL Rive Gauche coat (£120). The owner is approachable, knows her stock and is happy to haggle, so you'll get a bargain.

FASHION

East End Thrift Store

Unit 1A, Watermans Building, Assembly Passage, E1 4UT (7423 9700, www.theeastendthriftstore.com). Stepney Green tube. **Open** 11am-6pm Mon-Wed, Sun; 11am-7pm Thur-Sat. **Sells** M, W.

The clue's in the name – 'thrift' rather than 'vintage', which means you essentially get all the fab gear of yesteryear at prices that would get Del Boy all a-quiver. Most of the stock is around the £7-£10 mark, but if you splash out £15 you could get the one-of-a-kind turquoise evening dress with marabou trim on its hem (spotted on a previous excursion), or a Gloria Vanderbilt bomber jacket. It might not be as pretty as some of the other vintage shops, but the stripped warehouse space has a certain functional charm all of its own.

Episode

26 Chalk Farm Road, NW1 8AG (7485 9927, www.episode.eu). Camden Town tube. **Open** 11am-6pm daily. **Sells** M, W.

This easygoing store could do with a tidy up (Converse sneakers, £21, were strewn on the floor at our last visit), but it's a cheap and unpretentious place. Episode is an Amsterdam-based chain and stocks mostly European brands. There's a uniform price policy, so all dresses are £21, whether it's a Paula Yates-style fuchsia and black cocktail frock, or an on-trend orange and brown paisley shift. It's the place to go for knitwear and hats, especially berets (£7.50), and accessories in general; leather gloves are £9. Wax jackets are £29.50 and if you're lucky you'll bag a Barbour. This is a warehouse and dead-stock outlet, rather than a hand-picked experience, but everything is well displayed and it's easy to locate what you're looking for.

Fat Faced Cat

22-24 Camden Passage, N1 8ED (7354 0777, www.fatfacedcat.com). Angel tube. **Open** 11am-7pm Mon, Tue, Thur; 10am-6pm Wed, Fri, Sat; 11am-5pm Sun. **Sells** M, W.

Fat Faced Cat, run by husband-and-wife team Robert and Angela (a costume designer), was previously housed in a smaller space in nearby Pierrepont Arcade, but opened in this much larger unit on Camden Passage in 2011. Known for its creative window displays, it's a safe bet for good-quality, on-trend, colourful clothing from a variety of eras, with lots of well-known designers featuring. The well-edited range of clothing, shoes and accessories for both women and men is sourced from around the UK and from annual trips to Los Angeles. The shop is particularly strong on smart jackets, leather handbags, sunglasses and vintage jewellery, and also has an entertaining selection of ephemera, including an interesting range of old black-and-white photos (which might make entertaining greetings cards) and maps. Prices are fairly high, but not unreasonable for second-hand gear of this quality.

Frockney Rebel Vintage

242 Cambridge Heath Road, E2 9DA (8127 8609, www.frockneyrebelvintage.com). Cambridge Heath rail. **Open** noon-7pm Tue-Fri; noon-6pm Sat, Sun. **Sells** M, W.

Laura McAlpine and furniture designer Omid Asghari are behind this sleek outlet, set in a distinctive turquoise building on Cambridge Heath Road. Together, the pair look to source wearable vintage (that means no fancy dress prom dresses) from across Europe and make regular visits to Berlin, Milan and Paris to handpick their womens- and menswear. Despite the effort these two go to, prices are surprisingly reasonable, with almost all pieces (including coats and shoes) coming in under £50. Out-of-season pieces are held in the store room, so if you're after sunglasses and summer dresses in November, say, then you may still be in luck; call in advance, and they'll prepare some possible options for you to peruse.

The Girl Can't Help It

Alfie's Antique Market, 13-25 Church Street, NW8 8DT (7724 8984, www.thegirlcanthelpit.com). Edgware Road tube or Marylebone tube/rail. **Open** 10am-6pm Tue-Sat. **Sells** M, W.

Named after the Jayne Mansfield film, the Girl Can't Help It is classic Hollywood territory, personified by co-owner Sparkle Moore, an exuberant platinum-maned New Yorker who, with partner, Cad Van Swankster, sources most of her stock from the US. Always in stock are classic 1940s suits and 1950s circle skirts, decorated with everything from kitsch kittens to Mexican-style patterns. You can achieve the total look here, right down to the lingerie and glam accessories. Van Swankster presides over the suave menswear – Hawaiian shirts, gabardine jackets, slick 1940s and '50s suits, pin-up ties and camp accessories, such as tiki-themed bar glasses.

Lucy in Disguise

48 Lexington Street, W1F 0LR (7434 4086, www.lucyindisguiselondon.com). Oxford Circus or Piccadilly Circus tube. **Open** 10am-7pm Mon, Tue; 10am-8pm Wed-Sat; noon-6pm Sun. **Sells** W.

The vintage store of Lily Allen and half-sister Sarah Owen has really come into its own since moving to its Lexington Street location. The shiny black-and-white chequered floor, big 1950s-style television playing retro programmes, huge sky visual painted on the far wall, and vintage chandeliers create a cool and glamorous space in which to shop for good-quality vintage, from apparel from the likes of Pierre Cardin and Christian Dior, to lovely silk scarves and cool handbags. What's more, prices are surprisingly reasonable, with clothes starting around the £50 mark (although venturing into the hundreds). Highlights are the Hair and Make-Up Dept in the basement – perfect for a retro pin-up – and the VIP dressing room: pay £20 to book it and take your time to try on outfits, with a glass of champagne thrown in to get you in the party mood.

Shop Talk
Doug, co-owner of the Vintage Showroom

FASHION

Tell us about the shop
Our Earlham Street store opened in May 2009. We had already established our by-appointment showroom in west London, but as this was only open to design teams that we work with, a storefront was the natural progression. We felt that there was a big gap in menswear in London. There simply was not the quality of vintage shops for men that we had seen elsewhere on our travels in NYC or Tokyo, for example. A store with a beautifully curated collection of real one-of-a-kind vintage pieces. We hope we are some of the way, at least, to setting this right.

What's special about it?
The history. Before us, the store had been hardware store FW Collins since 1835 – one of the last of its kind in central London. A much-photographed and loved institution in its own right. Unfortunately it had to close in the end and we were delighted to be offered the space. We hope we have retained some of its charm and unique character. Also, the staff – we are very lucky to have an incredibly dedicated and enthusiastic team working with us who are all very passionate about what we do. This comes across in the shopping experience and creates a great oasis of calm in the middle of the West

End. Whether you have been buying vintage longer than us or are looking for your first piece, everyone gets looked after and hopefully finds something amazing to take away. Finally, the stock. We travel the world looking for amazing one-off pieces and our collection is constantly evolving and developing.

Who are your customers?
Having such a fantastic location, we get our fair share of actors and models, fashion designers and celebrities. The eccentric shop windows usually attract a lot of passing tourists just curious to see what we sell. The custom is probably split between wardrobe designers for film and theatre, clothing designers, diehard vintage enthusiasts and guys that are just looking for something cool and different.

What are your favourite shops in London?
Garbstore in Notting Hill, RRL on Mount Street for menswear, Selfridges for everything, Camisa Delicatessen on Old Compton Street for a great lunch and Monmouth Coffee Shop on Monmouth Street to start the day. Foyles is great for killing time – and the Vintage Showroom for the conversation and the music.

Merchant Archive Boutique

19 Kensington Park Road, W11 2EU (8969 6470, www.merchantarchive.com). Ladbroke Grove tube.
Open 10am-6pm Mon-Sat; noon-5pm Sun. **Sells** W.
Owner Sophie Merchant's discerning eye is evident in Merchant Archive's well-edited selection of beautiful one-off antique pieces, with vintage numbers from Lanvin, jumpsuits from the 1920s, antique velvet jackets, a good range of elegant dresses and some very special jewellery all waiting to be snapped up. The shop emanates an atmosphere of specialness as soon as you enter, and as a destination shop for both vintage and contemporary clothing, it takes pride of place in the address books of many a stylist, fashion designer and celebrity.

One of a Kind

259 Portobello Road, W11 1LR (7792 5284, www.1kind.co.uk). Ladbroke Grove tube.
Open 10am-6pm daily. **Sells** M, W, C.
Lindsay Lohan reportedly shelled out £10,000 in one visit here, selecting dresses and accessories sporting labels such as Chanel, Dior and YSL. No wonder owner Jeff Ihenacho plans to open a shop in LA. There are photographs of Jeff posing with various celebs in the window, and you certainly need an A-lister's wallet to shop here. Rare pieces are kept in a 'secret' room in the back,

to be viewed by appointment. During a previous visit, Jeff revealed sequinned Pucci harem pants and an early '70s YSL lace gown. One of a kind, without a doubt.

Painted Black

22 Veryan Court, Park Road, N8 8JR (www.painted black.co.uk). Crouch Hill rail. **Open** noon-6pm Mon-Fri; 11am-6pm Sat; noon-5pm Sun. **Sells** W, M.
Owner Amelia and her dog Rose can often be found behind the counter watching *The Good Life* in this beautifully presented shop just away from the main thoroughfare of Crouch End. The shop predominantly sells clothes, accessories and a few curios – such as Derek the taxidermied crow who, as we went to press, could be purchased for £150. If that's a little dear, evening classes in DIY taxidermy take place in-store. When this and the animal skulls on the wall are taken into account, Amelia's 'no fur or leather' policy can seem a little odd. Keen eyes can spot real vintage rarities, such as the £250 Christian Dior 'Beetlejuice' suit and the stunning £115 Jean Varon mint-condition dress we spotted. There is also a small collection of men's shirts and jackets, a variety of vintage cameras, old milk bottles and desk lights – including a cracking '60s white and gold lamp discarded by local actor James McAvoy.

Storm in a Tea Cup

Peekaboo

2 Ganton Street, W1F 7QL (7328 9191, www.peekaboovintage.com). Oxford Circus tube. **Open** 11am-7pm Mon-Sat. **Sells** W.

This central London boutique is headed up by the founders of Topshop's long-loved Peekaboo vintage concession, Emily Bothwell and Michael Caunter. From this central London base the pair look to move away from the colourful, second-hand party garb that made them so popular in Topshop and focus on the more grown-up, exclusive side of vintage. Delicate dresses, designer handbags and collectable accessories all feature in the simple, stylishly stark space. As you'd expect, prices reflect the chic ethos, though happily the bulk of the quality collection remains affordable.

Pennies

41A Amwell Street, EC1R 1UR (7278 3827, www.penniesvintage.com). Angel tube. **Open** 11am-7pm Tue-Fri; 11am-5pm Sat, Sun. **Sells** W.

Previously located just off Camden Passage, Pennies relocated to Amwell Street in 2011, and the shop is now housed inside owner Penny Ross's Georgian home. Together with her son Oliver she offers a mix of vintage clothing and accessories, and homewares new and old. The focus is on beaded flapper dresses from the 1920s, with some beautiful finds on display. If you're serious about this fashion era, and have the cash to splash – many of the dresses are rare items, with prices from around £80 to several hundred – then this shop is a don't-miss. Oliver is clearly passionate about the stock, sourcing items from far and wide, and making painstaking alterations and repairs himself. In addition to the flapper dresses, there's a well-edited selection of vintage lace wedding dresses from the Victorian era to the 1950s, as well as a range of vintage furs, jewellery and accessories, including some lovely clutches. Items also span new and old tea sets and retro cards, all lovingly displayed in the small space.

Reign Wear

12 Berwick Street, W1F 0PN (3417 0276). Oxford Circus or Tottenham Court Road tube. **Open** 11am-7pm Mon, Tue; 11am-8pm Wed-Sat; noon-6pm Sun. **Sells** W.

This Berwick Street store is well stocked with unique buys. The owners head to Austria, Germany and Italy (among other European countries) to source apparel, so items have a fresh feel compared to vintage dens that rely on American and British second-hand. There's also real attention to detail when it comes to arranging stock: items that work well together are paired on rails, and clothing is largely colour-coordinated – it makes the process of fashioning a complete outfit almost effortless. Prices are fair given the central London location, and you could walk away with a striking Nordic wool cardie for £30.

Rellik

8 Golborne Road, W10 5NW (8962 0089, www.relliklondon.co.uk). Ladbroke Grove or Westbourne Park tube. **Open** 10am-6pm Tue-Sat. **Sells** W.

Rellik (the Trellick Tower is opposite) is often cited as a favourite among the Kates and Siennas of the celebrity world, but neither the shop nor its price tags are intimidating. It's big enough for a lingering browse and small enough to get advice should you need it. The shop is run by three former Portobello market stallholders – Fiona Stuart, Claire Stansfield and Steven Philip – and their different tastes mean there's a good mix of pieces by the likes of Lanvin, Halston, Bill Gibb, Christian Dior and Ossie Clark. Philip's particular passion is the 1980s (Westwood, Alaïa) and he's popular with stylists (Kylie wore Rellik vintage in her Showgirl tour). There are earlier pieces too and one wall of the shop is dedicated to glam accessories, such as enormous Hermès sunglasses.

Rokit

42 Shelton Street, WC2 9HZ (7836 6547, www.rokit.co.uk). Covent Garden tube. **Open** 10am-7pm Mon-Sat; 11am-6pm Sun. **Sells** M, W.

As Rokit's flagship store – there's also one in Camden and two in Brick Lane – this branch stocks the most comprehensive selection of second-hand items, from tutus and military gear right through to cowboy boots and sunglasses. You won't find many well-known labels here, but it's still worth a rummage. There are also scarves, belts and hats galore. For men there are army jackets, Tees and shirts, as well as the usual male Americana – including a rail of wonderfully bashed-up Carhartt pieces.

Branches 101 Brick Lane, E1 6SE (7375 3864); 107 Brick Lane, E1 6SE (7247 3777); 225 High Street, NW1 7BU (7267 3046).

Storm in a Teacup

366 Kingsland Road, E8 4DA (8127 5471, www.storminateacuplondon.com). Haggerston rail. **Open** 11am-7pm Wed-Sat; noon-6pm Sun. **Sells** M, W.

On that no-man's-land stretch of Kingsland Road that seems to host nothing but takeaways is a shop that makes a lot of stylists' jobs a lot easier. Storm in a Teacup is the joint project of Joe Miller, who, by his own admission, has spent the past few years doing a bit of aimless this and that ('styling, erm, set design…erm') and his model girlfriend Claudia Raba. The small vintage store in Dalston is intended to sell off their sizeable combined fashion collection, and looks a little bit like the cast-offs of a troupe of 1980s supermodels. Silver Chanel onesies share the rail with cropped gold Escada jackets, and Alaïa showpieces worn on the catwalk by Linda Evangelista. Stock is not your common-or-garden See by Chloé, but rather collectors' pieces from more avant-garde designers – like Yohji Yamamoto or Comme des Garçons, and there's a stack of iconic Vivienne Westwood pieces. All this comes at a price – and it's not a cheap one. Most pieces are well into the three-figure mark. But for those fashion types paid to buy truly inspiring pieces of clothing (and yes, such professionals do exist), this place will be first on the must-visit list.

Victory Vintage

1st Floor, Whiteley's Shopping Centre, Queensway, W2 5LY (7792 9549). Bayswater tube. **Open** 11am-8pm Mon-Sat; 1-6pm Sun.

Fans of online vintage store Victory Vintage will love its roomy boutique on Queensway. Originally set up by Zoe Plummer (who you may remember as a star of 2010's *Junior Apprentice*) and her sister Rebecca, Victory Vintage stocks choice retro garb, hand-picked dresses, furs, shoes and accessories. It also now features menswear courtesy of Jake Hammond, a clothes trader who previously worked with David Saxby, the founder of now defunct vintage store Old Hat. Together, the trio draws die-hard East End vintage-shoppers to the West, as well as serving locals with a much-needed destination for good value, second-hand glamour. From its place amid mainstream big hitters Gap, H&M and Zara inside Whiteley's shopping centre, Victory Vintage also tempts hardened high street shoppers.

Vintage Emporium

14 Bacon Street, E1 6LF (7739 0799, www.vintage emporiumcafe.com). Shoreditch High Street rail. **Open** noon-7pm Mon-Fri; 10am-7pm Sat, Sun. **Sells** M, W.

In June 2010, partners Jess Collins and Oli Stanion opened their vintage-store-on-a-shoestring on Brick Lane back alley Bacon Street. With a well-edited range of clothing (in the basement) from the Victorian era through to the 1950s, its vintage time frame is tighter than that of nearby rivals, but all the better for it. Beautiful lace blouses, 1950s dresses, a great selection of hats, and top-notch accessories are all for sale, and, considering the age of most of the items, prices are very reasonable. What's more, the vibe of the Vintage Emporium is wonderfully relaxed, with the café – complete with bright yellow 1960s Gaggia coffee machine – a lovely spot to hang out in. A range of teas, excellent coffee, cakes and veggie lunches are served, and the venue also serves as an event space for life-drawing classes, poetry readings and the like.

Vintage Showroom

14 Earlham Street, WC2H 9LN (7836 3964, www.thevintageshowroom.com). Leicester Square tube. **Open** 11.30am-7.30pm Mon-Sat; noon-5pm Sun. **Sells** M

Striped 1940s sports blazers and racing coveralls, butter-soft motorcycle leathers, flight jackets and riding boots, droopy peasant jackets and a vast collection of worn-out denim, varsity T-shirts and Americana – the Vintage Showroom is a shrine to the crusty, crumpled and battered. The work of one-time market traders Roy Luckett and Doug Gunn, the Showroom has been almost a lifetime in the making, though it actually opened in 2007. Doug has been in the business for over a decade and Roy has been dealing in men's vintage for 25 years. The shop on Earlham Street is housed in an old ironmongers and stocks a tiny fraction of Roy and Doug's archive. There's also a traditional showroom in west London (open by appointment only), usually frequented by fashion designers and collectors. Stock is sourced from the US and Japan, Cambodian street markets and northern Canada – but there is an emphasis on Americana, denim, British tweeds and utility wear with a small range of rare tees and sweats.

What The Butler Wore

131 Lower Marsh, SE1 7AE (7261 1353, www.whatthebutlerwore.co.uk). Waterloo tube/ rail. **Open** 11am-6pm Mon-Sat **Sells** M, W.

This brilliantly named store specialises in 1960s and '70s fashion for men and women. Sandwiched between two cafés on Waterloo's Lower Marsh Street, the small but well-stocked shop sells everything you need to pull off a polished retro look, from Mary Quant-style shifts and floral flares to kitten heels and maxi dresses that we can picture south London native Florence Welch stepping out in. Prices are reasonable, with shirts from £25 and dresses from £50, while gentlemen's jackets go from £45 to £80 for velvet-trimmed suit jackets. Friendly staff are more than happy to let you rummage – particularly in the back where the furs, capes and evening dresses are kept alongside costume jewellery and accessories.

WilliamVintage

2 Marylebone Street, W1G 8JQ (7487 4322, www.williamvintage.com). Bond Street tube. **Open** 9am-5pm Wed-Fri (appointment only). **Sells** W.

As an expert voice on all things style, from wearing vintage with panache to dressing for the Oscars, former interior designer William Banks-Blaney is in demand. His advice comes by appointment only at this Marylebone boutique – a space he opened in November 2010 after his monthly fashion fairs became wildly over subscribed – and the two-floor store is a mecca for haute couture lovers. Banks-Blaney spends most of his time travelling the world sourcing timeless design pieces (which he then restores to immaculate condition) and his carefully edited stock features a discerning selection of vintage Ossie Clark, Jean Varon, Jean Dessès, Christian Dior and Balenciaga among others. An appointment will bag you a free run of the collection and the founder's own styling services.

WilliamVintage

FASHION

Lingerie, Swimwear & Erotica

Lingerie

The lingerie sections of many of London's department stores make great browsing grounds for underwear and bikinis. Our faves are **Liberty** and **Selfridges**.

Agent Provocateur

6 Broadwick Street, W1F 8HL (7439 0229, www.agentprovocateur.com). Oxford Circus or Tottenham Court Road tube. **Open** 11am-7pm Mon-Wed, Fri, Sat; 11am-8pm Thur; noon-5pm Sun. **Sells** W.

First port of call for the glamorous, decadent and fashion-forward lingerie fan, Agent Provocateur designs some of the most desirable bras, briefs and babydolls around. The first AP opened in Soho way back in 1994, and the brand now boasts an international reputation. Slip into the seductively lit shop, complete with saucy pink-uniformed staff, and lose a happy hour flipping through rails of wispy tulle and luxurious silk. It's a fine place to stock up on honeymoon fripperies (note for men: you cannot go wrong with a gift from this place); there's also a brilliant bridal range. Designs of the bras, briefs and thongs often feature sheer materials with bows and side ties. Nipple tassels, slips, suspenders and corsets are also on the menu.

Branches throughout the city.

Bodas

36 Ledbury Road, W11 2AB (7727 5063, www.bodas.co.uk). Notting Hill Gate tube. **Open** 10am-6pm Mon-Sat. **Sells** W.

There's a time and a place for seductive peepholes, side-tie knickers and marabou mules – and we urge you to embrace it. The rest of the time, boutiques such as Bodas are a real godsend. Head here for simple, well-cut and super-flattering bras and knickers. There are smooth padded bras in invisible 'maquillage' (a dark pink that works much better than nudes) for the perfect line under a flimsy frock, and sheer white soft-cup bras for stylish comfort. Cotton thongs start at around £11, and the lovely nightwear encompasses chic white pyjamas, nightdresses and kimonos. Great for cut-above essentials and wardrobe basics.

Branch 43 Brushfield Street, E1 6AA (7655 0958).

Myla

Westfield Shopping Centre, Ariel Way, W12 7GF (8749 9756, www.myla.com). **Open** 10am-9pm Mon-Fri; 9am-9pm Sat; noon-6pm Sun. **Sells** W.

Since it was founded in 1999, the luxury lingerie brand Myla has acquired a devoted following (its lace and freshwater pearl G-string acquired infamy after being featured in a classic Samantha *Sex and the City* scene). There are now lots of stores and concessions around town, which makes getting one's hands on the label's stylish, high-quality bras, knickers, toys and accessories a breeze. Seasonally updated collections always include fashion-forward colours and designs, though classics such as the signature silk and lace couture range are always in stock. There's a lovely swimwear range, elegant nightwear (like classic silk-satin pyjamas) and accessories such as candles, silk-bow nipple tassels and blindfolds.

Branches throughout the city.

Rigby & Peller

22 Conduit Street, W1S 2XT (0845 076 5545, www.rigbyandpeller.com). Oxford Circus tube. **Open** 9.30am-6pm Mon-Wed, Fri, Sat; 9.30am-7pm Thur. **Sells** W.

Unquestionably the Rolls-Royce of the bra-fitting world, Rigby & Peller – corsetière to the Queen, no less – continues to offer a service-oriented experience in its Mayfair boutique (despite being sold to Belgian company Van de Velde in 2011). Once you've seen the difference these properly fitting undergarments make, there'll be no returning to the grab-and-go guesswork and the greying rejects from the back of the drawer. Either arrive early or make an appointment if you want to be measured (it takes 45 minutes), and come prepared to splash some cash. Not because it's outrageously expensive – prices are, in fact, pleasingly affordable – but because you'll be dying to get your hands on the array of fabulous items. Brands include Spanx, Aubade and Fantasie as well as own-brand designs. Sports, mastectomy and maternity bras are available too. There are branches in Knightsbridge, Chelsea, Brent Cross and Westfield London.

Branches throughout the city.

Victoria's Secret

111-115 New Bond Street, W1S 1DP (7318 1740, www.victoriassecret.com). Bond Street tube. **Open** 10am-8pm Mon-Fri; 9am-8pm Sat; noon-6pm Sun. **Sells** W.

With its glossy quartz floors, black walls and leopard-print padded bras, Victoria's Secret is as different from Marks & Spencer's trusty undies department as you can get. The American lingerie giant, founded in 1977 by Roy Raymond, is known for its brash ad campaigns featuring scantily clad 'Angels' and saucy fashion shows. Being a Victoria's Secret Angel has kickstarted the career of many a young model, Miranda Kerr and Rosie Huntington-Whiteley included. With all this pomp and fizz, it makes sense that the brand's first UK stores do not do subtle – think polyester thongs and low-waisted briefs ('cheekies') many of them £10 a pop

Victoria's Secret

(or three for £24) in super-bright shades. A huge hit with teen shoppers.
Branch 111 New Bond Street, W1S 1DP.

What Katie Did

26 Portobello Green, 281 Portobello Road, W10 5TZ (0845 430 8943, www.whatkatiedid.com). Ladbroke Grove tube. **Open** 10am-6pm Mon-Sat; noon-6pm Sun. **Sells** W.
If you want to recreate Gemma Arterton's Bond girl look, get kitted out in WKD's Harlow Bullet Bra (not so much a push-up as a push-out). Even Gwynnie hasn't been able to resist the look (also snapped in Maitresse knickers by Mario Testino, no less, for *Vogue*). Vintage glamour is the USP here – think sexy corsets inspired by music hall and cabaret, seductive silks and satins (as well as velvet and leather, cotton and lace), and seamed stockings 'to bring out the showgirl in you'. Along with fabulous collections from the UK's top retro lingerie designers, WKD is now stocking Besame cosmetics in gorgeous retro-vintage packaging, so you can complete the look.

Swimwear

Biondi

55B Old Church Street, SW3 5BS (7349 1111, www.biondicouture.com). Sloane Square tube then bus 11, 22. **Open** 10.30am-6.30pm Mon-Sat. **Sells** W, C.

For the ultimate indulgence, and buckets of beach confidence, this luxury bikini boutique offers a fantastic on-site bespoke service, allowing you to make your dream one- or two-piece from a wide selection of luxurious fabrics and embellishments. Obviously, this comes at a price, but slightly less extravagant is the made-to-measure option (from £450), where staff produce tailored items from existing shapes and materials. There's also a great ready-to-wear selection of designer swimwear and beachwear from the likes of Vix, Karla Colletto, Debbie Katz, Fisico and Delfina, as well as hats, kaftans, tote bags, men's print shorts, sunglasses and other stylish beach accessories.

Heidi Klein

174 Westbourne Grove, W11 2RW (7243 5665, www.heidiklein.com). Notting Hill Gate tube. **Open** 10am-6pm Mon-Sat; noon-5pm Sun. **Sells** M, W.
The divine aroma of own-brand coconut candles at this glam beachwear store is enough to transport you to a world where stress-free grooming (there's an on-site Mystic Tanning booth), sampling beauty products (including the fabulous St Barth's range) and choosing the latest Missoni bikini are numbers 1, 2 and 3 on your to-do list. Own-brand bikinis start at £170 and come in classic black and white, with a choice of fashion-forward colours (snake, taupe, khaki) too. Also on offer are accessories by Anya Hindmarch, beach bags by Helen

Kaminski and Tom Ford and Tod's eyewear, as well as a host of own-brand kaftans, sandals and cover-ups. Robes and flip flops in every dressing room add to the VIP feel. A finer place to buy a bikini we can't imagine. **Branch** 123-124 The Arcade, Westfield Stratford City, E20 1EJ (8536 5700).

Odabash

48B Ledbury Road, W11 2AJ (7229 4299, www.odabash.com). Notting Hill Gate tube. **Open** 10am-6pm Mon-Sat; noon-5pm Sun. **Sells** W, C.
Slink into ultra-glam Odabash (white, white carpets, driftwood lamps) and even if the best you can hope for this summer is a week in a caravan in Wales, you'll feel like there's a yacht with your name on it somewhere. Frankly, nothing less would do justice to the kaftans, amazingly flattering bikinis (from about £158), sparkly flip flops and beachy glam jewellery. A range of Odabash flip flops is also available, while children get their own range of swimsuits, bikinis and kaftans. The shop's late summer sale is a fantastic way to stock up on high-quality swimwear on the cheap.

Pistol Panties

75 Westbourne Park Road, W2 5QH (7229 5286, www.pistolpanties.com). Westbourne Park tube. **Open** 9.30am-6pm Mon-Fri; 1-6pm Sat. **Sells** W.

If the eye-catching window displays don't draw you in, the flattering cuts certainly will. Started up by British/Colombian designer Deborah Fleming, Pistol Panties proved an instant success (her entire first collection was snapped up by Selfridges), attracting a loyal following for its fresh take on swimwear classics. Retro-style designs with polka dots, houndstooth patterns, paint splashes and frills create some of the most eye-catching, original and flattering designs available, while the perfectly formed can brave the stares in the cool cutaway swimsuits. Bright, oversized beach bags, attractive cover-ups (such as asymmetric dresses), flip flops and both new and vintage jewellery are also on offer, as are candles. Friendly and refreshingly honest staff will steer you in the direction of the perfect beachwear for you.

Erotica & fetishwear

Forget the stiff upper lip and British prudery; if it's latex, bondage and fetish gear you're after, London is the place to unleash your wildest fantasies. Visit the monthly **London Fetish Fair** (www.londonfetishfair.co.uk) for the last word in fetish fashion, or celebrate your sexual freedom at the **London Alternative Market** (www.london alternativemarket.com). Fetish fashionistas never miss the annual **Erotica** (www.eroticauk.com), an

Atsuko Kudo

exhibition that attracts around 80,000 visitors; and the high-end lingerie brand **Agent Provocateur** also has a continually expanding range of accessories (crystal whips, nipple tassels, metal cuffs) for sale in store and online.

Atsuko Kudo

64 Holloway Road, N7 8JL (7697 9072, www.atsuko kudo.com). Holloway Road tube or Highbury & Islington tube/rail. **Open** 10.30am-7pm Mon-Sat.

London's only retail outlet for latex couturier, *Vogue* favourite and fetish award-winner Atsuko Kudo, whose glamorous 'Hitchcock heroine' take on latex has led her to create one-offs for Lady Gaga, Beyoncé, Lara Stone, and, um, Kelly Brook. Holloway Road used to be fertile ground for fetish fiends, with Fettered Pleasures and House of Harlot close by. But the closure of both of those shops has left this small but stylish boutique to carry the leather-bound torch on its own, with a supreme selection of latex fashion.

Breathless

131 King's Cross Road, WC1X 9BJ (7278 1666, www.breathless.uk.com). King's Cross tube/rail. **Open** 11am-7pm Mon-Sat.

Owner and designer Dolenta and her team continue to expand the house label and explore beyond fetishwear essentials. The ranges lie somewhere between glam street and vintage-inspired couture – and there's plenty to choose from with around ten new designs emerging each year and a made-to-measure service. Women's lines nod to London's obsession with burlesque shapes (black and lilac mini-dresses with contrasting flared red petticoats and bow belts, and black-and-white striped Cruella deVil-esque tailored jackets that look divine with the Vogue range of latex miniature top hats). Classics include the 1930s-style baby doll dresses with latex rose detail and the bestselling straight- and flared-leg catsuits in a cornucopia of colours.

Coco de Mer

23 Monmouth Street, WC2H 9DD (7836 8882, www.coco-de-mer.com). Covent Garden tube. **Open** 11am-7pm Mon-Wed, Fri, Sat; 11am-8pm Thur; noon-6pm Sun.

This erotic emporium is London's most glamorous introduction to kink. The boudoir aesthetic creates an unmistakable vibe of refined naughtiness, and trying items on is a particular highlight, what with the peepshow-style velvet changing rooms that allow your lover to watch you undress from a 'confession box' next door. The jewelled nipple clips, jade cock rings and rose-decorated ceramic butt plugs and dildos are among the list of intriguing pieces. There's a deliciously large lingerie selection including Stella McCartney, Mimi Holiday, Lascivious and Coco de Mer's own range, as well as an array of leather masks, locking gauntlets and corseted

belts by Paul Seville and latex masks by Atsuko Kudo. The female-oriented book range includes an exclusive rare vintage selection, where you can find 1920s pornography and fiction originals, like *Lolita*. Started by Sam Roddick, the brand was sold to internet sex toy retailer Lovehoney in late 2011.

Expectations

75 Great Eastern Street, EC2A 3RY (7739 0292, www.expectations.co.uk). Old Street tube/ rail. **Open** 11am-7pm Mon-Fri; 11am-8pm Sat; noon-5pm Sun.

This leather, rubber and fetish store has an industrial, boiler-house setting that evokes a club-like vibe. You'll find plenty to wear to the ball. Premium jock straps, vivid rubber wrestling suits and cycling shorts, kilts and army surplus togs (such as combat pants) all make a statement, as do the sleek black rubber Adonis pouches and the rubber jeans and streetwear from Nasty Pig. For private play, there are over 100 electro-stimulation accessories, ranging from butt plugs to cock rings, in stainless steel and conductive plastic, and masked men can choose from a multiplicity of hoods in breath control, executioner or Hannibal styles, to name just a few. Other hardware includes restraints, collars, slings, harnesses, hogties, a quality metalwork series from Njoy, offering highly-polished metal dildos, and the new in-house range of stimulation aromas and herbal sex aids.

Honour

86 Lower Marsh, SE1 7AB (7401 8219, www.honour.co.uk). Waterloo tube/rail. **Open** 10.30am-7pm Mon-Fri; 11.30am-5pm Sat.

Honour's wide-ranging stock has something to suit all budgets. The ground level is home to a wealth of PVC and latex fashion, from tops, skirts and catsuits to classic uniforms such as nuns and maids to the 'high school honey' and 'flirty wench' look. Much of this is available up to size 26 and there's also a range of plus-size PVC and rubber. The latex menswear line includes a metallic red and blue fireman's costume and new olive-green military suit. Fetish magazine *Skin Two*'s sartorial offshoot, the popular, good-value rubber and PVC clothing range, is also available in store – fantastic for mistresses in the making. High, high heels, other shoes and boots are stocked up to size 10, and to complete the look you'll also find lingerie, wigs, eyelashes and long gloves. Hardcore guys and girls should venture upstairs to the 'bondage attic', where there's a no-nonsense display of toys, cuffs and collars, restraints and clamps.

House of Harlot

Unit 2B, 63-65 Princelet Street, E1 5LP (7247 1069, www.houseofharlot.com). Aldgate East tube or Shoreditch High Street rail. **Open** 10am-6pm Mon-Fri; noon-6pm Sat; 11am-5pm Sun.

Coco de Mer. See p105.

Now in a new location near Brick Lane, this leading hydra-headed latex boutique for both women and men now focuses almost exclusively on its own collections, including its new non-latex line, House of Harlot Stitched. The brand has become increasingly well established within the world of high fashion in recent years, collaborating with both Marc Jacobs and John Galliano, and worn on a number of occasions by Lady Gaga. The shop's own new lines have a more hardcore and retro-oriented feel, giving seasoned fetishists the extreme clothing they crave – whether in the form of latex catsuits, corsets, dresses short and long, uniforms or trousers. Prices may be commensurate with work-manship involved, but service is friendly and profes-sional. Clothing can be cut to measure at no extra cost, or created from scratch in around three to four weeks. Torture Garden's range is also stocked.

Liberation

49 Shelton Street, WC2H 9HE (7836 5894, www.libidex.com). Covent Garden tube. **Open** 11am-7pm Mon-Sat; also by appointment.
The flagship store for latex couturiers Libidex has con-siderably extended its range of glossy clothing delights, but you can still find intriguing accessories, all in *Little Shop of Horrors*-like surrounds. Pick up a hand-carved wooden cane, antique ivory dildos (£650) or a World War I operating table with original straps (and blood stains). Downstairs you'll find clothing,

accessories and hardware lines from Radical Rubber, Bondinage, hot new designer Bordello, Scarlet Diva, Prong, Slap Leather and a range covering classic fetish staples and 1940s Hollywood glamour puss and army-inspired couture. For men, ponytailed Leigh Bowery-esque hoods, extreme catsuits and shirts with vintage pin-up and intricate Japanese bondage designs feature, plus the usual collars, cuffs and neck corsets.

Sh!

57 Hoxton Square, N1 6PD (7613 5458, www. sh-womenstore.com). Old Street tube/rail. **Open** noon-8pm daily.
You don't have to be a woman to pass through the hal-lowed pink portals of London's only female-oriented sex shop, but you'll need to be chaperoned by one (though there's a gents-evening on Tuesday, 6-8pm). The capital's best sex shop for toys, Sh!'s strongest fea-ture is its friendly staff who give honest advice. Books, gifts and new kinky artworks are displayed alongside strap-on harnesses and three heart-shaped demo desks that feature own-range clitoral pumps, dildos and vibrators in numerous materials, styles and prices (our fave is the Lelo designer range). The Discretion Mini Vibe is a bargain. Even the fetish and lingerie lines downstairs in the basement have the feminine touch: handcuffs are suede-lined, collars are fit for a princess and bondage tape, crops and whips (some vibrating) are candy coloured.

Weddings

London has some of the best and most original bridal shops in the UK. These stores tend to operate on an appointment-only basis and booking ahead is essential. Also bear in mind that it can take up to a year to order a dress and have it made. Go along with a positive attitude, a strong idea of your budget and what you want, and an honest friend. Ask about fittings, alterations and extras to avoid any nasty financial surprises later on.

Vintage shops are an excellent starting point for brides and grooms; **Annie's Vintage Clothes** has some great gowns and accessories, as do vintage shop **Pennies**, in Islington, and the **Vintage Emporium**, just off Brick Lane. Many footwear designers, including **Emma Hope** and **Jimmy Choo**, have bridal collections and/or services.

One-stop wedding shop **Confetti** (0870 774 7177, www.confetti.co.uk) is good for wedding planning, affordable stationery, table decorations and even details of bridal fashion trends.

Dresses

Jenny Packham
75 Elizabeth Street, SW1W 9PJ (7730 2264, www. jennypackham.com). Sloane Square tube or Victoria tube/rail. **Open** by appointment 10.30am-4.30pm Tue-Sat.

With a string of design accolades to her name and a devoted celebrity following, Jenny Packham's brand of contemporary bridal glamour is in high demand. Appointments start with a lengthy discussion to determine exactly what the bride is looking for, and staff are experts in advising on styles to flatter. The look is romantic and Packham cites her inspiration as the iridescent beauty of nocturnal butterflies and circus lights (if that helps). Swarovski jewelled corsetry, French lace and silk chiffon are elegant elements of Packham's recent collection. Just along the road, at no.34, you'll find the Accessories Boudoir, selling a selection of lingerie, handbags, headdresses (including Swarovski tiaras by Polly Edwards) and handbags to complete the look.
Branch 3A Carlos Place, Mount Street, WIK 3AN (7493 6295).

Jenny Packham

FASHION

For the runaway bride

Fancy an off-roading kind of wedding day? Here are our ideas for a more maverick approach.

Dresses with a difference

Zoe Lem
Stylist and vintage expert Zoe Lem has a theory – the most important feature of a bride on her wedding day is her eyes. Zoe's vintage inspired creations leave ego to one side, favouring beautifully handcrafted dresses that focus on simplicity and silhouette, allowing the bride's beaming face to take centre stage. From the refreshingly welcoming chaos of her studio she'll talk you through the options, letting you know which era is most likely to suit your body shape.
www.zoelem.com

Fur Coat No Knickers
This Kingly Court shop specialises in vintage wedding frocks and has a big selection of 1950s prom-style dresses, for those of you whose style is more Scarlet O'Hara than Kate Middleton. Staff will tailor and tweak any of their existing dresses to make your perfect style, or start from scratch with a made-to-order service from £2,000. There's also an impressive selection of bags, shoes and general adornments from across the eras to perfect your look.
www.furcoatnoknickers.co.uk

The Pocket Library
Rebecca Denholm has one mission in life – to find you the perfect wedding dress. At her west London appointment-only studio she explains that she won't rest until she finds that dress that is uniquely 'you'. She has vintage couture from a range of eras with a focus on detailing and textiles. Once she knows what you're after, if there's nothing in her studio that suits, she'll keep her eyes peeled for a frock.
www.thepocketlibrary.co.uk

For dapper dandies

Beggars Run
Our favourite destination for suits for men who don't like suits, Beggars Run offers modern made-to-order two- and three-pieces in laid-back linens, corduroy and dogtooths, and fittings take place above a Victoria Park pub. From £300 for a made-to-measure suit.
www.beggarsrun.com

Hostem
If you fancy a more avant-garde approach to the morning suit, head to Hostem, where modern-minded gents will find labels such as Yang Li, Margaret Howell and Adam Kimmel providing off-the-peg tailoring for special occasions. We're particularly enamoured with the threads of Casely-Hayford – sharp, contemporary and oozing manly charm.
www.hotsem.co.uk

Marc Wallace
The go-to tailor for the peacock groom. Alongside the bespoke service, the Black Label collection offers three pieces in everything from baby blue to pin stripe rust. Floral ties finish off the look in requisite dandy flourish.
www.marcwallace.com

Hedonist's headware

Gina Foster
Make like a duchess and seek out this hatpin-sized millinery shop. Gina Foster makes hats for royalty and the like, but is no snob. If you take her a sample of a fabric you like, she'll re-make one of her chic little hats to match with material from Shepherd's Bush Market for no extra charge. From £180.
www.ginafoster.co.uk

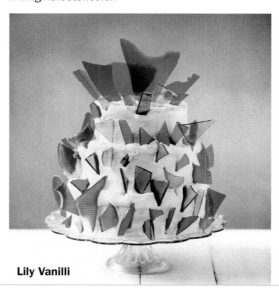

Lily Vanilli

Benefit meets Mad Hatters

The kitsch make-up brand gets together with eccentric milliner Mad Hatters to host hat-making and makeover classes, lubricated with cocktails and sweet treats. Email lisapd@benefit cosmetics.com to book. £38 per person including all materials.
www.katherineelizabethhats.com

The sweet spot

Lily Vanilli

Forget stodgy old fruit cake. Lilly Vanilli is currently London's darling of the decadent cake scene. She'll offer bespoke kitsch creations in flavours such as chocolate and avocado or rhubarb bakewell.
www.lilyvanilli.com

Choccywoccydoodah

Brighton's kings of cake camp have finally set up shop in Soho. The original bringers of lavish three-tiered tongue-in-cheek edible creations still offer the signature Sgt Pepper-inspired 'All You Need is Love' design. Or challenge their skills with a bespoke option.
www.choccywoccydoodah.com

Fancy feet

Hetty Rose

Hetty Rose will fashion you incredible wedding shoes from any fabric you choose. She hosts workshops for brides during which you can make your own pair.
www.hettyrose.co.uk

Shoes of Prey

If your need to micro-manage every aspect of your wedding stretches to footwear, try this: Shoes of Prey's easy-to-use website allows you to design every element of a bespoke pair of shoes and have them delivered in five weeks. Eat your heart out Nike iD.
www.shoesofprey.com

Something blue

Laura Lees Garters

Master embroiderer Laura Lees operates under the assumption that by the time the groom clocks your garter it'll be too late to turn and run.

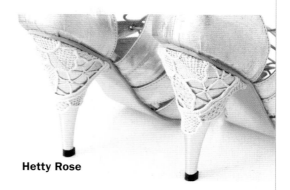

Hetty Rose

She makes them to order and stitches slogans such as 'TRAPPED' and 'I only married you for your money' into the blue silk. Email to order.
embroideryhouse@live.co.uk

The memories

Caught The Light

It's all in the name with Caught The Light photography. Rather than laborious staged line-ups of distant relatives, Chloe and Emma-Jane opt for natural shots. They capture stolen moments of laughter, dancing and silliness.
www.caughtthelight.com

Ellie Gillard Photography

Hunting for that filtered old-school look that your wedding has in your head? Ellie Gillard will oblige with photos in soft focus, black and white and muted tones. It's wedding fun with a vintage feel.
www.elliegillard.com

The flowers

Love Blooms

If a posy sounds passé, look to Love Blooms for a more creative take on your wedding stems: a headdress made of flowers, say, or a cake stand packed with plants.
www.loveblooms.co.uk

Amy Keeper

Add a discreet little twist to your bouquet with one of Amy Keeper's pendants. She'll place a picture of your choosing in a teeny frame and wrap it around your sprig for a bit of sentiment to accompany your flora.
www.amykeeperjewellery.co.uk

Luella's Boudoir

18 The High Street, SW19 5DX (8879 7744, www.luellasboudoir.co.uk). Wimbledon tube/rail. **Open** by appointment 10.30am-7.30pm Tue, Thur; 10am-6pm Sat; noon-5pm Sun.

A one-stop shop for every bride and bridesmaid (as well as mums, boys and guests), Luella's Boudoir features a handpicked selection from the very best accessories, lingerie, shoe and jewellery designers. Labels are constantly updated and could include Jacqueline Byrne, Charlotte Casadejus, Clara Bows, Caroline Atelier and New York-based designer Jessica Fontaine. The staff's wedding expertise is second to none and the shop offers a made-to-order bridesmaid collection with a choice of over 200 colours and the option of bespoke. The shop also offers a range of appointment-based services, including flower girl and bridesmaid outfits, and vintage dress adjustments and styling – where brides can bring along their vintage dresses to try on with accessories.

Morgan-Davies

25 Agdon Street, EC1V OAZ (7253 3007, www.morgandavieslondon.co.uk). Angel or Barbican tube or bus153. **Open** by appointment 10am-5pm Mon-Sat.

The boudoir-like interior of this Islington boutique is flanked with stunning gowns, all of them classic with a contemporary twist. British and European designers stocked include Augusta Jones, Jesus Peiro, Lusan Mandongus, Alan Hannah, Forget me Not and Watters & Watters. Shop manager Annalize has the remarkable ability to pick the perfect dress for your physique; keep your mind open, it's often not the one you expect. After initial fittings, you're looked after in the in-house atelier, where the seamstresses ensure you're fitted to absolute perfection. The shop also holds a range of accessories, including tiaras, brooches and earrings to complement your outfit.

Temperley London Bridal Room

2-10 Colville Mews, Lonsdale Road, W11 2DA (7229 7957, www.temperleylondon.com). Ladbroke Grove or Notting Hill Gate tube. **Open** by appointment 10am-6pm Mon-Wed, Fri; 10am-7pm Thur; 11am-6pm Sat.

Tucked away in a quiet Notting Hill mews, Alice Temperley's bridal room delivers superb service and attention to detail – offering champagne at appointments and even retailoring the dress to cocktail length after the big day to ensure you get as much wear and value for money as possible. As well as the extensive showroom of ready-to-wear creations in the label's signature romantic and ethereal style (silk georgette, hand-sewn pearls and sequins, embroidery), Temperley offers a fully bespoke service, giving a lucky few the opportunity to work with Alice herself to design a dream gown (from £10,000).

Luella's Boudoir

FASHION

Temperley London Bridal Room

Maternity & Unusual Sizes

Several high street chains offer trend-led maternity lines, including **Topshop** and **H&M**; **American Apparel** is a good choice for the style conscious, thanks to an abundance of stretchy, high-quality cotton items. Many of the shops listed below also sell baby clothes and gifts.

Maternity

Blossom Mother & Child

164 Walton Street, SW3 2JL (0845 262 7500, www.blossommotherandchild.com). South Kensington tube. **Open** 10am-6pm Mon-Sat; noon-5pm Sun.
This softly scented maternity wear specialist is a calming and reassuring place for hot and bothered mothers-to-be. As well as getting advice on everything from nursing bra sizes to local maternity wards, you can arrange a private evening appointment. The collection ranges from more affordable own-label day-wear (denim, workwear), eveningwear and sexy swimwear through to the popular customised jeans, and high-end designs by the likes of 7 for all Mankind and Citizens of Humanity. The lingerie collection is extensive and there are plenty of things for baby too, as well as luxury toiletries, lotions and potions. A concession can also be found in Harrods.
Branch 69 Marylebone High Street, W1U 5JJ (7486 6089).

JoJo Maman Bébé

68 Northcote Road, SW11 6QL (7228 0322, www.jojomamanbebe.co.uk). Clapham Junction rail. **Open** 9.30am-5.30pm Mon-Sat; 11am-5pm Sun.
Affordable and practical, with occasional flashes of French chic, JoJo is one of the most user-friendly maternity ranges around. Bestsellers include maternity jeans (possibly the cheapest to be found), easy-to-wear wrap dresses, kaftans and capsule officewear (linen shirts, trousers, dresses et al). There's loads of choice, plenty of style and it's all amazingly inexpensive – important when you're buying clothes that might not get much wear. Even so, only a selection of its huge stock is in-store – visit the website for further lines, including swimwear, nightwear, knitwear and jackets. It's also a good source of clothes for babies and children, gifts and nursery items.
Branches throughout the city.

9 London by Emily Evans

190 Pavilion Road, SW3 2BF (7730 1318, www.emily evansboutique.com). South Kensington or Sloane Square tube. **Open** 10am-6pm Mon-Sat; noon-5pm Sun.
This swanky maternity shop has a decidedly starry following – Kate Moss, Gwen Stefani and Laura Bailey are among the names choosing glamorous designs during their nine months – thanks to the names found here: True Religion, Minna, Faire Dodo, Pietro Brunelli and Gabby Harris. There are stylish maternity jeans, cute cashmeres and other elegant knitwear, and its own-label collection – 9 London – offers amazingly flattering and stylish evening and day dresses. There's also a range of lingerie and nightwear, lotions and potions and an unmissable children's collection – Tiny9 – for newborns through to nine-year-olds. There's also a concession in Harrods.

Blossom Mother & Child

Jojo Maman Bébé

FASHION

Pretty Pregnant

186 King's Road, SW3 5XP (7349 7450, www.pretty pregnant.co.uk). Sloane Square tube. **Open** 10am-6.30pm Mon-Sat; 10am-7pm Wed; noon-5pm Sun.
Now the concern of Dutch maternity wear brand Noppies, Pretty Pregnant is a one-stop shop for sensible maternity basics. Styles cover casual pieces and work outfits to swimwear and evening dresses. Keep an eye out for European brands including Queen Mum, Belly Button, Fragile and the slightly dubious sounding Hot Milk. The lingerie and nursing-wear sections are especially strong (with a large range of items from Boob), and staff are trained in bra fittings by Royal College of Midwives instructors, so can offer advice on anything from sizing to fabrics. Denim is another high point, with a large range of stylish maternity jeans, including pairs from 7 for All Mankind and Citizens of Humanity. If you're after skincare, check out the Mama Mio range (in particular the Tummy Rub Stretchmark Oil).
Branches 102 Northcote Road, SW11 6QW (7924 4850); 61 North Cross Road, SE22 9ET (8693 9010); 271 Upper Street, N1 2UQ (7226 9822).

Unusual sizes

On the high street, **New Look**, **Topshop**, **Dorothy Perkins** and **Next** all cater for both small and tall girls; **Principles**, **Austin Reed**, **Debenhams**, **Wallis** and **Miss Selfridge** all have a Petite range for women under 5ft 3in (in sizes 6-16).

High & Mighty

145-147 Edgware Road, W2 2HR (7723 8754, www.highandmighty.co.uk). Edgware Road or Marble Arch tube. **Open** 10am-6pm Mon; 9am-6pm Tue, Wed, Sat; 9am-9pm Thur, Fri; 11am-5pm Sun.
Sells M.
Since High & Mighty opened its first shop over 50 years ago on Edgware Road, trading as Northern Outsize Menswear, its reasonably priced contemporary and classic styles for men who struggle to fit into conventional high street sizes have gone from strength to strength. Catering to men over 6ft 2in, most trousers go up to 38in leg, and waist sizes up to 60in. Alongside its own labels there's a choice of brands such as Polo Ralph Lauren, Ben Sherman and Umbro. Covering most wardrobe necessities, including made-to-measure suits and wedding hire, there are accessories and shoes as well.
Branches The Plaza, 120 Oxford Street, W1N 9DP (7436 4861); 81-83 Knightsbridge, SW1X 7RB (7752 0665).

Long Tall Sally

21-25 Chiltern Street, W1U 7PH (7487 3370, www.longtallsally.com). Baker Street tube. **Open** 9.30am-6pm Mon-Wed, Fri; 9.30am-7pm Thur; 9am-6pm Sat; 11am-5pm Sun. **Sells** W.
Providing sartorial solutions for many a long-legged lass for over 30 years, Long Tall Sally's collections focus on comfortable, conventional and well-cut styles rather than high fashion. Prices are mid range, and there are clothes for every occasion. Tailored for ladies over 5ft 8in, trousers stretch from 34in to 38in, sleeves are longer, waists are cut lower and everything is offered in sizes 10-20. The range covers swimwear, maternity, knitwear, nightwear, accessories and shoes (sizes 7-11), and incorporates labels such as J Brand, Birkenstock, Converse and Hush Puppies.

Shoes

Many of the shops listed in the **Boutiques & Indie Labels** chapter stock a select range of stylish shoes, and both **b store** and **Folk** have their own lines of directional models for men and women. **Topshop**, **Selfridges** and **Liberty** are also good first ports of call with huge ranges; the former has a particularly good selection of Converse trainers.

On the high street, the ubiquitous **Office** (www.office.co.uk) is a good bet for a large selection of on-trend styles for men and women, while **Russell & Bromley** (www.russellandbromley.co.uk) is good for those with a bigger budget.

General

Black Truffle

4 Broadway Market, E8 4QJ (7923 9450, www.blacktruffle.com). Cambridge Heath or London Fields rail. **Open** 11am-6pm Tue-Fri; 10am-6pm Sat; noon-6pm Sun. **Sells** W, C.
Time Out has long sung the praises of Black Truffle, and for good reason. Selling some quirky yet wearable footwear for women and kids, the shop – a lovely space over two levels – has notched up a string of awards. The range of shoes is impressive, with brands such as Roby & Pier, Poetic Licence, Baltarini, Melissa, b store, Chie Mihara and Timeless represented. The shop also stocks tasteful bags from the likes of Abro, a small range of clothing that's especially strong on knitwear, and tasteful accessories, such as Falke tights, Dents gloves, Maniyak hats and affordable jewellery. It may be located on painfully trendy Broadway Market, but the stock here is more safely stylish rather than avant-garde, meaning that designs and materials have longevity. There's also a central London store on Warren Street, which now also has a lovely coffee bar inside.
Branch 52 Warren Street, W1T 5NJ (7388 4547).

British Boot Company

5 Kentish Town Road, NW1 8NH (7485 8505, www.britboot.co.uk). Camden Town tube. **Open** 10.30am-7pm daily. **Sells** M, W, C.
The British Boot Company was the first UK retailer for Dr Martens and became a favourite haunt of bands such as the Sex Pistols, the Buzzcocks and Madness in their late 1970s/early 1980s heydays. As well as the aforementioned DMs, the BBC offers all manner of big-soled, mean-looking, hard-wearing boots and shoes from the likes of Solovair, Gladiators, Grinders, NPS and Loake. This is also one of the few outlets where you can get your hands on a wide selection of George Cox shoes, the British brand famed for its brothel creepers and winklepickers, and newer Robot shoes.

Camper

34 Shelton Street, WC2H 9HP (7836 7973, www.camper.com). Covent Garden tube. **Open** 10am-8pm Mon-Sat; noon-6pm Sun. **Sells** M, W.
The successful Spanish eco footwear brand – one of Mallorca's best exports – has become more sophisticated in recent seasons, moving away from its funky but sensible image towards a more fashion-oriented aesthetic, particularly for the women's range. Each year, the label seems to flirt more with ankle boots and high heels (albeit rubbery wedgy ones) and girly straps. However, most of its styles are still distinctively recognisable, with the classic, round-toed and clod-heeled models still featuring. And the guys still have their iconic bowling shoes. Definitely worth another look if you've previously dismissed the brand.
Branches throughout London.

Christian Louboutin

23 Motcomb Street, SW1X 8LB (7245 6510, www.christianlouboutin.fr). Knightsbridge tube. **Open** 10am-6.30pm Mon-Sat; noon-6pm Sun. **Sells** M, W.
Celebrity favourite Christian Louboutin has been making truly exquisite footwear since 1992, and his shiny red-lacquered soles on his sought-after stilettos (which often have heels of over four inches) have become something of a trademark. He's more recently branched out into making equally covetable bags and creates catwalk shoes for everyone from Rodarte to Richard Nicoll. His London boutique brings a little drop of Paris to the big smoke and stocks key looks from his sleek and sexy collections, including sky-high platforms, Ms Turner-inspired ankle boots, stylish wedges and chic pumps. Prices (from £300) aren't for the faint-hearted, but then, perfection doesn't come cheap. A small menswear line is also stocked.
Branch 17 Mount Street, W1K 2RJ (7491 0033).

Emma Hope

53 Sloane Square, SW1W 8AX (7259 9566, www.emmahope.co.uk). Sloane Square tube. **Open** 10am-6.30pm Mon, Tue, Thur-Sat; 10am-7pm Wed; noon-5pm Sun. **Sells** M, W.
Having cut her teeth at Laura Ashley, Emma Hope's own-name designs nod to current trends yet remain every inch a reflection of her own dainty tastes; styles are the more sensible side of feminine, tending towards Kensington classics such as court shoes, ballet pumps and riding boots rather than sexy killer heels (although her snakeskin platforms are a little more in your face). Her unisex Joe sneakers are popular thanks to their natty juxtaposition of unusual uppers such as velvet and embroidered silk with stripes and simple rubber soles. Her straw weave and metallic leather ballet pumps are also bestsellers, while for evening there's a wide selection of slender courts and slingbacks. Men's styles mainly centre around trainers and a small selection of

F-Troupe. See p116.

casual shoes, boots and loafers. Quality materials and craftmanship mean steep prices, however, starting at around £259 for a pair of sneakers.

Branch 207 Westbourne Grove, W11 2SF (7313 7490).

F-Troupe

33 Marshall Street, W1F 7ET (7494 4566, www.f-troupe.com). Oxford Circus tube. **Open** 11am-7pm Mon-Sat. **Sells** M, W.

Previously solely a boutique favourite, British footwear label F-Troupe's first standalone store opened in August 2010 in Soho, providing a showcase for the full collection of men's and women's shoes and boots. In line with the inspiration for the shoes themselves, the shop was designed with a Dickensian curiosity shop in mind, with Victorian bric-a-brac dotted throughout. Boots are a particular F-Troupe focus, with styles managing to achieve a good mix between classic and innovative, with tassles, bows and unusual colours and textures – lots of tweed, suede and animal skins – providing interest. Given the original designs and high quality (some of the men's brogues are made in England), prices are reasonable, with most items between £85 and £200, and some as low as £20.

Jeffery-West

16 Piccadilly Arcade, SW1Y 6NH (7499 3360, www.jeffery-west.co.uk). Green Park or Piccadilly Circus tube. **Open** 10am-6pm Mon-Wed, Fri, Sat; 10am-7pm Thur; noon-4pm Sun. **Sells** M.

With its playboy vampire's apartment feel (red walls, velvet curtains, skulls in the window), this gothic Piccadilly store is the perfect showcase for Marc Jeffery and Guy West's rakish shoes. Still made to exacting traditional standards in Northampton – where both designers grew up – each shoe comes with an interesting twist, such as hand-burnished uppers, diamond broguing or a cleft heel, and are much loved by modern-day dandies about town. Classic shoes include the Brilleaux Wing Gibson in polished burgundy (£275). Shoe prices range from £175 to around £350, while boots go from around £295 up to £395 for the brand's Hannibal biker boots – a collaboration with Norton Motorcycles.

Branch 16 Cullum Street, EC3M 7JJ (7626 4699).

Kate Kanzier

67-69 Leather Lane, EC1N 7TJ (7242 7232, www.katekanzier.com). Chancery Lane tube. **Open** 8.30am-6.30pm Mon-Fri; 11am-4pm Sat. **Sells** W.

Adored for great-value directional footwear, Kate Kanzier is the place to come for brogues, ballerinas, and stylish boots in a huge range of colours. Sexy high-heeled pumps also feature strongly, in patent, suede, leather and animal prints, and with vintage designs dominating. The range is attractively arranged alongside a line of straightforward handbags and clutches in the spacious Leather

Kurt Geiger

Lane shop. The initial amazement at such low prices for such stylish designs is levelled when you inspect the quality a little more closely; however, the shoes are still good value for money – you'll be pushed to find knee-high leather boots as stylish as Kate Kanzier's for under £100 elsewhere – and it's a good bet for a splurge even when the bank balance is low.

Kurt Geiger

1 James Street, WC2E 8BG (7836 8478, www.kurt geiger.com). Oxford Circus tube. **Open** 10am-8pm Mon-Tue; 10am-9pm Wed-Sat; 11am-7pm Sun. **Sells** M, W.

Kurt Geiger has become the uncrowned king of the high street shoe chains in London, with its swanky products found in all the classiest department stores. Its mirror-clad Covent Garden flagship store remains the best place to see the full collection, however. Women's shoes cover a wide variety of styles, from the brand's signature, statement-making wedges and platforms to 'utility' urban boots, via a huge number of sexy stilettos, kitten heels, sandles and ballerinas. The men's lines are equally appealing, with a nice selection of desert-style suede boots, and a wide range of loafers, deck shoes and brogues. A good range of budgets are catered for too, with the Kurt Geiger diffusion lines, KG and Miss KG (stocked at concessions), catering to those with slightly thinner wallets. **Branches** throughout the city.

FIVE
Sneaker flagships

Adidas Originals

6 Newburgh Street, W1F 7RQ (7734 9976, www.adidas.com). Oxford Circus tube. **Open** 10.30am-6.30pm Mon-Sat; noon-5pm Sun.

This gallery-like space on Newburgh Street, just off Carnaby Street, houses Adidas Originals' limited edition collections, all with a smart, retro aesthetic – a more grown-up, less frenetic vibe than Adidas stores. There's also a branch on Earlham Street.

Nike Town

236 Oxford Street, W1C 1DE (7612 0800, www.nike.com). Oxford Circus tube. **Open** 10am-8pm Mon-Wed; 10am-9pm Thur-Sat; 11.30am-6pm Sun.

Nike's huge UK flagship bears down over Oxford Circus, housing an array of Nike collections, including high performance lines. Best bit? It's two Nike iD customisation spaces. Worst bit? Weekend daytime DJs.

Onitsuka Tiger

15 Newburgh Street, W1F 7RX (7734 5157, www.onitsukatiger.co.uk). Oxford Circus tube. **Open** 11am-7pm Mon-Sat; noon-5pm Sun.

This small store specialises in the original Tiger designs the Japanese manufacturer Asics first made its name in the 1960s.

Puma

51-55 Carnaby Street, W1F 9QE (7439 0221, www.puma.com). Oxford Circus tube. **Open** 10am-8pm Mon-Fri; 10am-7pm Sat; noon-6pm Sun.

This London flagship has the full range of Puma sneakers with limited-edition collections and exclusives.

Vans

47 Carnaby Street, W1F 9PT (7287 9235, www.vans.eu). Oxford Circus tube. **Open** 10am-7pm Mon-Wed, Fri, Sat; 10am-8pm Thur; noon-6pm Sun.

The original skate shoe brand is still going strong – with contemporary styles alongside adroit reissues of classic Vans and big-brand collaborations.

FASHION

The Other Side of the Pillow. See p121.

Manolo Blahnik

49-51 Old Church Street, SW3 5BS (7352 3863, www.manoloblahnik.com). Sloane Square tube then bus 11, 19, 22. **Open** 10am-5.30pm Mon-Fri; 10.30am-4.45pm Sat. **Sells** M, W.

Manolo Blahnik CBE has become one of the most prestigious shoe designers in the world. You have to buzz to gain admittance but once inside the service is impeccable as you rub shoulders with women happy to pay a month's rent for a pair of his timeless shoes. Best known for his killer heels, Blahnik's designs run the gamut from flat slip-ons to boots. The black patent high-heeled Erratic model (aka the Mary Jane), immortalised by Carrie Bradshaw in *Sex and the City* and often seen on the hoofs of Kate Moss, has now been brought back to the collection by popular demand. A small men's collection is also stocked.

Natural Shoe Store

21 Neal Street, WC2H 9PU (7836 5254, www.thenaturalshoestore.com). Covent Garden tube. **Open** 10am-7pm Mon-Wed, Sat; 10am-8pm Thur, Fri; noon-6pm Sun. **Sells** M, W.

A Covent Garden fixture for more than 30 years, and the first shop to introduce Birkenstocks to the UK. The store is dedicated to comfortable footwear... but don't let that put you off – models here are on the stylish end of the comfort shoe continuum, with a focus on classics such as Australia's iconic Blundstone boots and Grenson brogues. Other brands featured include the increasingly fashion-conscious Camper range; London-based brands Folk and Hudson; Patagonia, for good-quality walking shoes; Trippen, for leather boots and eccentric shoes; and Danish brand Duckfeet. There's also a cute collection of children's footwear, including sheepskin boots. Some vegan models are also stocked.

Branches 325 King's Road, SW3 5ES (7351 3721); 12 Eton Street, Richmond, Surrey TW9 1EE (8948 2626); (Issues) 181 Westbourne Grove, W11 2SB (7727 1122).

Old Curiosity Shop

13-14 Portsmouth Street, WC2A 2ES (7405 9891, www.curiosityuk.com). Holborn tube. **Open** 10.30am-7pm Mon-Sat. **Sells** M, W.

Built around 1567, this building can justifiably lay claim to being the oldest shop premises in central London – though whether it actually inspired the Charles Dickens novel of the same name is anyone's guess (though Dickens lived in nearby Bloomsbury and was known to have visited the shop). It's a joy to visit, anyhow, with small winding staircases and low wooden ceiling beams. These days, Japanese designer Daita Kimura creates unique handmade shoes in the basement workshop – his

avant-garde (and sometimes eccentic) styles for men and women start at around £160; the jazz shoe styles, such as the Paris model, are covetable, while the Hog Toe styles are particularly emblematic of his work. Duck as you go in to avoid bumping your head.

Oliver Spencer

58 Lamb's Conduit Street, WC1N 3LW (7269 6449, www.oliverspencer.co.uk). Russell Square tube. **Open** 11am-7pm Mon-Sat. **Sells** M.
The shoe and accessories shop from this modern British designer showcases Spencer's increasingly acknowledged range of Northampton-made men's footwear. The Oliver Spencer range comprises classic, hand-stitched shoes and boots with a contemporary twist, with a strong focus on brogues, desert boots and deck shoes. The quality of the materials (mainly leather and suede) and craftsmanship is high, and some of the newer models feature a comfortable Dainite sole, which has a superior grip and is said to minimise the collection and transfer of dirt. Prices start at around the £90 mark, going up to around £300. The shop also sells men's accessories, including colourful canvas and leather rucksacks and shiny leather wallets – and Spencer's womenswear collection. The brand's focus on decent, old-fashioned service makes shopping here a pleasure. The Oliver Spencer clothing range, meanwhile, is just down the road at no.62.

Oliver Sweeney

5 Conduit Street, W1S 2XD (7491 9126, www.oliversweeney.com). Oxford Circus tube. **Open** 10am-7pm Mon-Wed, Fri, Sat; 10am-8pm Thur; noon-6pm Sun. **Sells** M.
Oliver Sweeney makes beautiful men's shoes, which he sells from his gallery-like store on Conduit Street. In past collections, he's given classic styles such as the brogue, Chelsea boot and loafer fresh twists, including metal stud detailing, a toe-shape inspired by the clean lines of a Ford Mustang and new colourways including petrol blue and wine. The brand has recently been on a drive to refocus collections on more contemporary styles, launching the more trend-led London Collection and the Goodyear Welted line and collaborating with young designers like Matthew Miller. Both collections still adhere to Sweeney's high level of craftsmanship, with top-quality materials. Prices typically range from £165 to £325.
Branches 14 King Street, WC2E 8HR (7240 4549); 133 Middlesex Street, E1 7JF (7626 4466); 100 Cheapside, EC2V 6DY (7600 9200)

Poste Mistress

61-63 Monmouth Street, WC2H 9EP (7379 4040, www.office.co.uk/postemistress). Covent Garden tube. **Open** 10am-7pm Mon-Wed, Fri, Sat; 10am-8pm Thur; 11.30am-7pm Sun. **Sells** W.

Started by the Office Shoes chain as the more high-profile sister to its popular high street shops, Poste Mistress offers reasonably priced quality footwear in a decadent, retro boudoir setting. It's a sure bet if you're after a pair of on-trend shoes that will last you more than one season. As well as its own-brand range, the selection here – arranged attractively on shelves – includes designer favourites b store, Dries Van Noten, Chie Mihara, H by Hudson, Swear, Bruno Bordese, Fabio Rusconi, Acne, Opening Ceremony, Miu Miu, Jil Sander and Vivienne Westwood, and there's also a good range of more casual footwear from the likes of Converse and Melissa. The shop also stocks a small range of stylish accessories.

Tracey Neuls

29 Marylebone Lane, W1U 2NQ (7935 0039, www.tn29.com). Bond Street tube. **Open** 11am-6.30pm Mon-Fri; noon-5pm Sat, Sun. **Sells** W.

Footwear hangs from the ceiling on chains, sits on top of wooden stools and in fireplaces in Tracey Neuls' intimate and stylish studio shop on Marylebone Lane. The Cordwainers-trained Canadian is known for challenging the footwear norm with her unconventional yet comfortable designs and uses her equally conceptual shop to show off her wares. The eponymous main line (from £45) concentrates on her timeless yet trendy shapes in gorgeous tones and textiles, with her signature solid leather heels polished, slicked and even burnt. Her TN-29 brand (around £150) combines old and new so that vegetable-tanned leathers are paired with perspex, felt and hand-painted details. Recent lines have featured more affordable canvas shoes embellished with artists' prints (the likes of Le Gun). Other models, named after the cast of *Mad Men*, have been inspired by 1950s and '60s fashion, with a modern, distinctly Tracey Neuls twist.

Branch 73a Redchurch Street, E2 7DJ.

Bespoke

John Lobb

9 St James's Street, SW1A 1EF (7930 3664, www.johnlobbltd.co.uk). Green Park tube. **Open** 9am-5.30pm Mon-Fri; 9am-4.30pm Sat. **Sells** M, W.

In the shadow of the St James's Palace gate tower, this is a fitting site for one of the finest bespoke shoemakers in the world. The original John Lobb made his name as a cobbler during the reign of Queen Victoria, when he shod the feet of the Prince of Wales, later King Edward VII. Today, the company holds two royal warrants and has a fabulous range of classic shoes, boots, slippers and wellies. A pair of made-to-measure leather shoes will cost around £2,800 (plus VAT) but, if you've got deep pockets, this might be considered money well spent if you consider the craftsmanship involved and that the product is likely to last a lifetime.

Size?

Trainers

Skate shop Slam City Skates is good for limited-edition Nike SB's and Vans. Europe's first Supreme shop opened in Soho in September 2011, selling the full range of footwear from the cool New York streetwear brand.

Foot Patrol

80 Berwick Street, W1F 8TU (7287 8094, www.footpatrol.co.uk). Oxford Circus or Tottenham Court Road tube. **Open** 10am-7pm Mon-Sat; noon-5pm Sun.

Previously located on nearby St Anne's Court (where it was known for its shoes displayed in cages), Food Patrol reopened on Berwick Street in 2010 with a wooden bunker-like interior that feels simultaneously designed and understated. The trainer collection is similarly well edited to the previous shop, with a select range of lesser-seen Nike, Puma, Vans, New Balance and Adidas models, as well as shoes from the likes of Gourmet. Limited editions, exclusives and dead stock are a speciality, ensuring that the shop remains a first port of call for sneaker fiends from around the world. A small selection of T-shirts, hoodies, snapback caps and accessories from Veja, Herschel and Atmos is also stocked.

Kazmattazz

39 Hoxton Square, N1 6NN (7739 4133, www.kazmattazz.com). Old Street tube/rail or Shoreditch High Street rail. **Open** 11.30am-6.30pm Tue-Thur, Sun; 11.30am-8pm Fri, Sat.

A pit stop for both hardened trainer fanatics and anyone looking for rare pumps. Past treats found among the piles of boxes have included pairs of brown-and-white and purple-and-grey Adidas Flavours of the World as well as kicks from Greedy Genius, and new stuff comes in every week, sourced from all over the world. It also stocks more standard Nike (Dunks, Blazers, Air Max), Puma, Converse, Adidas (Stan Smith, Superstars) and Vans models, as well as Timberland boots and Keds. The shop is open until 8pm on Fridays and Saturdays, making the place a handy stop-off if you happen to be on your way to the bars and restaurants of Hoxton Square and around.

Branch 198 Brick Lane, E1 6SA (07973 145688).

1948

Arches 477-478, Bateman's Row, EC2A 3HH (7729 7688, www.1948london.com). Old Street tube/rail or Shoreditch High Street rail. **Open** 11.30am-6.30pm Tue-Fri; 10.30am-6.30pm Sat; 11.30am-5pm Sun. **Sells** M, W.

With Oxford Circus's Nike Town catering for the masses, it seems Nike's army of more refined sneaker freaks were feeling a little overlooked. The trainer brand's clubhouse for its most loyal (and obsessive) fans, 1948, is hidden under the railway arches on Bateman Row, a sidestreet connecting Great Eastern Street to Curtain Road. Its brick, wood and metal interior is complete with squishy sports-ready flooring made from recycled trainers, white neon football-pitch ceiling sculpture and plasma screens (which customers are often glued to when a big match is on). Another sizeable arch acts as a room for parties and Nike events; the library/chill-out area (sometimes hired out for meetings by local creatives) on the mezzanine floor has a large selection of art, fashion and music books to browse; and a decked garden with stadium-style tiered seating makes the most of the odd flash of sun.

The Other Side of the Pillow

61 Wilton Way, E8 1BG (mobile 07988 870508, www.theotherothersideofthepillow.blogspot.com). Hackney Central rail or bus 38, 242, 277. **Open** 11am-6pm Wed-Mon. **No credit cards.**

At first the name may seem strange, but not if you're into original Vans skate shoes and trainers, vintage sportswear and dead stock designer sunglasses (from the likes of Versace and Persol). Then you'll know why this shop, situated on whisper-quiet Wilton Way to the north of London Fields in Hackney, is mining a rich seam of cool. The Vans range from £65 to £250 (for rare and one-off needlepoint designs from the late 1960s), with a whole (retro) fridge full of Vans with exclusive Disney motifs and designs at around £95 a pair. Owners Henry Davies and Maurizio Di Nino have a passion for all kinds of collectibles from the 1960s to the mid '90s: cameras, line-dancing shoes, tea sets, '70s NOS Italian socks, 1980s Fisher Price record players, or even a first edition of Larry Clark's book *Teenage Lust*.

Size?

37A Neal Street, WC2H 9PR (7836 1404, www.size.co.uk). Covent Garden tube. **Open** 10am-7.30pm Mon-Wed, Fri, Sat; 10am-8pm Thur; noon-6pm Sun.

This hot-spot for London trainer fiends is unbeatable simply for its sheer variety of sneaker brands and colour combinations, thus making the too-cool-to-smile staff a necessary evil for punters looking for something a bit different. Old-school styles abound – there's no better place to pick up all-time classics like Converse All Stars, Puma Clydes, Adidas Gazelles and Nike Super Blazers. There are countless alternatives to the industry giants, like the more subdued Pointer and Clarks Originals, an array of British New Balance trainers, plus Asics, skate shoes from Vans. The small ground-level space is devoted to new arrivals; head to the surprisingly expansive basement for the rest.

Branches 33-34 Carnaby Street, W1V 1PA (7287 4016); 200 Portobello Road, W11 1LB (7792 8494).

Accessories Specialists

Many lifestyle/concept stores such as **Darkroom** (*see p35*) and **Luna & Curious** (*see p38*) stock avant-garde, affordable jewellery and accessories, while fashion boutiques such as **Diverse** and **Goodhood** (for both, *see p55*) are also good bets for pieces by an eclectic range of designers.

The shoe boutique **Black Truffle** (*see p114*) also has an excellent selection of bags, purses, tights, jewellery, hats and more. The bag collection at **Kate Kanzier** (*see p116*) is also extensive, stylish and affordable.

Bags & leather goods

Luxury British label **Mulberry** has long been recognised for its must-have leather bags, such as the Del Rey (named for Lana Del Rey).

Ally Capellino

9 Calvert Avenue, E2 7JP (7033 7843, www.ally capellino.co.uk). Liverpool Street tube/rail or Shoreditch High Street rail. **Open** 10am-6pm Tue-Sat; 11am-5pm Sun.

There's something quietly satisfying and delightfully unshowy about British designer Ally Capellino's bags, belts, wallets and purses, which appear in all the cool boutiques about town. Her signature pieces include understated, unisex satchels made from waxed cotton or canvas, with leather buckles: a classic Jeremy will set you back just under £224. Other offerings run from soft slouchy lambskin bags to more structured, vintage-style handbags with snap closures. The waxed cotton wash bags and laptop sleeves – including a luxury rucksack for Macbook users (a rare collaboration with Apple) – are other popular buys. The latest collection colours are shadowy and dark, inspired by ageing industrial buildings, with browns balanced by olives and rich reds. The brand celebrated its 30th anniversary in 2010, and a new branch opened in west London in 2011. The latter was celebrated with two limited-addition bags, the Golborne for men and the Portobello for women, in reference to the streets on which the new place sits.

Branch 312 Portobello Road, W10 5RU (8964 1022).

J&M Davidson

97 Golborne Road, W10 5NL (8969 2244, www.jandmdavidson.com). Ladbroke Grove, Notting Hill Gate or Westbourne Park tube. **Open** 10am-6pm Mon-Sat.

Anglo-French couple John and Monique Davidson's bags and leather accessories are made in their own Bolton factory, and the brand's slightly retro aesthetic has stood them in good stead for over 20 years. In the heart of Westbourne Park, the company faces some stiff competition from the neighbouring fashion boutiques, but holds its own thanks to traditional craftsmanship – high-quality leather, hand-stitching – combined with constantly evolving design. The brand steers clear of

Ally Capellino

FASHION

J&M Davidson

fly-by-night trends, however, so that the bags won't date – and helping to justify the prices. Small leather goods include belts, purses and wallets as well as a small range of classically stylish knitwear.

Lulu Guinness

3 Ellis Street, SW1X 9AL (7823 4828, www.luluguinness.com). Sloane Square tube. **Open** 10am-6pm Mon-Fri; 10am-6pm Sat.
Lulu Guinness's much-imitated signature style oozes femininity, matched with an irrepressibly playful streak. There's no mistaking her more extravagant handbag designs: bold, lip-shaped perspex or snake-skin clutches, say, or 'rose basket' bags, overflowing with pink satin appliqué blooms. Cheaper pieces are equally distinctive, running from retro-print laminated canvas vanity cases and make-up bags to gorgeously girly umbrellas, covered in her customary painted lips. **Branch** 23 Royal Exchange, EC3V 3LR (7626 5391); 42 Burlington Arcade, W1J 0QG (7491 9252).

Hats

Bates the Hatter

73 Jermyn Street, SW1Y 6JD (7734 2722, www.bates-hats.co.uk). Green Park or Piccadilly Circus tube. **Open** 9.30am-5.30pm Mon-Fri; 10am-5.30pm Sat.
Once, a man was not considered fully dressed if he went out without his hat. Having kept the tradition of gents' hats alive on Jermyn Street for over a century, Bates the Hatter clearly knows its niche, advising customers: 'Always wear a hat in inclement and sunny weather.' And sure enough, the shop sells headwear that covers all weather conditions: the straw panama is perfect for summer, while the deerstalker is ideal for those winter hunting expeditions. Well-crafted flat caps are a timeless classic, and chaps would do well to keep Bates in mind for formal occasions – Steed from *The Avengers* would be proud to wear the company's bowler hat, and the classy black top hat is a stunner in grey or black. This old-fashioned shop, with its wonderful topper-shaped sign, is one of London's finest surviving gems.

Bernstock Speirs

234 Brick Lane, E2 7EB (7739 7385, www.bernstock speirs.com). Liverpool Street tube/rail or Shoreditch High Street rail. **Open** 11am-6pm Tue-Fri; 11am-5pm Sat, Sun.
Paul Bernstock and Thelma Speirs met at Middlesex Polytechnic in 1979 and have been attiring east London's best-dressed heads since 1982. Everyone from Julie Christie and Boy George to Cheryl Cole and Victoria Beckham has bought one of their bonnets – creative reworkings of classic styles. Recent collections adhere to their witty and fashionable ethos, featuring bowlers topped with bobbles and wool-felt trilbys for men, as well as ribbon bow beanies and bunny-ear caps for women. The brand has also collaborated with designers Peter Jensen, Emma Cook, Antipodium, Agnès b, Jean Paul

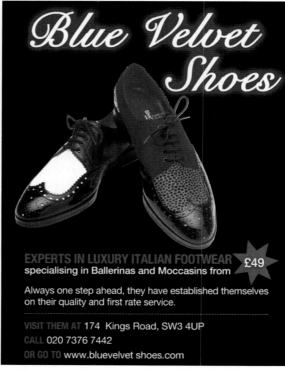
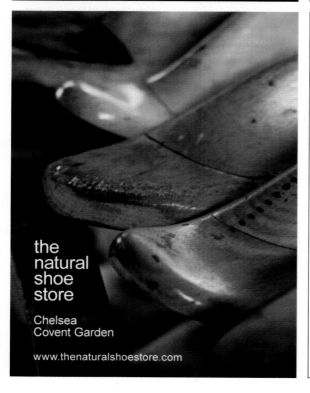

Gaultier and Richard Nicoll, and has a concession in Dover Street Market. *See also p126* **Shop Talk**.

Philip Treacy

69 Elizabeth Street, SW1W 9PJ (7730 3992, www.philiptreacy.co.uk). Sloane Square tube.
Open 10am-6pm Mon-Fri; 11am-5pm Sat.
Philip Treacy is one of London's most fashionable milliners. Much-loved by the late, great fashion editor Isabella Blow, he established his first studio in the basement of her house on Elizabeth Street in 1991 and his petite shop has since become a Belgravia hotspot a few doors down. Known for his ornate, attention-grabbing creations that often don't resemble a hat at all, designers like Karl Lagerfeld and Alexander McQueen have called on his services. Recent collections have featured funky colour and print design trilbys for men, fantastically feathered fascinators and neon berets, as well as oblong-shaped chic clutch bags for women. Treacy also designed and art directed Grace Jones's *Hurricane* tour in 2009, and returned to the London Fashion Week schedule in 2012 with a show starring Lady Gaga.

Jewellery

Ben Day

3 Lonsdale Road, W11 2BY (3417 3873, www.benday.co.uk). Ladbroke Grove tube.
Open 11am-6pm Tue-Sat; 11am-5pm Sun.

Ben Day has built up a loyal following for his exquisite, opulent creations over his 30 years in jewellery, fusing traditional hand-crafting skills with the latest technologies. Day creates his collections in the studio below his Notting Hill shop – each piece is a handmade one-off, adding to the air of exclusivity; for those who want something even more personal, Day will undertake bespoke work. His current collections feature opals, turquoise and volcanic stone and a range of more dramatic 'neon' stones.

Berganza

88-90 Hatton Garden (entrance in Greville Street), EC1N 8PN (7404 2336, www.berganza.com). Chancery Lane tube or Farringdon tube/rail.
Open 10am-5pm Mon-Sat.
Among the look-at-me sparkle and glitter of Hatton Garden, Berganza has a more subtle appeal, with its array of antique rings, rescued from home and abroad. With a speciality in engagement rings, the latest collection includes a wide array of diamond solitaire rings in line with most budgets. Rings are displayed in beautifully tattered velvet boxes in the shop window, next to hand-written labels describing their provenance. Georgian, Victorian, Edwardian and art deco treasures are all represented, in addition to a selection of stylish 1940s and '50s one-offs. Other pieces might include a 1970s Cartier money clip at £450, or a rather more expensive 15th-century gold sheriff's signet ring at £18,700. Prices start at just over £180.

FASHION

Ben Day

Shop Talk Thelma, co-owner and designer at Bernstock Speirs

Tell us about the shop.

The shop is situated on what we call 'upper Brick Lane'; away from the crowds and opposite a cute little green park. It is a hat shop for men and women, each piece invented in the workshop at the back of the shop. A fringe curtain separates the shop from the workshop and allows the customer an enticing glimpse into the world of Bernstock Speirs. The shop itself is painted clean white with white shelving, painted black wooden floors and a huge mirror on the wall. One wall has a display of bright bunny caps which looks very 1960s pop art. Backstage, in the workshop, the walls are a scrapbook of inspirational fashion images and the floor is concrete with a Jackson Pollock-effect finish.

What's special about it?

It is extremely chic and yet has a utility feel. We have the best visitors; artist and designer friends pop by for a cup of tea and a gossip or to talk about idea—s. We make things there, so it has a feeling of experimentation and industry. The hats are beautifully made and crafted with care. And the music is brilliant! Pop, disco, Motown and show tunes.

Who are your customers?

Our customers are very varied: they are usually fashion savvy, but there are exceptions. One of our favourite customers is a man in his early '60s, who is a delivery van driver. He must have seen the shop once when he drove past. He is intrigued by the hats and the atmosphere. He starts coming into the shop around September and he'll try hats on and choose which one he wants, then save up for it and buy it just before Christmas. Every year for the last few years he's done exactly the same thing.

What are your favourite shops in London?

Dover Street Market, Hunky Dory and Uniqlo.

What's the best thing about owning/ working in a shop?

It's a chance to engage with our customers… It's great to see people excited when they buy something they had no idea they even wanted until they saw it.

Comfort Station

FASHION

Comfort Station
22 Cheshire Street, E2 6EH (7033 9099, www.comfortstation.co.uk). Liverpool Street tube/rail or Shoreditch High Street rail. **Open** 11am-6pm Tue-Sun.

Fine art graduate and designer Amy Anderson is the creative talent behind this ladylike Cheshire Street boutique. Offbeat touches, such as birds painted on the door and a piano-turned-display cabinet, provide the ideal environment to showcase her handmade accessories. Alongside the beautiful, ethically made bags and bone-china crockery covered in wonderfully weird collaged prints is her jewellery line. The collection changes each season, with classically elegant but original designs in gold, silver, cord, wood and onyx. Favourites include the Sliced Poetry range – delicate leaf-shaped 'books' that fan open to reveal pages of Victorian poetry, and Anderson's Globe pendants – moveable silver rings that form a clever 3D sphere.

Cox & Power
35C Marylebone High Street, W1U 4QA (7935 3530, www.coxandpower.com). Baker Street tube. **Open** 10am-6pm Mon-Sat.

Sleek, beautifully crafted contemporary designs are the stock in trade at Cox & Power. Candy-bright gemstones mounted on simple silver and gold bands, strings of glinting sapphire beads and textured, invitingly tactile men's rings and cufflinks are among the goodies, while price tags start in the hundreds but soon run into the thousands. Wedding and commitment rings can be customised according to taste: choose the shape, finish and colour of the gold (from £295) and, if you really want to see how the whole process works, you can spend half a day in the workshop alongside goldsmith Power and even take part in the making of your jewellery (from £1,000, plus the cost of the piece created).

ec one
41 Exmouth Market, EC1R 4QL (7713 6185, www.econe.co.uk). Farringdon tube/rail. **Open** 10am-6pm Mon-Wed, Fri; 11am-7pm Thur; 10.30am-6pm Sat.

Husband-and-wife team Jos and Alison Skeates have a magpie's eye for good design, which makes for delightfully varied browsing in their shop. Over 50 designers are showcased: temptingly inexpensive trinkets include native New Yorker Alexis Bittar's colourful lucite bangles. Among the pricier standouts are Fiona Paxton's draped chain detailed neckpieces and Stephen Webster's darkly fantastical collection. Wedding and engagement rings are equally varied in price and style, running from simple stacking bands to shimmering, diamond-encrusted extravaganzas. An in-house bespoke service is available.
Branch 56 Ledbury Road, W11 2AJ (7243 8811).

Cox & Power. See p127.

Electrum Gallery

2 Percy Street, W1T 1DD (7436 2344, www.electrum gallery.co.uk). Goodge Street tube. **Open** 10am-6pm Mon-Sat.

Talent-spotting new jewellery design is made easy at Electrum, where a good deal of stock is conveniently under one roof. The gallery celebrated its 40th anniversary in 2011 and moved into its sister gallery's premises – Contemporary Applied Arts in Fitzrovia – in 2012. Designers from all around the world are represented, so the range of styles and budgets is huge, but with geometric form and fashion coming together as a guiding principle. Prices start at £200. Sharing a space with CAA (*see p160*) means Electrum's wares are exhibited alongside unique glass, ceramics and textile pieces. Note that CAA itself is on the move – most likely to Southwark, in March 2013 – so phone before visiting.

Kabiri

37 Marylebone High Street, W1U 4QE (7317 2150, www.kabiri.co.uk). Baker Street tube. **Open** 10am-6.30pm Mon-Sat; noon-5pm Sun.

Kabiri's admirable mission statement is to showcase the best in jewellery, regardless of its price, provenance or how well known the designer is – though many of its unknowns go on to become very successful indeed. Collections change with dizzying speed, but there are always a few things available for smaller budgets, such as the braided friendship bracelets and opulent crystal stud earrings, as well as the mid-range market, including young designer Kyle Hopkins' silver and gold pieces crawling with tiny toy-like men.

Branch 182 King's Road, SW3 5XP (7795 1559).

Lara Bohinc

149F Sloane Street, SW1X 9BZ (7730 8194, www.larabohinc107.co.uk). Sloane Square tube. **Open** 10am-6pm Mon-Fri; 10am-7pm Wed; noon-5pm Sun.

This Slovenian-born designer's talent for creating distinctive, dramatic pieces has stood her in good stead with the usually fickle fashionistas but her appeal went stellar when it was discovered that Samantha Cameron gave a Laratella bracelet (£320) from Bohinc's Essentials range to Michelle Obama. Elle Macpherson, Madonna and SJP are also fans. Glossy and sleek, with a high-fashion edge, Bohinc's creations make a real statement: think heavy, intricate yellow gold collars, sinuous interwoven bracelets and flowing, looped rose gold or platinum plate necklaces, all much imitated on the high street. Luxurious, supremely stylish bags, belts, shoes and sunglasses complete the look.

Lesley Craze Gallery

33-35A Clerkenwell Green, EC1R 0DU (7608 0393, www.lesleycrazegallery.co.uk). Farringdon tube/rail. **Open** 10.30am-6pm Tue, Wed, Fri; 10.30am-7pm Thur; 11am-5.30pm Sat.

All manner of inventive jewellery is showcased at this well-established Clerkenwell gallery, alongside delicate metalwork, decorative objects and textiles, all from designers worldwide. Yoko Izawa's knitted lycra and nylon yarn rings are among the quirky, highly individual offerings, while Jed Green's highly original pieces are created from glass in combination with other materials, such as silver, wood and pearls. Regular exhibitions highlight the work of selected designers, such as Australian jeweller Felicity Peters, who studied the Etruscan art of granulation to create her works of 18ct gold beads attached to onyx, tanzanite and tourmaline.

Maggie Owen

13 Rugby Street, WC1N 3QT (7404 7070, www.maggieowenlondon.com). Holborn or Russell Square tube. **Open** 11am-6pm Mon-Sat.

Lovers of costume jewellery flock to Maggie Owen's jewel of a shop located off Lamb's Conduit Street, and previously called French's Dairy. Behind the beautifully tiled frontage of London's first dairy, the shop showcases a lovely collection of bold, contemporary jewellery by the likes of French designer Philippe Ferrandis (whose distinctive necklaces started the story), along with innovative and talented designers such as style mag fave Anton Heunis, Stefanie Freydont, Simon Harrison and Karin Andreasson. The collection is enhanced by must-have lifestyle products: elegant fragrances and an array of scarves by local weaver Margot Selby.

Nicholas James

16-18 Hatton Garden, EC1N 8AT (7242 8000, www.nicholasjames.com). Chancery Lane tube.
Open 10am-5.30pm Mon-Fri; 10am-5pm Sat.

Owned by Nicholas Fitch (James is in fact his middle name), this spacious shop exudes sophistication even in classy Hatton Garden, London's famous jewellery quarter. Predominantly working with platinum and white diamonds, the designs are simple and contemporary but never boring: a deceptively simple rose-cut diamond sits in an ultra-modern, sharp-edged setting. Meanwhile, designs experimenting with more colour include rose gold rings embellished with natural brown diamonds. Bespoke jewellery, created using the latest CAD technology, is also available, for those who have a very specific piece in mind. And Nicholas James is, not surprisingly, also popular for engagement and wedding rings, as well as other wedding jewellery. While most of the designs in the shop are Fitch's own creations (designed and made in the UK), the shop also stocks a small selection of contemporary pieces from Henrich Denzel and Weissenstein.

FASHION

Tatty Devine. See p130.

Tatty Devine

236 Brick Lane, E2 7EB (7739 9009, www.tatty devine.com). Liverpool Street tube/rail or Shoreditch High Street rail. **Open** 10am-6pm Mon-Fri; 11am-6pm Sat; 10am-5pm Sun.

This east London company made its name with plastic fantastic jewellery: guitar plectrum charm bracelets, say, or kitsch anchor necklaces. Despite many imitators, it's still going strong – tribute to the designers' boundless inventiveness, which keeps it one step ahead of the competition. The foraging-themed collection is distinctly autumnal: think oversized beads, blackberries, leaves and colourful owls. Highlights include silk ivy leaf hair ribbons and a wooden brogue pendant. There are collaborations with the likes of Belle & Sebastian, Rob Ryan,

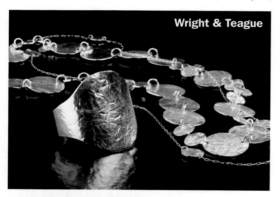

Wright & Teague

Tate, Selfridges and artists Gilbert & George, and the shop also stocks Smart Women products and Andrea Garland's beauty soaps, lotions and potions (handmade from scratch in Hackney). As well as a recently-opened branch in Covent Garden, there's now a concession on the ground floor of Selfridges too, where the distinctive 'name' necklaces are sold alongside other popular Tatty Devine motifs.

Branch 44 Monmouth Street, WC2H 9EP (7836 2685).

Wright & Teague

27 Burlington Arcade, W1J OEA (7629 2777, www.wrightandteague.com). Green Park or Piccadilly Circus tube. **Open** 10am-6pm Mon-Fri; 10am-5pm Sat.

Despite the boutique's smart setting, much of Gary Wright and Sheila Teague's much-imitated-but-never-matched jewellery is affordable for the average person: silver bangles hung with a single charm, say, or beaten silver studs. Prices rise for yellow and rose gold designs and rings set with gemstones. There's a pleasingly organic feel to many of the designs, which shun fussy detailing in favour of clean, simple lines. Some of the ranges look to other cultures and societies, and the latest features vintage, African, recycled and precious beads. The men's collection includes chunky chain bracelets, inscribed rings, pendants and tactile, pebble-like silver cufflinks.

Umbrellas

James Smith & Sons

53 New Oxford Street, WC1A 1BL (7836 4731, www.james-smith.co.uk). Holborn or Tottenham Court Road tube. **Open** 9.30am-5pm Mon, Wed-Fri; 10am-5pm Tue, Sat.

James Smith & Sons is one of the most visually striking of London's traditional shops. In the niche market of superior quality umbrellas, the store is unrivalled thanks to its lovingly crafted products, all built to last. This charming shop opened in 1830 and its original Victorian fittings are still intact. To say that it sticks out like a sore thumb would be unfair, but it's impossible to imagine New Oxford Street without it. Alongside the expected traditional brollies (such as a classic City umbrella with a hickory crook), there are high-tech folding models and sun parasols – including a dainty beechwood-handled number that's designed for weddings. Walking sticks and canes are the shop's other speciality, each one cut to the correct length for the customer. Furthermore, if you buy an umbrella here and the elements do get the better of it, James Smith has a repairs service to put it right again. The shop's staff are clearly proud to be carrying on a brand with such a long history.

Health & Beauty

Health & Beauty

London is now home to a selection of top-notch health and beauty boutiques that appeal to Londoners for their straight-talking approaches and high-quality products, and which eschew synthetic ingredients for purer concoctions. In this field, Australian skincare brand **Aesop London** (*see p134*) excels; the 'thinking person's' skincare brand opened shop on Mount Street a few years' back, and now has three branches in the capital, including one on east London's Redchurch Street. **Liz Earle Skincare** (*see p136*) is another don't-miss in this respect, with a large flagship in Chelsea's Duke of York Square. One of the pioneers of natural skincare products, meanwhile, was **Neal's Yard Remedies** (*see p136*), and the company is doing better than ever, with a clutch of new branches opened across the city.

Meanwhile, beauty and cosmetics shops have become more sophisticated, as consumers have become more savvy. Visit Primrose Hill's **Lost in Beauty** (*see p140*) for cult make-up and advice from expert staff, or **Space NK** (*see p141*) – now a common feature on London's retail landscape – for brands such as Eve Lom.

London's perfumeries now rival those in Paris for their indulgent atmosphere, and here, as with skincare, things have stepped up a notch, quality-wise, with **Miller Harris** (*see p142*) and US brand **Le Labo** (*see p142*) pioneering the trend for non-synthetic scents that can be sampled in their stylish boutiques. **Ormonde Jayne** (*see p142*), just off Sloane Square, is another don't-miss if you're after high-quality scents. The city's handful of herbalists, meanwhile, contains some lovely old gems – Green Park's **DR Harris** (*see p144*) first opened for business in 1790, while **G Baldwin & Co** (*see p144*) has been a feature of the Walworth Road since 1844.

Aesthetics are now as important a priority as eyecare at London's opticians and eyewear shops; visit **General Eyewear** (*see p146*), **Cutler & Gross** (*see p145*), **Mallon & Taub** (*see p147*), **Eye Company** (*see p145*) or **Opera Opera** (*see p147*), and you'll positively want to wear specs. (If you're lucky enough to have perfect vision, though, check out all three shops' highly covetable ranges of sunglasses.) **Kirk Originals** (*see p146*), meanwhile, is a visual experience you won't want to miss, with the interior of the Conduit Street flagship featuring winking eyes and artful displays of frames.

London's department stores also excel. **Selfridges** (*see p24*) and **Liberty**'s (*see p23*) beauty halls are two of the best, offering a huge range of cult products, and in 2012 **John Lewis** (*see p22*) revamped its Oxford Street beauty hall to offer a bigger, better space.

Aesop London

Skincare & Cosmetics

Skincare specialists

Space NK (*see p141*), **Cosmetics à la Carte** (*see p139*) and **Lost in Beauty** (*see p141*) all have good ranges of skincare products.

Aesop London
91 Mount Street, W1K 2SU (7409 2358, www. aesop.net.au). Bond Street or Green Park tube.
Open 11am-5pm Mon; 10am-6pm Tue-Sat.
A brand for the thinking person who wants to avoid heavily packaged and marketed products, Aesop eschews the dubious claims made by other skincare ranges, preferring instead to focus on quality, scrupulously researched natural ingredients and gorgeous scents, such as geranium, primrose and mandarin. This, the first stand-alone store in London, opened in 2008 in a former jeweller's shop in Mayfair, and is dominated by a huge circular sink (plucked from an old fish-paste factory), over which customers are encouraged to lather up body washes and smear on face creams. Lining the apothecary shelves, amid the mirrors and glass globe lights, is the entire collection of the Australian brand's skin, hair and body products. Highlights of the range include the Geranium Leaf body cleanser, the zingy Tahitian Lime cleansing slab and the Parsley Seed skincare range – although we defy you to find a scent you don't like here. Animal, a body wash for dogs, is a surprise big seller, but the Moroccan Neroli Shaving Serum might be used more often.
Branches Aesop Westbourne, 227A Westbourne Grove, W11 2SE (7221 2008); Aesop Shoreditch, 5A Redchurch Street, E2 7DJ (7613 3793).

Fresh
92 Marylebone High Street, W1U 4RD (7486 4100, www.fresh.com). Baker Street or Regent's Park tube.
Open 10am-7pm Mon-Wed, Fri, Sat; 10am-8pm Thur; 11am-5pm Sun.
Boston-based company Fresh does a very fine line in sophisticated health and beauty products, made with premium ingredients and dressed up in irresistible packaging. Co-founders Lev Glazman and Alina Roytberg are pioneers of sugar as a beauty ingredient, and the sensual Sugar range is among the brand's most covetable; the heavenly Brown Sugar Body Polish contains brown sugar crystals and essential oils, while the SPF15 Sugar lip treatment combines reparative oils and natural waxes with the sweet stuff. The passionate duo have also experimented with Umbrian clay, saké and soy to produce pricey but high-quality products. The most indulgent purchase has to be a pot of Crème Ancienne (£168/100g) – it's made entirely by hand in a monastery in the Czech Republic and is so rich that it banishes any dryness instantaneously. Other highlights from the range include

the Seaberry Restorative Cream and the pretty apothe-cary-style eaux de parfum, in enticing flavours such as Fig Apricot, Pink Jasmine and Citron de Vigne (also available as shower gel, body lotion and travel-handy roller-ball). There is an enticing make-up collection, plus a range of anti-ageing skincare products – we loved the rich-but-not-greasy Black Tea Age-Delay face cream, with its distinctive scent. Fresh also offers a holistic, customised facial treatment, the cost of which is redeemable against purchases of over £65.

Health and Beauty at Wholefoods

20 Glasshouse Street, W1B 5AR (7406 3100, www.wholefoodsmarket.com). Piccadilly Circus tube. **Open** 7.30am-9.30pm Mon-Fri; 9am-9.30pm Sat; 10am-9pm Sun.
Wholefoods, a health-oriented US supermarket that is popping up across London as fast as you can say 'organic', now has its own mini spa in Piccadilly. While it's not exactly a sanctuary (positioned next to one of the busiest tube stations in London, then past a stack of shopping baskets and checkouts) it's a handy beauty bolt-hole for the eco-minded. Effort has been made to separate the beauty area from the foodstuffs, with the beauty department dolled up with boutiquey wallpaper and neatly presented stacks of brilliant natural brands and lines – many of which you won't find anywhere else – from Studio 78 make-up to beautiful Palestinian soaps by Nablus. This considered approach to beauty is carried through to the treatment room, a cosy little spot tucked away off the shop floor.

Kiehl's

29 Monmouth Street, WC2H 9DD (7240 2411, www.kiehls.com). Covent Garden or Leicester Square tube. **Open** 10am-7pm Mon-Sat; noon-5.30pm Sun.

Liz Earle Skincare. See p136.

Ortigia. See p138.

With its quirky, inviting and brilliantly lit interior, the London flagship of the New York skincare company (established 1851) goes from strength to strength, with branches popping up on all the best shopping routes. Using only naturally derived ingredients and the minimum amount of preservative, Kiehl's products are suitable for some of the most sensitive skins. As well as products for face, body and hair, there are ranges specifically for men (from pre-shave to lip care), babies and children, and even sun protection. The lip balms and rich Crème de Corps (from £8.50/75ml) are cult products, while the Rosa Arctica regenerating face cream, Midnight Recovery Concentrate and the Facial Fuel range for men look set to join them.
Branches 20 Northcote Road, SW11 1NX (7350 2997); 186A King's Road, SW3 5XP (7751 5950); Units 14-15 Royal Exchange, EC3V 3LP (7283 6661); 9A Hampstead High Street, NW3 1PR (7443 7778).

Liz Earle Skincare

38-39 Duke of York Square, King's Road, SW3 4LY (7730 9191, www.lizearle.com). Sloane Square tube.
Open 10am-7pm Mon, Wed-Sat; 10.30am-7pm Tue; 11am-5pm Sun.
Former beauty writer Liz Earle launched her eponymous skincare brand in 1995, but it's only since the opening of her shop on Duke of York Square in 2007 that the brand has become better known. Based on botanical ingredients, most grown organically or harvested from sustainable wild sources, the streamlined range of products is, like Korres and Ortigia, pleasingly gimmick-free, as well as being notable for the absence of mineral oils and liquid paraffin waxes. Items are lovingly arranged in the spacious, well-staffed and fresh-feeling shop (think dove-grey tones, slate, greenery and wood), which is full of helpful leaflets and books on skincare and green beauty. The Superskin Moisturiser for mature skin contains cranberry and borage seed oils and rosehip oil to nourish and restore skin, while the Instant Boost Skin Tonic Spritzer uses the naturally active ingredients of pure aloe vera, camomile, cucumber and essential oils. The multi-award winning Cleanse & Polish Hot Cloth Cleanser (a cream used with a muslin cloth; £9 for a 50ml starter kit) has an avid following. The selection of 'minis' (from £5) in the shop is a great way to introduce yourself to the range, and facials are also available (signature facial, £85/90mins). Liz Earle Colour follows up its award-winning Sheer Skin Tint with a much anticipated range of make-up essentials, designed to enhance a wide variety of skin tones and colours. From this range comes the magical Healthy Glow Cream Blush, in seven gorgeous shades, guaranteed to perk up the dullest of complexions.

Neal's Yard Remedies

15 Neal's Yard, WC2H 9DP (7379 7222, www. nealsyardremedies.com). Covent Garden or Leicester

Shop Talk
Georgina Amador, owner of Hula Nails

Tell us about the shop
The salon is a pin-up – a cheeky tiki beauty emporium. We specialise in modern glamour in an old-school environment. We concentrate on chocolate-scented waxing treatments, Bio Sculpture 2-4 week gel manis, sparkling rosewater pedis, Minx foils, spray tans, lash extensions, vintage hair styling and make up.

What's special about it?
We're the friendliest beauty bunch in town, I think. We spend our days listening to Hawaiian music while beautifying and working with some of the best beauty brands around. We're a female-only salon and the atmosphere is busy but relaxed, happy and completely unique.

Who are your customers?
Our customers are professionals from all industries. Because of our location they are predominantly fashion, music, city and media clients. We also have a following of burlesque performers – although every single person who walks through the door gets to be a pin-up here. Because of the semi-permanent nature of our treatments, all of our busy clients want a glamorous experience and a result that lasts longer than average.

What are your favourite shops in London?
Collectif repro '50s boutique in Spitalfields – I just can't live without it. They dress me on a daily basis when I am not in Hula uniform. They have the best tiki and western-style pin-up dresses and the best pencil skirts in town. Stockings are really important for us as our uniforms sometimes allow a little glimpse of the tops and What Katy Did in Portabello do the sexiest sets of these. They also do the best retro vintage-style lingerie. I once picked up a silk gown from there for lounging at home and I feel super glamorous and very grown-up every time I put it on. Emerald Fontaine, our receptionist, is a burlesque performer by night, Hula girl by day and she can't live without her Ruby Woo red lipstick from M.A.C.

What's the best thing about owning/working in a shop?
The best thing is the daily interaction with our clients. The shop looks like a cross between a peep show, a vintage tiki hut and a salon, so we get a lot of intrigued walk-ins. From the moment our clients walk in, it's really enjoyable to see their stress disappear. I like to see their confidence grow too. All women feel better when they feel that they look great and my shop is about making that happen for them. I'm planning our Christmas activity currently so playing with glitter snow machines isn't a terrible job either...

HEALTH & BEAUTY

Nail bars

Beautiful Nails Studio

*28 Tottenham Street, W1T 4RH
(7580 5922). Goodge Street tube.*
This little nail bar sorts out your nails with little ceremony and only moderate cost attached (£15 gets you a good manicure and it's only £5 extra if you'd like some nail art). The only glossy thing about this place is the nails, but that means staff are happy to get stuck in with the power tools to file off dead skin; our tester left after a pedicure (£25) with feet half a size smaller. We're not the only ones to have discovered it: often the queue is out the door, so it's worth booking.

Hula Nails

*203-205 Whitecross Street, EC1Y 8QP
(07557142055, www.hulanails.com).
Old Street tube/rail.*
Georgiana Amador worked at M.A.C for many years – in contrast, Hula's boudoir-style beauty rooms are gloriously decked out in Hawaiian wallcoverings, with plush velvet sofas and burlesque flourishes. The salon specialises in luxurious grooming – come for a vintage-style pit-stop, with victory rolls and retro make up all on offer. Nail treatments take place in the window of the parlour, so you can sip on a free grated ginger tea and have a gossip as you watch the media types go by (waxes and spray tans are in cosily decked-out backrooms).

Square tube. **Open** 10am-7pm Mon-Wed, Fri, Sat; 10am-7.30pm Thur; 11am-6pm Sun.
A forerunner of the organic movement in the early 1980s, Neal's Yard has retained a loyal following despite competition from younger companies with similar ideologies. In recent years, the brand has expanded on to (smart) main shopping streets, such as Upper Street and King's Road, and most recently Westfield Stratford. Most stores are accompanied by luxury treatment rooms offering a wide range of therapies. The prettily packaged products, in their distinctive blue-glass bottles (to safeguard the ingredients), smell delicious without being overpowering, and prices are keener than for many organic products. Made in an eco-factory in Dorset, they run the gamut from soaps, hand washes and bath oils to sun creams, deodorants and essential oils, plus a mother-and-baby and men's range. There's also a dispensary for a huge range of dried herbs. Our top picks are the quick-absorbing Orange Flower Facial Oil, the Rehydrating Rose Daily Moisture Cream, the gently foaming Palmarosa Facial Wash, the replenishing Beauty Sleep Concentrate, award-winning Frankincense range and the Bee Lovely Hand Cream, of which 5% of the retail price is donated to a charitable cause. There is also an organic make-up range. Friendly and knowledgeable staff are on hand to help.
Branches throughout the city.

Ortigia

*55 Sloane Square, SW1W 8AX (7730 2826,
www.ortigia-srl.com). Sloane Square tube.*
Open 10am-6.30pm Mon-Sat.
Exotic, uplifting scents lure passersby into this eye-catching, beautifully arranged shop. Soaps, skincare products and perfumes come in handmade packaging inspired by Italian palazzos, mosaics and tiles (making them perfect for gifts). Named after a small island off Sicily's south-eastern coast known for its wonderful climate and rich volcanic soil, Ortigia uses plants indigenous to Sicily to create its luxurious but well-priced toiletries. There are 13 fragrances incorporating aromatic oils such as lavender, pomegranate, Sicilian lime, orange blossom and bergamot (the essential oil derived from the bitter orange tree), with base materials such as olive oil and almond oil strengthening the natural agenda. Each range includes bath oil, salts, soaps, room sprays and candles. The best-selling and most-loved Fico D'India range with fig, cedar, cactus and orange flower is divine, as is the classically packaged Almond Milk body cream. Mix and match minature versions to take on your travels or create your own gift box with the help of the welcoming, insightful staff. The firm's first stand-alone London boutique opened in spring 2008 in a fittingly elegant building in Sloane Square; a Marylebone shop followed suit shortly after.
Branch 23 Marylebone High Street, W1U 4PF (7487 4684).

Cosmetics & beauty shops

Becca

91A Pelham Street, SW7 2NJ (7225 2501, www.beccacosmetics.com). South Kensington tube.
Open 10am-6pm Mon-Wed; 10am-7pm Thur-Sat; noon-5pm Sun.

With its bright, elegant interior and seductive lighting, Becca has a luxurious, decadent feel. Australian founder Rebecca Morrice Williams, a former make-up artist, launched the brand when she couldn't find the perfect foundation, and is still very 'hands-on' in her approach; a key aspect of Becca is its inclusiveness – it caters for all skin colours and complexions, with a comprehensive collection of foundation and concealer shades. The focus is on achieving a radiant complexion, with a three-step system that begins with primer – a key product here, available in Hydrating or Mattifying versions – and a tinted base of Luminous Skin Colour or Shimmering Skin Perfecter. We're big fans of the Beach Tint Crème Stain for cheeks and lips, which imparts a dewy, natural-looking glow, as well as the mineral powder foundation. The final step is a dusting of very fine finishing powder. The smudge-proof Ultimate Mascara can be removed with just warm water. Make-up artists are on hand to give you a revamp (from £45) or lesson (£90; £45 redeemable against products), and there's a bridal service and a nail bar (from £15). The Becca Beauty Make Up Academy also offers a variety of courses for aspiring models and make-up artists.

Cosmetics à la Carte

19B Motcomb Street, SW1X 8LB (7235 0596, www.cosmeticsalacarte.com). Knightsbridge tube.
Open 10am-6pm Mon, Tue, Fri, Sat; 10am-7pm Wed, Thur.

Made by women for women for over three decades, Cosmetics à la Carte has enjoyed a steady following from local Sloane families throughout its lifetime; grandmothers bring their teenage granddaughters here for their first make-up lesson, thirtysomethings drop in for a seasonal make-up bag refresher, while brides-to-be visit in preparation for the big day. The intimate, stylish shop offers bespoke 'made-to-measure' make-up (it was the first company to offer this service) and skincare. However, this innovative and pioneering brand hasn't just limited itself to blending foundation and finishes (My Mix Skin Tint, £48); it also offers custom-made lipstick, gloss, powder and shadow, a Bespoke Colour Creation service for discontinued colours to match your old favourites and can reformulate almost any product to cater to allergies or sensitivities. Gone are the days of buying an eyeshadow trio because you like two of the shades: the click-in Colourbox system allows you to fill up a palette with whichever shades you fancy (eye, lip and cheek colours cost between £13 and £25). Make-up artists are on hand to give advice, even if you don't opt

MW Nails

3 Chichester Rents, WC2 A1EG (7242 4555, www.mwnails.com). Chancery Lane tube.

This wonderfully camp themed beautician's is decked out entirely, and authentically, from the salvaged innards of an American Airlines Boeing 747. Brightly lit beauty stations made up of roomy re-upholstered plane seats accommodate travel themed treatments such as the long lasting Two Weeks To Tahiti manicure (£39) or the quick file and polish Shanghai Shape (£12). And the fun's not just for the girls, male groomers can try out the Spruced Goose manicure (£29). The sense of silliness does not detract from the quality of the service, even if the the beauticians are dolled up like the cast of *Pan Am*.

WAH Nails

Topshop, 214 Oxford Street, W1D 1LA (7927 9844, www.wah-nails.com). Oxford Circus tube.

This edgy nail bar has made a big impact on the fashion scene in London in a short time. It's already established nail stations in Topshop, as well as just about every fashion launch party of the last few years, and brought nail art back to the fashion masses. The deft-of-hand nail technicians can rattle off a photo-real animal print on a nail in a matter of minutes, and are trained each season in the latest fashion prints.

Cosmetics à la Carte. See p139.

for one of the renowned lessons (£20-£180). Recent additions to the collection include the water-resistant Divine Lash Mascara, Hydra Lift energising eye gel, Hydra Smooth anti-wrinkle cream and Shine Illuminator Primer and Glow Enchancer. There are also regular seasonal updates.

Lost in Beauty

117 Regent's Park Road, NW1 8UR (7586 4411, www.lostinbeauty.com). Chalk Farm tube. **Open** 10am-6.30pm Mon-Sat; noon-5pm Sun.
Kitted out with vintage shop fittings, this chic Primrose Hill boutique, owned by renowned make-up artist Georgie Hamed, stocks a well-edited array of beauty brands, including award-winning British brand Oskia, Phyto, Caudalie, Dr Hauschka, Alexandra Soveral, Dr Alkaitis, Environ, REN, Shu Uemura, Art of Hair, Butter London nail polish with supremely covetable colours and, most recently, Antonia Burrell Skincare, whose signature Natural Face Lift Facial is available alongside a wide-range of other beauty treatments in the downstairs salon (booking essential). Other cult brands stocked include Becca make-up, Xen-Tan, the retro-packaged Rosebud Salve, Chantecaille make-up and skincare, Bumble and Bumble hair products, Jimmyjane candles and Belmacz Oyster Pearl translucent face powder. Illuminated theatre mirrors are perfect for sampling products, while the friendly staff are available to offer advice. Hamed herself (a regular on glossy fashion shoots) offers a bridal service, private lessons and parties. Prices start from £40 and head upwards. There's also a choice selection of vintage jewellery and clothing

Pak's

25-27 & 31 Stroud Green Road, N4 3ES (7263 2088, www.pakcosmetics.com). Finsbury Park tube/ rail. **Open** 9am-8pm Mon-Sat; 10am-6pm Sun.
Pak's is an Aladdin's cave of African and Afro-Caribbean hair and beauty products, with many exclusive and hard-to-find ranges. The flagship is a shop of two halves; the Wig Centre, on the left, offers an extensive array of wigs, weaves and extensions, both synthetic and human, alongside fake ponytails and hair pieces. Colours range from natural blond to black as well as kaleidoscopic blues, reds and pinks. The right-hand side Hair Centre is stocked to the rafters with hair and beauty products. Alongside names like Bedhead and Aveda are excellent moisturising haircare ranges Soft n' Free and Soft & Beautiful and various relaxers. Hair serums, oils, shines and polishers are a particular strength. Men are catered for with shaving oils, aftershaves and ingrowing hair treatments. The store also has a wide range of combs, brushes, straightening irons and rollers.
Branches throughout the city.

Screenface

48 Monmouth Street, WC2 9EP (7836 3955, www.screenface.com). Covent Garden, Leicester Square or Tottenham Court Road tube. **Open** 10.30am-6.30pm Mon-Sat; noon-5pm Sun.

Although on our visit the store looked as though it had been visited by a group of teenage girls on their way to a school disco (make-up smeared mirrors, missing lids, and messy, cluttered displays), professional make-up artists continue to seek out Screenface for its high-quality, long-lasting make-up and tools of the trade. Fardel face and body paints, Blink mascara, Lord & Berry eye and lip liners and Screenface's own range of make-up are all stocked. Haircare is of a similarly high standard (Joico, Fudge, Phyto), as are the make-up brushes and other tools. Special effects are big business: fake blood, raw flesh, adhesives and removers, plus all types of facial hair, from handlebar moustaches to mutton chops and an extensive array of false eyelashes. The latest products include French skincare range Embyolisse, tan-masters Fake Bake and, for those looking for knock-out effects for that forthcoming fancy dress party, torn skin gelatine prosthetics and werewolf double fangs.
Branch 20 Powis Terrace, W11 1JH (7221 8289).

Space NK

8-10 Broadwick Street, W1F 8HW (7287 2667, www.spacenk.com). Oxford Circus or Piccadilly Circus tube. **Open** 10.30am-7pm Mon-Fri; noon-6pm Sat.

With some 28 stores across London, Space NK could have easily become a soulless super-chain. The fact that it hasn't pays testament to founder Nicky Kinnaird's commitment to unearthing the latest cult beauty products from across the world. And not just any old products either – at Space NK, you can count on a meticulously edited range of top-quality items, produced by specialists in their field (Acqua di Parma, Nars, Nia 24, Tocca, Skeen, Michael Van Clarke, Laura Mercier among others). You'll find winners such as the legendary cleanser from celebrated facialist Eve Lom, perfect lipsticks by dedicated lip colour specialist Poppy King (aka Lipstick Queen), skincare by dermatologist Dr Brandt, and By Terry make-up and skincare from Terry de Gunzburg, who created YSL's celebrated light-reflective concealer Touche Eclat. And Space NK is showing no signs of resting on its laurels, with new lines being added all the time; recent additions include the 'gravity defying' make-up range Hourglass and award-winning Korean skincare range Erborian. At the heart of Space NK's philosophy is the idea that the consumer will be drawn to an eclectic range of products that are best suited to them, rather than investing in just one brand; we left the store with a very long wish-list.
Branches throughout the city.

Lost in Beauty

HEALTH & BEAUTY

Perfumeries & Herbalists

Perfumeries

See also p144 **Farmacia Santa Maria Novella**
and the shops in the **Skincare & Cosmetics**
chapter (*pp134-141*); **Space NK** (*see p141*)
is particularly good for scents.

Angela Flanders

*4 Artillery Passage, E1 7LJ (7247 7040, www.
angelaflanders-perfumer.com). Liverpool Street
tube/rail.* Open 11am-6.30pm Mon-Fri; 11am-6pm Sat.
This small perfumery is Angela Flanders' second shop
– a welcome addition to the Columbia Road branch. It is
redolent of her own creations as costume designer, offering perfumes in packaging that exude an air of
Victoriana. There are 16 signature scents, available in
eau de toilette, eau de parfum, perfumed candles, room
sprays, fragrant burning oils and perfumed lamp grains.
The heady aromas include woody Coromandel, vanilla-
scented Parchment and summery Hesperides. There's
also a range of colognes for men – look out for the new
Artillery range, created to commemorate the opening of
the new shop. Fragrances are also available in a more
concentrated form, in a handbag-sized 30ml bottle.
Branch 96 Columbia Road, E2 7QB (7739 7555).

L'Artisan Parfumeur

*Unit 13, Covent Garden Market, WC2E 8RB (3040
3030, www.artisanparfumeur.com). Covent Garden
tube.* **Open** 10am-7pm Mon-Wed; 10am-8pm Thur-Sat;
noon-7pm Sun.
It's no surprise to find that the stylish L'Artisan
Parfumeur is Parisian. The pretty Covent Garden store
is filled with scents – 'based on memories', as well as
interpretations of the natural world – grouped by
theme/mood. Les Voyages Exotiques features Timbuktu,
inspired by a trip to West Africa, while Les Insolites –
meaning the unusual – includes Tea for Two, evoking
the smoky aromas of Lapsang Souchong. Fragrances are
arranged in tealight holders filled with scented muslin,
which allow the perfume notes to breathe more easily
than a tester spray. What's more, all the fragrances are
designed to be used by both sexes. The classic fig, blueberry and mist are top sellers, along with Timbuktu for
men. New perfumes are added on a regular basis.

Le Labo

*28A Devonshire Street, W1G 6PS (3441 1535,
www.lelabofragrances.com) Baker Street tube.*
Open 10am-6.30pm Mon-Wed, Fri, Sat; 10am-7pm
Thur; noon-5pm Sun.

Joining New York, Tokyo and Los Angeles, London now
has its very own Le Labo perfume boutique. You may
have seen the austere bottles in Liberty, or spotted the
ultra-hip perfume bar in Paris's Colette, but if you've
never heard of it, even better – the brand has cultivated
a cult following among those who crave designer quality
but balk at purchasing anything mass-produced (Le
Labo's scents are freshly mixed at point of sale).
Handsome co-founder Edouard Roschi cites London's
eclectic vibe as to why it was the natural next step for
the brand, and accordingly he's taken over a 'superbly
ugly' former estate agent's in Marylebone and kitted it
out with a slick interior and Japanese mixing den. The
unisex perfumes start at £40 a bottle, and range from
the popular Rose 31 to the intense woody Santal 33. The
introduction of the Le Labo travel case means you can
carry your scent with you in style; another recent addition is shower gels. Note that if you bring an empty Labo
bottle back into store, staff will refill it for 20% off.

Miller Harris

*21 Bruton Street, W1J 6QD (7629 7750,
www.millerharris.com). Bond Street or Green
Park tube.* **Open** 10am-6pm Mon-Sat.
Lyn Harris, creator and founder of Miller Harris, is still
very hands-on when it comes to the running of her successful business. She has expanded the company to
incorporate not only perfumes but also teas, olive oils
and flower water. She uses the finest natural materials
in her unisex eaux de parfum, eaux de toilette, body oils
and body lotions (synthetic ingredients are only used
where they surpass natural sources, or where required
by legal regulations). Harris, who undertook years of formal training in both Paris and Grasse, sources raw ingredients from all over the world. Her iris comes from
Florence, the violet leaf from France, jasmine from
Egypt, while the particular orange flower she favours is
Tunisian. Perfumes from the original range of 12, divided
up by 'family' (citrus, floral, woody and oriental), are still
some of the bestsellers. Newcomers to the range include
Le Pamplemousse (limited edition), a grapefruit fusion
heightened with rhubarb and green melon, and La
Fumée (Arabie) with oriental notes.
Branches 14 Monmouth Street, WC2H 9HB (7836
9378); 14 Needham Road, W11 2RP (7221 1545).

Ormonde Jayne

*192 Pavillion Road, SW3 2BF (7730 1381, www.
ormondejayne.com). Sloane Square tube.* **Open**
10am-6pm Mon-Sat.
Shiny black walls and a plethora of mirrors give the
Ormonde Jayne flagship store a sumptuous look that
befits the rich scents created by Linda Pilkington.
Pilkington is passionate about her trade, sourcing ingredients herself in the Far East and Africa since starting
the company some 12 years ago. All components are free
from mineral oils, parabens and GM products, and staff

are happy to discuss which fragrance would best suit you, with the opportunity to be more exacting through a Perfume Portraits appointment. There are 12 gender-neutral scents to choose from; our favourites include the elegant Champaca, with pink pepper and bamboo, and the autumnal Tulu. An extended range of scents is now available in the form of Parfum d'Or Naturel – concentrated, alcohol-free gold perfume purées with a base of natural sugars; smooth it over the décolletage and shoulders for an incandescent effect with a lasting fragrance. There are also body lotions, bathing oils, shower creams, scented candles and travel/discovery sets, consisting of purse-size 10ml vials of fragrance. As well as the original shop in the Royal Arcade, Ormonde Jayne has concessions in Harrods and Fortnum & Mason.
Branch 12 The Royal Arcade, 28 Old Bond Street, W1S 4SL (7499 1100).

Les Senteurs
71 Elizabeth Street, SW1W 9PJ (7730 2322, www.lessenteurs.com). Sloane Square tube or Victoria tube/rail. **Open** 10am-6pm Mon-Sat.
The shelves of James Craven's pretty Belgravia boutique are laden with wares by prestigious perfumers, including stalwarts such as Annick Goutal and Creed, and lesser-known makes from traditional French and Italian perfume houses, such as Frédéric Malle's Editions de Parfums. Frédéric Malle's perfumes fly off the shelves, along with the classic Caron editions. New releases include Eau d'Italie, which evokes the elegant essence of Italy with intoxicating floral and woody notes. One of the shop's attractions is the care given to those selecting

gifts for others. Craven builds up a profile of the intended recipient by asking questions about looks, personality, favourite colours and even food. This personal approach is what sets the family-run business apart. Les Senteurs always supplies a sample with each sale so that the perfume can be tested before the bottle is opened.

Herbalists

Chinalife
99 Camden High Street, NW1 7JN (7388 5783, www.acumedic.com). Camden Town tube. **Open** 9am-8pm Mon-Sat; 9am-6pm Sun.
Created with the aim of bridging the gap between eastern and western healthcare, Chinalife is a modern holistic health shop with wooden shelves piled high with a selection of teas, supplements and aromatherapy oils. Stylishly packaged skincare and body ranges feature all-natural active ingredients, some familiar (gingko and ginseng), others, like the anti-ageing reishi or moisture-boosting Chinese angelica, less well known in the West. We particularly like the herbal foot bath, the flower water sprays and the jasmine face mask for dry skin. Tea-lovers are spoilt for choice, with an impressive array of medicinal blends and flower- and berry-filled sachets. A chic tea bar also offers exotic concoctions infused with pomegranate syrup and crushed rosebuds, and fragrant, spice-infused lattes. Sugar-free blends, green and caffeine-free teas are also sold, such as the much sought after Amachazuru tea, praised for its health-giving properties. Tea lectures and workshops have also proved

HEALTH & BEAUTY

Angela Flanders

popular. New additions include ornate china tea sets (£54.95). At the shop's rear, canvas panels suspended from the ceiling create an airy therapy room for the likes of acupuncture and Chinese meridian massage. Next door at the AcuMedic clinic, a team of experts from China can offer solutions to just about anything, from infertility through to smoking addiction.

DR Harris

29 St James's Street, SW1A 1HB (7930 3915, www.drharris.co.uk). Green Park or Piccadilly Circus tube. **Open** 8.30am-6pm Mon-Fri; 9.30am-5pm Sat.

In a city overtaken by characterless chain pharmacies, DR Harris has remained unfazed – it's hung on tight to its identity since 1790 and even boasts a royal warrant. A visit is much like stepping back through a door into times past. Polished wooden cabinets are filled with bottles and jars with old-fashioned shaving brushes and manicure kits. Its own elegantly packaged products have appealing names; there's Almond Oil Skinfood (£14.50/50ml), Bay Rum Aftershave (£21.95/100ml) and Old English Lavender Cologne (£29.50/100ml). Keep your eyes peeled, too, for Marvis toothpaste and Roger & Gallet soaps. Traditional it may be, but DR Harris appeals to modern sensibilities – none of the products are tested on animals and beauty editors continue to clamour over cult favourites such as the bright blue Crystal Eye Gel.

Le Labo. See p142.

Farmacia Santa Maria Novella

117 Walton Street, SW3 2HP (7493 1975). South Kensington tube. **Open** 10am-6pm Mon-Sat.

The minuscule London outpost of the famed Florentine pharmacy, founded by Dominican friars, sells beautifully packaged lotions, perfumes, eaux de colognes, exfoliating powders, pot pourri, scented paper and soaps. The shop can't compete with the Italian version, located in a 13th-century frescoed chapel, but the products from one of the world's oldest herbal pharmacies (the company was officially founded in 1612, though its origins date back as far as 1221) are the same; in fact, the lavender smelling salts and 'anti-hysteria' Acqua de Santa Maria Novella are practically unchanged formulas. Other renowned items include orange blossom water and pomegranate perfume. Melograno is its unisex signature scent. The bath salts, beautifully packaged in a vintage-style tin, make a great gift (£40).
Branch 1 Piccadilly Arcade, SW1Y 6NH (7493 1975).

G Baldwin & Co

171-173 Walworth Road, SE17 1RW (7703 5550, www.baldwins.co.uk). Elephant & Castle tube/rail.
Open 9am-6pm Mon-Sat.

This old-school apothecary, specialising in natural beauty products and health remedies, from oils and balms to herbs, has been open on the Walworth Road since 1844, making it one of London's oldest herbalists; there were originally 12 branches, but this is the only remaining shop. Swing by for top-notch dispensing advice and you might bump into long-time customers Michael Caine or Terence Stamp. Products include health tinctures, supplements, barks and flower remedies. You can also buy soap-making mould kits (£39.49, makes nine bars) and a range of unfragranced Baldwin bases to make your own face creams, shampoos or shower gels. The Synergy Range is based on the finest-quality essential oils combined with luxurious carrier oils; the store's bestseller is the relaxing, calming lavender oil (£5.89).

Nelsons Pharmacy

87D Duke Street, W1K 5PQ (7629 3118, www.nelsonspharmacy.com). Bond Street tube.
Open 9am-5.30pm Mon-Fri; 10am-5pm Sat.

There's something for every ailment at this homeopathic pharmacy – which was the first of its kind when Ernst Louis Ambrecht opened it in 1860. In the 1930s, Dr Edward Bach began to sell his famous Bach Original Flower Remedies here. Nowadays you'll also find pills and potions such as Menopause Care Tincture, Pills for Brain Fatigue and the Pure & Clear range for blemished skin. If you don't find what you're after, the friendly pharmacist will talk over symptoms and tailor-make a medicine for you using the vast 'potency bank' of more than 2,000 remedies. There's a peaceful clinic in the basement for massages, food-sensitivity testing, Alexander Technique lessons and homeopathy.

Eyewear

Chains **Dolland & Aitchison** (which has now merged with Boots Opticians; 361 Oxford Street, W1C 2JL, 7495 8209, www.danda.co.uk), **Optical Express** (65-72 the Strand, WC2N 5LR, 7436 5029, www.opticalexpress.com), **Specsavers** (Unit 6, 6-17 Tottenham Court Road, W1T 1BG, 7580 5115, www.specsavers.com) and **Vision Express** (263-265 Oxford Street, W1C 2DF, 7409 7880, www.visionexpress.com) also offer a wide range of frames, including budget-friendly options.

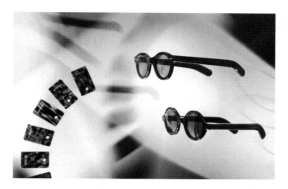

Cutler & Gross

16 Knightsbridge Green, SW1X 7QL (7581 2250, www.cutlerandgross.com). Knightsbridge tube.
Open 9.30am-7pm Mon-Sat; noon-5pm Sun.
Cool and quirky is the name of the game at this long-established outlet (founded in 1969), known for its innovative hand-built frames. A new collection is introduced twice a year, perhaps Warhol-inspired or the classic retro styling of the Belle de Jour range. C&G is renowned for its clever use of colour in its optical frames, while sunglasses run the gamut from leather-trimmed aviators to oversized tortoiseshell numbers. What characterises all of the frames is the high quality. Collaboration collections are big, with favourites including Maison Martin Margiela and Giles Deacon. Prices range from £130-£899.
Branch Cutler & Gross Vintage 7 Knightsbridge Green, SW1X 7QL (7590 9995).

Eye Company

159 Wardour Street, W1F 8WH (7434 0988, www.eye-company.co.uk). Oxford Circus or Tottenham Court Road tube. **Open** 10.30am-6.30pm Mon-Wed, Fri; 10.30am-7.30pm Thur; 11am-6pm Sat.
Supplying the film and TV industry, Soho's Eye Company is a hip independent intent on challenging the mediocrity of the high street chains. Its select range of mint-condition vintage frames (some dating back to the 18th century), its stylish own-brand frames and its selection of cherry-picked numbers from the likes of Dita, Mykita and Beau Soleil make you positively want to have to wear glasses – although the sunglasses provide plenty of excitement for those with 20/20 vision. If you have a favourite pair of frames that need a little TLC, Eye Company can also repair or copy them, or even design you a pair from scratch. Naturally, the full optical treatment is also available, including eye tests, contact lens fitting and aftercare.

Cutler & Gross

Eye Contacts

10 Chalk Farm Road, NW1 8AG (7482 1701, www.eyecontactscamden.co.uk). Camden Town or Chalk Farm tube. **Open** 10.30am-6pm Mon-Sat; 11am-6pm Sun.

HEALTH & BEAUTY

Tucked away in the lee of the Camden Lock railway bridge, this relaxed optician's has been tending to the optically challenged of NW1 since Camden's 1980s heyday. Spec-themed stained-glass windows provide a nice touch of colour to a stylish, pared-back bare-brick space housing a small but well-chosen frame selection. Frames from Alain Mikli and Lindberg are displayed alongside less familiar designers such as LA's Dita eyewear. British designs include Cutler & Gross (*see p145*), Booth & Bruce and Tom Ford. Eye tests are reasonably priced and friendly staff are on hand to help with the difficult frame-choosing process.

General Eyewear

Arch 67, Stables Market, NW1 8AH (7428 0123 /www.generaleyewear.com). Camden Town or Chalk Farm tube. **Open** 10am-6pm daily.

The company formerly called Arckiv now consists of two lines; the original brand name now refers to the new menswear label, while the eyewear part of the business is now called the more generic General Eyewear. Supplying frames and lenses to the theatre, TV and film industries, the company specialises in beautiful and unusual eyewear designs, antique (from 1800 onwards) and modern: you'll find monocles and lorgnettes, flying and biking goggles, glam rock or space-age designs, as well as the usual suspects (Mikli, Ray-Ban, Persol) and a few high-end names associated with fashionable over-sized sunglasses (Pucci, Courrèges, Cardin). The shop also supplies anti-reflection lenses and can add metallic and other coatings. Plus, head here to have bespoke frames created using in-house materials, so you know exactly what you're going to get (£285 including lenses).

Kirk Originals

6 Conduit Street, W1S 2XE (7499 0060, www.kirk originals.com). Oxford Circus tube. **Open** 11am-7pm Mon-Wed, Fri, Sat; 10am-8pm Thur.

Set up by Jason Kirk after he found some glasses made by his great uncle over 90 years ago, this shop takes a witty approach to the art of specs. This is exemplified in the store on Conduit Street, now the flagship since the company moved from the Covent Garden base it had occupied since the beginning. The interior of the new store, designed by design studio Campaign, is about as flash as they come, with prints of winking eyes, slate-grey walls and floors that artfully display the frames, and a space-age feel that points to the brand's avant-garde approach. Kirk's own-brand frames dominate, mixing simple old-school styling with bright colours. Ranges include the new Twenty collection, celebrating the store's 20th anniversary. Other standouts are Beam and Sunbeam, the only entirely acrylic optical collections on the market. Free coffee also helps with the decision-making.

Kirk Originals

Spex in the City

Mallon & Taub

35D Marylebone High Street, W1U 4QB (7935 8200, www.mallonandtaub.com). Baker Street or Regent's Park tube. **Open** 10am-6.30pm Mon-Wed, Fri, Sat; 10am-7pm Thur; 11am-5pm Sun.

This independent optical boutique is run by experienced optometrists Joan Mallon and Shanah Taub. A stylish interior – slate floors, fresh flowers – is complemented by friendly and knowledgeable staff, who talk customers through eye-care issues as well as new developments. Specs on offer include all the main brands, such as Oliver Peoples, Cutler & Gross, Dita, Thom Browne and many more, and glasses are often ready to wear in a few hours. Modern, classic and vintage frames, and unusual colours and styles, create a 'candy store' vibe. There's also a nice range of sunglasses.

Opera Opera

98 Long Acre, WC2E 9NR (7836 9246, www.opera opera.net). Covent Garden tube. **Open** 10am-6pm Mon-Sat.

Dispensing for over three decades from its corner site near the Royal Opera House, this family-run business exudes an old-fashioned sense of pride in optical crafts-manship, and even has its own factory turning out the shop's Harpers range – making it one of the few remaining British frame manufacturers. Control of production not only allows touches like old-fashioned hinges, but also means the shop is geared for bespoke frames – whether to replicate some treasured old specs or copy something you've seen perched on a famous nose (John Lennon, Johnny Depp, Buddy Holly). The shop stocks frames based on designs from the 1930s through to the

'80s; its range of rare vintage and retro sunglasses is unbeatable, if you have the cash to splash.

Spex in the City

1 Shorts Gardens, WC2H 9AT (7240 0243, www. spexinthecity.com). Covent Garden tube. **Open** 11am-6.30pm Mon-Fri; 11am-6pm Sat; 1-5pm Sun.

This small and friendly Seven Dials outlet, run by Gillian Caplan, offers sight tests, lens fitting, fabulous frames and, perhaps most importantly, really good style advice. Staff pride themselves on taking as much time as necessary to help you into the right frames, taking into account face and eye shape, even hairstyle. A carefully chosen range includes frames by European designers Epos, Reiz and Cazal, plus Japanese brand Yellows Plus. Also check out Caplan's line of bespoke own-brand frames as well as the ultra cool sunnies by the likes of Jeremy Tarian and Randalf Engineering.

36 Opticians

36 Beauchamp Place, SW3 1NU (7581 6336, www.36opticians.co.uk). Knightsbridge or South Kensington tube. **Open** 10am-6pm Mon-Sat.

There's an eclectic range of over 5,000 frames at this appealing store run by opticians Ragini Patel and Sveta Khambhaita. The enormous range stretches from the simple (with super-low starting prices to match) to the exclusive limited-edition handmade beauties by the likes of US designer Barton Perreira (as seen in a cool ad campaign featuring Giovanni Ribisi) along with a host of other fabulously famous-name frames for the four-eyed. A growing range of cool accessories includes stylish lorgnettes and spectacle chains made of stone.

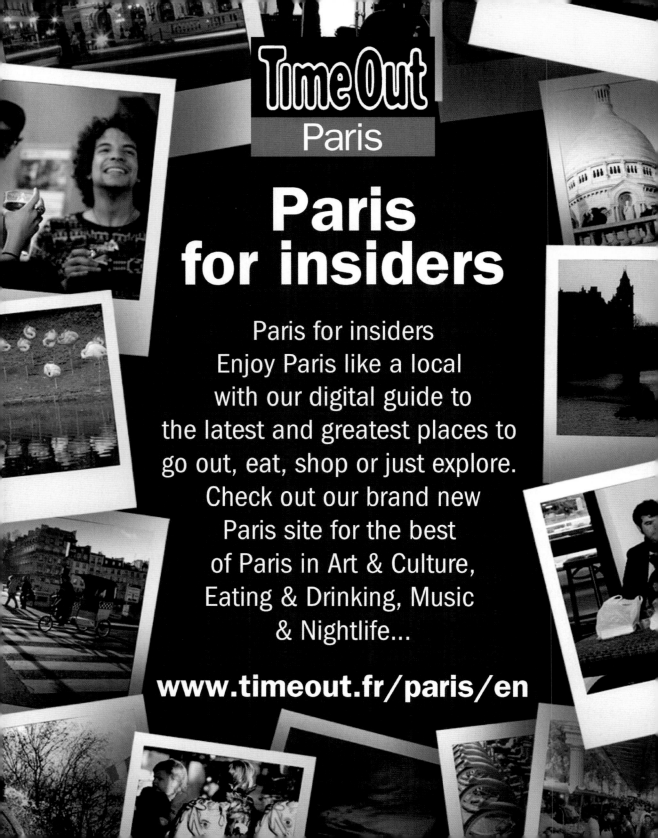

Home

THE WORLD CAN BE AN UNJUST AND TREACHEROUS PLACE, BUT THERE ARE THOSE WHO STRIVE TO MAKE IT SAFE FOR EVERYONE.

Operating in some of the world's most dangerous and oppressed countries, **Human Rights Watch** conducts rigorous investigations to bring those who have been targets of abuse to the world's attention. We use strategic advocacy to push people in power to end their repressive practices. And we work for as long as it takes to see that oppressors are held accountable for their crimes.

KNOWLEDGE IS POWER. LEARN ABOUT LIFE-CHANGING EVENTS IN YOUR WORLD THAT DON'T ALWAYS MAKE THE HEADLINES AND HOW YOU CAN HELP EFFECT POSITIVE CHANGE.

Stay informed, visit HRW.org

HUMAN RIGHTS WATCH

Home

The division between vintage and new furniture and homewares shops in London is now sometimes blurred. The city's contemporary design shops, such as **SCP** (*see p156*), **Aria** (*see p152*) and **Aram** (*see p152*), are still highly enticing prospects, however, offering a charming array of fun, interesting and well-designed products that are often talking points. Design classics never go out of style, and London's stylish furniture emporiums – many of which are clustered around Islington and Clerkenwell, as well as Brompton Road, such as the **Conran Shop** (*see p152*) and **Skandium** (*see p156*) – excel in this area.

Individually made objects once only found in crafts outlets or bought direct from makers are now sold in the large interiors stores; but if you're still one for browsing the boutique independents, you're in for a treat – London's small home accessories shops are better than ever before. Islington is a good hunting ground, with one-offs such as **Atelier Abigail Ahern** (*see p152*) and **Folklore** (*see p154*). East London's **Columbia Road** and **Redchurch Street** host a fair number of them, too – don't miss **Labour & Wait** (*see p161*) or **Treacle** (*see p162*).

London is also a fantastic place to hunt for antiques and vintage pieces, although the landscape has shifted in recent years. Camden Passage, once lined with creaky dealers, has yielded to new (albeit lovely) independent shops, selling everything from chocolate to jewellery – although some of the old guard remain, especially in idiosyncratic Pierrepoint Arcade. Church Street in Marylebone, home of the excellent **Alfie's Antique Market** (*see p169*), has blossomed into antiques row. Meanwhile, shops selling 20th-century furniture are flourishing; excellent neighbourhood shops include **Two Columbia Road** (*see p176*) and **Fandango** (*see p174*). A trend for curiosities has seen the likes of **Peanut Vendor** (*see p174*) and **Pelicans & Parrots** (*see p40*) selling stuffed animals, framed butterflies and other odd items, alongside more familiar – and very stylish – retro homewares.

Note that many of the shops listed in the **Lifestyle Boutiques & Concept Stores** chapter (*see pp33-41*) have a good range of furniture and items for the home: independent retailer **Smug** (*see p41*), is particularly worth seeking out, as is – at the other end of the scale – transatlantic import **Anthropologie** (*see p33*). It's also worth remembering that fashion designers, such as **Orla Kiely** (*see p85*) and **Paul Smith** (*see p83*), also have increasingly well-established homewares lines.

Furniture & Homewares

Contemporary & design classics

Aram

110 Drury Lane, WC2B 5SG (7557 7557, www.aram.co.uk). Covent Garden or Holborn tube. **Open** 10am-6pm Mon-Wed, Fri, Sat; 10am-7pm Thur.

Back in the 1960s, design champion Zeev Aram introduced the likes of Alvar Aalto, Marcel Breuer, Le Corbusier and Arne Jacobsen to UK homes through his long-gone King's Road store. This impressive five-storey space replaced it, stocking furniture, lighting, textiles and other home accessories. Alongside the classics, Aram also stocks contemporary works by both established designers – Ronan and Erwan Bouroullec and Hella Jongerius – and emerging ones. Lighting comes from top manufacturers such as Artemide and Flos, furniture from brands like Vitra and Cassina. Aram is the only UK stockist of authorised Eileen Gray designs. It also often stocks special editions.

Aria

Barnsbury Hall, Barnsbury Street, N1 1PN (7704 1999, www.ariashop.co.uk). Angel tube or Highbury & Islington tube/rail. **Open** 10am-6.30pm Mon-Sat; noon-5pm Sun.

Aria is located in an atmospheric space in Islington's Barnsbury Hall. Many of the building's original features have been restored and they now contrast beautifully with the über-modern lines of contemporary furniture and homewares. High-quality design pieces are here, such as the ever-popular angle-poise lamps (from £99), as are more unusual pieces, like the Bourgie table light by Ferruccio Laviani (£196). This mix, teamed with a very nice in-store café, makes Aria a pleasure to visit. Chairs are a speciality, with Patricia Urquiola and Patrick Jouin well represented. Smaller stand-outs include Custom mugs and cushions, polaroid cameras and pretty Taika bowls (£17) that would make a great gift, especially if it had some of Aria's very tempting selection of toiletries (Cowshed, Savon de Marseilles) nestled inside it.

Atelier Abigail Ahern

137 Upper Street, N1 1QP (7354 8181, www.atelier abigailahern.com). Angel tube or Highbury & Islington tube/rail. **Open** 10.30am-6pm Mon-Sat; 12.30pm-4.30pm Sun.

This tiny interiors shop may not have a huge range, but what it lacks in quantity is more than made up for in quality. Abigail Ahern is revered as one of the UK's top interior designers, and her selection of both her own-brand items and stock from international designers is both inventive and original. Textiles are particularly strong; as well as some striking merino wool ottomans (£898.50), there is a selection of stand-out rugs. Colour ranges are muted but striking, summing up a store that's a delightful departure from the sparse lines of many design stores. Fun and affordable items for the home are also, somewhat surprisingly, in abundance – the pineapple wall sconce (£100), the golden gun vase (£17.50) and Ahern's own bulldog lamps (£295) are destined to be talking points of any room, while the wonky bookcase wallpaper is for any homeowner looking to make a statement.

B&B Italia

250 Brompton Road, SW3 2AS (7591 8111, www.bebitalia.com). South Kensington tube. **Open** 10am-6pm Mon-Sat; noon-5pm Sun.

Few London interiors stores exhibit the pzazz of B&B Italia; if you've ever fancied yourself as a catwalk model, the long runway that guides you into the cavernous showroom offers plenty of opportunity to try out a few moves. B&B's sleek furniture is displayed in classic room-sets that are bigger than most London flats. Over its 40 years, the Italian brand has maintained a strong interest in working with inventive designers – recent collections have seen new versions of Patricia Urquiola's Husk chair, a new dynamic sofa system called Bend and a raft of additions to Antonio Citterio's Maxalto range, including a new sofa. Alongside these traditionally proportioned pieces are more sculptural forms – Naoto Fukasawa's Papilio collection, for example, offers the likes of a high back chair and a love seat.

Conran Shop

Michelin House, 81 Fulham Road, SW3 6RD (7589 7401, www.conran.co.uk). South Kensington tube. **Open** 10am-6pm Mon, Tue, Fri; 10am-7pm Wed, Thur; 10am-6.30pm Sat; noon-6pm Sun.

While Terence Conran pioneered the idea of modernism in Britain back in the 1960s, he's always had an impressively sharp eye for the decorative too, and nowhere is this more evident than at the Fulham Road flagship (which celebrates 25 years at Michelin House in 2012). The furniture here ranges from design classics, such as the Eames Dar chair, to collaborations with established designers, such as the colourful Oswald sofa with Squint (*see p156*), to more prosaic but well-designed armchairs, tables, storage units and beds. Much stock is exclusive and Conran mixes these pieces in among classics to create inspirational room settings on the ground floor. The basement is home to a vast array of lighting, tableware and accessories. There's also a new kids' department here, with its own reading room and mini haberdashery.
Branch 55 Marylebone High Street, W1U 5HS (7723 2223).

Aria

HOME

Designers Guild

267-271 (store) & 275-277 (showroom) King's Road, SW3 5EN (7351 5775, www.designersguild.com). Sloane Square tube then bus 11, 19, 22. **Open** *Store* 10am-6pm Mon-Sat; noon-5pm Sun. *Showroom* 10am-6pm Mon-Sat.

Interior designer Tricia Guild launched Designers Guild in 1970, and the firm quickly became the best of its type, with colourful fabrics and wallpapers offering modern takes on traditional patterns. The store now also has a great selection of homewares, including a sizeable range of paint colours selected to complement the fabrics, wallpapers, home furnishings, tableware, rugs, stationery and all the other design-led accessories. It also stocks a great range of contemporary and vintage furniture, which you can choose to cover with fabrics from the vast Designers Guild range or select from other brands such as Jasper Conran and William Yeoward, even combining different fabrics on the same piece. Cushions go from around £50, while bedlinen starts at £60 for a single duvet set. There's also a range of children's homewares.

Folklore

193 Upper Street, N1 1RQ (7354 9333, www.shopfolklore.com). Highbury & Islington tube/rail. **Open** 11am-6pm Tue-Sun.

Joining some chichi neighbours, Folklore brings simple, modern homewares to Upper Street. With its white painted floorboards and pale wooden shop fittings it has an ever-appealing Scandinavian feel. Owner, trained interior designer Danielle Reid, sources stock from across Europe, the US and London, and she has a knack of spotting fresh home-grown design talent. Recent finds include Dalston-based Naomi Paul, who makes pendular chrochet lampshades and Peckham designers Hendzel and Hunt, who use reclaimed wood in their beautiful bespoke furniture. The emphasis is on sustainable design, exemplified by the giant lampshades made from rolls of discarded cardboard boxes or papier mâché table lamps by Trash Me, £79. Looking for a smart, original house-warming gift? Start here.

Geoffrey Drayton

85 Hampstead Road, NW1 2PL (7387 5840, www.geoffreydrayton.com). Warren Street tube. **Open** 10am-6pm Mon-Sat.

Geoffrey Drayton has been pioneering modern furniture, lighting and homewares in London for almost five decades. The shop's success (it has recently expanded into the shop next door) is partly down to the knowledgeable staff and partly to a terrific range of high-end, made-to-order classic furniture from the world's best brands and designers. B&B Italia, Cassina, Interlübke,

Kartell, Knoll, Porro, Vitra and Ycami are all stocked, along with smaller makers like E15 and Rexite. Classics stocked include Ludwig Mies van der Rohe's Barcelona chair and Harry Bertoia's Diamond chair (both manufactured by Knoll), and there's a good range of beds and stylish storage furniture.

Heal's
196 Tottenham Court Road, W1T 7LQ (7636 1666, www.heals.co.uk). Goodge Street tube. **Open** 10am-6pm Mon-Wed, Fri; 10am-8pm Thur; 9.30am-6pm Sat; noon-6pm Sun.

Heal's may be the grand old dame of interiors stores, but its happy combination of excellent sourcing, helpful staff and a layout that's constantly being reinvented means it manages to stay relevant. Heal's commitment to sourcing new designers is impressive, while established names such as Orla Kiely, Clarissa Hulse, LSA and the Designers Guild are also well represented among the mirrors, rugs, bedlinen, clocks, cushions, art and photography available. The store's ground floor is the most fun for casual browsers, offering a cornucopia of table- and kitchenware, toiletries and gift items, plus a terrific lighting department boasting such delights as Tom Dixon's Beat pendant shades range. First and second floors house the bulk of the furniture, and for mid-century modernist fans, there's a great selection of vintage Danish furniture.

Branches 234 King's Road, SW3 5UA (7349 8411); 49-51 Eden Street, KT1 1BW (8614 5900).

Lifestyle Bazaar
11A Kingsland Road, E2 8AA (7739 9427, www.lifestylebazaar.com). Hoxton rail. **Open** 11am-7pm Mon-Sat; noon-5pm Sun.

Lifestyle Bazaar, the creation of London-based design team Laurent Nurisso and Christopher Curtis, was originally based in central London's Newburgh Street, before moving to more design-centred Shoreditch. The shop specialises in a selection of fun and stylish homeware items, such as bowler hat sugar bowls and Hamlet skull tea-light holders, which are perched on or around larger pieces such as storage systems, lighting and retro-contemporary chairs. There are lots of bright and original ideas, with products sourced from around the world. There's a nice selection by big-name designers too, including Starck and Marcel Wanders, but this is definitely a place to discover new names and, with any luck, pick up future design classics.

Mint
2 North Terrace, SW3 2BA (7225 2228, www.mintshop.co.uk). South Kensington tube. **Open** 10.30am-7pm Mon-Wed, Fri, Sat; 10.30am-7.30pm Thur.

Conran Shop. See p152.

Mint feels like a Dalí painting come to life, with its hand-picked and specially commissioned furniture, glassware, textiles and ceramics arranged like an avant-garde curiosity shop. Owner Lina Kanafani fills her two-level space with international designs, and form and colour play a large part in her selections. Each year she exhibits new designers, taking on the most popular items in the shop the following year. Much of Mint's stock could be considered as art with a capital 'a', a fact reflected in the prices. Louise Hindsgavl's stunning porcelain one-off piece Everyday Scenario, Surgery Suggestion (£1,400), would be hard to define as anything other than sculpture, and Ezgi Turksoy's limited edition sterling silver spoons (from £550) are hardly everyday items, but the vintage pieces add to the sense of the unique, and there are plenty of smaller, more affordable items too; Katie Lilly's hand-decorated plates are adorable (£60).

Pitfield London

31-35 Pitfield Street, N1 6HB (7490 6852,
www.pitfieldlondon.com). Old Street tube/rail.
Open 11am-7pm daily.
A new addition to Shoreditch's ever-growing design and interiors outlets, Pitfield is a lifestyle store in its truest sense. The colourful shop is a perfectly organised chaos of high-end homeware. You'll find quirky Jonathan Adler ceramics perched next to Iittala glassware and Red Decker cleaning brushes. Look out for the vintage finds among the contemporary offerings, all sourced both at home and internationally by owner Shaun Clarkson. A gallery space offers six-weekly rotating exhibitions, often with related collaborations sold in the shop. The adjoining café is a bright and airy space selling specialist coffees, pastries and daily-changing salads.

SCP

135-139 Curtain Road, EC2A 3BX (7739 1869,
www.scp.co.uk). Old Street tube/rail or Shoreditch
High Street rail. **Open** 9.30am-6pm Mon-Fri;
9.30am-6pm Sat; 11am-5pm Sun.
SCP attempts to showcase the very best of contemporary furniture, lighting and homewares. Overseeing it is Sheridan Coakley, who sources globally and stocks a clutch of respected designers – among them Robin Day, Terence Woodgate, Matthew Hilton, Konstantin Grcic, Donna Wilson and Michael Marriott. Furniture and storage solutions are all bold lines and slick minimalism, exemplified by Kay + Stemmer's Edith and Agnes shelving and Jasper Morrison's global lights. Accessories broaden out to take in everything from the highly decorative to the fun and quirky, with staples including the pigeon clip-on lights, the Acapulco chair and a cool range of ceramics, with pieces from Marimekko and Rob Ryan. Textiles, cushions and blankets are another strong point, and it's a great place for unusual gift items. SCP also retails the George Nelson Bubble lights by Modernica. Produced by Howard Miller until 1979, these shades are

part of the permanent collection of the Museum of Modern Art in New York – you can own one for £350.
Branch 87-93 Westbourne Grove, W2 4UL
(7229 3612).

Skandium

247 Brompton Road, SW3 2EP (7584 2066,
www.skandium.com). South Kensington tube.
Open 10am-6.30pm Mon-Wed, Fri, Sat; 10am-7pm
Thur; 11am-5pm Sun.
With two shops in London – a two-storey space in Marylebone and this 700sq m flagship – Skandium fans are spoilt for choice. Most people know the store for its gorgeous ranges of Scandinavian home- and tableware (Marimekko features strongly), but there's also classic furniture from manufacturers like Asplund, Artek, Fritz Hansen, Swedese and Knoll, and even broader European wares from the likes of German design house Vitra and big names Cappellini and Cassina. Lighting comes courtesy of top names like Louis Poulsen, Secto and Le Klint. What makes Skandium special, however, is its commitment to excellence in contemporary design; textiles, chairs, storage units, mirrors, candle holders, hooks, phones and a range of coffee-table books on Scandinavian design are all available, to ensure attention to detail across the home. Skandium has a concession in Selfridges, and also operates the Republic of Fritz Hansen store (www.skandium.com/republic-of-fritz-hansen.asp), which opened in Fitzrovia's Margaret Street in autumn 2011. The latter sells the entire Fritz Hansen furniture collection, together with accessories hand-picked by Skandium, including Danish vintage glass and ceramics, lighting, fashion, bags, sunglasses, books, magazines and Skandium furniture classics.
Branch 86 Marylebone High Street, W1U 4Q
(7935 2077).

Squint

178 Shoreditch High Street, E1 6HU (7739 9275,
www.squintlimited.com). Shoreditch High Street
rail. **Open** 10am-6pm Mon-Fri; by appointment Sat;
1-5pm Sun.
Squint's products – easily recognisable by the colourful and distinctive patchwork designs – are now stocked in Harrods, Liberty, the Conran Shop and the Designers Guild, but this is its only stand-alone shop and showroom, where you can see a selection of its 'ready to go' fabrics, wallpaper, mirrors and lighting, as well as order one of its trademark bespoke Chesterfield sofas (from £4,500), iconic Egg chairs and other upholstered furniture. The beautiful coverings – made up of both contemporary and vintage textiles – cover the items completely, including chair legs and even entire chests of drawers, and all of the pieces are handmade in England. The Shoreditch Collection, which launched in May 2010, features a range of contemporary shapes inspired by designs from the 1950s and '60s.

Folklore. See p154.

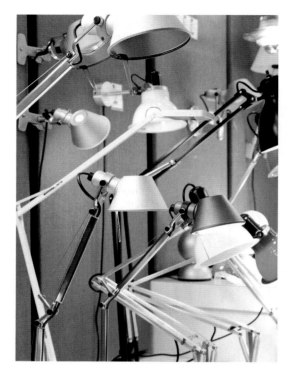

SCP. See p156.

Tobias & the Angel

68 White Hart Lane, SW13 0PZ (8878 8902, www.tobiasandtheangel.com). Hammersmith tube then bus 209 or Barnes Bridge rail. **Open** 10am-6pm Mon-Sat.

This lovely shop has the kind of interior many of us strive to create at home: careful, but unfussy, cosy yet airy. The furniture, a sleeker Scandinavian take on English country, is all handmade to measure in its workshop in Surrey. Constructed in wood (including solid pine and oak), the range includes tables, chairs, drawer units, chicken-wire linen cupboards, desks and benches – painted in a choice of colours and priced per square foot. The freestanding furniture, such as the superb housekeeper's cupboard, provides a flexible alternative to a fitted kitchen. Chairs and sofas are covered in antique and vintage cloth, which is also for sale in lengths, as is a lovely hand-block-printed cloth. The accessories are particularly attractive, from pretty cushions to delightful cat doorstops. The place also has a good selection of lamps, shades, bags, aprons and table linen. Come Christmas, it's the place to head to for unusual decorations for the tree.

Twentytwentyone

274-275 Upper Street, N1 2UA (7288 1996, www.twentytwentyone.com). Angel tube or Highbury & Islington tube/rail. **Open** 10am-6pm Mon-Sat; 11am-5pm Sun.

Twentytwentyone furniture and homewares shop has long been held in high esteem by *Time Out* for its mix of vintage originals, reissued classics and contemporary designs. Big-name brands such as Arper, Artek, Cappellini, De Padova, Flos, Swedese and Vitra are stocked, but founders Simon Alderson and Tony Cunningham are also keen to foster new talent, stocking designs by exciting new leading British designers. Stock is divided between two locations; the River Street showroom houses most of the larger items, while the Upper Street outpost – brilliant for home accessories and gifts – has been expanded and now includes a basement showroom to display lighting, as well as a few larger items. **Branch** 18C River Street, EC1R 1XN (7837 1900).

Unto This Last

230 Brick Lane, E2 7EB (7613 0882, www.untothislast.co.uk). Shoreditch High Street rail. **Open** 10am-6pm daily.

Nestled snugly in an old East End workshop that exudes Dickensian quaintness, this small furniture maker produces a distinctive range of birch plywood and laminate pieces, transforming raw materials into decidedly modern furniture. Named after the 1862 John Ruskin book advocating the principles of local craftsmanship, Unto This Last does exactly that – combining simple design with sophisticated computer software to produce well-priced cabinets, bookcases, chairs and beds, plus a small range of accessories like tealight holders, fruit bowls and placemats. The finished products have a beautifully fluid, organic appearance, and are bold enough to act as statement pieces. A new service allows you to add bright laminte to the products for a colour pop. We particularly liked the Step Shelves (from £90) that can be free-standing or wall-mounted. Look out too for the facet chair (from £150), the best-selling Kumu chair (from £65) and the 4ft Standing lamp (£90).

Wawa

1 Ezra Street, E2 7RH (7729 6768, www.wawa.co.uk). Hoxton or Shoreditch High Street rail. **Open** 10am-6pm Mon-Fri; 10am-3pm Sun.

Wawa sells bright and bold tailor-made sofas designed and handmade by Richard Ward, whose love of curves, lines and colour is obvious in his work (think contemporary takes on old classics). Each sofa is unique and upholstered with great attention to detail using hand-tied springs. Prices start at around £800 for an armchair, rising to around £2,500 for a large chaise longue; choose your fabric from the large collection that takes in ranges by the Designers Guild, Zimmer & Rohde and Lelieve. The shop also stocks a gorgeous selection of plates and trays, as well as mirrors, lamps and lampshades, tableware and clocks. Head to the showroom on a Sunday and have a mooch around the flower market afterwards; if you're visiting during the week, it's always worth phoning to check it's open (note that Wawa is closed on Saturdays).

Accessories & specialists

Ben Pentreath

17 Rugby Street, WC1N 3QT (7430 2526, www.benpentreath.com). Holborn or Russell Square tube. **Open** 11am-6pm Mon-Sat.

It's always a tight squeeze in this petite boutique just off Lamb's Conduit Street. But despite its diminutive scale, there's plenty packed in at Ben Pentreath, from kitchenware and stationery, to cushions and candles. You'll find exclusives such as Peter Hone plasterworks and Bridie Hall decoupage. True, this place is an ideal gift destination, but as you're buying your mate a gorgeous glass tray lacquered with a vintage map of London, you just might find yourself stocking up on those trendy Kilner jars you suddenly need. Come in November for the eagerly awaited Cabinet of Curiosities, each year housing a different exhibition of exciting and buyable treats.

Casa Mexico

1 Winkley Street, E2 6PY (7739 9349, www.casamexico.co.uk). Bethnal Green tube/rail or Cambridge Heath rail. **Open** 10am-6pm Mon-Fri; 10am-5pm Sat, Sun.

For all things Mexican, this Bethnal Green store is a must-visit: the product list covers the usual kitchenware – from

Twentytwentyone. See p159.

little *cazuelas* (bowls) to *chimineas* (wood-burning stoves), lamps, rugs and blankets, and 'ranch-style' furniture (made from seasoned pine). But it also features Mexican folk art, reproduction Mayan and Aztec terracotta masks and funerary urns, sisal and straw bags and baskets, ponchos, pots and planters for the garden and a range of beautiful handmade tiles. Of course, no Mexican outpost would be complete without a full range of Day of the Dead products, and Casa Mexico doesn't disappoint: skull posters, skull candle-holders, Loteria de Luna playing cards, and that essential articulated clay skeleton. The selection of food and drink is also unparalleled, with a kitsch display of canned and dried beans, chillis and sauces, as well as Mexican beers and tequilas, and a freezer full of tortillas made with the traditional *masa harina*. The clothing range has also expanded in recent times; the *guayabera* shirts are particularly covetable.

Celia Birtwell

Unit 5, Baseline Studios, Whitchurch Road, W11 4AT (7221 0877, www.celiabirtwell.com). Latimer Road tube. **Open** by appointment Mon-Fri.
The work of this celebrated textile designer has long been in vogue. Her latest foray into bright, breezy colourful interiors, Pop Story, keeps her in the trendy bracket, while the delightful classic lines Beasties and Jacobean are hardy perennials. This studio is mainly about the textile collection, launched in partnership with her former husband, fashion designer Ossie Clarke, in the 1960s, and which later became a witty range of furnishing fabrics

and wallpapers. Classic collection prints cost from £55/m, and voiles, silk cushions (from £75 each) and upholstered chairs are also available, as is a bespoke upholstery service.

Contemporary Applied Arts

2 Percy Street, W1T 1DD (7436 2344, www.caa.org.uk). Goodge Street or Tottenham Court Road tube. **Open** 10am-6pm Mon-Sat.
The CAA is consistently inventive with its exhibitions of its 300-plus makers. The applied arts here embrace the functional in the form of unique pieces of jewellery, textiles and tableware as well as ceramics, glass, metal, paper, silver and wood, but there are also purely decorative pieces such as wall-hangings made of recycled ceramic and mosaic shards. The ground-floor gallery space houses solo or themed exhibitions, while the large basement shop area has pieces for all pockets, from both established members and newcomers. If you can't find exactly what you're looking for, CAA will probably be able to direct you to a maker who undertakes commissions with whom you can discuss your specific requirements. Note that CAA is on the move – most likely to Southwark, around March 2013 – so phone to check before visiting.

Divertimenti

227-229 Brompton Road, SW3 2EP (7581 8065, www.divertimenti.co.uk). Knightsbridge or South Kensington tube. **Open** 9.30am-6pm Mon, Tue, Thur, Fri; 9.30am-7pm Wed; 10am-6pm Sat; noon-5.30pm Sun.

Cooks will salivate in this fantastic store. If you need something to blanch, zest, grate, glaze or dust, then you're almost guaranteed to find it here. There's a good range of top-quality kitchen classics such as the Waring Juice Extractor and the KitchenAid Artisan, while attractive chunky earthenware is another speciality – the Mediterranean colours of the Poterie Provençale give an instant hit of sunshine. Venture down to the basement for staggeringly pricey cookers by La Cornue and an Aga showroom, plus copper pans, enormous mortar and pestles, super-thick wooden chopping boards and old-fashioned ice-cream scoops. The baking section is exhaustive. If you don't think you merit fancy cooking tools yet, then enlist in its cookery school to hone your skills.
Branch 33-34 Marylebone High Street, W1U 4PT (7935 0689).

Labour & Wait
85 Redchurch Street, E2 7DJ (7729 6253, www.labourandwait.co.uk). Shoreditch High Street rail. **Open** 11am-6pm Tue-Sun.
This retro-stylish store, which recently relocated to London's trendiest street, sells the sort of things everybody would have had in their kitchen or pantry 60 years ago: functional domestic goods that have a timeless style. Spend any time here and you'll be filled with the joys of spring cleaning. Who'd have guessed that a scrubbing brush could be so appealing? For the desk proud, there's a pig and goat hair bristle computer brush, while for the kitchen there are some great simple classics like a steel wall-mounted bottle opener, enamel milk pans and jugs in retro pastels, and lovely 1950s-inspired Japanese teapots. You can garden beautifully with ash-handled trowels, pale suede gauntlets, and a dibber and label set. Our favourite, though, is the chubby flowerpot brush. There is a small range of classic vintage clothing (work jackets, aprons), vintage Welsh wool blankets, classic basic toiletries, and some great old-fashioned gifts for children, such as a pinhole camera kit and vintage-style satchels, and a lovely range of handmade notebooks from Portugal. Hard to leave empty-handed.

Limelight Movie Art
313 King's Road, SW3 5EP (7751 5584, www.limelightmovieart.com). Sloane Square or South Kensington tube. **Open** 11.30am-6pm Mon-Sat.
Limelight Movie Art sells original movie artwork from all over the world. The clientele includes collectors looking for the work of a particular graphic artist, such as Saul Bass or Ercole Brini, as well as film buffs or fans hunting down images of their favourite star. Buying a piece of movie artwork can prove a wise investment, as it's a product that never seems to go out of fashion. Foreign posters can be less expensive – *Certains l'aiment chaud* (rather than *Some Like It Hot*) can be bought for £1,100. All the posters, lobby cards and inserts on sale are in excellent condition.

HOME

Moomin

43 Covent Garden Market Building, WC2E 8RF (7240 7057, www.moomin.com). Covent Garden or Leicester Square tube. **Open** 10am-8pm Mon-Sat; 11am-5pm Sun.

Ever dreamt of owning a bath towel, napkin or lunchbox emblazoned with a Moomin? No? We can scarcely believe it. But there's apparently sufficient demand to warrant a store dedicated entirely to Finnish artist Tove Jansson's lovably strange hippo-like trolls. Based under the grandeur of Covent Garden Market's iron and glass roof, the dinky boutique stocks a raft of Moomin merchandise. You'll find fantastical treats from cookie cutters to kids' rompers, as well as more grown up memorabilia-like copper pill boxes and beautiful printed trays.

Rug Company

124 Holland Park Avenue, W11 4UE (7229 5148, www.therugcompany.info). Holland Park tube. **Open** 10am-6pm Mon-Sat; 11am-5pm Sun.

The designer collection here reads more like a fantasy wardrobe than a selection of rugs, with collaborations from Vivienne Westwood, Diane von Furstenberg, Paul Smith, Jonathan Adler and Matthew Williamson among others. Founded in 1997 by Christopher and Suzanne Sharp, the company is dedicated to traditional methods of rug-making; the hand-knotting is done by weavers in Kathmandu, using hand-spun wool from Tibet and northern India. It also sells antique rugs, sourced from around the globe. Bespoke commissions are undertaken.
Branch 555 King's Road, SW6 2EB (7384 0980).

Ryantown

126 Columbia Road, E2 7RG (7613 1510, www.misterrob.co.uk). Hoxton or Shoreditch High Street rail. **Open** noon-6pm Sat; 10am-4pm Sun.

Printmaker Rob Ryan opened this lovely gallery/shop in summer 2008. Tiles, printed tissue paper, screenprints, paper cut-outs, cards, wooden keys, limited-edition prints, cushions, vases, Easter egg cups, even skirts and T-shirts, all bear his distinctive, fun graphics and words – with phrases such as 'I thought you didn't like me' or 'You can still do a lot with a small brain' – printed on many of the covetable items. Collaborations have seen his work appear on skateboards, necklaces and even Paul Smith pumps. Aside from his shop work, Rob has also recently customised a Lomo Diana camera, relocated his entire workshop to Somerset House for two weeks, and auctioned his work for the Marine Conservation Society; details of his latest exploits can be found on his blog http://rob-ryan.blogspot.com.

Treacle

110-112 Columbia Road, E2 7RG (7729 0538, www.treacleworld.com). Hoxton or Shoreditch High Street rail. **Open** noon-5pm Sat; 9am-4pm Sun.

Treacle started off as a cake shop, quickly expanding to cater for those looking to uphold the traditions of the great British teatime by selling a range of retro paraphernalia, such as cake stands, teapots (plus hand-knitted tea cosies) and tea towels. There's an impressive stock of original china tea sets from the British post-war era (with brands such as Midwinter and Meakin often featuring), mixed alongside some innovative contemporary brands, such as Yoyo Ceramics, Donna Wilson, SJM Ceramics, Cornishware ceramics and Repeat Repeat English bone china. The cupcakes should help to appease any market crowd-provoked stress.

W Sitch & Co

48 Berwick Street, W1F 8JD (7437 3776, www.wsitch.co.uk). Oxford Circus or Tottenham Court Road tube. **Open** 9am-5pm Mon-Fri; 9.30am-1pm Sat. **No credit cards.**

This strangely old-fashioned shop has been trading in this Soho townhouse for more than 100 years. Managed by Ronald Sitch and his sons James and Laurence, its business is the reproduction and restoration of antique lights, though there are also fittings for sale. The company's own range of wall lights and lanterns is made using traditional methods. This may be a small-scale operation, but its prestige and skill are far-reaching – W Sitch supplied the light fittings for the film *Titanic* and it also looks after the wall brackets that grace the state dining room at No.10. For the rest of us, W Sitch will repair, rewire and repolish most period lighting or convert a favourite vase into a lamp.

Bathrooms & kitchens

Aston Matthews

141-147A Essex Road, N1 2SN (7226 7220, www.astonmatthews.co.uk). Angel tube or Essex Road rail. **Open** 8.30am-5pm Mon-Fri; 9.30am-5pm Sat.

This bathroom emporium has been trading since 1823 and the showroom, stretched over several shopfronts on the Essex Road, is packed floor to ceiling with a huge selection of bathroomware, showerheads, screens, taps and accessories. Every taste is catered for, from Empire-style cast-iron baths, such as the Brunel, through to art deco-inspired taps and the latest Philippe Starck-designed bidet. You'll also find cloakroom-sized basins and, for very bijou spaces, corner WCs. The extensive range means anyone with lavatory pretensions will be happy here, yet the store maintains the reassuring, competent feel of an old-fashioned plumbers' merchant's.

CP Hart

Arch 213, Newnham Terrace, Hercules Road, SE1 7DR (7902 5250, www.cphart.co.uk). Lambeth North tube or Waterloo tube/rail. **Open** 9am-5.30pm Mon-Sat.

HOME

Labour & Wait. See p161.

A visit to CP Hart's flagship showroom underneath the Waterloo arches is rather like going on an exciting outing. Filled with gleaming room-sets, a fountain of shower heads and sanitaryware that is more Salvador Dali than Thomas Crapper – this is a place like no other. Here, bathrooms are courtesy of Starck, Foster, Massaud, Wanders, Urquiola, Hayón and Citterio. For boutique hotel-style decadence, there are freestanding baths with tapered legs that look like pieces of antique furniture. Showering has possibilities you never knew existed: FeOnic sound technology turns glass shower screens into speakers, and Power Glass has invisibly wired LED lights that appear to float. If your main bathroom concerns are to wash and go, there are simple classics such as CP Hart's own London range – ideal for period homes. Our only gripe is that nothing is priced, not even on the website, but for products alone, expect to pay from £4,000 for an average bathroom. The design service is £500.
Branches throughout the city.

Czech & Speake
39C Jermyn Street, SW1Y 6DN (7439 0216, www.czechspeake.com). Green Park or Piccadilly Circus tube. **Open** 9.30am-6pm Mon-Fri; 10am-5pm Sat.
Located on the street that's renowned for purveying the finer things in life to gentlemen of means – shirts, cologne, cigars – Czech & Speake is perhaps the poshest bathroom

shop in London. Its bathroom furniture is terribly smart and includes a mahogany Edwardian-style range of fittings and bath panels. From its art deco-inspired Cubist range, an octagonal black lacquer-framed mirror costs £1,400 plus VAT, while a set of chrome basin taps will set you back £705 plus VAT (more for the platinum option, obviously). We spotted a chrome toilet brush for £340 plus VAT and a pair of robe hooks for £150 plus VAT – both beautifully designed, but you'd have to spend a lot of time in your smallest room to justify it. If you can't afford the hardware, you can always treat yourself to some of the elegant own-brand lotions and potions, including the No. 88 bath oil in a chic black frosted bottle for £49. The shop also stocks Edwardian kitchen fittings.

David Mellor
4 Sloane Square, SW1W 8EE (7730 4259, www.davidmellordesign.com). Sloane Square tube. **Open** 9.30am-6pm Mon-Sat; 11am-5pm Sun.
This well-established two-storey shop in Chelsea first opened its doors in the swinging sixties, when the area was something of a hub for artists and designers. It stocks the full range of cutlery from Britain's best-known cutlery designer. Born in Sheffield – a city that was the centre of the UK's steel industry – the late David Mellor originally trained as a silversmith, but went on to successfully blend traditional craftsmanship with modern

Water Monopoly

cutlery design, with the result that his eponymous brand is today synonymous with quality, heritage and forward-thinking design. As well as cutlery, the shop sells a large collection of stylish tableware and kitchenware, both own-brand and from top-notch international companies. The wedding list service is also recommended.

Plain English

41 Hoxton Square, N1 6PB (7613 0022, www.plainenglishdesign.co.uk). Old Street tube/rail. **Open** 10am-6pm Mon-Sat.
Plain English's bespoke kitchens are based on 18th- and 19th-century Georgian examples and handmade in Suffolk. Designs are beautifully simple; the London-popular Spitalfields Kitchen is timeless without being olde worlde, and can be adapted to suit contemporary living. The Shaker-inspired Williamsburg Kitchen was designed for the Shaker Shop in London, while the Longhouse was inspired by a Georgian butler's pantry. The newest design, the Osea Kitchen, takes the Essex coastline as its starting point for a naturally rugged aesthetic. The designs differ slightly, but are very much in the same restrained – and yes, plain – mould. Look around and the displays ooze craftmanship and longevity. Drawers are hand-dovetailed and cupboards can have 'Wapping holes' or a 'Spitalfields hole fret' for ventilation. Three coats of paint are applied by hand before installation plus a final

coat once the kitchen is in place. You'll pay £45,000 for an average kitchen, including appliances and fitting. **Branch** 28 Blandford Street, W1U 4BZ (7486 2674).

Water Monopoly

10-14 Lonsdale Road, NW6 6RD (7624 2636, www.watermonopoly.com). Queens Park tube/rail. **Open** 9am-6pm Mon-Thur; 9am-5pm Fri.
The Water Monopoly certainly has the wow factor, in its new 5,500sq m showroom. The company, based in a converted stables, specialises in restored English and French antique sanitaryware. Choose from over 200 baths and basins, from copper tubs to polished-iron wash stands, all expertly restored to your chosen finish. Our last visit unearthed a French 1930s art deco double basin and an Edwardian canopy shower bath complete with body sprays. There's no need to worry about dodgy old plumbing – each item comes complete with fittings converted for modern pipes, and smart new taps in classic designs, such as its Bistrot or Carpe & Lyre ranges, work perfectly with the antique baths and basins. As well as original pieces, there's a selection of reproductions such as the beautiful freestanding Paris bath based on a French stone tub (from £5,600 plus VAT), or the fireclay Hanley bath (£5,750 plus VAT). Children – or exhibitionists – will appreciate the Porthole bath (£3,710 plus VAT) with its two glazed portholes on the side.

HOME

Floral Hall. See p169.

Vintage Furniture & Homewares

Antiques

Angell Antiques

22 Church Street, NW8 8EP (07775 968016, www.angellantiques.com). Edgware Road tube or Marylebone tube/rail. **Open** 10am-5.30pm Tue-Sat by appointment only.

'Decorative without being fussy' is how the owners describe their stock. A large, attractive space houses an expansive collection of furniture and objects. Industrial furniture and old shop fittings are specialities. Typical items include 18th-century rustic farmhouse tables alongside bold pieces of sculpture, lockers and cupboards. You'll also find pairs of 1930s leather armchairs for around £2,200 and good-quality chaises longues. Smaller items include vintage advertising signs and tins.

Antique Trader at Millinery Works

85-87 Southgate Road, N1 3JS (7359 2019, www.millineryworks.co.uk). Old Street tube/rail then bus 76, 141 or Haggerston rail. **Open** 11am-6pm Tue-Sat; noon-5pm Sun.

This former Victorian hat factory is packed with Arts and Crafts furniture and objects from the Cotswold School – all of which can be picked up at reasonable prices. Even the most basic dining tables and chairs are sturdy and of good quality. Expect to pay £1,000 for an oak Arts and Crafts table and four chairs by an unknown maker. Specialised pieces that you wouldn't be surprised to see in the V&A are a real draw – and some are strictly POA. Top-drawer makers include Morris, Dresser and the Barnsley Workshop. Heal's furniture is often in stock and look out, too, for smaller items such as Liberty & Co dressing-table sets and ceramics. There are regular exhibitions as well as excellent Arts and Crafts shows twice a year.

Chesney's

194-202 Battersea Park Road, SW11 4ND (7627 1410, www.chesneys.co.uk). Battersea Park rail or bus 344. **Open** 9am-5.30pm Mon-Fri; 10am-5pm Sat.

An international fireplace empire that began when Paul Chesney and his brother Nick realised the value of discarded antique fireplaces 25 years ago. Chesney's Battersea showroom stretches over four shopfronts, providing ample space to display an impressive variety of antique and reproduction chimney pieces, alongside wood-burning stoves. Made in China and Europe from limestone and marble, there are over 50 period-inspired styles (£500-£100,000) to choose from. Modern designs come courtesy of partnerships with designers such as

Streetwise **Columbia Road, E2**

Come on a Sunday for the popular flower market and a winning array of quirky, one-off shops.

If you can drag yourself out of bed on Sunday morning and make it down to Columbia Road, you'll find London's sweetest-scented and most colourful market, with flower stalls and an excellent range of boutique-style shops. If you want to avoid the crowds and you're not after any blooms, many of the shops also open on Saturday afternoons – though the lively Sunday exchanges are often the best part of the experience.

The market is open from 8am until 2pm (or thereabouts – many of the shops shut betweeen 3pm and 4pm). Given the early start needed to bag the choicest bouquets (or herbs, cacti, tropical blooms and, from November, Christmas trees), you might need some sustenance. Grab some breakfast on Ezra Street, at characterful **Jones Dairy Café** (www.jonesdairy.co.uk), then wander down to the yard where stalls tout vintage items. If you're looking for upmarket homewares, **Wawa** (*see p159*) sells customised handmade sofas, lamps and accessories. On your way back up Ezra Street to Columbia Road, you pass the Courtyard. There you can drool at the retro items in **Ben Southgate** (*see p170*).

Back on Columbia Road, you'll be swept along by the market throng. When you've had your fill of flower traders, check out the attractive shops that run either side of the street.

The Ezra Street end of Columbia Road is best for art. **Elphick's** (no.160, 7033 7891, www.elphicksshop.com) sells contemporary prints. **Nelly Duff** (no.156, 7033 9683, www.nellyduff.com) has an affordable array of more graphic art, and **Start Space** (no.150, 7729 0049, www.startspace.co.uk) showcases large-scale paintings and photography.

L'Orangerie (no.162, 8983 7873) is an accessories shop on the corner of Barnet Grove. Gems include chunky bead necklaces, trendy straw sun-visors and fat glass rings; staff are very friendly. At no.152 is **Open House** (07979 851593, www.openhouseretail.co.uk), a pretty shop selling reproduction home- and gardenwares. **Jessie Chorley & Buddug** (no.158, 07708 921 550) is an unashamedly twee and romantic shop stocking a collection of vintage-inspired jewellery and accessories. **Laird of Glencairn** (no.128, 7613 3842) is a heritage-focused men's headwear store, stocking classic fedoras, bowlers, caps and trappers. **Marcos & Trump** (no.146, 7739 9008) stocks fair trade fashion such as People Tree and Melissa. Retro-inspired beauty boutique the **Powder Room** (7729 1365, www.thepowderpuffgirls.com) is at no.136; pop inside for reasonably priced hair dos, manicures and make-up sessions. Sweet-toothers can indulge at old-fashioned sweetshop **Suck & Chew** (no.130, 8983 3504, www.suckandchew.co.uk) and cupcake and retro kitchenware shop **Treacle** (nos.110-112; *see p162*).

Columbia Road institution **Milagros** (no.61, 7613 0876, www.milagros.co.uk) has Mexican curiosities and trinkets. Particularly covetable are the *retablos* (allegorical folk art). A more recent addition, **Ryantown** (no.126, *see p162*), sees Rob Ryan's crafty motifs cover tiles, perspex keys, screenprints and mugs. **Supernice** (no.106, 7613 3890, www.supernice.co.uk) has Blik wall art (removable stickers) in a great range, with images ranging from robots to birds on telegraph wires.

You're coming to the end of the main drag, but don't miss modern jewellers **NumberNinetyFour** (no.94, 07776 358583), perfumer **Angela Flanders** (no.96; *see p142*) and **Vintage Heaven** (no.82, 01277 215968, www.vintageheaven.co.uk), where the charming retro china is piled high. Further on, at the junction with Hackney Road, is **Two Columbia Road** (*see p176*), a stalwart for 20th-century furniture.

HOME

French House

Furniture arcades & covered markets

Alfie's Antique Market

13-25 Church Street, NW8 8DT (7723 6066, www.alfiesantiques.com). Edgware Road tube or Marylebone tube/rail. **Open** 10am-6pm Tue-Sat.
Alfie's occupies a building that started life as the Edwardian department store, Jordan's. After falling into disrepair, it reopened as an antique market in 1976 and is now home to around 60 dealers, including vintage clothes store The Girl Can't Help It (*see p96*). For 20th-century furniture, venture into the area known as the Quad, as well as Decoratum's (7724 6969, www.decoratum.com) vast space in the basement. On the first floor, don't miss Dodo (7706 1545) for 1920s and '30s advertising posters and signs, and Louise Verber (7569 8770), which has mirrors, lighting and mercury glass. Vincenzo Caffarella's (7724 3701, www.vinca.co.uk) impressive showroom of 20th-century Italian lighting takes up the second floor mezzanine. Finally, rest up at the pleasant rooftop café, before one last rummage through the vintage trimmings at the charming Persiflage (7724 7366).

Bermondsey Square Antiques Market

Corner of Bermondsey Street & Long Lane, SE1 (7525 6000). Borough tube or London Bridge tube/rail. **Open** 5am-1pm Fri.
Following the redevelopment of Bermondsey Square, the ancient antiques market – good for china and silver as well as furniture and glassware – continues in an expanded space that accommodates 200 stalls that now include food, fashion and craft stalls. Arrive early.

Grays Antique Market & Grays in the Mews

58 Davies Street, W1K 5LP & 1-7 Davies Mews, W1K 5AB (7629 7034, www.graysantiques.com). Bond Street tube. **Open** 10am-6pm Mon-Fri; 11am-5pm Sat.
Stalls in this smart covered market – housed in a terracotta building that was once a 19th-century lavatory showroom – sell everything from art, antiques and rare books to jewellery, dolls and vintage fashion. This is one of the most diverse markets of its kind, though not all the stalls are open every day the market trades.

Jasper Conran, Jane Churchill and Biba's Barbara Hulanicki. Chesney's also has a licence to recreate a collection of chimney pieces from the archives of the Sir John Soane's Museum. A bespoke service is also available; call for details.
Branch 734-736 Hollway Road, N19 3JF (7561 8280).

Core One

The Gas Works, 2 Michael Road, SW6 2AN (7731 7171, www.coreoneantiques.com). Fulham Broadway tube. **Open** 10am-6pm Mon-Fri; 11am-5pm Sat.
This large industrial building is an unlikely setting for a collective of antique and 20th-century furniture dealers. Head through the gates, keep going past the rusting gasometer, and you're there. There are ten dealers in total who inhabit the space: Blanchard, Christophe Edwards and Andrew Webb, Christopher Jones, Daniel Mankowitz, Dean Antiques, Glaisher + Nash, James Graham-Stewart, Richard Steenberg, Roderic Haugh and Ted Wolter. The only theme here is eclecticism – among the collections you'll find everthing from lighting to works of art and furniture, spanning the 17th to 20th centuries.

Floral Hall

Corner of Crouch Hill & Haringey Park, N8 9DX (8348 7309, www.floralhallantiques.co.uk). Finsbury Park tube/rail then bus W7 or 91. **Open** 10am-5pm Tue-Sat; also by appointment. **No credit cards.**

With its old-fashioned window, Floral Hall is a constant in Crouch End, its shop floor creaking with faded French grandeur. Gilt overmantel mirrors may not be in top-notch nick but, with prices starting from around £300, they are ideal for those in search of the battered look – and a bargain. Early 20th-century chandeliers range from £250 to £3,000 and there's normally some nice furniture pieces too – an art deco bedside table, say, or a pair of French café chairs, as well as a good range of original lamps. Phone before visiting in August as, in true French style, the shop usually closes.

French House

41-43 Parsons Green Lane, SW6 4HH (7371 7573, www.thefrenchhouse.co.uk). Parsons Green tube. **Open** 10am-6pm Mon-Sat.
The French House has the sort of stock you'd like to discover in France yourself. Most of the furniture is displayed in its original state with two prices: restored and as seen. The on-site workshop has been integrated into the showroom so you can watch the experienced upholsterer at work; for your own piece, you can choose from a selection of lovely French fabrics, exclusive to the shop. A restored 1860s chaise longue will cost around £1,800. Large gilt mirrors are good enough to hang as they are and mid-century Italian lighting has recently been added to the list of collected treasures. Thanks to monthly buying trips, there's always something new

LASSCo

and unusual to check out. Pretty 19th-century single bed prices start at £600, more masculine *lits bateaux* from around £950.

Lacquer Chest & Lacquer Chest Too

71 & 75 Kensington Church Street, W8 4BG (7937 1306, www.lacquerchest.com). Notting Hill Gate or Kensington High Street tube. **Open** 9.30am-5.30pm Mon-Fri; 10.30am-4pm Sat.
Gretchen Anderson and her husband Vivian have been in the business for well over 40 years and the ordered clutter of their 18th- and early 19th-century household antiques creates a more intimate atmosphere than that found in the shop's smarter neighbours. Think William Morris rush chairs, Welsh milking stools and early 19th-century, three-legged cricket tables (£500-£2,000). Most of the business is carried out behind the scenes, however; five floors hold an extraordinary library of antiques, with pieces hired out to film makers and stylists.

LASSCo

Brunswick House, 30 Wandsworth Road, SW8 2LG (7394 2100, www.lassco.co.uk). Vauxhall tube/rail. **Open** 9am-5pm Mon-Fri; 10am-5pm Sat; 11am-5pm Sun.
This 18th-century Vauxhall mansion and its vast warehouse are packed with architectural relics from the capital and beyond, such as Victorian stained-glass windows, a cell door from the Clerkenwell House of Detention (£975 plus VAT), and doors that came from the NatWest bank in York House (£8,250). Baltic pine floorboards from an ex-Salvation Army building were £38/sq m. The Parlour houses baths and basins of the sort Hercule Poirot might have used and there are also ornate art nouveau radiators. Head downstairs for Victorian basins and fireplaces. The branch in Bermondsey specialises in flooring.
Branch Millstream Road, SE1 3PA (7394 8061).

La Maison

107-108 Shoreditch High Street, E1 6JN (7729 9646, www.lamaisonlondon.com). Shoreditch High Street rail. **Open** 10am-6pm Mon-Sat.
This classy shop makes you want to get under the sheets – and stay there. The beds here are the stuff of French costume dramas and perfect for *liaisons dangereuses*. If you don't know your Louis XVI from your Louis Philippe, the charming staff will guide you through some bedroom history. Don't be put off by the rather cramped dimensions of the antique doubles; La Maison provides a seamless extension service. Single Louis XVI beds go for £500 and doubles from £700. Armoires start at £1,200 and bedside tables at £250. The shop also sells its own reproduction beds – expect to pay around £2,000 for a simple Louis XV-style double.

20th-century design

Ben Southgate

4 The Courtyard, Ezra Street, E2 7RH (mobile 07905 960792, www.bsouthgate.co.uk). Hoxton or Shoreditch High Street rail. **Open** 9am-3pm Sun.
Ben Southgate spent over a decade as a furniture restorer before opening this stylish grown-up boys' paradise among the blooms of Columbia Road. Stock includes vintage board games from around £30, the kind of 1950s football tables you see in French bars and cafés, clubby 1930s and '40s leather armchairs, enamel lampshades and polished medical cabinets (around £1,250). Prices are reasonable; huge 1940s eight-drawer plan chests sell for around £600. Southgate has also added lighting to his collection, so head to the shop in search of stylish studio desk lamps and the like.

Birgit Israel

251-253 Fulham Road, SW3 6HY (7376 7255, www.birgitisrael.com). South Kensington or Gloucester Road tube. **Open** 10am-6pm Mon-Sat.

HOME

Ben Southgate

Peanut Vendor. See p174.

Vintage furniture fairs

BADA Antiques and Fine Art Fair

Uber-rich, international antique collectors can be found musing on the worth of fine furniture at this British Antique Dealers' Association fair. Get your credit card ready if you fancy dropping in to browse larger pieces for the home, paintings, silverware, jewellery and ceramics.
Duke of York Square, SW3 4LY (www. bada-antiques-fair.co.uk).

Midcentury Modern

Mid-twentieth-century design nuts and Londoners casually looking for authentic vintage pieces tend to pitch up at this regular event. Dozens of dealers bring a hand-selected mix of beautifully restored furniture, lighting and accessories, and most are happy to talk you through an item's heritage.
(www.modernshows.com).

Vintage Home and Interiors Fair

Small furniture items (footstools, bedside tables and the like) join textiles, crockery, glassware, mirrors and lighting at this cheery little fair. Sellers are pretty crafty, so expect a few handmade items – tote bags, greetings cards, vintage fabric draught excluders – among the mix.
Cecil Sharp House, 2 Regents Park Road, NW1 7AY (www.vintagefashionfairlondon.co.uk).

Vintage Home Show

An appealing fusion of mid-twentieth century design classics and shabbier retro homeware, this new west London fair joins the established circuit of vintage markets. Scope out affordable options in furniture, textiles, ceramics and plenty of kitsch.
Chiswick Town Hall, Heathfield Terrace, W4 4JN (www.vintagehomeshow.co.uk).

Still on Fulham Road but now in a new space, Birgit Israel's smart, timeless 20th-century furniture store attracts collectors, interior designers and stylists looking for period pieces in mint condition. Birgit sources much of the stock herself from around the world. Lights are a particular passion, with the likes of Murano glass-tiered chandeliers and Venini glass disk wall lights often gracing the shop with their presence. Furniture is understated – what Israel calls 'casual luxury' – encompassing, for example, a set of four 'Eden Roc hotel' chairs (£1,750), say, or a pair of acrylic cube tables, fresh from the 1960s (£645). The store also makes bespoke and collection piece furniture to order and an interior design consultancy is available. Israel's clothing boutique is just along the road.

D&A Binder

34 Church Street, NW8 8EP (7723 0542, www.dandabinder.co.uk). Edgware Road tube or Marylebone tube/rail. **Open** 10am-6pm Mon-Sat.
D&A Binder looks rather like the ghost of Grace Brothers past. It's where old shop fittings come to rest, no longer needed for perfumery, haberdashery and wigs. David Binder rents props for films and theatre and sells to the likes of Hackett and Agent Provocateur, but private individuals shop here too. The huge 1920s mahogany shirt cabinets are perfect for the shirted man about town. Chrome and glass display cabinets from the 1940s work well in modern bathrooms. Museum cabinets are often in stock too. Look out for 1920s hat moulds, tailors' mannequins and corsetry advertising figures for manufacturers like Regent Corsetry, and mahogany bow-end glass wall shop cabinets. And, of

course, chrome shoe stands will do a fine job displaying your treasured Manolos.
Branch 101 Holloway Road, N7 8LT (7609 6300).

De Parma

247 Fulham Road, SW3 6HY (7352 2414, www.deparma.com). South Kensington tube. **Open** 10am-6pm Mon-Sat.
Gary de Sparham concentrates on mid 20th-century design in this new white space in south-west London. Almost everything is Italian and, in the main, by well-known designers such as Ico Parisi, Giò Ponti, Adnet, Fortana Arte and Fornasetti. Special pieces have been spotted here in the past, such as a 1969 Maurice Calka fibreglass Boomerang desk, one of only 35 (£34,000), and a 1940s Osvaldo Borsani commode in black lacquer and sycamore (£5,200). But there are also more affordable items, such as a chic 1940s black lacquered armchair (£1,450). De Parma also has a small selection of artworks, sculpture and photography for sale.

Dog & Wardrobe

Unit 3B, Regent Studios, 8 Andrew's Road, E8 4QN (mobile 07855 958741, www.thedogandwardrobe. com). London Fields rail or bus 55. **Open** 11am-5pm Thur-Sun.
Jane Money and Vishal Gohel's tiny retro furniture and design emporium is hidden just past Broadway Market, in a ground-floor unit of artists' hub Regent Studios. It's crammed with artfully presented vintage furniture (with lots of 1960s-style chairs and tables) and curios such as retro alarm clocks, desk lamps,

HOME

Planet Bazaar. See p176.

stylish coat stands, framed insects, animal skulls, shop-keepers' display cabinets, classic tins and bottles, and old typewriters, as well as a selection of framed contemporary art. Get here early on a Saturday for rich pickings before E8's fashionistas wake up. Money and Gohel also provide a design service.

Fandango

2 Cross Street, N1 2BL (mobile 07979 650805, www.fandangointeriors.co.uk). Angel tube or Highbury & Islington tube/rail. **Open** 11am-6pm Wed-Sat; also by appointment.

The selection of 20th-century furniture and objects here is very thoughtful. The shop specialises in post-war design from the 1950s and '60s, such as an orange Theo Ruth sofa or a Neil Morris cloud table, and you'll usually find pieces by well-known designers such as Arne Jacobsen. But it's not all about names here. Stock is interesting even if it is anonymous. There are attractive 1940s Murano glass chandeliers that have been resin-coated to bring them up to date and give them more masculine appeal (around £900) and neon works of art by Chish and Fips.

Gallery 1930

18 Church Street, NW8 8EP (7723 1555). Edgware Road tube or Marylebone tube/rail. **Open** 10am-5pm Tue-Sat.

The shop is a must for art deco enthusiasts and a particularly good hunting ground for those furnishing small flats, with dinky occasional tables and silver or chrome deco photograph frames, nostalgically filled with pictures of silver screen stars like Grant and Garbo (from £85). The drinks trays from the 1920s and '30s – mirrored or in black Vitriolite – make classy wedding gifts. For more movie glamour, there's 1930s polished steel film-set lighting on wheels – some lights are huge (prices range from £700 to £1,500) and all are reconditioned and rewired. Susie Cooper ceramics are always in stock, as are other big names such as Clarice Cliff and Lalique.

Peanut Vendor

133 Newington Green Road, N1 4RA (7226 5727, www.thepeanutvendor.co.uk). Canonbury rail or bus 73. **Open** 10am-7pm Tue-Thur; 10am-6pm Fri, Sat; noon-6pm Sun. **No credit cards**.

This local fave sells a well-edited range of charming yet affordable vintage furniture, curiosities and household knick-knacks. The affable owners, Barny and Becky, have a passion for good design and recognised a gap in the London market for aesthetically pleasing furniture that doesn't cost the earth. The eclectic selection often includes classic designs, such as Ercol pieces. Enamel light shades, 1960s coffee tables and folding stools, original wall hooks, industrial salvage items, early 20th-century chests, display/storage cabinets, old telephones, enamel bread bins and school-style chairs also crop up

More furniture treasure troves

Aladdin's Cave

72 Loampit Hill, SE13 7SX (no phone).
St Johns rail. **Open** 9am-6pm daily.
South-east London's premier treasure trove is
easy to spot from the road – the lifesize metallic
model of Predator is a slight giveaway. Inside
what feels like a giant shed hang a variety of
chandeliers. The far back wall, covered by
paintings and prints in mismatched frames,
can't be seen from the doorway because
of the sheer volume of wing-backed chairs
and dressers.

Crystal Palace Antiques & Modern

Imperial House, Jasper Road, SE19 1SJ
(8480 7042, www.crystalpalaceantiques.com).
Crystal Palace rail. **Open** 10am-6pm Mon-Sat;
10am-5pm Sun.
There are more than 15 dealers selling across
four storeys at this warehouse-style showroom.
Each floor has its own character: if you like artily
arranged mid-20th-century furniture, head down
to the basement; if it's Victorian antiques you're
after, negotiate the tangle of chests, tables and
accessories on the first floor.

Decoratum

31-33 Church Street, NW8 8ES (7724 6969,
www.decoratum.com). Marylebone tube/rail.
Open 10am-6pm Tue-Sat.
A stone's throw from Regent's Park, Decoratum
has the air of a museum or a gallery. The classy
layout is a fine setting for the quality original
vintage furniture from the 1950s, '60s, '70s and
'80s, and is a favourite among interior designers
and private collectors. There's also a branch in
Alfie's Antique Market.

Do Shop

34 Short's Gardens WC2H 9PX (7836 4039,
www.do-shop.com). Covent Garden tube. **Open**
10am-6.30pm Mon-Wed, Fri, Sat; 10am-8pm
Thur; noon-6pm Sun.
A bright, sunny shop in the heart of Covent
Garden, selling a mix of contemporary
homewares from a wide range of up-and-coming
designers. The owners support young designers
through their Do Masters programme, which
handpicks design school graduates to sell
through the store, and gives them a generous
profit return.

East London Furniture

46 Willow Walk, SE1 5SF (07709 429687,
www.eastlondonfurniture.co.uk). Bermondsey
or Borough tube. **Open** 10am-6pm Mon-Fri.
This recently opened store recycles locally
sourced wood and furniture, to make rustic-
looking new pieces. Everything on sale
represents something diverted from landfill,
but you wouldn't necessarily know it – a stylish
floor lamp (£500) is made from a doorframe,
a hip little block lamp (£55) is made from an
old pallet. There are cheap buys too, with a
simple book stand just £8.

The Old Cinema

160 Chiswick High Road, W4 1PR (8995
4166, www.theoldcinema.co.uk). Turnham
Green tube. **Open** 10am-6pm Mon-Sat;
noon-5pm Sun.
Housed in a building that was a cinema from
1912 to 1933, this vintage and antiques store
is a great spot for finding striking furniture
pieces; think utilitarian lockers, steel desks
or mid-20th-century sideboards, as well as
smaller items including battered old trunks
and Anglepoise lamps. There's plenty here
for Danish design lovers.

Retrovius

2A Kensal Green, NW10 5NR (8960 6060,
www.retrouvius.com). Kensal Green tube/rail.
Open 10am-6pm Mon-Sat.
In the secret address book of many interior
designers, Retrouvius is a salvage shop that
specialises in sourcing quirky reclaimed goods.
A batch of 50 French school chairs (£39 each,
with discounts for bulk buys), a perfectly
preserved lute, and a painted timber surveyor's
pole were all available on our last visit.

HOME

regularly. All items are originals, sourced and hand-selected from the UK and Europe. There's also a little vintage bike shop at the back, selling some lovely old racing models. Note that the place is sometimes closed on Tuesday mornings.

Planet Bazaar

Arch 68, The Stables Market, Chalk Farm Road, NW1 8AH (7485 6000, www.planetbazaar.co.uk). Camden Town or Chalk Farm tube. **Open** noon-5pm Tue-Fri; 10am-5.30pm Sat, Sun; also by appointment.

Proprietor Maureen Silverman remarks that Planet Bazaar's atmospheric digs beneath Victorian railway arches are the sort of place that people pop into to cheer themselves up as much as to do any shopping. You can see why. The place is crammed with everything from unusual ceramic animals and Murano glass vases, to vintage furniture and a huge selection of lighting, including 1960s Danish wooden lamps, plastic mushroom lamps from the 1970s, and industrial metal desk lamps. There's also a good range of rosewood coffee tables and chests of drawers from the 1960s, and the sort of sideboards that would have been laden with platters of cheese and pineapple in *Abigail's Party*. Chairs range from industrial stools to classic Danish armchairs and cool plastic numbers. Pop art is usually in stock too, with prints by Peter Blake, and Jamie Reid, who produced iconic artwork for the Sex Pistols.

Themes & Variations

231 Westbourne Grove, W11 2SE (7727 5531, www.themesandvariations.com). Notting Hill Gate or Westbourne Park tube. **Open** 10am-1pm, 2-6pm Mon-Fri; 10am-6pm Sat.

Liliane Fawcett's enduringly chic gallery has a strong focus on French and Italian decorative arts and furniture, especially from the 1970s. It takes its name from Italian designer Piero Fornasetti's series and is the exclusive UK agent for the Fornasetti studio. Plates from the series, featuring a woman's head in one of 365 positions, are £125. Stylish post-war and contemporary furniture is a speciality. We witnessed the arrival of a 1970s Pierre Cardin desk – on sale for an eye-watering £32,000. Themes & Variations has an annual themed exhibition, bringing together 20th-century pieces with furniture and objects from contemporary designers.

Two Columbia Road

2 Columbia Road, E2 7NN (7729 9933, www.two columbiaroad.com). Hoxton or Shoreditch High Street rail. **Open** noon-7pm Wed-Fri; noon-6pm Sat; 10am-3pm Sun.

Well-selected pieces are the order of the day here, whether it's 1970s chrome pendant lights or collectable Charles Eames wooden chairs. Some 20th-century shops can feel like a bit of a mixed bag, but there's a definite style here. The appealing corner site is owned by Tommy Roberts (who made his name with the cult Carnaby Street interiors shop Kleptomania in the 1960s) and is run by his son Keith. Expect to find well-known names such as Arne Jacobsen and Willy Rizzo among the stock as well as more affordable pieces (Danish 1960s leather sofas in slender, elegant shapes for around £850, and rosewood desks of the same period for £1,500).

Themes & Variations

HOME

Gardens & Flowers

Columbia Road Market (*see p46* **Markets**) is London's dedicated plant market, and the best bet for a combination of variety and keen prices, although your local street market is likely to sell workaday bedding plants and blooms for even less. **New Covent Garden Flower Market** (Covent Garden Market Authority, Covent House, SW8 5NX, 7720 2211, www.newcoventgardenmarket.com) covers three-and-a-half acres and sells blooms from all over the world; there's a £5 entrance fee if you bring your car, but it's free for pedestrians. Turn up before 7am for the best choice.

Garden centres & nurseries

Clifton Nurseries

5A Clifton Villas, W9 2PH (7289 6851, www.clifton. co.uk). Warwick Avenue tube. **Open** *Apr-Oct* 9am-6pm Mon-Sat; 11am-5pm Sun. *Nov-Mar* 8.30am-5.30pm Mon-Sat; 11am-5pm Sun.

Few garden centres have credentials as impeccable as Clifton. For a start, it's been a neatly planted urban arcadia since Victoria was on the throne. Longevity apart, it commands respect for the expertise of the staff, the quality of the plants on sale and the fact that it is a consistent medal winner at the RHS Chelsea Flower Show. The managing director, Matthew Wilson, is a familiar byline in the horticultural press and a regular panellist on Radio 4's *Gardeners' Question Time*. His staff are equally well qualified to tell you the best time for pruning your recently acquired wisteria and answer any number of other queries. Come in summer for a stunning rose collection – there's one for the most unpromising of backyards – or in winter to get the benefit of the hothouse full of tender tropical specimens. When we visited the café was being refurbished, but it was always a favourite tea-time spot, where you could eat cake and admire the container planting. The landscaping and design service is gold standard: any number of London gardeners aspire to the 'Clifton Look'. The garden shop is lovely, not just for seeds and secateurs, but for books and imaginative gardeners' gifts.

Petersham Nurseries

Church Lane, off Petersham Road, Petersham, Richmond, Surrey TW10 7AG (8940 5230, www.petershamnurseries.com). Richmond tube/rail. **Open** 9am-5pm Mon-Sat; 11am-5pm Sun.

The best way to approach this most bucolic of suburban garden centres is along the river bank to Petersham meadows, where you'll discover this horticultural idyll at the end of the glorious (private) garden of Petersham House, owned by Gael and Francesco Boglione. They established the centre in March 2004, with the aim of creating a place where plant lovers could find unusual varieties for the urban garden, and enjoy being inspired by artistic groupings of plants and reclaimed garden antiques at the same time. The happy result is that there isn't a corner of this celebrated nursery that isn't ravishing, but if you need practical gardening advice on varieties and soil types, you can rely on the staff to help. The cottage garden perennials, shrubs, herbs and climbers are displayed in a series of antique timber-frame greenhouses, and grouped together aesthetically in old-fashioned handcarts, weathered clay pots and timber boxes. The new garden shop carries a pleasingly wide range of stock for the garden-proud and is the scene of regular Saturday morning garden events and workshops. We planned our visit around a talk on guerilla gardening with the Man who Sows, blogger and author Richard Reynolds. The much-lauded restaurant is now in the capable hands of chef Greg Malouf – book ahead for a table – but the Tea House is lovely for cakes and pastries. Visitors are required to leave their cars at home, so if you're planning to buy a shed-load of stuff, ask about the delivery service.

Garden shops

Hortus

26 Blackheath Village, SE3 9SY (8297 9439, www.hortus-london.com). Blackheath rail. **Open** 10am-6pm Mon-Fri; 9.30am-6pm Sat; 10am-4pm Sun.

A pleasing garden store at the south end of Blackheath Village, Hortus is mostly about accessories and design, but also has an outdoor patch (with a black bunny in a hutch). This backyard shows off the specimen trees (pittosporums, olives) and the understated container range. There's a wide variety, including Crescent's cleverly heavy looking lightweight stone-effect jobs. Hamilton Landscapes runs a garden design and maintenance service from a summerhouse here too. The rest of the plant selection is limited to seasonal container fillers (summer herbs, autumn cyclamen, spring bulbs) and is prettily displayed on pavement tables. The shop is fab for unusual and covetable accessories: any number of lovely watering cans for the house and garden, designer trowels by Sophie Conran, pretty garden lights and nifty slug and wasp traps masquerading as ornaments. Stock changes seasonally, but trugs, cards, tools, vases and quality outdoor furniture are usually available.

Judy Green's Garden Store

11 Flask Walk, NW3 1HJ (7435 3832). Hampstead tube. **Open** 10am-6pm Mon-Sat; noon-6pm Sun.

The fact that Judy Green's pretty little store has been proclaimed a 'garden boutique' should tell you all you need to know about the more rarefied type of horticulture that it caters for. There'll be no hefting sacks of well-rotted farmyard manure from here. Instead, take a stroll to Flask Walk, one of London's most winsome shopping streets, to see a garden store burgeoning prettily with seasonal container-planting candidates: violas, campanulas, cyclamen, narcissi, ivies and summer lavenders and pelargoniums, as well as eye-catching pots and boxes to arrange them in. Step indoors for Tamara Fogle's bags, designer gumboots, indoor orchids, crockery, vases and quality garden tools.

Flowers

Absolute Flowers

12-14 Clifton Road, W9 1SS (7286 1155, www.absoluteflowersandhome.com). Warwick Avenue tube. **Open** 8am-6.30pm Mon-Sat; 10am-5.30pm Sun.
Come here for statement-making bunches, hand tied into a perfect multi-headed sheaf, or carefully placed in a designer container. AF is modish, always in vogue (and *Vogue*) and has now extended its interiors remit to include homewares: furniture, lamps, luggage. Walking into the shop can be a little intimidating, as you watch the chic artists (seems belittling to call them florists). The shop specialises in English blooms, and bouquets are kept simple: a beautiful collection of mop-headed hydrangeas for example, in a colour range like dawn, from pale blue to washed pink, are held with ribbon in co-ordinating hues. Homewares and accessories are also sold. Given the number of starry events the company cuts a flowery dash for, the staff are kept extremely busy, but they take time to discuss your needs all the same.

Angel Flowers

60 Upper Street, N1 0NY (7704 6312, www.angel-flowers.co.uk). Angel tube. **Open** 9am-6pm Mon; 9am-7pm Tue-Sat; 11am-5pm Sun.
Globetrotting Belgian Marco Wouters cultivated his love of flowers and plants working with his grandma in the vegetable garden when he was a mere stripling of seven. Having travelled widely, making a study of plants in their natural environments, he has now put down roots here and created this, Islington's flowery bower. His blooms are imported from Dutch flower markets four times a week and there's always a massive variety available. There are hot tropicals and orchids, and buckets full of cottage-garden lovelies in season. The shop is a blaze of colour all year round, and the staff are as happy to sell you a perfect bunch of sweet peas for the kitchen table as a great swishy armful of a mixed bouquet.

Bloomsbury Flowers

29 Great Queen Street, WC2B 5BB (7242 2840, www.bloomsburyflowers.co.uk). Covent Garden tube. **Open** 9am-5pm Mon; 9am-6pm Tue-Fri.
The Royal Ballet dancers-turned-florists Stephen Wicks and Mark Welford have been creating displays of extraordinary grace for 17 years from this Covent

Angel Flowers

La Maison des Roses

Garden stage. They're well known in the area for event floristry, but we're most enamoured of the glossy and unusual seasonal tied bunches that can be arranged for you (or some lucky recipient) while you wait. There's always something fresh and fragrant blooming in store: when we visited, big, flame-petalled dahlias were busting out all over, alongside late roses, hypericum berries, orange-scented bergamot and other more herbal mixtures. Read the Bloomsbury boys' blog to see what's in season and why flowers make life worth living. You can buy their flower arranging book online, too.

Jane Packer Flowers

32-34 New Cavendish Street, W1G 8UE (7935 2673, www.jane-packer.co.uk). Bond Street tube. **Open** 9am-6pm Mon-Sat.

The victory bouquets given to medal winners at the London 2012 Olympics were not only beautiful; they were also a tribute to the internationally celebrated florist, who died in November 2011. Jane Packer's creative director, Susan Lapworth, designed the bouquets, whose components all had to be British-grown blooms. The Jane Packer empire continues to thrive: a new shop has opened in John Lewis, a walk away from this flagship store and flower school. It's a lovely place to watch the experts; flower fans are invited to regular demonstrations that take place here throughout the year (see website for details). A great deal of the business is given over to high-profile and event clients, but the individual and eye-catching bunches designed for casual buyers are put together with care and flair.

La Maison des Roses

48 Webbs Road, SW11 6SF (7228 5700, www.maison-des-roses.com). Clapham South tube or Clapham Junction rail. **Open** 10am-6pm Tue-Sat.

Clearly the best time to visit this glorious boutique is during early summer, when English roses are at the height of their velvety splendour and their fragrance hits you as you cross the threshold. It's a pretty place, and when the short home-grown season is over, the imports are just as lovely. You can buy your roses in lovely tied bunches or in pretty containers, or have the Maison decorate your *maison* with roses for a special occasion. Rose-scented unguents, candles and room sprays are also sold. Check the website to find out about the flower arranging courses that are held here at the height of each season.

McQueens

70-72 Old Street, EC1V 9AN (7251 5505, www.mcqueens.co.uk). Old Street tube/rail. **Open** 8.30am-6pm Mon-Fri.

Kally Ellis launched this pioneering flower shop 21 years ago and its glamour has burgeoned ever since. Here, McQueens protégés create fantastic bouquets and bunches from a huge range of flora and foliage, from traditional darlings of each season (narcissi and fritillaria, roses and dahlias, violas and chrysanths, cyclamen and ivies) to hothouse exotica such as strelitzia, protea and gardenia. If you fancy treating yourself to one of Luis da Silva's floristry courses, book yourself a place on the website.

Scarlet & Violet

*76 Chamberlayne Road, NW10 3JJ (8969 9446,
www.scarletandviolet.com). Kensal Green tube.*
Open 8.30am-6pm Mon-Sat.

Vic Brotherson is best described as an 'artisan florist'
and her arrangements, whether for a wedding or a
glossy magazine shoot, are testament to her skill. The
look is deliciously seasonal. Cottage garden blooms (the
likes of delphiniums, sweet peas, peonies and scabious
in season) and evergreens are favoured candidates for
arrangements, and the casual displays, in reclaimed
containers such as pickle jars, buckets, antique jugs and
bottles, give an impression of boldness and generosity.
You can rely on friendly, personal service and an
imaginatively tied bunch of happiness when you buy
flowers here.

Wild at Heart

*Turquoise Island, 222 Westbourne Grove, W11
2RH (7727 3095, www.wildatheart.com). Notting
Hill Gate or Westbourne Grove tube.* **Open** 8am-6pm
Mon-Sat.

The listed building known as Turquoise Island,
designed by Piers Gough, has had a wild side for nearly
20 years – since Nikki Tibbles won the contract for a
retail outlet on its outside edge. She opened her much-
lauded flower shop here and went on to create a whole
Wild at Heart homewares brand, with flowers at its core,
of course. The flagship store is on Pimlico Road and
there are concessions in Harrods and Liberty, but we
love this branch best. The blooms are fresh and
vibrant – seasonal English flowers are favoured, with
plenty of bold colourful foliage to get you through the
winter and the most beautiful tulips and other spring
bulbs to celebrate an early spring, even when the rain
keeps sloshing down.
Branch 54 Pimlico Road, SW1W 8LP (3145 0441).

You Don't Bring Me Flowers

*15 Staplehurst Road, SE13 5ND (8297 2333,
www.youdontbringmeflowers.co.uk). Hither Green
rail.* **Open** 8am-6pm Tue-Fri; 9am-6pm Sat; 10am-
5pm Sun.

A leading player in Hither Green's reinvention as an arty
enclave to rival Brockley, You Don't Bring Me Flowers is
like a homely kitchen where all the blooms and foliage
are clustered round a large butler sink and spill out on
to the pavement. The effect is cottagey, but alongside the
strikingly beautiful English garden favourites such as
roses, peonies, delphiniums and larkspur, there are more
shrubby and herbacious specimens to add structure and
fragrance to a bouquet: dill, eryngium, rosemary, glossy
leaved elaeagnus and bay. The company does a fair bit
of wedding and event floristry but staff are just as happy
devising tied bunches according to customers' tastes
while they sit in the lovely café. YDBMF also sells a small
number of gifts and greetings cards.

Scarlet & Violet

Leisure

Leisure

Despite a struggle to survive within the independent music and book trade, things aren't totally bleak. Music stores and bookshops have been at the forefront of the trend for more experience-led shopping, having traditionally been places where customer-staff interaction is particularly valued; now, enjoying a free in-store gig at one of the city's record shops is a regular experience for many a music buff, while a great many of London's bookshops have frequent in-house talks and events, and continue to excite those who enjoy the quality browsing experience that can never be replicated by online shops. Cherish lovely independents such as the **Big Green Bookshop** (*see p184*), **Lutyens & Rubinstein** (*see p187*) and **Honest Jon's** (*see p201*) while you still can.

Photography and electronics buffs keen to get their hands on the latest gadgetry will also have a field day in the capital, with Covent Garden's **Apple Store** (*see p204*) – the largest of its kind in the world – something of a destination for technology geeks. In a completely different vein is second-hand audio specialist **Audio Gold** (*see p204*), a true neighbourhood independent, run by passionate staff who will set you up with a hi-fi system for just a few hundred pounds.

Most of the shop's stock is composed of products made during the UK's audio heyday in the 1960s, '70s and '80s.

London's excellent second-hand camera shops proferring vintage models also cater to those who feel that modern equipment lacks the romance of yesteryear. Don't miss **Classic Camera** (*see p206*) and **MW Classic Cameras** (*see p207*).

Londoners have become a crafty lot. Knitting and other traditional handicrafts have fitted in nicely with the eco-conscious move towards cottage industries. Modern haberdasheries can now be found in various spots around London, and the likes of Forest Hill's craft store **Stag & Bow** (*see p216*) and Islington's knit shop, **Loop** (*see p216*), have been a great success, with regular workshops and a community atmosphere.

We've also become bike-crazy, with fixed-gear bikes now a common sight on the city's roads; Soho's **Tokyo Fixed** store (*see p233*) is central London's trendy emporium for 'fixie' obsessives, while **Foffa Bikes** (*see p229*) epitomises a new breed of cycle stores. If you're after a vintage racer, meanwhile, get yourself over to Finsbury Park – the steel frames at the tiny **Sargent & Co** (*see p233*) evoke the romanticism of cycling's pre-1990s golden eras.

Books

General & local

Central branches of the big chains include the massive **Waterstones** flagship (203-206 Piccadilly, SW1Y 6WW, 7851 2400, www.waterstones.co.uk), which has a bar/restaurant, and the academic bookseller **Blackwell's** (100 Charing Cross Road, WC2H 0JG, 7292 5100, www.blackwell.co.uk).

The **British Library Bookshop** (British Library, 96 Euston Road, NW1 2DB, 7412 7735, www.bl.uk/bookshop) stocks some good literature and history titles based on the collections.

Big Green Bookshop
Unit 1, Brampton Park Road, N22 6BG (8881 6767, www.biggreenbookshop.com). Turnpike Lane tube.
Open 9am-6pm Mon, Tue, Thur-Sat; 10.30am-6pm Wed; 11am-5pm Sun.
A bookshop deserving of accolades, Big Green Bookshop is a community effort in every way. The owners decided to go it alone when the only bookshop in Wood Green, a Waterstones, closed down. They enlisted locals to help them turn a defunct internet café into a bookshop in little over two weeks, and when it launched in March 2008 decisions regarding the shop's name, stock and events were made by the customers themselves. In return, patrons have access to comfy chairs, free coffee and wonderfully enthusiastic staff. As well as a fine stock of local bookshop usuals, it's strong in children's titles, multicultural books and fiction, and recently launched a second-hand books department. What's more, the events programme is unparalleled. There are weekly writers' workshops and children's author events, storytelling mornings, knitting days, boardgames and comedy nights once a month, and the odd festival. The energy is infectious. The shop has tight links with indie newcomer Gallic Books (www.gallicbooks.co.uk), the Belgravia Books initiative that opened on Ebury Street in September 2011.

Broadway Bookshop
6 Broadway Market, E8 4QJ (7241 1626, www.broadwaybookshophackney.com). London Fields rail or bus 26, 55. **Open** 10am-6pm Mon-Sat; 11am-5pm Sun.
This Hackney independent benefits from its position on the canal end of popular Broadway Market. A smart layout and intelligently weighed stock boost its appeal further. The shop is a thoughtful enterprise, promoting small publishers like Eland and stocking lots of *New York Review* titles, plus interesting reprints of forgotten gems. There's plenty of top-drawer literary fiction and a large travel section that's strong on London and local history. The second-hand collectibles have become more

popular in the last couple of years, with punters keen to get their hands on old 1930s and '40s hardbacks. The shop is also a permanent exhibition space, promoting local artists.

Daunt Books
83-84 Marylebone High Street, W1U 4QW (7224 2295, www.dauntbooks.co.uk). Baker Street tube.
Open 9am-7.30pm Mon-Sat; 11am-6pm Sun.
Though not strictly a travel bookshop, this beautiful Edwardian shop will always be seen first and foremost as a travel specialist, thanks to its elegant three-level back room complete with oak balconies, viridian-green walls, conservatory ceiling and stained-glass window – home to row upon row of guidebooks, maps, language reference, history, politics, travelogue and related fiction organised by country. France, Britain, Italy and the United States are particularly well represented; go downstairs to find more far-flung destinations. It's a particularly valued collection now that the specialist Travel Bookshop in Notting Hill is no longer. Travel aside, Daunt is also a first-rate stop for literary fiction, biography, gardening and much more. James Daunt's commitment to providing proper careers for his workers ensures an informed and keen team of staff. What's more, the no discounting, no three-for-twos policy creates an atmosphere much more in keeping with traditional local bookshops than with overdone marketing schemes.
Branches 51 South End Road, NW3 2QB (7794 8206); 193 Haverstock Hill, NW3 4QL (7794 4006); 112-114 Holland Park Avenue, W11 4UA; 158-164 Fulham Road, SW10 9PR (7373 4997); 61 Cheapside, EC2V 6AX (7248 1117).

Foyles
113-119 Charing Cross Road, WC2H 0EB (7437 5660, www.foyles.co.uk). Tottenham Court Road tube.
Open 9.30am-9pm Mon-Sat; 11am (until noon browsing only)-6pm Sun.
Probably the single most impressive independent bookshop in London, Foyles has been selling books in London since 1903 and built its reputation on the sheer volume and breadth of its stock (with 56 specialist subjects in the flagship store). Going against the tide of bookshop closures, it now boasts five stores in central London, with its flagship due to move to a huge space (that formerly housed Central Saint Martins) down the road from its current site, in 2014. The five hugely comprehensive storeys of its present building accommodate other shops too: there's Ray's Jazz and café, a fine concession of Unsworth's antiquarian booksellers, and the Grant & Cutler foreign-language bookstore on the first floor. Fiction at Foyles should be lauded, along with an impressive range of teaching materials, computing software and the comprehensive basement medical department. Elsewhere, there's an extensive music department, a large gay-interest section, a fine range of foreign fiction,

Lutyens & Rubinstein. See p187.

Gosh!. See p190.

law and business, philosophy and sport. The shop hosts regular events featuring well-known faces such as Billy Bragg, Sophie Dahl and Christopher Priest.
Branches Southbank Centre, Riverside, SE1 8XX (7440 3212); St Pancras International, Euston Road, N1C 4QL (3206 2650); Westfield London, W12 7GE (3206 2656); 74-75 Lower Ground Floor, The Arcade, Westfield Stratford City, E20 1EH (3206 2671).

Hatchards

187 Piccadilly, W1J 9LE (7439 9921, www.hatchards.co.uk). Piccadilly Circus tube.
Open 9.30am-7pm Mon-Sat; noon-6pm Sun.
Holding court with Fortnum & Mason and other Piccadilly royalty is London's oldest surviving bookshop, dating back to 1797. Its old-school charm and refined aura have helped it maintain an ambience all its own (even though it's now owned by Waterstones). The grand shop is extensive in its stock, but particularly good for travel and biography, and new hardback fiction. Benjamin Disraeli, Lord Byron and Oscar Wilde are former fans. These days, celebrated authors come to sign the books –

recent visitors include Peter Ackroyd, Will Self and Clare Balding. Mowbray's religious booksellers is located on the third floor. Hatchards prides itself on its knowledge-able staff and its comprehensive range of signed and special editions.

John Sandoe

10 Blacklands Terrace, SW3 2SR (7589 9473, www.johnsandoe.com). Sloane Square tube.
Open 9.30am-6.30pm Mon-Sat; 11am-5pm Sun.
John Sandoe founded the shop in 1957 and, though he has passed away, his legacy is one of the best local inde-pendents in London, with a loyal and ever-growing clien-tele, professional staff and enviably broad stock. New and classic releases rub spines with more unusual items – books with no ISBN or that have been privately printed, for example. These are bought safe in the knowledge that certain customers will be interested – a testament to the personal relationship here between staff and visitors. There's a high proportion of quality hardbacks, a very full travel section upstairs and a fun children's section in the basement. Half the ground floor is devoted to art, photography and architecture.

London Review Bookshop

*14 Bury Place, WC1A 2JL (7269 9030,
www.lrbshop.co.uk). Holborn or Tottenham
Court Road tube.* **Open** 10am-6.30pm Mon-Sat;
noon-6pm Sun.

If you're looking for a place to inspire you to get reading then this is it, from the inviting and stimulating
presentation to the clear quality of the books chosen.
Politics, current affairs, fiction and history are well represented on the ground floor, while downstairs, exciting poetry and philosophy sections sit alongside
essays and literary criticism – everything you'd expect
from a shop owned by the *London Review of Books*.
The LRB's events programme has seen authors such
as Robert MacFarlane, Will Self and Ian Sinclair visit,
while all sorts of writers and journalists stop by at the
adjoining London Review Cake Shop, a breezy coffee
shop. The shop also co-publishes signed limited editions
by writers such as Julian Barnes and Ian McEwan.

Lutyens & Rubinstein

*21 Kensington Park Road, W11 2EU (7229 1010,
www.lutyensrubinstein.co.uk). Ladbroke Grove tube.*
Open 10am-6pm Mon-Sat; 11am-6pm Sun.

Founded in 2009 by literary agents, Lutyens &
Rubinstein sells a beautifully arranged and well-edited
selection of literary fiction and general non-fiction, over
two floors. Although there are special sections for children's books, poetry and art titles, the focus is on excellence in writing across a broad range of subject areas.
The core stock of titles was put together by the owners
canvassing hundreds of readers on which books they
would most like to find in a bookshop, and thus every
book stocked is sold because somebody has recommended it. The result is an appealing alternative to the
homogeneous chain bookshops, with some unusual
titles available. As well as books, the shop stocks its own
range of stationery, greetings cards, paperweights, local
honey and home-made jam, and a range of literary-
inspired scents from CB I Hate Perfume. A bespoke service offers the option to be sent monthly titles in
accordance with your personal tastes. What's more,
there's an active and engaged events programme. It's all
very Notting Hill, but charming with it.

Owl Bookshop

*209 Kentish Town Road, NW5 2JU (7485 7793).
Kentish Town tube/rail.* **Open** 9am-6pm Mon-Sat;
11am-5pm Sun.

A clever rearrange has made Kentish Town's Owl
Bookshop easier to negotiate: classic fiction has been
given room to expand, becoming the store's main focus,
and there are now some armchairs to help you relax while
you mull over your choices. Trading for a good three
decades, the shop covers food and drink, gardening, sport
and fiction, with all stock judiciously laid out. There's a
strong children's section to the right as you come in and

a smart selection of stationery for sale. Owl also stocks
DVDs – mainly world, cult and classic films, with an
impressive selection for the kids. All in all, a valuable
local resource in this part of north London.

Woolfson & Tay

*12 Bermondsey Square, SE1 3UN (7407 9316,
www.woolfsonandtay.com). London Bridge tube/
rail.* **Open** 11am-7pm Mon-Fri; 11am-5pm Sun.

This bookshop-cum-gallery-cum-café was created by
literary duo Shivaun Woolfson and Frances Tay to be a
space for expression, with a focus on writing that serves
to 'entertain, enlighten and educate'. The store opened
in September 2010, but, with its carefully chosen stock
and modern, engaged ethos, it already harbours some
real treasures. In particular, it has an intriguing international section, promoting everything from Soseki
Natsume's *I Am a Cat* to Diego Marani's *New Finnish
Grammar*. There is some unusual and socially conscious
stock, too, with a politics section and a world affairs and
social action area. The travel section contains few guidebooks, encouraging a more esoteric form of travel, as
illustrsted in books such as Rebecca Solnit's *A Field
Guide to Getting Lost*. There's also a great selection of
classic travel-themed novels published by Eland. The
interior itself is a symphony to minimalism, while the
spacious gallery/café space, serving home-made Asian
meals, is spartan and monochrome, but livened up by
the artworks. The (strongly female) clientele make the
most of a busy roster of events and activities, including
tai chi classes, LGBT discussion forums and storytelling for kids.

Special interest

London's main art galleries, such as **Tate Britain**,
Tate Modern, the **Design Museum** and the
National Gallery, should also be ports of call
for books on art.

Note that foreign-language specialist **Grant
& Cutler** (www.grantandcutler.com) has merged
with Foyles, and can be found on the first floor
of the company's flagship on Charing Cross Road
(*see p184*).

Artwords Bookshop

*69 Rivington Street, EC2A 3AY (7729 2000,
www.artwords.co.uk). Old Street tube/rail.*
Open 10.30am-7pm Mon-Fri; 11am-7pm Sat.

Partly thanks to its location in artist-dense Hoxton but
also due to its knowledgeable staff, Artwords has its finger firmly on the pulse when it comes to publications on
contemporary visual arts. As well as offering a vast
collection of up-to-date books from Britain, the bookshop
regularly imports new works from Europe, North
America and Australia. Stock relating to contemporary
visual culture dominates, but there are also plenty of

LEISURE

architecture, photography, graphic design, fashion, advertising and film titles. It's also worth heading here if you are on the look-out for a rare magazine - you'll find a range of creative magazines and periodicals, including the painting-specialist *Turps Banana,* industry favourite *Elephant* and the interdisciplinary *Cabinet.*
Branch 20-22 Broadway Market, E8 4QJ (7923 7507).

Atlantis Bookshop

49A Museum Street, WC1A 1LY (7405 2120, www.theatlantisbookshop.com). Holborn or Tottenham Court Road tube. **Open** 10.30am-6pm Mon-Sat.
London's oldest independent bookshop on the occult (it opened back in 1922) sells new and second-hand titles on everything from angels and fairies, vampires, werewolves, earth mysteries and magic, to meditation, healing, green issues, spiritualism and psychology. The shop also hosts regular events such as 'An evening with...' and the popular 'Psychic Café' series. The physical shop is petite in size, but a much larger range of stock is available from the company's e-shop (see the website listed above). The shop's in-store noticeboard is a useful resource for finding out about practitioners of alternative therapies, as well as external events.

Bookmarks

1 Bloomsbury Street, WC1B 3QE (7637 1848, www.bookmarks.uk.com). Tottenham Court Road tube. **Open** noon-7pm Mon; 11am-7pm Tue-Sat.
From each according to his ability, to each according to his reads: Bookmarks is London's premier socialist booshop, going strong for more than three decades,
despite constant threats from, well, global capitalism (Amazon is 'the Starbucks of the booktrade', say staff). Bookmarks (almost a pun) sees itself as a home for ideas and an enabler of those ideas in a practical manner, regularly 'taking ideas to the movement' by setting up stalls at rallies, providing information about activism and hosting author events; China Mieville, Owen Jones and Hamid Dabashi have all been guests. The shop's spacious, airy interior (replete with replica Soviet sculpture) holds a fabulous collection of left-wing writing – lots of history and politics of course, but also a small but well-chosen fiction section, left-wing second-handers and a great, thought-provoking children's section. As official bookshop for near-neighbour the TUC, there are also many trade union publications.

Books for Cooks

4 Blenheim Crescent, W11 1NN (7221 1992, www.booksforcooks.com). Ladbroke Grove or Notting Hill Gate tube. **Open** 10am-6pm Tue-Sat.
The astute book shopper will have noticed the number of London bookshops opening coffeeshops to attract customers. Books for Cooks puts them all to shame – it has its own kitchen in the back, where recipes from a massive stock of cookery books are put to the test and sold from midday until the food runs out (no reservations). The most successful of them are compiled into the shop's own publications (£5.99 each). The front room is stacked high with books covering hundreds of cuisines, chefs and cookery techniques, as well as food-related fiction, culinary history, foodie biographies and nutrition. Workshops and evening classes with the shop's resident cooks are another way to get stuck in (see website for details).

Magma. See p190.

Forbidden Planet

179 Shaftesbury Avenue, WC2H 8JR (7420 3666, www.forbiddenplanet.com). Covent Garden or Tottenham Court Road tube. **Open** 10am-7pm Mon, Tue; 10am-7.30pm Wed, Fri, Sat; 10am-8pm Thur; noon-6pm Sun.

Self-confessed geeks (and otherwise) get together at London's megastore for sci-fi, fantasy and comic-related books and memorabilia. Forbidden Planet stocks thousands of books – covering science fiction, animation, graphic arts, computer games, film, horror, sport, super-heroes and more – as well as a huge range of graphic novels, from classic *Marvel* comics, to obscure small publishers from around the world, to *Viz* annuals. The store also stocks a good number of signed books, as well as a huge range of DVDs, action figures, posters, clothing, games, and other genre-related merchandise. What's more, author events take place here regularly. A first port-of-call for *Star Wars* and *Doctor Who* obsessives and the place to head to for Marvel and DC action figures.

Gay's the Word

66 Marchmont Street, WC1N 1AB (7278 7654, www.gaystheword.co.uk). King's Cross St Pancras tube/rail or Russell Square tube. **Open** 10am-6.30pm Mon-Sat; 2-6pm Sun.

In 2010, when Camden council threatened a rent hike of 25%, the future looked uncertain for Britain's only dedicated gay and lesbian bookshop (established in 1979), but somehow Gay's the Word soldiers on. After a financial crisis in 2007, the shop launched a shelf-sponsorship programme called Cash for Honours, which drew support from loyal customers including Sarah Waters, Ali Smith and Simon Callow. Stock covers fiction, history and biography, as well as more specialist holdings in queer studies, sex and relationships, children, and parenting – plus a selection of possibly the funniest greetings cards in London. In addition to regular author readings and book-signings (think Alan Hollinghurst, Armistead Maupin, Stella Duffy, Mark Doty), there are weekly writing groups, plus monthly trans discussion groups.

Goldsboro

23-25 Cecil Court, WC2N 4EZ (7497 9230, www.goldsborobooks.com). Leicester Square tube. **Open** 10am-6pm Mon-Sat.

Now in a new, larger Cecil Court space (which housed Nigel Williams' shop, until he passed away in 2011), Goldsboro stands out from the crowd along this street of antiquarian booksellers. The shop is the largest signed, first-edition specialist in the UK, with some 5,000 good-quality titles in stock. Writers regularly sign consignments of first editions (mostly from the 1960s onwards), which often sell for the same price as unsigned editions elsewhere; big names include Ian Rankin, Wilbur Smith, Peter Ackroyd and Bernard Cornwell. Goldsboro is also responsible for one of the world's

Persephone Books. See p190.

LEISURE

largest first-edition book clubs; there's a new title each month and many are exclusive to the store and bound in limited-edition slipcases.

Gosh!

1 Berwick Street, W1F 0DR (7636 1011, www.gosh london.com). Tottenham Court Road tube. **Open** 10.30am-7pm daily.

There's never been a better time to take up reading comics – and there's nowhere better to bolster your collection than at this Soho specialist, which moved into its new, larger Berwick Street space from Bloomsbury in 2011. Half of the basement room is given over to comics and back issues while the other holds a fine stash of Manga. A new exhibition spaces houses the works of regularly changing artists. It's graphic novels that take centre stage, though, from early classics like *Krazy Kat* and *Little Nemo* to Alan Moore's *Peter Pan* adaptation, *Lost Girls*. The legendary Moore is one of many high-profile authors to have signed here. Bryan Talbot (*Alice in Sunderland*) is another. Gosh! has begun to sell exclusive bookplated editions of some works – authors sign tip-in sheets that collectors can then add to their copies; plates upcoming when we visited included Brian K Vaughan and Fiona Staples' *Saga Volume 1*, Brandon Graham's *Prophet*, and Will Bingley and Anthony Hope-Smith's *Gonzo*. Classic children's books, of the *This is London* vein, are also a plus point here.

Koenig Books

80 Charing Cross Road, WC2H 0BF (7240 8190, www.koenigbooks.co.uk). Leicester Square tube. **Open** 11am-8pm Mon-Fri; 10am-8pm Sat.

An inspiring, German-owned independent bookshop specialising in art, architecture, fashion, design and photography tomes. Koenig's first London branch is based in the Serpentine Gallery, and the other is the newest addition to the capital's traditional literary artery – Charing Cross Road. The latter shop is done out stylishly in black and every book is given respectful prominence – products are displayed with their covers rather than spines facing customers to ensure their full effect. Head downstairs for year-round special offers. Both branches of Koenig have full access to the stock of mammoth arts bookshop Buchhandlung Walther Koenig in Cologne, so can order you just about anything you can think of.
Branches Serpentine Gallery, Kensington Gardens, W2 3XA (7706 4907); Whitechapel Gallery Bookshop (managed by Koenig Books), 77-82 Whitechapel High Street, E1 7QX (7522 7897).

Magma

117-119 Clerkenwell Road, EC1R 5BY (7242 9503, www.magmabooks.com). Chancery Lane tube or Farringdon tube/rail. **Open** 10am-7pm Mon-Sat.
There are all the design, architecture, graphics and creative magazines you could want here, from large-format art and design books to prints, T-shirts and design gifts. The shop's objective is to blur the boundary between bookshop and exhibition space, making visits interactive and educational experiences. As well as the usual look-at-me coffee-table books, there are lots of in-depth essay collections, plus obscure and fun tomes. If you can visualise it, there's probably a book on it here, with stock covering everything from Banksy to a whole range of bike-culture publications. There are also numerous unbookish design-related items, such as the blank Russian dolls, Magma's own Bird Bingo and a wide range of stationery. Try the nearby arty products sister store for trendy bicycle clips, Moomin-print kitchenware or make your own ukelele sets.
Branches 8 Earlham Street, WC2H 9RY (7240 8498); 16 Earlham Street, WC2H 9LN (7240 7571).

Persephone Books

59 Lamb's Conduit Street, WC1N 3NB (7242 9292, www.persephonebooks.co.uk). Russell Square tube. **Open** 10am-6pm Mon-Fri; noon-5pm Sat.

The main office of this publisher and bookseller is piled high with lovingly restored reprints of unfairly neglected women writers, mainly from the interwar period. These beautiful objects are covered in identical plain dove grey, but each book's endpapers comprise wonderful re-creations of patterns – wallpapers, fabrics, clothing or suchlike – contemporary to the book. More importantly, they make for fascinating reading. Some are by well-known names – Penelope Mortimer, Katherine Mansfield, Virginia Woolf – while others offer the chance to get to know quick-witted women who, by virtue of the time in which they lived, were not given the respect they might otherwise have gained in their own lifetimes. There's *William – an Englishman*, Cicely Hamilton's 1919 exploration of war; or *Someone at a Distance* (1953), in which Dorothy Whipple traces the effects of a man's infidelity on his family. Persephone's bestseller is *Miss Pettigrew Lives for a Day* (1938) by Winifred Watson, and it's worth checking out its 100th publication – a new collection of short stories.

Stanfords

12-14 Long Acre, WC2E 9LP (7836 1321, www.stanfords.co.uk). Covent Garden or Leicester Square tube. **Open** 9.30am-8pm Mon-Sat; noon-6pm Sun.

Escape the throngs of tourists on Long Acre by ducking for a breather into this inspirational travel shop. Stanfords is almost as essential to your trip as suntan lotion. In addition to every kind of travel guide, you'll find background literature on every conceivable destination, a specially selected fiction range, world music, a children's section and navigation software. The selection of equipment such as medical kits, binoculars and torches has also grown in recent years. Check out the giant maps on each floor, then go to the first floor and

Jarndyce. See p193.

have your very own customised map or aerial photo-graph printed out in poster form. Adding even more character, Stanfords stocks atlases and reproduction antique maps and guides. There's a café, too.

Watkins Books
19-21 Cecil Court, WC2N 4EZ (7836 2182, www.watkinsbooks.com). Leicester Square tube.
Open 10.30am-6.30pm Mon-Wed, Fri; 11am-7.30pm Thur, Sat; noon-7pm Sun.
This specialist in mysticism and spirituality is some-thing of an institution, having been established in 1897, and with the likes of occultist Aleister Crowley on its customer roll call. The company was on the brink of going bust in 2010, but the shop was saved by American entrepreneur Etan Ilfeld, who retained the former staff, and brought the shop back to life – a testament to people with passion. It stocks an exceptional selection of books on esoterica, including self help, alternative therapy, witchcraft, oriental religion, astrology and occultism titles from around the world. There's a large collection of good-quality second-hand (sometimes rare and col-lectable) titles, plus audiovisual material, personal talis-mans, healing crystals, jewellery and even daily-changing in-house astrologers and tarot readers.

Second-hand & antiquarian

The book stalls underneath Waterloo Bridge, near BFI Southbank, are a hotspot for browsers. **Goldsboro Books** (*see p189*) also sells some old first editions.

Any Amount of Books
56 Charing Cross Road, WC2H 0QA (7836 3697, www.anyamountofbooks.com). Leicester Square or Piccadilly Circus tube. **Open** 10.30am-9.30pm daily.
This Charing Cross stalwart seems to have smartened up a little over the last year; fear not, the bare floorboards and wooden shelving remain, but the stock seems easier to negotiate than in times past. Specialising principally in arts and literature, Any Amount is jam-packed with decent quality books on all subjects. Prices range from £1 to £2,000 (including, amusingly, a 'medium-rare' sec-tion). The shop had a scoop in 2007 by acquiring the library of Angela Carter; more recently, the books of noted *bon viveur* Norman Douglas and the late great Jeremy Beadle have made their way here. Diversifying a little never hurts business either, and the shop has devel-oped a sideline selling collections of leather bindings to interior decorators and set designers.

Bernard J Shapero

32 St George Street, W1S 2EA (7493 0876, www.shapero.com). Bond Street or Oxford Circus tube. **Open** 9.30am-6.30pm Mon-Fri.

Bernard J Shapero's interesting collection of antiquarian and out-of-print texts is enticingly displayed over four floors in these smart Mayfair premises. Specialisms here include travel (with a comprehensive collection of Baedeker guides) and colour-plate books. The shop's newest department deals with books from and about Russia, some of which are in Russian. There are also rare atlases and monographs of early photography. The shop began in Grays Antiques Market in 1979 and moved to Notting Hill before settling here over a decade ago; the range, presentation and, above all, quality of its beautiful volumes are second to none. One for the serious collector – though by no means unapproachable to the rest of us.

Henry Sotheran

2-5 Sackville Street, W1S 3DP (7439 6151, www.sotherans.co.uk). Green Park or Piccadilly Circus tube. **Open** 9.30am-6pm Mon-Fri; 10am-4pm Sat.

A fine old-fashioned place, Henry Sotheran combines quality, class and tradition – established in York back in 1761, the business moved to London nearly 200 years ago, in 1815 – with a surprisingly relaxed ambience. The extraordinary range of stock covers English literature (specialising in first and important editions of works from the 17th to the 20th centuries), children's and illustrated titles, travel and exploration, art and architecture, science and natural history. Departments are run by specialists, so novices can be assured of being guided by informed hands, while opportunities for collectors are abundant (past acquisitions have included the libraries of Laurence Sterne and Charles Dickens). Prices fittingly often run into the thousands here – a first edition of *The Origin of Species* sold for £82,000 recently – though they start at around £20. In recent years, greater emphasis has been placed on the shop's fine collection of prints and posters downstairs; two or three exhibitions are put on per year – vintage travel posters were a recent attraction.

Skoob

Jarndyce

46 Great Russell Street, WC1B 3PA (7631 4220, www.jarndyce.co.uk). Holborn or Tottenham Court Road tube. **Open** 11am-5.30pm Mon-Fri.

In Dickens's *Bleak House* Jarndyce and Jarndyce was the law case that consumed all the money the litigants were fighting over. In contrast, the stock in this charming bookshop, which is housed in a building dating back to the 1730s and located opposite the British Museum, is most reasonably priced, with exciting finds from £10. The shop does maintain its links to the great man himself, though, with a suitably large collection of Dickens that had been freshly catalogued on our last visit. The owners believe strongly in the durability and good value of 18th- or 19th-century titles – the focus of this fine institution. Other specialisms here include pamphlets, street literature, women writers, literature on London and chapbooks from the period. Proprietor Brian Lake is known for his publication *Fish Who Answer the Telephone And Other Bizarre Books* (co-edited with Russell Ash), along with other amusingly titled tomes.

Marchpane

16 Cecil Court, WC2N 4HE (7836 8661, www.marchpane.com). Leicester Square tube. **Open** 10.30am-6pm Mon-Sat.

Opened in 1989, London's longest-serving specialist for children's books, Marchpane, is the only bookshop we know with its own BBC Dalek. Other features are signed photos of Russian cosmonauts, punk fanzines and circuit board fixtures. Stock includes classics such as *Winnie-the-Pooh* and *The Wind in the Willows*, and the shop specialises in Lewis Carroll, with a collection of illustrated editions of *Alice's Adventures in Wonderland*, but you don't need to be a serious collector to appreciate the stock, which starts at around £10 and includes some real gems. Downstairs, near the gramophone and chaise-longue, are drawers housing periodicals from the 1930s to '60s.

Natalie Galustian Rare Books

22 Cecil Court, WC2N 4HE (7240 6822, www.nataliegalustian.com). Leicester Square tube. **Open** 10am-6pm Mon-Thur; 11am-7pm Fri-Sat.

A Cecil Court relative newcomer – open since 2010 in the former site of Red Snapper books – Natalie Galustian is a welcome new addition to the street, with some unique offerings. Specialising in first edition books, manuscripts and letters from 19th- and 20th-century English and American literature, it's also the place to head to for books and poetry focusing on the African-American and Caribbean experience, the Beat generation, early French exotica, Olympic Press editions and photography, vintage cookery and cocktails. There is an extensive collection of rare and new gambling books, with a particular focus on poker throughout the 18th, 19th and 20th centuries. Head downstairs for a gallery housing art and photography exhibitions.

Quinto/Francis Edwards

72 Charing Cross Road, WC2H 0BB (7379 7669, www.francisedwards.co.uk). Leicester Square tube. **Open** 9am-6pm Mon-Sat; 11.30am-5.30pm Sun.

A stalwart of Charing Cross Road, in 2010 Quinto and Francis Edwards moved from their premises at no.48A just up the road to no.72, but their remit remains the same: to sell antiquarian, rare, second-hand and collectable books and to continue their deservedly famous monthly wholesale change of stock, with new books brought regularly from Hay-on-Wye; lines of customers still extend down the street at 2pm on the chosen Sunday. There's a rolling stock of around 50,000 titles, so you'll really feel like you've earned your find, especially if you're rooting around the assortment of titles in the basement.

Skoob

Unit 66, The Brunswick, WC1N 1AE (7278 8760, www.skoob.com). Russell Square tube. **Open** 10.30am-8pm Mon-Sat; 10.30am-6pm Sun.

In 2008, Skoob returned to business in the Brunswick Centre and we're delighted to say it's still going strong. The 2,500sq ft of floor space may be in a basement with concrete walls and exposed piping, but the operation is light and airy, and recent reshuffles have made it easier to navigate the 60,000 titles on display, which cover almost every subject imaginable – from philosophy, biography, maths and science to languages, literature and criticism, art, history, economics and politics. Holdings are regularly refreshed with stock from the 950,000-volume warehouse in Oxford that's also run by personable owner Chris Edwards. Unlike its name, Skoob is not backward in coming forwards, and long may it continue. Note that there's a discount for students and Curzon cinema-goers.

Travis & Emery

17 Cecil Court, WC2N 4EZ (7240 2129, www.travis-and-emery.com). Covent Garden or Leicester Square tube. **Open** 10.15am-6.45pm Mon-Sat; 11.30am-4.30pm Sun.

Specialist second-hand music shops are thin on the ground in London; it's no surprise that the best one should be in Cecil Court, home of antiquarian publications and convenient for customers popping in for a browse before going to the nearby Coliseum Opera House. It stocks mostly collectors' music and related publications: libretti for operas, music history and theory books and collectable programmes and play-bills. Travis & Emery is strong on piano, violin, flute and organ music, but all music is catered for. Staff are musicians and very knowledgeable – ask them if you can't find something as they may have it in the basement storeroom. Upstairs is mainly sheet music, with reference works behind the counter. It's good for out-of-print music, and is popular with students; much of the second-hand stock is as good as new.

LEISURE

Records & CDs

General

Brill

27 Exmouth Market, EC1R 4QL (7833 9757, www. clerkenwellmusic.co.uk). Angel tube or Farringdon tube/rail. **Open** 7.30am-6.30pm Mon-Fri; 9am-6pm Sat; 10.30am-4pm Sun.

It's no misnomer: this small CD store/café has a strong local following and is a great place to add to your collection without being patronised by record fascists. Stock is CD-only; not all back-catalogue records make the cut and new releases only do if they're suitably interesting. You'll find a rock section that mixes classic albums by Joni Mitchell with newer releases from the Magnetic Fields, a soul rack where Marvin Gaye snuggles up to Frank Ocean, and eclectic jazz, reggae, pop, country and world sections. Overseeing the operation is Jeremy Brill himself, as affable as he is informed, cheerfully dispensing excellent coffee, daily-purchased Brick Lane bagels and locally produced baked goods for consumption at a smattering of seats (that now include a small back yard area).

Fopp

Fopp

1 Earlham Street, WC2H 9LL (7845 9770, www.foppreturns.com). Leicester Square or Tottenham Court Road tube. **Open** 10am-10pm Mon-Wed; 10am-11pm Thur-Sat; 12.30-7pm Sun.

Fopp's road has been a rocky one. The indie music store began its life as a one-man stall in a Glasgow arcade. At the height of its glory there were over 100 branches across the UK, now stripped back to the eight that were saved from administration by big uncle HMV. London's main three-storey branch in Covent Garden has arguably benefitted from the downsize – staff are knowledgeable and the atmosphere is calm and welcoming. Browse the ground floor for deals on classic CDs, DVDs and records that'll often leave you change from a fiver. Head upstairs for specialist music – the legendary 'suck it and see' policy replaces listening posts, giving you 21 days in which to sample your audio purchases at home before deciding whether you want to return them for a full refund. The basement holds an impressively in-depth cinema selection.

Branch (in Waterstones) 82 Gower Street, WC1E 6EQ (7636 8371).

HMV Megastore

150 Oxford Street, W1D 1DJ (7631 3423, www.hmv.com). Oxford Circus or Tottenham Court Road tube. **Open** 9am-8.30pm Mon-Wed, Fri, Sat; 9am-9pm Thur; 11.30am-6pm Sun.

Oxford Street's only remaining megastore – now that Virgin/Zavvi and Borders have bitten the dust – the HMV flagship is a first and last stop for CDs, records and DVDs covering all genres. The sensory overload may be too much for those who prefer the more relaxing and personalised atmosphere of some of the small independents, but there's no denying the width and breadth of the stock available here. Plus, if you head downstairs, the separate sections for classical and jazz and blues are quiet oases away from the hubbub. And if you're feeling lost, staff are always on hand to locate discs for you. With competitive seasonal sales, cut-price box sets and hundreds of rarities and imports, there's little chance you'll leave this world-beating behemoth of a store empty-handed.

Rough Trade East

Dray Walk, Old Truman Brewery, 91 Brick Lane, E1 6QL (7392 7788, www.roughtrade.com). Shoreditch High Street rail. **Open** 8am-9pm Mon-Thur; 8am-8pm Fri; 10am-8pm Sat; 11am-7pm Sun.

This infamous temple to indie music has never looked more upbeat, its new-found impetus provided by its venture east in August 2007. Rough Trade East's truly inspiring 5,000sq ft loft-style store, café and gig space offers aural beats and treats for Shoreditch's scenesters. The café boasts its own monthly-changing art gallery, sells smoothies, sarnies and beer; rock portraits

LEISURE

LEISURE

Rough Trade East

Kristina Records. See p198.

are hung around the seating area, while nu-psychedelic pop often floats out of the speakers. Both the vinyl and CD collections are dizzying in their range, spanning punk, hardcore, American and British indie, reggae, dub, funk, soul, post punk and new wave, with a large row of dance 12-inches, the highlight of which is the 'bastard pop' mash-up section. With 16 listening posts and free in-stores nearly every night of the week you can't get much closer to music nirvana.
Branch Rough Trade West 130 Talbot Road, W11 1JA (7229 8541).

Sister Ray

34-35 Berwick Street, W1F 8RP (7734 3297, www. sisterray.co.uk). Oxford Circus or Piccadilly Circus tube. **Open** 10am-8pm Mon-Sat; noon-6pm Sun.
Previously Selectadisc, Sister Ray remains a mecca for Berwick Street's beat obsessives on their lunchbreaks, with its flatscreen TV, customer turntables and turquoise walls – not to mention a hugely broad stock. Much of the music is on vinyl (over 20,000 plates and counting) and the shop's dedication to back-cataloguing albums in genres such as drum'n'bass, gothic, industrial and hip hop (with UK talent well represented) albums puts most megastores to shame. The selection of second-hand sixties and seventies records, covering everything from folk to prog rock, draws a specialist crowd. Staff are well informed and there are plenty of new-release CDs, music DVDs, T-shirts and books should the vinyl not appeal to you. If in doubt, check the tacky (and cheap) Sleeve of the Week outside for inspiration.

Second-hand

Note that retro electronics shop **Audio Gold** (*see p204*) has a second-hand vinyl department.

Flashback

50 Essex Road, N1 8LR (7354 9356, www. flashback.co.uk). Angel tube then 38, 56, 73, 341 bus. **Open** 10am-7pm Mon-Sat; noon-6pm Sun.
Flashback's mostly second-hand stock is treated with utmost respect. There are usually a few boxes of bargain basement 12-inches going for pennies outside the front door, but inside stock is scrupulously organised. The ground floor is dedicated to new-release vinyl and second-hand CDs, with rock and pop alongside dance, soundtracks, soul, jazz and metal. The large selection of 1960s psych, garage and hip hop is a well-kept secret among DJs. The basement is vintage vinyl only: an ever-expanding jazz collection jostles for space alongside soul, hip hop and an astonishing selection of library sounds (regularly plundered by producers looking for samples). Those not inclined to rummage can search out long-lost gems on its website.
Branch 144 Crouch Hill, N8 9DX (8342 9633).

Shop Talk
Shop Talk
Jack, co-owner of Kristina Records

Tell us about the shop
Kristina Records is a vinyl-only record shop in Dalston, which we opened in July 2011. We sell new and second-hand records across a wide spectrum of genres, mainly concentrating on underground music, for want of a better term. There are three of us who own and run the shop together: me (Jack Rollo), James Thornington and Jason Spinks. We all spent many years working behind the counter of other record shops and felt that east London was the perfect place to start our own shop. We also all grew up avidly collecting vinyl and the physical record shop has a very special place in our hearts. We see it not only as somewhere to buy but also as a social space, a place to talk about music, get recommendations and see bands and DJs perform. One year on, it really feels like we have become part of the flourishing community of musicians, labels and promoters who make up the thriving DIY music scene in east London.

What's special about it?
The key idea behind Kristina is that all the stock is curated. We only carry records that we love. It seems obvious, but we want to have a record shop with only good records in it. We aim to have a constantly changing high-quality stock, ranging from classic albums, obscure rarities and great reissues to the latest dance and underground rock releases. The way the shop looks and feels is also really important to us; the cliche of the specialist record shop is surly staff and dusty clutter and we hope to debunk this by providing a clean, well-designed space and friendly service. So many people are realising the joys of buying vinyl at the moment and I would hope our customers, from the ones who have just started collecting to the seasoned veterans, feel that Kristina is an approachable and exciting place to feed their vinyl habit. We also have regular in-store gigs and events: over the past year we've had some fantastic shows from the likes of Veronica Falls, Beautiful Swimmers, Raime, Ital, DJ Qu, Subway Sect, Comet Gain and Patrice Scott, to name just a few.

Who are your customers?
Our customers are, to put it simply, people who love vinyl. There's no real specific demographic. Dalston has a brilliant community of music lovers and it feels great to be a local shop providing them with great music old and new. We also get lots of customers from further afield. We sell a lot of records online as well as in the shop and we love it when our customers from around the world visit the shop when they are passing through London. It's really important for a shop like ours to build up regular customers and get to know people's tastes.

What are your favourite shops in London?
Being a record nerd I often find myself in record shops on my day off and there are still so many great ones: Phonica, Soul Jazz, Honest Jon's, Intoxica and Rough Trade. I buy books like crazy so Cecil Court is paradise. There are some great places around us in Dalston for clothes and furniture, like Pelicans & Parrots, Huh, and the Peanut Vendor.

What's the best thing about owning/ working in a shop?
Getting to get up every day and come into work to listen to and talk about music. Retail is all I've ever done and I love the relationships you build with your customers. From behind the counter of a shop I think you get a weird but very special insight into people's lives and meet people you never would otherwise.

LEISURE

On the Beat

Intoxica!

231 Portobello Road, W11 1LT (7229 8010,
www.intoxica.co.uk). Ladbroke Grove tube.
Open 10.30am-6.30pm Mon-Sat; noon-5pm Sun.
One of London's most idiosyncratically decorated
shops, Intoxica! – a vinyl-only store – is kitted out with
bamboo wall coverings and tribal masks. It makes for a
browsing experience that's as big on character as it is
on classic records. The ground-floor shelves are stacked
with everything from reggae, funk and '60s beat to exotica and easy listening; there's also a good range of alternative and new wave from the 1970s to today and a great
soundtrack selection. The basement is packed with soul
and blues, and its jazz section is especially big on British
artists. Note that the shop's future is uncertain, so phone
before making a special journey.

Kristina Records

44 Stoke Newington Road, N16 7XJ (7254 2130,
www.kristinarecords.com). Dalston Kingsland rail.
Open noon-8pm Mon-Fri; 11.30am-8pm Sat, Sun.
This Dalston record shop opened in July 2011, much to
the excitement of local music fans. Expect to find anything from funk, soul and indie to reggae and post-punk.
One of the strongest draws, however, is the contemporary

dance music section, which features all conceivable sub-
genres and styles of house and techno. Whether you're
inclined to the more industrial sounds of Detroit, or the
more soulful deep house of Europe, there is bound to be
something to excite your ears here. The owners are keen
to help you with your choices, and the atmosphere is
relaxed, with a listening point available to preview any
potential purchases. The shop also has a regular programme of in-store gigs from up-and-coming bands;
check the website or facebook for details.

On the Beat

22 Hanway Street, W1T 1UQ (7637 8934).
Tottenham Court Road tube. **Open** 11am-7pm
Mon-Sat.
Put thoughts of Norman Wisdom's 1967 police comedy
to one side: On the Beat is for record collectors of all
stripes. Spend 15 minutes thumbing here and you'll definitely come out with something you'd forgotten you
always wanted. The well-priced, mostly vinyl collection
is crammed into a small room, walls lined with posters
and dog-eared music mags that date back decades. In
manager Tim Derbyshire's words, the large collection
covers 'everything but classical' – you'll find a wealth of
old funk and soul albums, a huge number of library

LEISURE

sound compilations and a good range of jazz, country, folk and 'girl singers' records; the rock section covers everything from 1960s psychedelia to '90s pop.

Out on the Floor

10 Inverness Street, NW1 7HJ (7485 9958).
Camden Town tube. **Open** 11am-6pm daily.
This two-level, two-shop operation is a sanctuary for serious record collectors. In the basement you'll find Rok Pete's, specialising in guitar music – there's a particularly interesting selection of heavy metal seven-inches and plenty of punk, prog and 1960s and '70s rock. The ground floor hosts Up at Out on the Floor, home to the in-house reggae label, Tuff Scout Records, and boasting a well chosen collection of 12-inch reggae, 1960s soul and a limited array of CDs. Despite the unwieldy name, hand-drawn psychedelic signs for the 12-inches give the place a particular charm.

Reckless Records

30 Berwick Street, W1F 8RH (7437 4271, www.
reckless.co.uk) Oxford Circus tube. **Open** 10am-7pm Mon-Sat.
Duncan Kerr, general manager of Reckless Records, has been a loyal keeper of the company for over 25 years. When the company went bust in 2009 he bought up some of Reckless's old stock and opened on the location of the mini-chain's former dance music branch in Soho's Berwick Street. It sells everything from rare rock vinyl to classic drum'n'bass, as well as punk, reggae, jazz and a good range of original Mo' Wax and Blue Note vinyl. Reckless will buy most kinds of music and will make house calls for large buys. It also buys CD box sets, and limited editions.

Classical

Gramex

25 Lower Marsh, SE1 7RJ (7401 3830). Waterloo
tube/rail. **Open** 11am-7pm Mon-Sat.
Browsing here is as comfortable as flicking through a friend's collection; battered sofas and cuppas abound. The vast selection of quality used LPs and CDs is so constantly in flux that hundreds of records are cluttered on the central table while they await sorting. This is done by affable owner Roger Hewland, whose photographic memory is probably the only thing stopping the store sliding into chaos. The majority of the CD stock is taken up with a catalogue of composers past and present, with opera also well represented and an assortment of jazz comprising half the stock. Venture down to the basement for vinyl.

Harold Moores Records

2 Great Marlborough Street, W1F 7HQ (7437
1576, www.hmrecords.co.uk). Oxford Circus tube.
Open 10am-6.30pm Mon-Sat.

Honest Jon's. See p201.

LEISURE

Sounds of the Universe

Harold Moores is not your stereotypical classical music store: young, open-minded staff (including Tim Winter of Resonance FM) and an expansive stock of new and second-hand music bolster its credentials. This collection sees some great old masters complemented by a range of eclectic contemporary music, including plenty of avant-garde and electronic work from independent labels like Touch. Soft lighting, carpets and wood panelling create a cosy atmosphere, and there's plenty to appeal to amateur enthusiasts as well as aficionados. There's a suitably studious basement dedicated to second-hand classical vinyl and CDs, including an excellent selection of jazz.

Jazz, soul & dance

Kristina Records (*see p198*) has new and second-hand vinyl covering most genres, but is particularly strong on dance music.

BM Soho

25 D'Arblay Street, W1F 8EJ (7437 0478, www. bm-soho.com). Oxford Circus tube. **Open** 11am-7pm Mon-Wed, Sat; 11am-8pm Thur, Fri; noon-6pm Sun.
Junglist Nicky Blackmarket's BM Soho has kids queuing up to snag his latest promos. Don't come expecting anything other than upfront club music. On the ground floor you'll find house, minimal and techno. The basement remains London's most reliable dispenser of new and pre-release drum'n'bass, dubstep, bassline and UK garage. Downstairs is now also home to a small Dub Vendor concession – London's legendary dub and reggae peddlers. Both are kitted out in a futuristic black metallic finish that only amplifies the apocalyptic bass sounds emanating from the sound system. Come on a Friday afternoon when turntablists nod into their headphones trying out white labels for the weekend's sets and it can feel like you're already clubbing. DJs also head here for last-minute equipment – slip mats, needles, speakers and record bags reside at the back.

Honest Jon's

278 Portobello Road, W10 5TE (8969 9822, www.honestjons.com). Ladbroke Grove tube.
Open 10am-6pm Mon-Sat; 11am-5pm Sun.
This legendary record shop's owner had the good foresight to lend former hired hand James Lavelle £1,000 to set up Mo' Wax records in the early 1990s. Prints of old blaxploitation posters crowd the technicolour walls, a sign that jazz, soul, revival reggae and global sounds remain the house specialities. Honest Jon's has also branched out into many of the genres that for years relied on this very store for their samples: Berlin techno is well represented and peripheral dance genres like dubstep, post-dubstep and exotica also get a look in. The majority of the store's CD and vinyl collection is reserved for luminaries such as Parliament, Prince and Burning Spear.

Phonica

51 Poland Street, W1F 7LZ (7025 6070, www.phonicarecords.co.uk). Oxford Circus or Tottenham Court Road tube. **Open** 11.30am-7.30pm Mon-Wed, Sat; 11.30am-8pm Thur, Fri; noon-6pm Sun.
This is the go-to spot for London's club DJs looking for latest release records – there's no second-hand vinyl here. The doors are always flung open and staff are DJs-about-town – happy to help you dig out a hard-to-find disc or advise on the latest releases to suit your tastes. Finger through rack upon rack of pristinely selected records favouring the deeper and edgier side of electronic music. The broad focus is on house, disco, techno and dubstep but selections also journey through nu jazz, exotica, broken beat and hip hop flavours, and there are turntables in the store on which to listen to records. CDs are displayed on antique wooden tables, boasting the latest alt-indie and electronic releases, and box sets take pride of place in a glass cabinet.

Sounds of the Universe

7 Broadwick Street, W1F 0DA (7734 3430, www.soundsoftheuniverse.com). Tottenham Court Road tube. **Open** 11am-7.30pm Mon-Sat; 11.30am-5.30pm Sun.
Bright and breezy, this stylish sound store in the heart of Soho has universal appeal. Its affiliation with reissue kings Soul Jazz records means its remit is broad. This is especially true on the ground floor (new vinyl and CDs), where grime and dubstep 12-inches jostle for space alongside new wave cosmic disco, electro-indie re-rubs, Nigerian compilations and some electronic madness. A good number of listening posts offer insights into a diverse mix of new releases from Venetian Snares to Soul II Soul legend Jazzie B, while the second-hand vinyl basement is big on soul, jazz, Brazilian and alt-rock.

Soundtracks, shows & nostalgia

Dress Circle

57-59 Monmouth Street, WC2H 9DG (7240 2227, www.dresscircle.co.uk). Leicester Square tube. **Open** 10am-6.30pm Mon-Sat; noon-5pm Sun.
This OTT luvvy-magnet and temple to show tunes is still a West End hit after more than 30 years. It continues to wow professional thesps and drama queens alike with its staggering collection of show tunes on CD and DVD (featuring popular classics like *The Sound of Music* and plenty of more obscure gems). A range of posters celebrates productions past and present; Stephen Sondheim, Barry Manilow and Barbara Cook are regulars here. Plus, there's specialist memorabilia – an old programme signed by Noel Coward might just be perfect gift. Note that Dress Circle may re-locate in 2013 – phone to check before making a special trip.

LEISURE

Electronics & Photography

Despite quite a few recent economy related shop closures, the Oxford Street end of Tottenham Court Road is still electronics heaven, and includes the **Sony Centre Galleria** (no.22-24), the specialist **Samsung-Bose Centre** (no.20-21), **Shasonic**'s Panasonic store (no.28) and **Ask** (*see below*).

General Electronics

Ask

248 Tottenham Court Road, W1T 7QZ (7637 0353, www.askdirect.co.uk). Tottenham Court Road tube. **Open** 10am-7pm Mon-Wed, Fri, Sat; 10am-8pm Thur; noon-6pm Sun.

Ask is a virtual palace in comparison with the other shops along this stretch of Tottenham Court Road, providing four floors of stock, more assistants than you can shake a stick at and a lofty, uncluttered feel. Staff are very helpful but not overly pushy – they're trained by the manufacturers themselves so they're kept up to date with new technology and are always willing to impart their knowledge. A 'try before you buy' policy is a further plus. Ask also has a comprehensive and competitively priced online store supplying some 10,000 different lines, with an emphasis on popular items like home-cinema packages, hi-fi equipment, laptops (no Macs though – although iPads and iPods are sold), digital cameras, camcorders, sat navs, MP3 players and DAB radios. Online customers can opt for either a delivery or pick-up service.

Maplin

166-168 Queensway, W2 6LY (7229 9301, www.maplin.co.uk). Bayswater or Queensway tube. **Open** 9am-8pm Mon-Fri; 9am-6pm Sat; 11am-6pm Sun.

The beauty of this popular nationwide chain is the sheer scale of random electronics kit available, from satellite systems, speakers, hard drives, motherboards and computer cables to wireless phone line extenders, USB turntables and roll-up pianos. Mixers, turntables, amps and disco lighting do a roaring trade with the capital's DJs, while gadget fiends are well catered for with metal detectors, a variety of radio-controlled toys, solar-powered battery chargers, even underwater CCTV surveillance systems (honestly). The size of the shop often dictates the range of gear on offer (this branch has two floors), but you can safely expect a decent smattering of essentials at most of the 40 spacious stores located throughout the London area (dial 0844 557 6000 for HQ enquiries or go to the Maplin website). Note: because there's such a mind-boggling choice, use the power of the internet to narrow your preferences and check for stock availability before setting off (the more centralised shops tend to be smaller).
Branches throughout the city.

Computers

Apple Centre

Selfridges & Co, 400 Oxford Street, W1A 1AB (7318 1361, www.squaregroup.co.uk). Bond Street tube. **Open** 9.30am-10pm Mon-Sat; 10am-8pm Sun.

Recently relocated to Selfridges, the Apple Centre is an authorised reseller of Apple products, hard, soft and in between. iMacs start from £999, MacBook Airs from £849 and MacBook Pros from £999. The centre also sells iPods and iPads, as well as a tempting selection of accessories. To get the full sonic effect, high quality Bose speakers are on offer, as well as top-notch headphones from Sennheiser and B&W. The store also provides training courses in using Apple products (including tutorials on iWeb and iMovie software) and there's a quick turnaround repair service too that, unlike Apple Stores, requires no pre-booked appointment. Extended warranties are available on most products.

Apple Store. See p204.

LEISURE

Audio Gold. See p204.

Apple Store

1-7 The Piazza, WC2E 8HA (7447 1400, www.apple.com). Covent Garden tube. **Open** 9am-9pm Mon-Sat; noon-6pm Sun.

The three-storey London flagship for one of the world's most successful companies is also, at the time of writing, still the biggest Apple Store in the world. Sitting opposite Covent Garden Market in a grade II-listed columned building, it's as hip and beautiful as one might expect, with exposed brickwork, big oak tables and stone floors. All the latest Apple products can be found here – compact MacBook Pro and MacBook Air notebooks, iMac desktops, the ubiquitous iPhone and iPad, the full range of iPods and the impressive Apple TV system. The store also stocks a vast range of accessories, including speakers, headphones and app-enabled toys and games. Head to the long Genius Bar for free one-to-one technical support (pre-bookable), or wise up on technical matters with the help of free workshops in the Community Room. There's also a Start Up Room, where staff will help set up your new iPad, iPhone, iPod or Mac, or transfer files from your old computer to your new one – all for free. This is the kind of futuristic store you dreamed about as a kid. If you were a nerdy kid.

Branches 235 Regent Street, W1B 2EL (7153 9000); Westfield London, W12 7GF (8433 4600); Brent Cross, Upper West Mall, NW4 3FP (8359 1050); The Arcade, Westfield Stratford City, E20 1EQ (8277 2200).

Hi-fi

Audio Gold

308-310 Park Road, N8 8LA (8341 9007, www. audiogold.co.uk). Finsbury Park tube/rail then W7 bus. **Open** 10am-6pm Mon-Sat.

With its mix of used, new (mainly DAB radios) and hireable audio products – as well as second-hand vinyl – Audio Gold is one of the best places in London to track down old-school equipment, from ghetto blasters to amplifiers from the 1960s, '70s and '80s (Britain's golden decades of audio production). The shop, located in an old bank building, is a well-known haunt for Crouch End's community of musicians, who are often seen in the space chatting to the affable owners, Richard and Ben, over a coffee. The extensive 'prop hire' section is not only a celebration of all the 'strange and beautiful' machines the owners have picked up over the years but it's a boon for those in the media and film industries looking to set the scene with an original Walkman or a genuine 1980s clock-radio. Equipment is also rented out for parties and events. The list of audio manufacturers covered includes typical brands like Sony, Toshiba, Denon, Tivoli and Pure but, by and large, most of the products here are comprised of names from a realm well beyond the high street's vocabulary: turntables by Linn, speakers by Quad and Spendor, amps by Sugden and Meridian, and reel-to-reel tape machines by Teac and Akai. Audio Gold also buys your second-hand equipment – as long as it works.

Aperture Photographic

Grahams

*Unit 1, Canonbury Yard, 190A New North Road,
N1 7BS (7226 5500, www.grahams.co.uk). Essex
Road rail or 271 bus.* **Open** 10am-6pm Tue, Wed;
10am-8pm Thur; 9am-6pm Fri, Sat.

Hidden away in the backstreets of De Beauvoir Town,
Grahams certainly won't be doing any casual business
with passing pedestrians. Those who come here make
the pilgrimage because they are ready to compile a top-
quality hi-fi/home-cinema system with a lot of care and
deliberation – there are four demo rooms available for
this purpose – and are willing to spend a very large
sum of money in the process. Probably the longest-
established of all competitors in town (its predecessor,
Grahams Electrical, opened in Clerkenwell in 1929), the
shop is guided by a policy of uncompromising quality,
whatever the cost. Consequently, the majority of its
components (amps, speakers, HD TV equipment and
wireless streaming audio) demand four-figure sums.
Grahams' carefully crafted list of manufacturers
includes Linn, Loewe, Miller & Kreisel, B&W, Spendor,
Classe, Naim, Rega, Meridian and a few others that
share the same lofty and rarefied tier.

Oranges & Lemons

*61-63 Webb's Road, SW11 6RX (7924 2040,
www.oandlhifi.co.uk). Clapham Junction rail.*
Open 10am-6pm Mon, Tue, Thur-Sat; (late
opening Thur by appointment only).

Laid-back and friendly, Oranges & Lemons is one of the
better places in south London to buy hi-fi separates
(individual units that combine to make up a complete
audio system) and home-cinema equipment. The test
rooms are cosy and homely, serving as both a pleasant
environment for your shopping experience and, more
importantly, a fairly accurate representation of how a
particular audio set-up will work in an average living
room. Systems of any size, complexity and price range
can be assembled – right up to a full, wireless multi-room
AV solution – but you could also come here to upgrade
just one component of an existing system. O&S's current
line includes prestigious brands like Sonos, Linn, Naim,
Arcam, B&W, Rega, Neat and PMC. Bear in mind that
the shop is often busy so you may not get a test room
immediately – you can, however, book a demonstration
in advance.

Photography

Aperture Photographic

*44 Museum Street, WC1A 1LY (7242 8681,
www.apertureuk.com). Holborn or Tottenham
Court Road tube.* **Open** 11am-7pm Mon-Fri;
noon-7pm Sat.

Frequented by camera enthusiasts and paparazzi
downloading their latest scoops, this retail store-

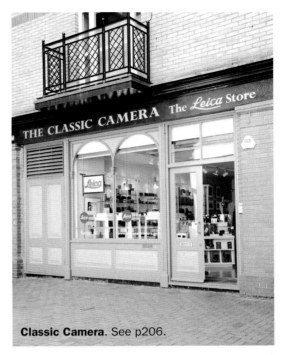

Classic Camera. See p206.

LEISURE

cum-café has a buzzing atmosphere. The photographic side centres on an excellent selection of vintage manual and autofocus Nikons, Leicas, Canons and Hasselblads, along with a sprinkling of other brands. Prices are reasonable too, while offers for unwanted gear are among the more generous in town. The café serves coffees, teas and juices, as well as sandwiches, stir-fries and cookies, giving you something to chew on while jawing over the relative merits of Leica lenses and Canon zooms. Most of the staff are photography enthusiasts and are happy to answer any questions.

Camera City

16 Little Russell Street, WC1A 2HL (7813 2100, www.cameracity.co.uk). Tottenham Court Road tube. **Open** 10am-6pm Mon-Fri; 10.30am-2pm Sat; 11am-2pm Sun.

One of a cluster of second-hand photography outlets to be found within a stone's throw of each other, this diminutive Aladdin's cave is a great place to grab a classic Pentax, Canon, Nikon or Olympus camera. Its range of vintage accessories includes small-but-important things such as replacement tripod bushes and flash adaptors. Apart from retail sales, the store has a well-regarded and generally speedy repair service for both film and digital cameras; a postal service is available if you can't come in personally. Note that credit cards aren't accepted but debit cards are fine.

Classic Camera

2 Pied Bull Yard, off Bury Place, WC1A 2JR (7831 0777, www.theclassiccamera.com). Holborn tube. **Open** 9.30am-6pm Mon-Fri; 10am-4.30pm Sat.

This isn't the place for anyone on a tight budget, since 90% of the stock here is of Leica origin – we're talking £3,000 plus for a camera. The rest of the stock isn't exactly light on the wallet either, with esoteric brands like Voigtlander rubbing shoulders with top-of-the-range compacts from household names like Panasonic, Nikon, Sony and Fuji. There's a big focus on rangefinder cameras here, which have traditionally been the snappers of choice for street photographers, à la Henri Cartier-Bresson. Apart from cameras and lenses, you'll find binoculars by Leica, Zeiss, Steiner and Minox, and accessories including Billingham bags, Gitzo tripods and Artisan & Artist straps, as well as a decent selection of photographic books by famed Leica users such as Korda and Brassaï. Staff service and repair Leica cameras too, promising to try and fix anything made by the German company.

Lomography Gallery Store

Jessops

63-69 New Oxford Street, WC1A 1DG (0845 458 7201, www.jessops.com). Tottenham Court Road tube. **Open** 9am-8pm Mon-Sat; noon-6pm Sun.

This country-wide chain is an ideal one-stop shop for most photographic needs. All 21 London branches specialise in consumer-based products but you'll also find a decent range of 'prosumer' equipment too. As most of the cameras are on display and not tucked behind a counter, it's easy to get some hands-on experience with your intended purchase, whether it be a quality SLR, a slim compact or that sharp new lens you've been dying to try. All the major Japanese camera and lens brands are stocked, along with a decent selection of accessories. Prices are very competitive, which isn't surprising given the ever-threatening online marketplace. Jessops also runs an excellent, tried-and-tested personal printing service for photographic books, calendars, canvases and wall art. **Branches** throughout the city.

Lomography Gallery Store

3 Newburgh Street, W1F 7RE (7434 1466, www.lomography.com). Oxford Circus tube. **Open** 10am-7pm Mon-Sat; noon-6pm Sun.

The Lomography movement was a phenomenon that began in the 1990s when a group of art students from Austria rediscovered the Lomo LC-A 35mm Soviet-era compact; and so began a nostalgia for the 'good old days', when Polaroid cameras were considered cutting-edge and no holiday pic collection was complete without the oddly framed, weirdly lit or unfocused snapshot. Opened in 2009, with its logo 'The Future is Analogue', Lomography stocks a collection of reissued 'toy' cameras such as the Diana from Hong Kong, the Chinese Holga and the Russian Lomo, as well as fisheyes, pinholes, film stock and some lovely accessories. Check out the Lomowall with over 14,000 'Lomographs'. A film processing lab is located at the Commercial Street branch.
Branch 117 Commercial Street, E1 6BG (7426 0999).

MW Classic Cameras

Unit 3K, Leroy House, 436 Essex Road, N1 3QP (7354 3767, www.mwclassic.com). Angel tube then 38, 73, 341, 476 bus. **Open** by appointment only Mon-Sat.

The owners of MW Classic Cameras, Mahendra Modi and David Woodford (hence the company name), are enthusiastic and knowledgeable. Their much-visited website sells rare and collectable cameras and photographic equipment, with a wide range of brands stocked, including Leica, Hasselblad, Pentax, Rollei and

LEISURE

Teamwork

Voigtlander, as well as an interesting selection of old Soviet-era cameras. Of course, pride of place goes to Leica, and there are many collectable examples for sale. MW also sells some fascinating examples of old plate and box cameras. This is ostensibly a mail order firm but you're welcome to pop into the office, as long as you call first to make an appointment.

Nicholas Camera Company

15 Camden High Street, NW1 7JE (7916 7251, www.nicholascamera.com). Mornington Crescent tube. **Open** 10.30am-6pm Mon-Sat.

An interestingly shambolic buy-sell-exchange emporium, the Nicholas Camera Company sells all sorts of old and modern cameras dating from as far back as the 1800s. It's best to have a clear idea of what you want before you visit – rather than browsing, you have to tell the shopkeeper what you're after and he goes off and has a look. In addition to stock from the more familiar SLR brands (Canon, Nikon, Pentax), you'll also find large-format giants by the likes of Horseman, Linhof and Sinar, medium-format cameras from Hasselblad and Mamiya, and a range of accessories, darkroom kits and used top-drawer digital equipment. The shop also runs a repair service.

Teamwork

41-42 Foley Street, W1W 7JN (7323 6455, www.teamworkphoto.com). Goodge Street tube. **Open** 9am-5.30pm Mon-Fri.

Teamwork specialises in high-end digital camera backs and medium- to large-format models, as well as light meters, flash guns, photographic filters, reflectors, video equipment, panoramic cameras, tripods and monopods, bags, backgrounds and props. There is also a large selection of Hasselblad equipment. Although the shop caters mainly to the professional market, the knowledgeable and helpful vendors are more than happy to advise and help amateurs too – just not where compact cameras are concerned. Along with a selection of quality used equipment, Teamwork also runs a rental service for cameras, video rigs, lighting equipment and computers. Repairs are also undertaken.

York Cameras

18 Bury Place, WC1A 2JL (7242 7182, www.york cameras.co.uk). Holborn tube. **Open** 9.30am-5pm Mon-Fri; 10am-3pm Sat.

Staffed by a team of seasoned experts, each of whom is a dedicated photographer, York Cameras (a Canon Pro Centre) stocks an impressive selection of both new and used cameras, as well as lots of accessories like lenses, filters, tripods and gadget bags. The shop was first established in 1971 on York Road (which explains the name) before moving to its current address in 2000. Factor in the attentive service, and it's little wonder this trusted store continues to attract such a loyal, discerning clientele.

Crafts, Hobbies & Parties

Art & craft supplies

Atlantis European

Britannia House, 68-80 Hanbury Street, E1 5JL (7377 8855, www.atlantisart.co.uk). Aldgate East or Whitechapel tube or Shoreditch High Street rail. **Open** 9am-6pm Mon-Sat; 10am-5pm Sun.

Fine artists at all stages of their careers, from primary school children after pots of glitter paint right up to professionals looking for Sennelier oils in the most obscure hue head to this great art warehouse in the East End. It caters mostly for the sketcher and painter, rather than the craftsperson. There are thousands of tubes of paint from familiar names such as Winsor & Newton, Old Holland and David Hockney's favourite, Michael Harding Oils. Then there are pencils, brushes, cutting tools and adhesives, and big-money purchases such as easels. Pretty much everything and anything that an artist might need is sold at competitive prices. The staff are lovely and students can ask for a 10% discount. Frames are sold downstairs, but ring ahead to check the size you need is in stock.

Cass Art

66-67 Colebrooke Row, N1 8AB (7354 2999, www.cassart.co.uk). Angel tube. **Open** 10am-7pm Mon-Wed, Fri, Sat; 10am-8pm Thur; 11am-5.30pm Sun.

Not only artists, but stationery fetishists everywhere just love Cass for cheer-up fineliners and quality pocket sketchbooks. This is the flagship store, where the Cass legend – 'let's fill this town with artists' – really holds true. On the three floors are all the sketchbooks, easels, modelling clay, paints, inks, pastels you'll ever need to live a more creative life. Here, and in the Hampstead branch, there are regular events and workshops to inspire and assist participants – some are free, others provide the materials you'll need. Look out for the regular student days, when your card gets you 15% discount on the already competitive prices. The best thing about Cass is its young, friendly 'can do' vibe, which is infectious. **Branches** 13 Charing Cross Road, WC2H 0EP (7930 9940); 24 Berwick Street, W1F 8RD (7287 8504); 220 Kensington High Street, W8 7RG (7937 6506); 58-62 Heath Street, NW3 1EN (7435 5479).

Green & Stone

259 King's Road, SW3 5EL (7352 0837, www.greenandstone.com). Sloane Square tube, then 11, 19, 22 bus. **Open** 9am-6pm Mon-Fri; 9.30am-6pm Sat; noon-5pm Sun.

Cass Art

L Cornelissen & Son

This venerable artists' institution celebrated 85 years in Chelsea in 2012. It opened in 1927, and has been in its current location on the King's Road since 1934, when what was a framing business for the many local artists, with art supplies attached, set up shop in a former women's suffrage movement shop. When you visit you feel like you're stepping back in time – and not just because you're treated with the utmost politeness, even if you're only after birthday card-making materials for your child (there's a small children's department in the craft and modelling area downstairs). The emphasis is on quality: you'll find only the finest art supplies here. Expect oil paints by Michael Harding, Sennelier, Charvin and Winsor & Newton; watercolours by Schmincke; and acrylics by Goldren, Liquitex and Daler Rowney. As well as the paints, there's a comprehensive selection of calligraphy tools and paper, along with print-making paraphernalia, graphic design gear and brushes of every size and specification. There's still a framing service, one of the best in London, but these days the arts supplies branch of the business has caught up with it.

L Cornelissen & Son

105 Great Russell Street, WC1B 3RY (7636 1045, www.cornelissen.com). Tottenham Court Road tube. **Open** 9.30am-5.30pm Mon-Sat.
The original 'artists colourmen', this is a most delightful (Grade II-listed) shop to visit. It was established by Louis Dieudonne Cornelissen in 1855 and still looks like some old apothecary from a storybook. Staff are, gratifyingly, most polite and eager to help you find the pigment and quality of paint you require, even if you're just a dauber. The store attracts serious artists, and always has done (Ford Madox Brown and Dante Gabriel Rossetti bought their burnt umbers and rose madders here). Specialities include gilding, printmaking and restoration, and of course hundreds of paints. As well as top-quality printing and painting materials, the shop also sells calligraphy equipment, paper, painting sets and feather quills. A worldwide mail order service is available.

London Graphic Centre

16-18 Shelton Street, WC2H 9JL (7759 4500, www.londongraphics.co.uk). Covent Garden or Leicester Square tube. **Open** 10am-6.30pm Mon-Fri; 10.30am-6pm Sat; noon-5pm Sun.
These supply stores for graphic artists exist where media types tend to congregate. This is the flagship store for a company that has become one of London's biggest players in the art and design community. You can fit out a studio with plan chests, drawing tables and lightboxes, as well as buy supplies of board and paper, printing equipment and stationery. Hobby artists and designers should find all they need in the way of pens, brushes, craft materials, paints and adhesives. The shop also houses sporadic exhibitions (a free mould-making for plaster cast models class was coming up

when we visited), and special 20%-off student days. It's good for gift items too – think Lomography cameras, old-fashioned wind-up tin toys, Eames mugs and Moleskine notebooks, journals and bags.
Branches 13 Tottenham Street, W1T 2AH (7637 2199); 86 Goswell Road, EC1V 7DB (7253 1000); 54 York Way, N1 9AB (7833 8782).

Shepherds Falkiners

76 Southampton Row, WC1B 4AR (7831 1151, www.bookbinding.co.uk). Holborn or Russell Square tube. **Open** 10am-6pm Mon-Fri; 10am-5pm Sat.
This branch of the long-established bookbinding suppliers is now known as Shepherd's Falkiners. Here, in this atmospheric store, you can learn to bind a book, make prints, indulge in Turkish marbling or make pop-up cards. The range of decorative paper for craft projects, bookbinding and present-wrapping is superb: Japanese and Nepalese tissues and fine lightweights in gorgeous silk-screened designs are beautifully delicate and there are some striking marbled English patterns from the 18th century among the French, Florentine and Dutch decoratives. If you want actual bookbinding services, head to the bindery in Victoria (which also undertakes restorations and framing). Here you can get a photograph album bound in one of 150 choices of book cloth (do make an appointment before you visit, though). If you want to do the binding yourself, however, you can find the sewing thread, glue, paper-making equipment and tools you'll need here and at the Mayfair branch, along with stationery, framing services and decorative papers.
Branches 76 Rochester Row (The Bindery), SW1P 1JU (7233 6766); 46 Curzon Street, W1J 7UH (7495 8580).

Beading & jewellery-making

Beadworks Bead Shop

21A Tower Street, WC2H 9NS (7240 0931, www.beadworks.co.uk). Covent Garden or Leicester Square tube. **Open** 10.30am-7pm Mon-Sat; 11am-5pm Sun.
Back in the 1970s the original Covent Garden Bead Shop was where the resident hippy-dippies procured the wherewithal for multicoloured bracelets and dread-beads. Since then, several city bead merchants have combined to form Beadworks and the stock has became a tad more sophisticated, with semi-precious stones, crystals and all the accessories, tools, chains and findings jewellery makers need to create original pieces. There are still little bags of bog-standard mixed plastic beads, or novelty types in the shape of skulls or Christmas trees or Easter chicks (depending on the season). More serious baubles include the precision-cut crystal beads by Swarovski or the vintage rose freshwater pearls: they're for amateur jewellers who want

their pieces to look professional. To that end, Beadworks also holds £92 one-day beading classes. Check the website for free beading and jewellery making demos, which show you how to make the most of the wide-ranging stock: at more than 6,000 items it's one of the largest ranges in Europe.

Fabrics

Soho's **Berwick Street** has been home to some of the best textile shops in town for decades.

Berwick Street Cloth Shop

14 Berwick Street, W1F 0PP (7287 2881, www.theberwickstreetclothshop.com). Oxford Circus tube. **Open** 9am-6pm Mon-Fri; 9am-5pm Sat.
The knowledgeable materialists know their cloth here, and are only too willing to fossick about among the rolls of unusual and beautiful fabrics to find what you're after. The staff are, after all, used to dealing with demanding customers, as their legendary shop is a leading supplier of fabrics to the film, theatre, interior design, fashion and bridal industries. The range is second to none, and includes some real stars: delicate beaded tulle, gossamer-thin, intricate lace, soft velvets, satin brocades and embroidered silks, along with all the taffetas, chiffons, nettings and wool blends to suit all occasions. There's also a bespoke service, so you can commission a fabric you've seen in a picture, or design your own pattern to be made up for a one-off dress. It's also possible to have your own fabric beaded to your specifications. BSCS's sister companies, Broadwick Silks (9-11 Broadwick Street, 7734 3320, www.broadwicksilks.com) and the Silk Society (44 Berwick Street, 7287 1881, www.thesilksociety.com), are both a stone's throw away, and carry some show-stopping brocades, feather fabrics and specialist sequins.

Borovick Fabrics

16 Berwick Street, W1F 0HP (7437 2180, www.borovickfabricsltd.co.uk). Oxford Circus tube. **Open** 8.30am-6pm Mon-Fri; 8.15am-5pm Sat.
Costume designers on big budget movies and West End shows, fashion students from Central St Martins, small-scale dressmakers and hobby crafters all rate this place highly. The 80-year-old Borovik family name is a byword for excellent fabrics, for soft furnishings as well as fashion. Any kind of material can be found here: luxurious silks (an extensive range of Bennett silks is displayed) and crushed velvets, fine lace for weddings and party dresses, workaday corduroy and twill, and fancy embroidered tulles, beaded fabrics and brocades.

Cloth House

47 Berwick Street, W1F 8SJ (7437 5155, www.clothhouse.com). Oxford Circus tube. **Open** 9.30am-6pm Mon-Fri; 10.30am-6pm Sat.

Even if your textiles experience is limited to unpleasant school needlework memories, the Cloth Shop will pique a new-found interest in dressmaking. Its irresistible window displays draw you in to examine great rolls of delicately dyed cheesecloth and muslin, hand-woven cotton, soft silks and satins, woollens and denims. Materials are sourced from around the world, so you can use block-printed Indian cotton or Thai hand-printed hemp to create unusual home accessories. Then there are all the trimmings – bobbins and spools of them – alongside enticing trays of buttons.
Branch 98 Berwick Street, W1F 0QJ (7287 1555).

Joel & Son Fabrics

73-83 Church Street, NW8 8EU (7724 6895, www.joelandsonfabrics.com). Edgware Road tube. **Open** 8.30am-5.30pm Mon-Sat.
Away from the Berwick Street axis is this high-fashion fabric collection. For many couture fans, this is the finest fabric shop in the world. The range of stock is indeed breathtaking. The luxury stuff excites: there are so many different types and weights of silk and satin in a fabulous range of colours and prints from Italy and Switzerland, and bolts of exclusive beaded and printed ballgown material. As well as all this high-end stuff, though, there are well-priced printed cottons and suitings for tailors and dressmakers, alongside accessories, buttons and trims. The staff are helpful and can make suggestions if you're not sure what you're after.

Haberdashery & buttons

John Lewis (*see p22*) has a strong haberdashery department, while **Cloth House** (*see left*) and **Persiflage** (at Alfie's Antiques Market – 7724 7366, 13-25 Church Street, NW8 8DT), have great selections of vintage buttons.

Button Lady

12 Heath Street, NW3 6TE (7435 5412, www.buttonladyhampstead.co.uk). Hampstead tube. **Open** 10.30am-5pm Tue-Fri; 10am-6pm Sat; 11.30am-5.30pm Sun.
Antique buttons arranged in pretty jars are now the stock in trade of interior decorators of the vintage variety, but this tiny boutique has been charming its visitors with that look for more than 30 years. A nightmare for koumpounophobics she may be, but the Button Lady is a delight to spend time with. Riffle through the little tins, stands and cardboard boxes to find the button of your dreams and ask its price. Don't be shocked, some of these antique beauties are superbly detailed. Exquisite antique finds glint amid the piles of stock: tiny enamelled designs, hand-painted with roses, say, or Bohemian pressed glass buttons. The art deco button collection has some particularly stylish options. As well as buttons, velvet and silk scarves, shawls and pashminas are also stocked, along with smart bags, hats and jewellery.

Button Queue

76 Marylebone Lane, W1U 2PR (7935 1505, www.thebuttonqueen.co.uk). Bond Street tube.
Open 10am-5.30pm Mon-Fri; 10am-3pm Sat.
Queen Toni of the buttons has retired, but her son and his partner have taken over this 60-year-old button business. There are so many buttons, ancient and modern, valuable and available for small change, all prettily displayed in cases and cupboards. Dressmakers and accessorisers browse long and hard to find the exact shade, material, size and shape for their needs. You can find 19th-century picture buttons, 1920s antique art nouveau designs and art deco plastics, not to mention Bimini glass buttons, enamels and oversized contemporary styles. Away from the decorative, there are sensible blazer buttons, tailors' buttons, understated dinner jacket styles and toggles for a duffel. Beautiful pearl and silver buttons turn an ordinary cashmere cardigan into a semi-precious object, and if you can't find the exact style you're after, staff will cheerfully hunt that button down. A button-covering service is also offered, and the company can even arrange to have buttons dyed to match the colour of a fabric.

Kleins

5 Noel Street, W1F 8GD (7437 6162, www.kleins.co.uk). Oxford Circus or Tottenham Court Road tube.
Open 10am-5pm Mon-Fri.

Button Queen

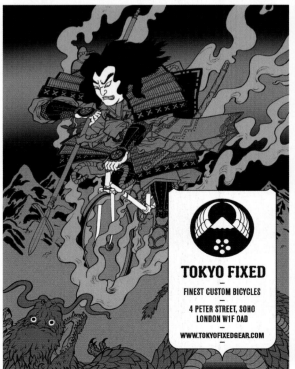
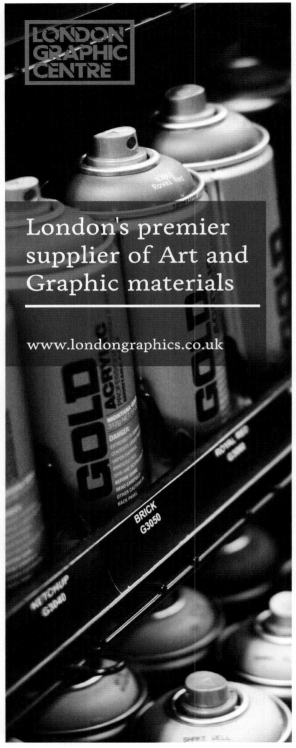

Those among us who are handy with our needles cannot rave enough about this Soho haberdashery. It has all the trimmings, from essentials, such as bias bindings and zips, to the frivolous: you never know when you might need a fun fur edging on something. The range of braids, ribbons, lacy and silky trims, beaded edgings and sparkling diamante buckles and buttons satisfies magpie crafters, and then there are all the tools for the trade, too: pincushions, needles, handles and frames for bag making, hooks for corsetry and dyes and glues for clothes customising.

MacCulloch & Wallis

25-26 Dering Street, W1S 1AT (7629 0311, www.macculloch-wallis.co.uk). Bond Street or Oxford Circus tube. **Open** 10am-6pm Mon-Wed, Fri; 10am-7pm Thur; 10.30am-5pm Sat.

This handsome shop has everything for the amateur and professional stitcher. It's lovely for a browse, especially for those little essential trims you never thought you'd need: sparkly sew-on feather fringes, furry pom-poms, beaded floral sprays. The fabric department is extensive and attractive, then there are the big money purchases, such as tailors' dummies and Bernina sewing machines. There's a load of obscure stuff too: for those interested in corsetry, it has steel boning, while milliners after wires and hat blocks are also spoilt for choice. It's a source of fascination for young textile students, too: the very young might fancy cutting their tailoring teeth on a craft kit, to make their own cuddly toy.

VV Rouleaux

102 Marylebone Lane, W1U 2QD (7224 5179, www.vvrouleaux.com). Bond Street tube. **Open** 9.30am-6pm Mon, Tue, Fri, Sat; 10.30am-6pm Wed; 9.30am-6.30pm Thur.

Rolls and rolls of ribbons, in so many lovely colours; it's almost impossible to resist them and they go down a storm in the festive season. Of course, ribbons aren't just for Christmas, or just to tie up your bonny brown hair, as VVR has proved, having been awarded 'cool brand status' in 2004. Ribbons finish off outfits, trim hats and cushions and turn a bunch of flowers into a piece of art. As well as the ribbons (the VV Rouleaux range is also sold at John Lewis), there are braids, trimmings, feathers, butterflies and eye-catching corsages. Downstairs you'll find furnishing trimmings, including ties, tassles and fringing, as well as jewellery, vintage bridal headdresses, veils and flowers. Staff are happy to offer decorating tips and ideas.

Knitting & needlecraft

Fabrications

7 Broadway Market, E8 4PH (7275 8043, www.fabrications1.co.uk). London Fields rail. **Open** noon-5pm Tue-Fri, Sun; 10am-5.30pm Sat.

Fabrications

The likeable Barley Massey is the force of nature behind this ecologically sound shop, studio, gallery and public workshop. The unusual pieces in the haberdashery and knitting stock are all carefully chosen to inspire customers to make do and mend, salvage stuff they would throw away, customise and revitalise and be creative. This is known as 'upcycling' (one up from recycling and a whole lot cheaper and more sustainable than buying new). Among the regularly changing offerings, you might find beautiful knitted flowers and toys, bags, or Massey's cushions made from vintage fabrics. The shop also does a good line in seasonal items, cards and gifts, often from local creatives, as well as Hackney mementoes. There's a lovely eco classroom and events space, and the workshops, where everyone gets together to learn to knit, or make toys and clothes, or even find their way round a sewing machine, are brilliant. Check the events calendar to find out more.

I Knit London

106 Lower Marsh, SE1 7AB (7261 1338, www.iknit. org.uk). Waterloo tube/rail. **Open** 10.30am-8.30pm Tue-Thur; 10.30am-6pm Mon, Fri, Sat.
This purl of a shop is a close-knit community indeed. At its centre are Gerard Allt and Craig Carruthers, whose skill with the needles has led to what amounts to a woolly, liberal salon, where anyone who loves to knit can foregather on a Wednesday and Thursday night from 6pm and talk designs, patterns and basically have a good yarn, and a drink or two. Then there's the Sunday Knit Roast, the Saturday Classes and the Sock Club. It's all very sociable, but for people who just want to buy needles, wool and accessories it's all here, beautifully displayed. The emphasis is on good-quality wool, with an appealing selection of wools and yarns from British independent yarn producers, knitting patterns, both vintage and modern, and a range of how-to books.

Loop

15 Camden Passage, N1 8EA (7288 1160, www.loopknitting.com). Angel tube. **Open** 11am-6pm Tue, Wed, Fri, Sat; 11am-7.30pm Thur; noon-5pm Sun.
Loop will get your needles clicking in no time. The breadth of stock, the inspirational creations (knitted by homeware and knitted toy designers such as Sally Nencini and Catherine Tough) and, of course, the classes, patterns, magazines and tools, make this lovely Islington shop a pleasure to spend time in. Best of all, as far as experienced crocheters and knitters are concerned, is the obvious care and attention given to sourcing quality yarn. There are so many appealing shades, weights and textures. We love Artisan Yarns from Herefordshire: their colours come from natural dyes made from organic plant extracts, and the wool is 'kettle dyed', which means only small batches are coloured together. The subtle variations in colour in each mean that you feel like you're buying one-offs. Other delights are the pastel-coloured linen lace yarns, for cool summer knits, Adriafil's llama yarn, and soft cashmere yarns for very special jumpers.

Prick Your Finger

260 Globe Road, E2 0JD (8981 2560, www. prickyourfinger.com). Bethnal Green tube/rail. **Open** 10.00am-6.30pm Tue-Sat.
Rachael Matthews's right-on 'textile art collective' thrums with creative activity. It looks like a gallery, celebrating British crafts and textiles throughout history. The speciality is yarn spun in-house, as well as sourced from small farmer producers who 'are doing it for themselves': these include wools from Wensleydale Sheep Shop, Coldharbour Mill and UK Alpaca. Other delights include embroidery silks, crochet hooks and knitting needles as well as all the trimmings: buttons, ribbons, darning equipment and drop spindles. Most exciting are the classes for beginners and improvers and the regular events that go on in the gallery space. We're tempted to sign up for the next 'Knit your first jumper' course. Check the blog for the next PYF happening.

Stag & Bow

8 Dartmouth Road, SE23 3XU (8291 4992, www.stagandbow.com). Forest Hill tube/rail. **Open** 11am-6pm Tue, Thur-Sat; 10am-6pm Wed; 11am-4pm Sun.
Expect a relaxed approach to craft and textiles at this charming craft store and workshop. Classes include crochet, needle felting, embroidery, fabric printing and button-making among a raft of others. There's a hint of wit in some – such as Emergency Hat, which sees a milliner teach you how to make a hat in three hours – as well as history. Founders Pascale and Cyrus love local, as well as craft-history and you may well find yourself learning how to make fabric buttons while listening to a talk about their provenance from an expert. Stock includes haberdashery (from trimmings to felt) and quality yarns, all beautifully displayed, and there's a newly added rail of carefully selected vintage clothing to further tempt the denizens of SE23.

Models & games

See also p189 **Forbidden Planet**.

Comet Miniatures

44-48 Lavender Hill, SW11 5RH (7228 3702, www.comet-miniatures.com). Clapham Common tube or Clapham Junction rail. **Open** 9.30am-5pm Mon-Sat.
The shop's shutters are emblazoned with some sort of drooling alien, which gives a hint as to what's behind them. Sci-fi and fantasy models, toys and collectibles are a big draw. There are plastic models of Alien, Predator, Godzilla and various dragons, kits so that you can make

Stag & Bow

Angels

and paint your own, and obscure board games inspired by cult TV series and films. As well as the covetable *Star Wars*, *Captain Scarlet* and *Stingray*-type nostalgia, there are more contemporary fixations, such as *Avatar* and *Pirates of the Caribbean* figures and toys. A first port of call for all sci-fi, film, TV, military and weaponry related paraphernalia, and for model-making kits. There's also a good range of books and magazines for fans, and a range of kits for those who want to try their hand at building their own figures, robots and vehicles.

Compendia

10 Greenwich Market, SE10 9HZ (8293 6616, www.compendia.co.uk). Cutty Sark DLR. **Open** 11am-5.30pm daily.

This shop inspires you to turn off screens and phones and communicate through cards, counters, dice and tiles. The busy window display bespeaks a proud tradition of strategic games playing: handsome wooden chess sets and tables skittles, polished boules and croquet clubs and attractive variations on a theme: Mapominos looks like a geographers' version of dominos. Then there are the big award winners, such as Seven Wonders. It has the big-names too: Scrabble, Monopoly, Cluedo; the pub games: cribbage, Shove Ha'penny, skittles, and the complicated strategic games of great beauty, such as backgammon and Mah Jong. Top cult board games such as Carcassonne and the Settlers of Catan are still bestsellers. Then there are the jigsaw puzzles: the lovely ones by Escher are a challenge, but completing a 4,000-piece Birth of Venus is an achievement indeed. Computer games or those that require plugs or batteries are banished from this rarefied territory.

Playlounge

19 Beak Street, W1F 9RP (7287 7073, www. playlounge.co.uk). Oxford Circus or Piccadilly Circus tube. **Open** 11am-7pm Mon-Sat; noon-5pm Sun.

Toyshops aren't just for children, say the key players in this leisure lounge. There's plenty to amuse the junior customers, but grown-ups are invited to join in the fun. To that end, the playthings sold in this shop may be design classics or innovations, and there are gadgets and games that are out of the ordinary. By the same token, you're not going to find every toy of the moment here. It's packed with action figures, gadgets, books and comics, as well as T-shirts and clothing. You can buy a vinyl figure of Periwinkle (the Playlounge bubble gum boy logo), strange cuddly animals by Noferin, Hayao Miyazaki's Totoro toys or any number of appealing and unusual picture books, such as an unabridged version of *Alice in Wonderland*, with dark and disturbingly beautiful illustrations by Camille Rose Garcia.

Parties & magic

Angels

119 Shaftesbury Avenue, WC2H 8AE (7836 5678, www.fancydress.com). Leicester Square or Tottenham Court Road tube. **Open** 9.30am-5.30pm Mon, Tue, Thur, Fri; 10.30am-7pm Wed.

Angels is the undisputed doyenne of fancy-dress hire for adults and children in the capital. The range – spanning everything from splendid Tudor robes to a sequinned showgirl outfit from *Octopussy* – and quality are unparalleled. Some of the handmade costumes from the massive collection Angels has created for films over the years have even found their way to the six-floor hire shop. There's also a selection of cheap superhero costumes for sale (Superman, Spider-Man), starting at £28.99. Costumes for hire start from £60 + VAT (currently £72) and individual items for hire start from £20+VAT (£24). The expanding range of packet costumes, sold via the website, is also good quality, with Winnie the Pooh, Captain Caveman and Hong Kong Phooey all new for 2012.

Branch 1 Garrick Road, NW9 6AA (8202 2244).

Davenports Magic Shop

7 Charing Cross Underground Shopping Arcade, WC2N 4HZ (7836 0408, www.davenports magic.co.uk). Charing Cross tube/rail. **Open** 9.30am-5.30pm Mon-Fri; 10.30am-4.30pm Sat.

Davenports was established back in 1898, and today is staffed by professional magicians who are able to demonstrate the most suitable magic for your level of experience and budget. The equipment for beginners, such as trick card decks, starts from £7; for more advanced magicians, there's everything from trick Top Hats to crafty tables. Posters and collectibles (such as a hand-painted representation of Tommy Cooper mounted on a wooden board) are also for sale, and there's a wide range of how-to instruction DVDs and books (including an interesting second-hand section). If you really want to learn the tricks of the trade, though, then enrol in one of Davenports magic courses or head to one of its magic shows (see the website for details).

International Magic

89 Clerkenwell Road, EC1R 5BX (7405 7324, www.internationalmagic.com). Chancery Lane tube or Farringdon tube/rail. **Open** 11.30am-6pm Mon-Fri; 11.30am-4pm Sat.

This delightful family-run shop, in operation for over 50 years, is an Aladdin's cave for wannabe and professional magicians and those who just want to learn a few party tricks to impress and baffle their friends. Impromptu tricks and gimmicks include a huge range of playing cards and coin tricks, while the large selection of stage tricks ranges from floating light bulbs to vanishing cabinets. Arcane books and tutorial DVDs will show you the ropes and, for those who want to go one step further, there's the opportunity to undertake courses, catering to a range of different levels, plus attend lectures by professional magicians, such as John Archer and Etienne Pradier. The shop also runs an annual week-long magic convention that is now in its 41st year.

Party Party

9-13 Ridley Road, E8 2NP (7254 5168, www.pp shop.co.uk). Dalston Junction or Dalston Kingsland rail or 67, 76, 149 bus. **Open** 9am-5.30pm Mon-Thur; 9am-6.30pm Fri, Sat.

This cheap and cheerful three-floored party shop – the area's best – is packed to the brim with dressing-up outfits and props (wigs, beards, gorilla outfits, hats, masks, professional outfits, Halloween costumes, fat suits) and party supplies. There's a large area dedicated to equipment for cake-making and decorating – everything from icing and candles to cake stands and pillars – and a massive range of balloons, glitter, banners, confetti, flags of the world, bunting and decorations. A must-visit if you need an injection of garish kitsch for a hen party, wedding or birthday celebration, and for colourful tableware and instruction books on flower arranging and cake decorating. Don't leave without a six-foot paper palm tree.

Branch 206 Kilburn High Road, NW6 4JH (7624 4295).

Stationery

Blade Rubber Stamps

12 Bury Place, WC1A 2JL (7831 4123, www.blade rubber.co.uk). Holborn or Tottenham Court Road tube. **Open** 10.30am-6pm Mon-Sat; 11.30am-4.30pm Sun.

A stone's throw from the British Museum, this shrine to wooden-handled rubber stamps has something for every eventuality and taste, from arty stamps depicting chandeliers and cityscapes to London buses, *Alice in Wonderland* characters, cutesy puppies and telephone Homework stamps ('Check spelling', 'Keep trying') make handy purchases. Unmounted sheets of rubber stamps, ink pads in every imaginable shade, glitters, decorative paper glues, stencils, stickers, sticks of sealing wax, and a range of magazines and books complete the stock. Blade also has a made-to-order service for personalised stamps. And if you fancy having a bash yourself you can buy a kit or carving rubber to make your own stamps.

Mount Street Printers & Stationers

4 Mount Street, W1K 3LW (7409 0303, www.mountstreetprinters.com). Bond Street or Green Park tube. **Open** 9am-6pm Mon-Fri.

With a telltale whiff of glue and ink permeating up from the printworks downstairs, this shop means business – and claims to offer the fastest stationery turnaround in town. You'll find everything from crisp white invitation cards to thank-you notes with matching tissue paper-lined envelopes. Even the most imaginative commissions are affordable, and the company takes particular pride in its special design techniques, which include ornate die-stamping and engraving. A small selection of ready-made stationery runs from invitation and correspondence cards to visitors' books.

Paperchase
213-215 Tottenham Court Road, W1T 7PS (7467 6200, www.paperchase.co.uk). Goodge Street tube. **Open** 8.30am-8pm Mon-Fri; 9am-7pm Sat; 11.30am-6pm Sun.
The ground floor at Paperchase's three-floor flagship store sells greetings cards of every description, along with all manner of present-wrapping paraphernalia (tissue paper, gift wrap, bows, tags and lengths of velvety ribbon). Photograph albums and frames, notebooks (including Moleskines), pencil cases, diaries and gift items are artfully arrayed towards the front of the store, while the little shelves at the back are filled with writing paper and envelopes in a multitude of colours and sizes. Upstairs, prices climb, with luxury Filofaxes, pens, leather bags and passport wallets (including Mimi) and a select homewares range. Plus, come Christmas time, it's packed chock full of the quirkier end of seasonal decorations. The top floor stocks top-notch art materials including a lovely selection of interesting paper. **Branches** throughout the city.

Tobacconists

JJ Fox
19 St James's Street, SW1A 1ES (7930 3787, www.jjfox.co.uk). Green Park tube. **Open** 9.30am-5.45pm Mon-Fri; 9.30am-5pm Sat.
A prestigious, family-owned tobacconist with expert and enthusiastic staff, who hold great pride in the brand's heritage – the business was started as far back as 1881, and is reportedly the oldest cigar merchant in the world. JJ Fox only stocks cigars with an unquestioned provenance and that meet the highest standards. Among many Cuban brands are the popular Montecristo No.4 and Cohiba Robusto. You can also find a wide selection of New World cigars, such as Ashton from Dominican Republic and Padron from Nicaragua. The great pipe selection features Stanwell and Meerschaum models. There's also a good range of vintage and limited-edition cigars, gift items – such as cigar cutters, pipe-shaped cufflinks, and pewter flasks – and the shop has an excellent website. One for the seriously discerning and enthusiastic smoker.

Party Party. See p219.

Come to see and be seen on one of east London's most style-conscious streets.

Since its revamp in 2004, the few surviving traders of this once run-down market – one of London's oldest – have been joined by a new wave of gourmet food sellers and stallholders flogging anything from handmade undies and vinyl records to vintage kidswear, old books, bric-a-brac and cupcakes. The place is constantly evolving, with relatively new spillover areas – Schoolyard Market and Netil Market – fast forming their own distinct personalities.

Food offerings on Broadway Market include lunch options such as Vietnamese baguettes, posh beefburgers, thalis and salads, plus an array of baked goods. Fresh meat, fish, cheese and classic fruit and veg stalls also line the street. Alongside are a number of restaurants, cafés and traditional shops – a hardwear store, a butcher's, a launderette, an old-style barber shop and even a pie and mash shop, F Cooke (no.9, 7254 6458).

Other useful shops include fishmonger **Fin & Flounder** (no.71, 07838 018395, www.finand flounder.com); deli/café **L'Eau a la Bouche** (nos.35-37, 7923 0600); florist **Rebel Rebel** (no.5, 7254 4487, www.rebelrebel.co.uk), which sells lovely hand-tied bouquets; and independent bookseller the **Broadway Bookshop** (no.6; *see p184*). **Buggies & Bikes** (*see p262*) sells funky kids' clothes, organic baby lotions and even paddling pools. At no.49, there's haberdasher **Our Patterned Hand** (7812 9912, www.patterned hand.co.uk) and at no.7, **Fabrications** (*see p215*), where you'll find contemporary 'eco-friendly' textiles and knitting materials.

There's also a clutch of shops that reflect Broadway Market's fanbase – London's style blogging, fixed-wheel bike-riding style obsessives. **69b** (no.69b, 7249 9655) is an excellent womenswear boutique, founded by stylist

and one-time *i-D* magazine fashion editor Merryn Leslie, whose stock is handpicked from sustainable labels. **Hub** (*see p55*) on Ada Street does a great line in simple and stylish men's and women's brands, from Acne to Barbour, while nearby **Strut Broadway** (2B Ada Street, 7254 8121) is an upscale vintage and used fashion store that focuses on big labels and rare pieces. At **Black Truffle** (no.4; *see p114*), designer shoes sit amid covetable handbags, gloves and other accessories in a deceptively large space. **Artwords** (no.20-22, 7729 2000) is a light, airy bookstore stocking photobooks and style mags; **Donlon Books** (no.77, 7684 5698) is a tiny art, photography and culture bookstore with new and rare books, mags and 'zines.

Vintage homewares are stocked at **Stella Blunt** (no.75), while **MacBlack & Vine** (no.47, 07968 333328, www.macblackandvine.co.uk) displays a regularly changing stock of classic and retro furniture, as well as fine wine. Just around the corner, opposite the Regent Canal is interiors and furniture store the **Dog & Wardrobe** (*see p173*).

LEISURE

Musical Instruments

Most shops listed in this section deal in second-hand as well as new equipment. There are many music shops clustered around Denmark Street and Charing Cross Road.

All-rounders

Barbican Chimes Music Shop

Silk Street, EC2Y 8DD (7588 9242, www.chimes music.com). Barbican tube or Moorgate tube/rail. **Open** 9am-5.30pm Mon-Fri; 9am-4pm Sat (9am-5pm during term time).

An invaluable resource for Guildhall students and soloists performing at the Barbican, Chimes – at the base of Cromwell Tower, right next to the main entrance of the Barbican – has a large stock of sheet music, manuscript paper, reeds, strings, bows, mouthpieces, classical CDs, books and more. There's also a limited selection of guitars (classical, acoustic, electro-acoustic) and ukes, plus rhythm instruments and novelty children's items. The South Ken branch has more for-hire instruments, while the Academy Chimes, located at the Royal College of Music, stocks printed and examination music, but is a bit more of a tourist museum shop.

Branches Academy Chimes Music Shop Royal Academy of Music, York Gate Building, Marylebone Road, NW1 5HT (7873 7400); **Kensington Chimes Music** 9 Harrington Road, SW7 3ES (7589 9054); **Ealing Chimes Music** 11 Queens Parade, W5 3HU (8997 4088).

Chappell of Bond Street

152-160 Wardour Street, W1F 8YA (7432 4400, www.chappellofbondstreet.co.uk). Oxford Circus or Tottenham Court Road tube. **Open** 9.30am-6pm Mon-Fri; 10am-5.30pm Sat.

It's retained its old name, but in 2006 Chappell moved from Bond Street (its home for nearly 200 years) to this amazing three-storey temple in Soho. The shop is Yamaha's flagship UK music store, with a great range of digital, acoustic and hybrid pianos, electric and acoustic guitars, brass, woodwind and music production equipment. Prices start at around £7 for a recorder and head into the stratosphere (around £19,000) for a double bass. The basement houses the largest selection of printed music for sale in Europe, and the shop also supplies music books and backing tracks. Past and present customers include Beethoven, Chopin, Jamie Cullum, Jools Holland and Coldplay. The store hosts free fortnightly Lunchtime Recitals.

Umbrella Music

0845 500 2323, www.umbrellamusic.co.uk.

Check the website for the whereabouts of Umbrella Music, as it was on the move as we went to press. The long-established Umbrella is known for stocking a very reasonable collection of new electronic keyboards,

Duke of Uke

Bridgewood & Neitzert. See p225.

acoustic and digital pianos, guitars (classical, bass, electric and electro-acoustic), plus plenty of beginners-level brass, woodwind, strings, drums (including the SpongeBob three-piece junior set) and percussion, amplifiers, recorders, ukes and banjos. It also holds studio equipment (mics, stands, PAs and mixing desks, computer soft- and hardware), plenty of sheet music, hosts education courses and has an on-site workshop for basic repairs.

Guitars, banjos & ukuleles

See also p222 **Barbican Chimes Music Shop** and **Chappell of Bond Street**, and p226 **Hobgoblin**. Denmark Street is a first port-of-call for guitar shops.

Bass Gallery
142 Royal College Street, NW1 0TA (7267 5458, www.thebassgallery.com). Camden Town tube or Camden Road rail. **Open** 10.30am-6pm Mon-Thur; 10.30am-5.30pm Fri; 11am-5pm Sat.
An alternative to the Denmark Street gang – and with an ever-growing reputation – is north London's Bass Gallery. Opened in 1992, it offers a wide range of new, used and vintage instruments as well as amps and accessories. Staff here pride themselves on their friendly service and expertise and make a point of trying to keep ahead of the curve by road-testing new products before deciding what to stock. There's an in-

house workshop where guitars are built that also offers set-ups, repairs and maintenance. The store will also sell your old gear for you.

Chandler Guitars
300-302 Sandycombe Road, Kew, Surrey TW9 3NG (8940 5874, www.chandlerguitars.co.uk). Kew Gardens tube/rail. **Open** 9.30am-6pm Mon-Sat.
The fact that Chandler Guitars has survived for so long in its remote, sleepy Kew Gardens locale is a testament to the quality of the service and instruments here. The catalogue covers new electric guitars from Paul Reed Smith, Gibson and Fender, high end acoustic models by Martin and Breedlove, as well as a superb range of vintage models (acoustic, classical, left-handed). There are plenty of pedals, amps and accessories, too, and the workshop will sort out any setting up modifications or repairs. Chandler is the servicing workshop of choice when the Killers, Paul Weller or Dave Gilmour are in town.

Duke of Uke
88 Cheshire Street, E2 6EH (3583 9728, www.dukeofuke.co.uk). Shoreditch High Street rail. **Open** noon-7pm Tue-Fri; 11am-6pm Sat, Sun.
When eccentric musician Matthew Reynolds decided that London needed a specialist ukulele shop, he ploughed his life savings into Duke of Uke. The shop, now in a new larger space in Cheshire Street, stocks a fair few banjos, guitars, mandolins and harmonicas, but

LEISURE

TW Howarth. See p226.

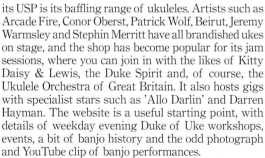

its USP is its baffling range of ukuleles. Artists such as Arcade Fire, Conor Oberst, Patrick Wolf, Beirut, Jeremy Warmsley and Stephin Merritt have all brandished ukes on stage, and the shop has become popular for its jam sessions, where you can join in with the likes of Kitty Daisy & Lewis, the Duke Spirit and, of course, the Ukulele Orchestra of Great Britain. It also hosts gigs with specialist stars such as 'Allo Darlin' and Darren Hayman. The website is a useful starting point, with details of weekday evening Duke of Uke workshops, events, a bit of banjo history and the odd photograph and YouTube clip of banjo performances.

London Guitar Studio/ El Mundo Flamenco
62 Duke Street, W1K 6JT (7493 0033, www.london guitarstudio.com, www.elmundoflamenco.co.uk). Bond Street tube. **Open** 10am-6pm Mon-Wed, Fri, Sat; 10am-7pm Thur; 10am-5pm Sun.
If you're looking for an acoustic guitar, whether classical or flamenco, the centrally-located London Guitar Studio is the place to come. Hang out in the Spanish-inspired patio area and strum on a few of their offerings. A wide range of traditionally made instruments by manufacturers such as Alhambra, Goya, Burguet,

Camps and Granados can be found here, along with cases, strings, music, stands and tuners. There's also a decent selection of recordings, books and DVDs to provide inspiration and, perhaps not surprisingly, El Mundo Flamenco can supply the rest of the essential extras – from the shoes (150 nails are tapped into the sole one by one) all the way up to the fans, flowers, castanets and hats.

Wild Guitars
393 Archway Road, N6 4ER (8340 7766, www. wildguitars.com). Highgate tube. **Open** 10am-7pm Mon-Sat.
Opened in 1996, Wild Guitars specialises in rare, vintage and often bizarre second-hand guitars, amps, effects and echo machines. Dave Wild – owner, and guitar repair-man – opened his shop with the intention of providing a service for professional musicians, and WG remains a firm favourite with north London's rock aristos (including members of Coldplay, Bombay Bicycle Club and Pink Floyd). Expect HiWatt, old Vox, Selmer, Gibson, Fender and Epiphones. But stock moves quickly and new pieces are coming in all the time, so for a full list of what's available, take a look at the regularly updated website.

Pianos & organs

J Reid & Sons

184 St Ann's Road, N15 5RP (8800 6907, www. jreidpianos.co.uk). Seven Sisters tube/rail or South Tottenham rail. **Open** 9am-5.30pm Mon-Fri; 10am-5pm Sat. **No credit cards.**

Britain's largest piano store has been selling pianos since the 1920s and here you'll find brand new Bluthners, Bösendorfers, Kawais and Yamahas; reconditioned Steinways and Bechsteins; shiny new Czech uprights (Petrof, Weinbach, Zeidel, Riga Kloss); and scores of restored second-hand models. Reid also makes its own-brand grands and uprights – Reid-Sohn – which are built in Korea and Indonesia. There's also a specialist professional range – Reid-Sohn Academy – manufactured in Germany. The company runs a busy workshop repairing and restringing pianos, but if you decide your current piano is no longer suitable, Reid will value, sell or part-exchange your model for another. The shop also offers rentals and hire-to-buy schemes, deducting any hire charges from a subsequent purchase.

Markson Pianos

5 - 8 Chester Court, Albany Street, NW1 4BU (7935 8682, www.marksonpianos.com). Great Portland Street or Regent's Park tube or bus C2. **Open** 9.30am-5.30pm Mon-Sat; 10am-4pm Sun.

As well as selling pianos, this family-run business has been providing restoration, polishing and tuning services for over 100 years. Pianos from the British manufacturer Kemble are sold alongside Bechstein's high-end professional uprights and grands. Other brands include Yamaha, Waldstein, Steingraeber, Hoffmann and Bösendorfer. Some pianos cost well into the thousands, although there are plenty from around £500. The store sells a number of pre-owned models that have been fully examined and set up, with necessary parts being replaced and any repairs, such as casework damage, being dealt with by its own repairers and polishers.

Pro audio/electronics

Westend DJ

10-12 Hanway Street, W1T 1UB (7637 3293, www.westenddj.com). Tottenham Court Road tube. **Open** 9.30am-6.30pm Mon-Sat; noon-6pm Sun.

An exhaustive range of cutting-edge DJ and audio-visual equipment and accessories is stocked at Westend DJ. The complete hardware catalogues for all of the leading brands, including Technics and Pioneer, are available, plus industry names like Stanton, Numark and Denon. As well as the latest turntables, mixers, CD decks, video decks, effects units, amplifiers and speakers, you can pick up headphones, slipmats, styli, microphones, stands, record boxes and a whole lot more.

Service is informative and not pushy; and it may well be possible to barter for a deal if you're buying a package of several items. It's worth browsing the comprehensive website before you visit.

Branches Atlantic Electronics 970 North Circular Road, NW2 7JR (8208 6988); **WestendProduction** 11 Great Russell Street, WC1B 3NH (7631 1935).

Stringed instruments

Bridgewood & Neitzert

146 Stoke Newington Church Street, N16 0JU (7249 9398, www.londonviolins.com). Stoke Newington rail or bus 73. **Open** 10am-6pm Mon-Fri; 10am-4pm Sat.

Having started out as makers of lutes, viols and baroque violins, this respected duo has an impeccable knowledge of the stringed instrument. Bridgewood & Neizert sells violins, violas, cellos and double basses in both modern and classical styles with prices for a modern violin starting at around £200 and rising to the thousands for high-end models. It also stocks a wide variety of specialist strings. There are seven full-time members of staff to deal with guaranteed repairs and restorations of modern as well as period instruments (including lutes and viola d'amores) and B&N also offers valuations, commission-based sales and part-exchange services.

John & Arthur Beare

30 Queen Anne Street, W1G 8HX (7307 9666, www.beares.com). Bond Street tube. **Open** (preferably by appointment) 10am-5pm Mon-Fri.

With over 140 years' experience in selling Stradivaris, Guarneris and other Italian masters, J&A Beare's collection of instruments is of the highest calibre. Many of the world's top musicians frequent the place. In 1998, Beare's joined forces with Morris & Smith, London dealers, and together the firm offers expertise and advice in the buying and selling of stringed instruments and bows as well as valuations for insurance purposes. The majority of the violins, violas and cellos are antiques, but there are a few new items. There are experts on hand to appraise and advise on restoration and repair.

Woodwind, brass & percussion

See also p226 for **Hobgoblin**, and for the **Early Music Shop**, which specialises in musical instruments and sheet music from the 18th century, and stocks harps, flutes, baroque cellos, zithers, crumhorns, folk and world instruments.

Foote's

www.footesmusic.com

Founded in 1920 by Charles Ernest Foote, this central London store (see the website for the new Soho premises,

LEISURE

which were unconfirmed as we went to press) houses a great selection of instruments: maple ply snare drums, Schlagwerk cajons handmade in Germany, a host of World and Latin percussive instruments (ganzas, tambourines, berimbaus, pandeiros, bells, whistles and more), as well as woodwind, brass and string instruments. Staff are knowledgeable and passionate about the instruments they play and sell. A decent stock of books, DVDs and CDs covers a wide range of instruments; the online site is useful but a store visit is recommended. There's a rent-to-buy scheme as well as hands-on tuition offered (on request) in an in-store demo room.

TW Howarth

31-35 Chiltern Street, W1U 7PN (7935 2407, www.howarth.uk.com). Baker Street tube or Marylebone tube/rail. **Open** 9.30am-5.30pm Mon-Fri; 10am-4.30pm Sat.

Britain's leading outlet for woodwind instruments and accessories operates across three separate storefronts selling clarinets, saxophones, bassoons and oboes. It stocks sheet music and specialist accessories like instrumental microphones and mouthpieces. There are five full-time staff who look after repairs. Yamaha remains the market leader, but the best saxes and clarinets are French (Selmer, Buffet, LeBlanc), while the best bassoons tend to be German (Gebrüder Mönnig, Puchner, Oscar Adler and the like). The shop also sells second-hand instruments and runs a rental scheme.

World, early music & folk

See also above **TW Howarth**.

Early Music Shop

11 Denmark Street, WC2H 8TD (7632 3960, www.earlymusicshop.com). Tottenham Court Road tube. **Open** 10am-5.50pm Mon-Wed, Fri, Sat; 10am-7pm Thur.

Ever fancied yourself as one of those musicians you see serenading lost loves in Shakespearian comedies? If so, head to the Early Music Shop to find the necessary tools. Specialising in instruments from the medieval to the baroque periods, staff here are the go-to guys for lutes, harps, flutes and crumhorns. A particularly large collection of recorders runs from a tenor for a plastic one up to £3,500 for a Paetzold cherrywood model. There's a wide range of specialist facsimiles and sheet music to choose from. Try out the annual Early Music Festival in Greenwich in November for a taster of what this scene is all about.

Hobgoblin

24 Rathbone Place, W1T 1JA (7323 9040, www.hobgoblin.com). Tottenham Court Road tube. **Open** 10am-6pm Mon-Sat.

The diverse stock at this remarkable folk shop covers a mix of traditional, World and folk instruments covering woodwind (bagpipes, flutes), stringed instruments (fiddles, harps, zithers) and fretted instruments (banjos, mandolins, ukuleles), as well as free reed (melodeons, harmonicas, concertinas), percussion and guitars. More unusual finds like the Irish bodhrán drum, a double-reed Chinese flute or the Siberian jaw harp make this shop unique. Vintage and second-hand items are for sale, as are a host of books, CDs and accessories (amps, cases, tuners), and every Friday an on-site luthier makes lutes, ouds and guitars and does repairs. The website lists a host of items that have been reduced to clear.

Jas Musicals

14 Chiltern Street, W1U 7PY (7935 0793, www.jas-musicals.com). Baker Street or Bond Street tube. **Open** 11am-6pm Mon-Fri; 10am-6pm Sat.

Marylebone's Chiltern Street is the central London outpost of the original Southall shop that was opened over 25 years ago by Harjit Singh Shah. His original intention was to apply high-class western technology to Indian instruments while maintaining traditional standards of the old ways of craftmanship, and those impressed with the success of this enterprise have included Jimmy Page, Talvin Singh, John McLaughlin, Zakir Hussain and David Gray. The shop specialises in classical and folk instruments from all over India, stocking tablas, dhols, harmoniums, veenas and sitars, among others. The shop also offers a repair service and a host of accessories, instrument bags, music and books. Instrument prices are surprisingly low compared to those for most western instruments.

Branch 124 The Broadway, Southall, Middx, UB1 1QF (8574 2686).

Ray Man

54 Chalk Farm Road, NW1 8AN (7692 6261, www.raymaneasternmusic.co.uk). Camden Town or Chalk Farm tube. **Open** 1-5pm Mon; 10.30am-6pm Tue-Sat; 11am-5pm Sun.

A family-run business for over 30 years, Ray Man sells a unique variety of traditional instruments from all over Asia, Africa, the Middle East and South America. More recognisable items like sitars and darbuka drums share the space with Chinese zithers and Indian fiddles. There is a wide selection of the shop's best-selling item – the ukelele (from £21.50), plus several smaller and even more affordable objects such as the Vietnamese frog box and Indian monkey drums, tam tam and nipple gongs, singing bowls, bells, cymbals and shakers. The Vietnamese Jew's harp (as heard on Morricone spaghetti western soundtracks) fits nicely into your pocket. Ray Man also runs a service that tracks down specialist overseas instruments.

Ray Man

Streetwise Camden Passage, N1

Angel's pedestrianised crooked alley mixes 19th-century charm with some thoroughly modern shops.

One of the attractions of antiques and boutique shopping is that very special thrill of a unique or unusual find, and visitors to Islington's Camden Passage are unlikely to be disappointed on that score: expect to stumble across Marmite truffles, mid-century-modern ornaments and hand-tailored Nigerian waistcoats, not to mention stalls selling all manner of bits and pieces. The narrow alleyway, running between Islington High Street and the tip of Essex Road, is a glorious throwback to 19th-century London, with Victorian lamp posts, wonky paving, traditional shopfronts and a time-warp pub, the Camden Head. Coming from Angel tube, your first stops might include **Esme** (no.6, 07810 382 565) for unique antique jewellery, then **Smug** (no.13, *see p41*), Lizzie Evans' lifestyle boutique with great ceramics and gifts, vintage furniture, Casio watches, cards and a range of interesting exclusives. Next door is **Loop** (*see p216*), a four-storey knitters' paradise that stocks high-quality yarns and runs regular workshops. At no.12 sits Camden Passage's most iconic vintage shop, **Annie's** (*see p90*), which is strong on wedding dresses from the Victorian era to the '50s. **Fat Faced Cat** (no.22-24, 7354 0777), another vintage store, has a more contemporary feel, plus just as much ephemera as fashion – it has an excellent men's vintage selection, too. At the far end is the **African Waistcoat Company** (no.33, 1493 4917), selling bright, handwoven Nigerian fabrics tailored into waistcoats. **Susy Harper** (no.35 7704 0688) sells equally stylish but more subdued womenswear. The tiny **Pierrepont Arcade**, just off the main drag, houses Camden Passage's real

oddities – tiny units packed with crockery, silverware and collectibles. Modern additions such as the **Blow Bar** (no.25, 7354 1551) and frozen yoghurt bar **Frae** (no.27, 7704 6538) work well alongside the 1950s-themed **Issy's Milky Way** (no.28), with its soda fountain classics, and comfort food specialist the **Breakfast Club** (no.31, 7226 5454). Austrian café **Kipferl** (no.20, 7704 1555) sells a few groceries, such as sweets and gourmet sausages. Finally, **Paul A Young Fine Chocolates** sits temptingly at no.33, serving up London's most daring chocolate flavours. Hold the Marmite.

Sport & Fitness

Of all the major department stores, **Harrods** has the biggest selection of sports and fitness equipment, with much of the store's fifth floor given over to golf simulators, ski, riding and biking equipment and plenty of designer sportswear to complete the look. **John Lewis** stocks table tennis, snooker and pool tables, as well as exercise machines and accessories for other sports. **Selfridges** has a range of Gocycle electric bikes and a concession for Cycle Surgery. See also the trainer shops listed in the **Shoes** chapter.

Cycling

London's bike shops are getting better and better, with more and more small businesses (as well as branches of the big chains, such as Evans and Cycle Surgery) opening all the time; below is a selection of the best.

Bikefix

48 Lamb's Conduit Street, WC1N 3LJ (7405 1218, www.bikefix.co.uk). Holborn tube. **Open** 8.30am-7pm Mon-Fri; 10am-5pm Sat.

If you're looking for a machine that'll make fellow cyclists stop and stare, or need a three-wheeler to take your ice-cream business into the parks, head for Bikefix. The fantastically quirky and original selection of bikes includes utility models, recumbents and folding bikes – the recumbent style is significantly more aerodynamic as well as eye-catching. But if you're not keen on eccentric bike models, there's also an excellent choice of more familiar-looking rides, from less well-known manufacturers such as Fahrrad Manufaktur and touring specialist Tout Terrain. Bike Fix first started as a repair and maintenance workshop, and it continues to fix bikes, on a first come, first served basis.

Brick Lane Bikes

118 Bethnal Green Road, E2 6DG (7033 9053, www.bricklanebikes.co.uk). Bethnal Green tube/rail or Shoreditch High Street rail. **Open** 9am-7pm Mon-Fri; 11am-6pm Sat; 11am-5pm Sun.

Fixed-wheel and single-speed bikes have become essential urban-hipster accessories in recent years, and you'll find a wide selection at Brick Lane Bikes. The stock includes their own BLB range of pre-built ready to go set-ups, plus a variety of vintage track and road frames (Cinelli, Leader) in most shapes and sizes, all of which can be built to order. Prices for custom-builds are quite high and customer service can range from fairly helpful to crushingly indifferent; it helps to have some idea what you're after before going in.

Brixton Cycles

145 Stockwell Road, SW9 9TN (7733 6055, www.brixtoncycles.co.uk). Brixton tube/rail. **Open** 9am-6pm Mon-Wed, Fri, Sat; 10am-7pm Thur.

A Brixton fixture since the 1980s, this co-operative offers a fine range of bicycles and a well-regarded workshop. Bikes from Trek and Specialized keep commuters happy, as do the Bromptons. The workshop can also undertake custom-builds, including fixed-wheel and single-speed machines. It provides a daily on-the-spot repair service in the first hour of opening; otherwise you'll need to book, up to a month in advance. The service options range from a £40 (plus parts) checkover to a £120 (plus parts) service that sees the bike taken apart, cleaned, lubricated and put back together again. Brixton Cycles also stocks a range of skateboards and longboards.

Condor Cycles

49-53 Gray's Inn Road, WC1X 8PP (7269 6820, www.condorcycles.com). Chancery Lane tube. **Open** 9am-6pm Mon, Tue, Thur, Fri; 9am-7.30pm Wed; 10am-5pm Sat.

The USP of this family-run London legend, in business since 1948 and still in excellent health, is its own range of road bikes, built to order on a bespoke basis. Having chosen a model, prospective purchasers are propped on a fitting jig and measured for the correct frame and components, with clued-up staff adding appropriate parts according to the buyer's budget. But while Condor is heaven for the serious road cyclist, there's plenty for casual riders too. The basement showroom also has some off-the-peg bikes from other manufacturers, and the range of accessories on the main floor is perhaps the best in town.

Foffa Bikes

Unit 9, Pinchin Street, E1 1SA (7481 2516, foffabikes.com). Shadwell tube/DLR. **Open** 11am-7pm Tue-Fri; 11am-6pm Sat, Sun.

Dani Foffa started working on old bikes in 2007 from his tiny flat in east London while keeping his day job in the City. A couple of years later he quit and teamed up with photographer Tyson Sadlo to create Foffa bikes. Since then they've launched four models, including the Ciao, a light, comfortable and compact commuter bike; the Gears, a multi-purpose racing bike ideal for lightweight touring; the single speed Prima, perfect for city cruising; and the women's commuter bicycle, the Grazia. Every one of these bikes can be customised in any way you want from a range of artist-designed stickers and paint jobs. This service is also available on the store's website, allowing you to get cycling creative from the comfort of your own home. Finally, the store has also introduced a new innovative hire scheme. From £29 per day and £70 per weekend, you can take out any bike you want on a trial basis. If you decide to purchase the bike, Foffa will refund the cost of the hire.

Tokyo Fixed. See p233.

MiCycle

47 Barnsbury Street, N1 1TP (7684 0671,
www.micycle.org.uk). Highbury & Islington tube/
rail. **Open** 8.30am-6.30pm Mon-Fri; 10am-6pm Sat;
noon-6pm Sun.

This bike store and workshop caters for both Bobbin-
type (vintage-loving, slow-rolling) and Bianchi-type
(speedy) riders, and accordingly stocks just these two
brands. MiCycle pitches itself as a cycling club, encouraging its customers to become members and participate
in the various workshops and classes that it runs. Two
annual memberships are offered. At £2.95, the silver
membership gives you access to the store's workshop
and 10% off all classes and courses, while the gold membership, £29.95, gives you all this, plus a free bike service
and 10% off all future bike purchases for that year.

Mosquito Bikes

123 Essex Road, N1 2SN (7226 8765,
www.mosquito-bikes.co.uk). Angel tube or
Essex Road rail. **Open** 9am-6pm Mon-Wed,
Fri; 9am-7pm Thur; 10am-6pm Sat.

Stockist of high-end road and mountain bikes from
manufacturers such as Surly, Kinesis and Kuota,
Mosquito Bikes is a dream shop for the serious cyclist.
It's not cheap, however, with frame-building masters
like Pegoretti, Cinelli and Independent Fabrication generally charging well into four figures for their products.
Since you're spending a lot on the bike, it should fit
your body, and as part of its service Mosquito will pro-
fessionally fit your custom-built bike to your frame,
having determined your cycling history and aspira-
tions, measured you from top to toe, and checked your
flexibility and feet. The workshop operates a booking
system and provides a standard service for £75.
Mosquito also stocks an interesting range of clothing
from the likes of Café du Cycliste, Levis, Morvelo and
Showers Pass.

Push Cycles

35C Newington Green, N16 9PR (7249 1351,
www.pushcycles.com). Canonbury rail or bus 21,
73, 141, 236, 341. **Open** 8am-6pm Mon-Fri; 9am-
5.30pm Sat.

One of our favourite bike stores, Newington Green's
Push delivers a small but nicely chosen range of bikes –
including Mercians, the classic English brand, as well
as models from Italians Bianchi and Cinelli. The accessories stocked are of the quality, niche-brand ilk – so,
saddles by Brooks, skate-style helmets by Bern and
Nutcase, locks from Kryptonite, bags from Belk, and
lights from CatEye as well as the cool, detachable rubber lights from Knog. Urban bike fanatics are also
catered for with limited-edition graphics-based bike
posters, and the possibility of joining in with the sociable bike rides that leave from the shop every Sunday. A
downstairs workshop will sort out any bike casualties.

Shop talk
Jody Leach, Cycle Club manager at Rapha

Tell us about the shop

It's a meeting place for all road cyclists and fans of road racing to watch the latest races among a wealth of cycling memorabilia, shop from the full emporium of Rapha clothing and accessories, including an exclusive Cycle Club collection, enjoy the finest coffee, pre- and post-ride food, a beer or two, free WiFi and international cycling magazines. Rapha's CEO, Simon, conceived the Rapha Cycle Club back in 2010 as the place he would most like to hang out to watch racing and share the love of the sport with others. We have now opened seven clubs around the world and have enjoyed meeting like-minded fans, watching the racing and consuming cycling culture, while being surrounded by beautiful things. It is the ultimate Rapha experience.

What's special about it?

Everything is anchored in road cycling, from the memorabilia on the walls to the food and drink in the café (we serve delicious coffee made by one of Germany's top baristas and bike food such as a specially created fig roll). The shop and the café flow seamlessly into one another so you can sit and nurse an espresso while watching the Tour de France and reading some cycling literature, or you can browse the Rapha collection.

Who are your customers?

It's varied as we're in the heart of Soho, but generally they're road cyclists who are coming to get a fix of road cycling. We've also built up a great reputation for our coffee so have a core of regular customers that we see every morning.

What are your favourite shops in London?

Condor Cycles, one of the oldest bike shops in London and still the best; Paul Smith for their simple style (I got married in a Paul Smith suit), beautiful merchandising and interesting retail environments; and Postcard Teas. We serve their tea, so I'm biased, but it has the reputation of being the best in the UK and the shop is an Aladdin's Cave of amazing teas.

What's the best thing about owning/working in a shop?

In general I love working in retail as it's so varied. No two days are the same due to a varied customer base. With the Rapha Cycle Club it's great to be able to set the standards for how we, Rapha, will develop the Cycle Club and retail globally across the brand.

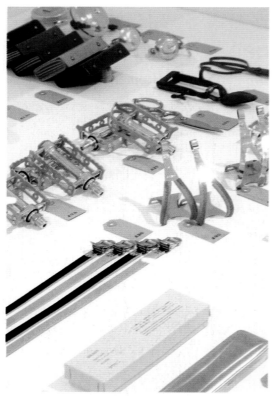

Tokyo Bikes

Rapha CC

85 Brewer Street, W1F 9ZN (7494 9831, www.rapha.cc). Piccadilly Circus tube. **Open** 7.30am-9pm Mon-Fri; 8.30am-7pm Sat; 10am-6pm Sun.

The 'CC' in Rapha CC stands for Cycle Club. For the team at Rapha, road riding is a way of life and this shop/café is a meeting place where cyclists can hang out before hitting the streets en masse (check out the website for how to get involved in the evening rides). Whether you're a seasoned racer or simply a cycling commuter, there are accessories and clothing here to suit your every need. The Technical range is for competitive cyclists while the City range offers more relaxed alternatives. There's even something for the dapper dandy – a suit jacket with special features that make it possible to cycle in. Once you've finished browsing the stylishly minimal shop, kick back in the café with a Square Mile espresso and a focaccia roll.

Sargent & Co

74 Mountgrove Road, N5 2LT (7359 7642, www.sargentandco.com). Finsbury Park tube/rail. **Open** varies; phone to check. **No credit cards**.

Owner Rob Sargent has an off-kilter sense of humour – 'No mountain bikes, high breads (sic), or modern carp (sic)' – but his message is clear: to promote, revive and facilitate the pastime of cycling. Sargent's love of all things cyclical means that his lovely Finsbury Park shop, guarded by Cassius the cat, is bedecked with frames (photo- as well as bike-) and accessories from the glory days of cycling. Services range from puncture repairs or a wash-and-brush-up to a full customisation or restoration, 'All carried out at very competitive prices, usually with a smile, and occasionally a cup of tea.' Beware, though, Sargent's has been known to close for substantial periods of time at short notice. It's best to check the website, or ring ahead, before making the trip.

Tokyo Bikes

87-89 Tabernacle Street, EC2A 4BA (7251 6842 www.tokyobike.co.uk). Old Street tube/rail. **Open** 11am-7pm Tue-Sat.

Simplicity equals beauty – the philosophy behind a Tokyo Bike creation. Based on the concept of 'Tokyo Slow', the bikes are designed to be light to ride with an emphasis on comfort over speed. Made from Cr-Mo steel, and featuring thinner than standard 650mm wheels, these bikes are perfect if you're drawn to the idea of cruising around the city in style. The store, which moved from Tokyo to London only this year (and is no relation to Tokyo Fixed), will furnish you with one of its bikes for between £490 and £600. It also sells style-savvy extras.

Tokyo Fixed

4 Peter Street, W1F 0AD (7734 1885, www.tokyo fixedgear.com). Piccadilly Circus tube. **Open** 11am-7.30pm Mon-Fri; 11am-6pm Sat; noon-6pm Sun.

Foffa Bikes. See p229.

LEISURE

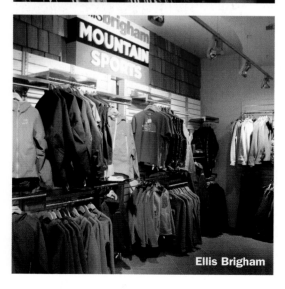

Ellis Brigham

The fixed-wheel cycling scene – or cycling on a bike that has no freewheel so cannot coast – has seen an explosion in popularity and, in response, bike nuts Tokyo Fixed have moved from exporting keirin frames from Tokyo (back in 2007), to opening its two-storey Soho store in 2009. The shop stocks all things fixed-wheel, including frames, wheels, and high-end exclusive brands such as Cherubim, Enigma, Nagasawa, Nari Furi, Milani and CCP. Fixed-wheel bikes first became popular with cycle couriers due to their simplicity and ease of maintenance, but have more recently become something of a craze, and one that Tokyo Fixed intends to foster in the city.

Outdoor pursuits & multi-sport shops

Covent Garden has a cluster of shops located near Ellis Brigham (*see right*) that will appeal to (and kit out) hikers, climbers, campers and snowsports enthusiasts.

Ace Sports & Leisure
6 Fortress Road, NW5 2ES (7485 5367, www. acesportsdirect.com). Kentish Town tube/rail. **Open** 9.30am-6pm Mon-Sat.
Established in 1949, Ace Sports is a proper old-school sports shop that covers all sports but has a particular emphasis on football gear; the store stocks plenty of official home and away premiership strips, as well as international shirts, football boots, balls and souvenirs. As well as a rugby section, the store has a small rack of boxing gloves and accessories, a few snooker cues and cricket whites, gloves and pads, as well as tennis and badminton equipment. It also offers an embroidery service, and will customise any sports top of your chosing. Most of the products are available online and can be sent overseas.

Decathlon
Canada Water Retail Park, Surrey Quays Road, SE16 2XU (7394 2000, www.decathlon.co.uk). Canada Water rail. **Open** 9am-9pm Mon-Fri; 9am-7pm Sat; 11am-5pm Sun.
The warehouse-sized London branch of this French chain offers London's biggest single collection of sports equipment. You'll find a vast array of reasonably priced equipment and clothing for all mainstream racket and ball sports as well as for swimming, running, surfing, fishing, horse-riding, mountaineering, ice-skating, skiing, even archery and petanque. The company boasts a 'try before you buy' testing service on its golfing woods and irons. Separate premises host bicycle sales and repairs, along with all sorts of cycling paraphernalia. There's an extensive range of hiking and camping equipment (tents, clothing and accessories). Note that Decathlon will make deliveries all over the country.

Ellis Brigham

Tower House, 3-11 Southampton Street, WC2E 7HA (7395 1010, www.ellis-brigham.com). Covent Garden tube. **Open** 10am-8pm Mon-Fri; 9.30am-6.30pm Sat; 11.30am-5.30pm Sun.

With countless racks of outdoor clothing upstairs and climbing, hiking, skiing and snowboarding equipment downstairs in the basement, this is the largest of the mountain sports shops on Southampton Street. It also houses London's only ice-climbing wall, 26ft high. The wall is in a refrigerator, starting in the basement and rising through the ground floor, where there are viewing windows. Two people can climb at any one time (£50 per person per hour, £25-£35 if you have your own kit and don't need instruction). Book at least a day ahead for weekdays, and around six weeks in advance for weekends.

Branches Unit 2003, Westfield Shopping Centre, W12 7GF (8222 6300); 178 Kensington High Street, W8 7RG (7937 6889); 6 Cheapside Passage, EC2V 6AF (3170 8746); Unit 2092, Westfield Stratford City, W12 7GF (8740 3790).

Niketown

236 Oxford Street, W1C 1DE (7612 0800, www.nike.com). Oxford Circus tube. **Open** 10am-9pm Mon-Sat; 11.30am-6pm Sun.

Four-storey Niketown is big on clothing. It may be low on equipment but it stocks an excellent selection of football boots and has a well-stocked running department as well as a customisation lab on the second floor where, with many of the designs, you can choose your material (cracked leather, metallic) and colour (even colour of 'swoosh') and then personalise it with an embroidered ID. There are also plenty of shirts (baseball, cycling, rugby, football) and accessories (bags, gloves, socks). In keeping with the trend for interactive retail, Nike Town hosts DJs and in-store events on Saturdays throughout the summer. For Nike's 1948 store, selling rarer trainer models, *see p121.*

Wigmore Sports

39 Wigmore Street, W1U 1PD (7486 7761, www.wigmoresports.co.uk). Bond Street tube. **Open** 10am-6pm Mon-Wed, Fri, Sat; 10am-7pm Thur; 11am-5pm Sun.

If it's got strings and it swings, you can buy it here. The most impressive racket sports specialist in London, Wigmore Sports has a whole room stacked full of tennis, squash and badminton rackets. This is high-end gear so don't expect to find more than a dozen tennis rackets among the hundreds on display for much under £50; most are over £100. All the extras are here, plus specialist clobber like tennis-specific sunglasses with teal tinted

Run & Become. See p236.

lenses that mute all light except optic yellow. The footwear choice is also extensive, with something for every surface. There's a 24-hour stringing service and an in-store practice wall so you can try before you buy. There's also a concession in Harrods.

Specialists

For the **Supreme** skateboard shop, *see p63*.

Arthur Beale

194 Shaftesbury Avenue, WC2H 8JP (7836 9034). Tottenham Court Road tube. **Open** 9am-6pm Mon-Fri; 9.30am-1pm Sat.

There are some odd shops in London, but few beat the surprise factor of finding a yacht chandler in Shaftesbury Avenue. Arthur Beale is a retail survivor, hanging on long after many of the other chandlers went bust. It may look old-fashioned – and it stubbornly holds out against this new-fangled internet thing – but the stock is as useful now as it ever was for sailors. On the ground floor you'll find everything from reels of rope, ship's bells, barometers and brass navigation lights to basic boating hardware such as cleats, fairleads and lacing hooks. On the first floor you'll find books, boots and lifejackets.

Bloch

35 Drury Lane, WC2B 5RH (7836 4777, www.blochshop.co.uk). Covent Garden tube. **Open** 10am-6pm Mon-Sat; noon-5pm Sun.

Feet are important for everyone, but vital for a dancer. Bloch, a renowned dance footwear and apparel manufacturer that was founded in 1932, continues to sell shoes for ballet, tap, hip hop, jazz, latin and ballroom, but it has recently gone into partnership with Australian designer Jozette Hazzouri, producing a range of high-fashion shoes and sandals. Its own brand of day shoes features a striking range of colours and funky, dance-inspired designs, and Baby Bloch will ensure your child has shoes to die for before he or she can even crawl – thus ensuring the shoes stay clean as well. Bloch's own-brand active-wear clothing line is great for yoga and Pilates practitioners, as well as dancers.

Freed of London

94 St Martin's Lane, WC2N 4AT (7240 0432, www.freedoflondon.com). Leicester Square tube. **Open** 9.30am-5.30pm Mon-Fri; 10am-4.30pm Sat.

If you've ever seen a ballet, you'll have seen a Freed pointe shoe. The company was founded in 1929 by Frederick Freed and today supplies shoes to prominent dance companies and schools, including the Royal Ballet, New York City Ballet and the Royal Ballet School. Darcey Bussell and Margot Fonteyn wore Freed shoes. The shoes are mostly still made by hand in the traditional turn shoe method, where most of the stitching is done with the shoe turned inside out. If you can't stand en pointe, you can still enjoy wearing the company's ballroom, jazz and Latin shoes, plus a range of clothing. All products are Freed branded.

Run & Become

42 Palmer Street, SW1H 0PH (7222 1314, www.runandbecome.com). St James's Park tube. **Open** 9am-6pm Mon-Wed, Fri, Sat; 9am-8pm Thur.

Tony Smith opened Run & Become in 1982 on its present site, and improving sales allowed him to buy the next-door shop a few years later. Although Tony himself died in 2006, his daughters had already joined him in running the business and it remains family run. The experienced staff, most of them enthusiastic runners, are determined to find the right pair of shoes for your particular physique and running style, with wide selections of road, off-road, fell, spiked and barefoot shoes for sale, including Saucony, Brooks, ASICS, Nike, Puma and Adidas. Apart from shoes, the full gamut of running kit, from clothing to energy snacks to speed monitors, is also available.

Slam City Skates

16 Neal's Yard, WC2H 9DP (7240 0928, www.slamcity.com). Covent Garden tube. **Open** 11am-7pm Mon-Sat; noon-5pm Sun.

Slam City Skates is a legendary name on the British skate scene, as much a part of the London skateboarding identity as doing kickflips and railstands on the walkways beneath the Southbank Centre. It's also the best-stocked shop for decks, trucks, wheels and almost any skateboard accessory – with makers such as Palace, Blueprint, Girl, Chocolate and Deathwish well represented – as well as footwear and clothing by Krew, Vans, Altamont, Nike SB and Supra, including the shop's own unique T-shirt and hoodie range. All the staff are skaters and you can see some of them doing their stuff on the company website under the 'team' link.

Soccer Scene

56 Carnaby Street, W1F 9QF (7439 0778, www.soccerscene.co.uk). Oxford Circus tube. **Open** 10am-7pm Mon-Wed, Fri, Sat; 10am-8pm Thur; noon-6pm Sun.

Soccer fans are nothing if not tribal, and you can get most of the requisite club and country replica kits here. Arsenal, Chelsea and Spurs team kits are available (from £30-£55 for the shirts, £15-£30 for the shorts), along with strips for Aston Villa, Bolton Wanderers, Everton, Liverpool, Manchester (United and City), and Newcastle – basically all the premier league clubs, along with a wide range of national team outfits. There are children's sizes for not much less (£30 £45). Apart from shirts, football accessories are for sale and, naturally, football boots – and not just the mainstream brands: come here for Lotto, Uhlsport and Joma. **Branch** 156 Oxford Street, W1D 1ND (7436 6499).

One of central London's most interesting shopping streets.

Partially pedestrianised, with a slew of good pubs and cafés, Lamb's Conduit Street has a gentle pace that seems far from the bustle of the West End. There's a nice mix of traditional and hip retailers, and residents and shopkeepers stick together – there are organised street festivals, and chains remain a rarity. It's a good location for the **People's Supermarket** (no.72-78; *see p251*), a volunteer-run alternative to the big supermarkets.

Close to Virginia Woolf's old stomping grounds, **Persephone Books** (no.59; *see p190*) is a treasure. Both a small press and retail shop, it specialises in rescuing and elegantly reprinting neglected 20th-century women's fiction. Just a bit further along, the **Lamb Bookshop** (no.40, 7405 6536, www.thelambbookshop.co.uk) stocks a good range of fiction and an even better selection of children's books.

In keeping with the slightly old-fashioned feel of the strip, there are a couple of gentlemen's outfitters that seem to belong to a bygone era, selling suits, waistcoats, tweeds, ties and socks. **Sims & Macdonald** (no.46, 7430 1909, www.simsandmacdonald.com) has been on the street for seven decades, while **Connock & Lockie** (no.33, 7831 2479) offers tailoring for women as well as men.

A few doors down at no.49 and no.53 is **Folk** (7404 6458, *see p55*). The first shop is given over to menswear – the look is casual with a twist and stock is dominated by the in-house label, plus a smattering of other brands such as Our Legacy and Han. No.53 is now a dedicated womenswear store, heavy on stylish Scandinavian labels, such as Acne and WhyRed, with lovely coats from Sessùn. At no.55 is the flagship store of men's brand **Private White V.C.** (7831 3344, www.privatewhitevc.com),

with its quality, everyday menswear using the finest British materials and craftsmanship. **Universal Works** (no.37, 3632 2115) is a similiarly high-quality label for men, while ultra-dapper menswear and accessories label **Simon Carter** (no.36a, 7242 9772) sells bags, cuff-links, wallets, luggage and stand-out shirts.

Just around the corner on Rugby Street is **Ben Pentreath** (no.17; *see p159*), the interiors and oddities store, and the lovely 1920s shopfront of **Maggie Owen**, formerly French's Dairy (no.13; *see p128*). The jewellery and accessories shop housed within showcases European designers such as Philippe Ferrandis and Anton Heunis. For more accessories, carry on to 7 Rugby Street, where **Susannah Hunter**'s (7692 3798, www.susannahhunter.com) handmade leather bags and furniture are decorated with her signature appliquéd flowers.

Back on Lamb's Conduit Street, **Oliver Spencer**'s upmarket menswear boutique is at no.62 (7269 6444, www.oliverspencer.co.uk), while his shoe boutique is at no.58 (*see p119*). Nearby is one of the newer and most exciting shops: concept store **Darkroom** (no.52; *see p35*). Inside the stylish black-walled space you'll find an intriguing selection of unisex fashion and jewellery, designer ceramics and artwork for sale. At no.50 is the **French House** (7831 1111), selling country-style duvets, linens, Provençal baskets and lavendar soap. Reliable repairs outfit **Bikefix** (*see p229*) is next door, stocking a good range of accessories, plus unusual urban bikes and fold-ups if you're in the market for a new ride.

Round off your shopping trip with a fragrant bouquet at **Dawson Flowers** at no.43 (7404 6893, www.dawsonflowers.net).

LEISURE

Pets

Holly & Lil
*103 Bermondsey Street, SE1 3XB (3287 3024,
www.hollyandlil.co.uk). London Bridge tube/rail.*
Open 11am-6pm Mon; 10.30am-6.15pm Tue,
Fri; 10.30am-7pm Wed, Thur; 10.30am-5pm Sat;
11.30am-3.30pm Sun.
Holly & Lil's dog collars and leads are all handmade, luxurious and on-trend. There are limited-edition collections
– the star of award winning silent film *The Artist*, Uggie,
had a custom collar designed for the red carpet, complete
with patent black bow and gold piping. The new Cool
Britannia coat comes all sizes (fit for even the biggest of
bulldogs, and in all sorts of materials (leather, tartan,
Harris tweed). Extra touches include 'charm collars'
adorned with beads, tiny multicoloured dice, or semi-
precious stones. Prices start at around £40, rising to £132
for the hand-stitched Union Jack models. The shop also
sells a range of harnesses and charity collars, and cats
get a look in, too, with their own line of collars. If nothing
seems quite fancy enough, owners can commission
something ultra-outrageous themselves.

Kings Aquatic & Reptile World
*26 Camden High Street, NW1 0JH (7387 5553,
www.kingsreptileworld.co.uk). Mornington Crescent
tube.* **Open** 10am-6pm Mon-Sat; 10am-2pm Sun.
Reptile expert Simon King set up this exotic pet shop,
supplying arachnids, snakes, amphibians, invertebrates
and reptiles, in 1997. Any squeamish readers out there
can relax, though – all the creatures are safely ensconced
in their cages. Prices vary widely depending on the rarity
of the specimen; a tarantula will set you back between
£10 and £200, lizards go for £8 to £800 and baby corn
snakes start at £45. Kings also breeds rare monitor
lizards and runs a pet-sitting service. Crickets, locusts
and frozen mice are for sale for pets' snacks, and there
are all sorts of cages. A modest selection of cold-water
and tropical fish is available downstairs.

Mungo & Maud

Mungo & Maud
*79 Elizabeth Street, SW1W 9PJ (7467 0820,
www.mungoandmaud.com). Sloane Square tube
or Victoria tube/rail.* **Open** 10am-6pm Mon-Sat.
A boutique with a touch of French sophistication, this
is the ultimate 'dog and cat outfitters'. Fed up with their
dog's outmoded accessories clashing with their modern
home, dog-lovers Michael and Nicola Sacher decided to
design their own to fill the niche. Stylish and minimalist,
pooch products include washable dog beds, collars and
leads, and a new range of super chic cashmere pullovers,
as well as the 'petite amande dog fragrance'; for kitty,
there's catnip and embroidered wool cat blankets.
Humans won't feel left out and can browse book titles
like *Lump: The Dog Who Ate A Picasso* and *Is Your Cat
Gay?* There's also a concession in Harrods' Pet Kingdom.
Branch 51 Ledbury Road, W11 2AA.

Mutz Nutz
*221 Westbourne Park Road, W11 1EA (7243
3333, www.themutznutz.com). Ladbroke Grove or
Westbourne Park tube.* **Open** 9am-6pm Mon, Fri,
Sat; 9am-7pm Tue-Thur; 11am-5pm Sun.
As the name suggests, the treats from this attractive boutique will drive cats and dogs (or their owners) crazy. On
the shelves you'll find toys, leads, handmade
jewel-encrusted collars (£50-£200), organic nibbles,
toothbrushes – even dog nappies. There are also special
dog car seats and, bizarrely, wedding dresses with veils.
Cats are equally well catered for, with catnip spray and
a three-sided 'scratch lounge'. The nearby newly renovated same-owned Dog Spa (22 Powis Terrace, W11 1JH,
7243 3399) offers Italian baths: pets are tended to with
all-natural products by personal groomers and leave
fully coiffed, perfumed and ribbon clad. At the pet supermarket, goodies and titbits can be taken away.

Primrose Hill Pets
*132 Regent's Park Road, NW1 8XL (7483 2023,
www.primrosehillpets.co.uk). Chalk Farm tube.*
Open 9.30am-6.30pm Mon; 9am-6pm Tue-Sat;
11am-5pm Sun.
The UK's finest quality leads and collars are available
here (check out the Puppia range), as well as some very
swish numbers from Germany (Hunter) and the US (Miro
& Makauri): they come in all sizes, in leather, fabric or
nylon, plain or diamanté. There is also a range of coats
(all sizes, some exclusive), beds (faux suede, vet bed), air-
line-approved pet carriers (Sherpa) and a range of
grooming products (including ones for sensitive skins
and allergies), plus there's a treatment service for cats
and dogs (by appointment). Food here is a best-seller and
focuses on organic and hypo-allergenic ranges such as
Lily's Kitchen and Pet Munchies. Informed staff give
advice on diets, food, supplements and treats and they
will readily point you in the direction of local breeders
and shelters.

LEISURE

Food & Drink

Food & Drink

As one of the world's most cosmopolitan cities, London has an unparalleled range of international food shops offering every conceivable type of produce, and with specific neighbourhoods to visit for each; so, for instance, Shepherds Bush is the place to head to for Middle Eastern foodstuffs, Hackney has a host of places selling Turkish and Vietnamese produce, while Soho is home to two much-loved Italian delis (**Lina Stores** and **I Camisa & Son**). London's many food markets are also definite highlights of its culinary landscape; London chefs are often found trawling the famous **Borough Market** (*see p42*), while Hackney's **Broadway Market** (*see p46*) and Bermondsey's **Maltby Street Market** (*see p48*) have become Saturday hangouts for many of the city's foodies.

Traditional institutions are another highlight: **Allens of Mayfair** (*see p243*) has been in business since the 1720s, while Jermyn Street's **Paxton & Whitfield** (*see p246*) has been selling fine cheeses for over 200 years. The newer wave of upscale outfits has solidified the city's enthusiasm for high-quality food, with **Daylesford Organic** (*see p248*), **La Fromagerie** (*see p245*) and the **Ginger Pig** (*see p244*) three popular don't-misses. For a more radical approach

on how to shop in the 21st century, head to **Unpackaged** (*see p251*), the grocer's that eschews packaging wherever possible. The **People's Supermarket** (*see p251*) on independents-filled Lamb's Conduit Street is similarly revolutionary in its fight against food waste and in its staffing system, whereby members work as volunteers in the shop for a discount on produce.

Sweet treats, meanwhile, come in the form of posh chocolate shops **Prestat** (*see p248*) and **Paul A Young** (*see p247*), and retro sweet haven **Hope & Greenwood** (*see p247*).

Oenophiles and coffee lovers are also spoilt for choice. From 17th-century wine companies selling traditional vintages (**Berry Bros & Rudd**, *see p254*) to friendly and passionate neighbourhood wine boutiques, such as **Borough Wines** (*see p254*) and **The Sampler** (*see p256*), London's wine sellers offer both expertise and variety. Caffeine addicts should make a beeline for the **Algerian Coffee Stores** (*see p257*), a stalwart of Soho's Old Compton Street for well over a century. And for a proper – and we really do mean proper – cup of tea, don't miss the lovely **Postcard Teas** (*see p258*) in Mayfair, home to a superb range of high-quality tea leaves, as well as tasting sessions.

Food

Bakeries & pâtisseries

De Gustibus
4 Southwark Street, SE1 1TQ (7407 3625,
www.degustibus.co.uk). London Bridge tube/rail.
Open 7am-5pm Mon-Fri; 7am-4pm Sat.
Dan and Annette Schickentanz started the highly
esteemed De Gustibus bakery business in the kitchen of
their Oxfordshire home. While the shops tend to look like
sandwich joints (and the sandwiches are indeed terrific),
it's the modest displays of expertly made breads that
really shine. The huge rounds of Six Day Sour are worth
a trip across town as this deliciously tangy, even-textured
white bread keeps well and upgrades your daily toast
and sarnies to gourmet status. The walnut loaf has
gained the pair royal recognition, with Prince Charles
praising its wholesome, rich and nutty texture. The salt
beef sandwiches are very highly rated, but a choice of
rye loaves and others in the American and Italian traditions mean everyone will be able to find something to sat-
isfy. Bread-making classes for all levels are also on offer.
Branch 53-55 Carter Lane, EC4V 5AE (7236 0056).

Konditor & Cook
22 Cornwall Road, SE1 8TW (7261 0456,
www.konditorandcook.com). Waterloo tube/rail.
Open 7.30am-6.30pm Mon-Fri; 8.30am-3pm Sat.
Gerhard Jenne caused a stir when he opened this bakery on a South Bank side street in 1993, selling rude
gingerbread people for grown-ups and lavender-
flavoured cakes. It's now a mini chain with a few
branches (including a swanky café in the Gherkin).
Signature products are magic cakes, miniature iced
pictures that can be pieced together to create an 'edible
patchwork quilt' – perfect for parties. The distinctive
folds of the whisky and orange bombe make it one of
the best-known cakes in the range. Look out especially
for seasonal treats such as pumpkin pie in October
and mince pies in December, and don't miss the terrific
hot chocolate, made with double cream and Valrhona
couverture. The bespoke wedding cakes are adorned
with intricate hand-painted designs. Quality pre-
packed lunchtime salads, sandwiches and sausage
rolls are also available.
Branches throughout the city.

Poilâne
46 Elizabeth Street, SW1W 9PA (7808 4910,
www.poilane.fr). Sloane Square tube or Victoria
tube/rail. **Open** 7am-7pm Mon-Fri; 7am-6pm Sat.
Founded in Paris in 1932 by Pierre Poilâne, this company achieved international repute under his son Lionel
and is now run by granddaughter Appollonia. The

London branch produces bread satisfyingly similar to that made in Paris and distributes to many other shops in the capital, including Selfridges and Waitrose. The bread is baked in environmentally friendly wood-fired ovens using waste wood. Although prices are premium, the chewy, dense and remarkably sour loaves have long keeping qualities, so score on value. The branch at Cadogan Gardens has a café, where alongside classic French dishes, Poilâne pastries and tartines are served. **Branch** 39 Cadogan Gardens, SW3 2TB (3263 6019).

Butchers

Allens of Mayfair

117 Mount Street, W1K 3LA (7499 5831, www.allensofmayfair.co.uk). Bond Street or Green Park tube. **Open** 7am-7pm Mon-Fri; 7am-5pm Sat; 11am-3pm Sun.

A Mayfair institution operating for nearly 180 years from the same site, though not with the same owners – Justin Preston and David House (both butchers by trade) saved the business from imminent closure when they bought it in spring 2006. Beef and game remain the fortes; in season you'll find snipe, teal and widgeon as well as more common species such as pheasant and grouse, and for a small charge Allens will process birds you have acquired. The range of smoked meats

includes venison, ham and chicken. Helpful staff are on hand to recommend appropriate cuts of meat, along with an accompanying condiment. Meat boxes are also available, including a gourmet weekend selection, barbecue banquet box, exotic kebab box and a weekly meat box (available online) for two or four people. Butchery classes cost £150 per person.

C Lidgate

110 Holland Park Avenue, W11 4UA (7727 8243, www.lidgates.com). Holland Park tube. **Open** 7.30am-7pm Mon-Fri; 6.30am-6.30pm Sat.

The butchers at C Lidgate have run this store for over 150 years – and have kept the cleavers in the same fam-

FOOD & DRINK

Poilâne

C Lidgate. See p243.

ily's hands for four generations. That's right: the Lidgates truly have butchery in their blood. The meat here is organic and free range, and a great deal of it is sourced from prestige estates, including Prince Charles's Highgrove. But the family have also kept up with the times; the window is crammed with tempting dishes such as saddle of lamb with pesto. The scotch eggs (made with quail eggs and wrapped in Lidgate's own cumberland sausage mince), speciality sausages and pies (made to order in ceramic dishes) go down a treat. A selection of desserts (apple and pecan pie, say) are also on offer.

Ginger Pig

99 Lauriston Road, E9 7HJ (8986 6911, www.thegingerpig.co.uk). Mile End tube then bus 277, 425. **Open** 9am-5.30pm Tue; 9am-6.30pm Wed-Fri; 9am-6pm Sat; 9am-3pm Sun.
The east London outlet for the celebrated farm-based butcher of rare-breed meats that came to national attention via Borough Market in the late 1990s. You'll find cuts from longhorn cattle, Swaledale and Black Face sheep, Gloucester Old Spot and Tamworth pigs, plus own-made bacon, sausages, pork pies and terrines. All the meat comes from animals that have been raised to a high standard of welfare. There's also an excellent deli downstairs, with sausage rolls, duck and pistachio pâté,

handmade pies and cooked meats, as well as non-meat fodder such as fresh veg, olives, fish, bread, quiches, pickles, chutneys, and decent wine and beer. You can even order custom-made pork pie 'wedding cakes'. Butchery and sausage-making classes are also offered.
Branches Borough Market, SE1 1TL (7403 4721); 8-10 Moxon Street, W1U 4EW (7935 7788); 27 Lower Marsh, SE1 7RG (7921 2975); 137-139 Askew Road, W12 9AU (8740 4297).

Fishmongers

Sandys

56 King Street, Twickenham, Middx TW1 3SH (8892 5788, www.sandysfish.net). Twickenham rail. **Open** 7.30am-6pm Mon-Wed, Sat; 7.30am-7.30pm Thur; 7.30am-7pm Fri; 9am-5pm Sun.
Easily one of London's best fishmongers, this large and popular store is an established family-run business, and offers a wide range of sustainably sourced species, from Cornish sardines and lemon sole to wild sea trout and Sri Lankan red snapper. The selection of shellfish is also exemplary, with New Zealand mussels, English cockles, whelks, live and cooked lobsters and crabs, king scallops and North Atlantic prawns. Smoked produce comes from

prestigious Scottish company Inverawe, and include a range of hot and mild smoked salmon, eel, halibut and trout. You'll also find own-made sausages and game in season. As well as the normal services (skinning, boning, filleting et al), the fishmongers will also vacuum pack your fish for you on request (and free of charge). Catering platters are also available.

Steve Hatt

88-90 Essex Road, N1 8LU (7226 3963). Angel tube. **Open** 8am-5pm Tue-Thur; 7am-5pm Fri, Sat.
There's nothing new to report about Steve Hatt: just expect first-class fresh fish from this long-established fishmonger and you won't be disappointed. A wet fish display stretching along the wide front window affords queuing customers plenty of opportunity to check out what's available and, once you've made your selection, you can have your fish skinned, boned and filleted on request by the cheery staff. Labels highlight deals, such as sea trout 'lowest price of the season'. Expect prime examples of wild Scottish halibut, bluefin tuna, gilthead bream, prawns, scallops and smoked fish (from the shop's own smokehouse), plus fresh samphire. Frozen fish is available, but extras are kept to a minimum.

Cheese shops

La Fromagerie

2-6 Moxon Street, W1U 4EW (7935 0341, www.lafromagerie.co.uk). Baker Street tube. **Open** 8am-7.30pm Mon-Fri; 9am-7pm Sat; 10am-6pm Sun.
A large window piled with regal wheels of comté, gouda, emmental, unpasteurised cheddar and more offers a taster of the delicious delights to be found beyond the black wooden door of this chic deli-café with refrigerated cheese rooms. Patricia Michelson and team hand-select cheeses from small artisan makers for sale alongside speciality seasonal produce (Brogdale heritage apples, Roscoff onions, San Marzano tomatoes), sweet things (orange and almond cake, brownies with Piedmontese hazelnuts), freshly baked breads, quality olive oils and traiteur dishes made on the premises to take away or enjoy in the café. Helpful staff offer advice on cheese board selections, and wine pairings from their range. Check the website for tasting events.
Branch 30 Highbury Park, N5 2AA (7359 7440).

Neal's Yard Dairy

17 Shorts Gardens, WC2H 9UP (7240 5700, www.nealsyarddairy.co.uk). Covent Garden tube. **Open** 10am-7pm Mon-Sat.
A thoroughly British shop with a traditional French attitude to cheese retailing in that, like an *affineur*, Neal's Yard buys from small farms and creameries in Britain and Ireland, and matures the cheeses in its own cellars until ready to sell in peak condition. It's best to walk in

Ginger Pig

and ask what's good today – you'll be given various tasters by the well-trained staff. Also on sale are oat cakes, jam, honey, pickles, chutney, English apples (in season) and top-drawer books on cheese and other food. Around Christmas time, the queue for Montgomery's cheddar and stilton often runs down the street.
Branch 6 Park Street, SE1 9AB (7367 0799).

Paxton & Whitfield

93 Jermyn Street, SW1Y 6JE (7930 0259, www.paxtonandwhitfield.co.uk). Green Park tube.
Open 9.30am-6pm Mon-Sat; 11am-5pm Sun.
In business for over 200 years, and based on this site since 1894, Paxton & Whitfield sells a wide range of British and continental European cheeses, plus excellent hams, biscuits and real ale. The shop underwent a major refurbishment during summer 2011, giving the interior a whole new look, providing more space for tastings, and expanding and modernising the maturing cages in the cellar. Service remains exemplary and delightfully unstuffy – a rare pleasure on Jermyn Street. Among the unusual English varieties to look out for are Oxford isis (washed in mead), caradon blue from Cornwall and naturally smoked 'ceodre' cheddar, and the shop now has an extended range of French cheeses, courtesy of Androuet, a traditional Parisian cheese shop. P&W is also known for its celebration 'cheese cakes' – contrasting tiers of artisan cheese rounds made to look like traditional wedding cakes. Spectacular hampers can be filled with everything from cheese and chutney to cheese knives and cheese boards. Sandwiches are available at lunchtime. Expect long queues at Christmas.

La Fromagerie. See p245.

Confectioners

L'Artisan du Chocolat

89 Lower Sloane Street, SW1W 8DA (7824 8365, www.artisanduchocolat.com). Sloane Square tube.
Open 10am-7pm Mon-Sat; noon-5pm Sun.
L'Artisan du Chocolat's Gerard Coleman and Anne Weyns launch a new collection each season as well as special designs for festive occasions such as Valentine's Day, Christmas, Easter and Halloween, making this an ideal destination for those times when you want to give something original and tasteful but lack inspiration. Best known for liquid salted caramels, chocolate coated popcorn and chocolate 'pearls', they also offer a range of bars made from scratch in Kent using ground cocoa beans, cane sugar and cocoa butter; the green tea bar is particularly innovative, while the ginger and lemongrass bar is designed as a harmonious experience. Sugar-free, dairy free and vegan bars are available. The company has a concession in Selfridges and a stall at Borough Market.
Branch 81 Westbourne Grove, W2 4UL (0845 270 6996).

Hope & Greenwood

20 North Cross Road, SE22 9EU (8613 1777, www.hopeandgreenwood.co.uk). East Dulwich rail.
Open 10am-6pm Mon-Sat; 11am-5pm Sun.
Saturday queues are almost inevitable at this small vacuum for pocket money. Everything from chocolate gooseberries to sweetheart candies is prettily displayed in plastic beakers, cellophane bags, glass jars, illustrated boxes, porcelain bowls and cake tins. Relive sweet childhood memories by indulging in a bag of sherbert Flying Saucers, gobstoppers or rhubarb and custard 'rations', as well as Double Dips, sugar mice, Curly Wurlys, Love Hearts and a new range of candyfloss in flavours such as green apple or strawberry. Posher chocolates are also available, including lavender and geranium truffles. Gift possibilities include Union Jack mints, retro gumball machines and the refills for them. Ice-cream is available in the warmer months. Space is also found for a select range of homewares, including aprons, mixing bowls and baking paraphernalia. The branch in Covent Garden is a good pre-theatre pitstop.
Branch 1 Russell Street, WC2B 5JD (7240 3314).

Ladurée at Harrods

Harrods, 87-135 Brompton Road, SW1X 7XL (3155 0111, www.laduree.fr). Knightsbridge tube.
Open 9am-9pm Mon-Sat; 11.30am-6pm Sun.
The London flagship of this famous Parisian macaroon chain is made up of a collection of individually designed rooms set into a corner of Harrods. A long and elegant marble counter proudly displays Marie Antoinette-worthy multi-coloured delicacies. Alongside the classics, look out for seasonal specials, in flavours such as blood

L'Artisan du Chocolat

orange, ginger or green apple. In the café, afternoon tea comes complete with finger sandwiches, mini viennoiseries and pastries. From the low, brick-coloured velvet chairs of the mezzanine, you can catch glimpses of the street or look over the chandelier to the pastel greens and pinks of the shop counter, where all manner of boxes are stacked ready to hold take-home treats.
Branches 71-72 Burlington Gardens, W1J 0QX (7491 9155; 1 The Market, Covent Garden, WC2E 8RA (7240 0706; 14 Cornhill, EC3V 3ND (7283 5727).

Paul A Young Fine Chocolates

33 Camden Passage, N1 8EA (7424 5750, www.payoung.net). Angel tube. **Open** 10am-6.30pm Tue-Thur, Sat; 10am-7.30pm Fri; 11am-6pm Sun.
A gorgeous boutique on Islington's Camden Passage, with almost everything – chocolates, brownies, cakes, ice-cream – made in the downstairs kitchen and finished in front of customers. Young is a respected pâtissier as well as chocolatier and has an astute chef's palate for flavour-combining. Valrhona and Amedei are his favoured couvertures, which he combines in different blends and origins to match his other ingredients. Summer sees plenty of temptations, such as Pimm's cocktail truffles featuring cucumber, strawberry and mint flavours, and white chocolate blondies made with raspberries and blueberries. The shop is a first port of call for Valentines Day and Mothers' Day gifts. The firm

FOOD & DRINK

has also produced an exclusive brownie collection for Fortnum & Mason.
Branches 20 Royal Exchange, EC3V 3LP (7929 7007); 143 Wardour Street, W1F 8WA (7437 0011).

Prestat
14 Princes Arcade, SW1Y 6DS (7494 3372, www.prestat.co.uk). Green Park tube. **Open** 9.30am-6pm Mon-Fri; 10am-5pm Sat; 11am-4.30pm Sun.
England's oldest chocolatier – the brand has been around for more than a century – is up to the minute when it comes to promoting the health advantages of chocolate. Prestat's Choxi+ bars (dark, milk, ginger, orange, mint) are processed gently to maximise antioxidant content – the claim is that they contain two to three times more of these nutrients than standard milk or dark chocolate. This bijou boutique also offers unusual and traditional chocolates in elegant, brightly coloured packaging, making them lovely gift options. Aside from the straight-up choices, there are boxes of dark chocolate-covered apricots, indulgent champagne truffles, hot chocolate flakes and a range of chocolate wafers (try the Earl Grey ones). The friendly and passionate staff make this an upbeat shopping experience. All Prestat's chocolates are manufactured in the UK from top-quality ingredients. There is a Prestat concession within Harrods.

Rococo
5 Motcomb Street, SW1X 8JU (7245 0993, www.rococochocolates.com). Knightsbridge tube. **Open** 10am-6.30pm Mon-Sat; noon-5pm Sun.
Don't be fooled by the novelty bags of chocolate maize and mushrooms, Rococo is a serious chocolatier, pioneering artisan manufacture, unusual flavour combinations and ethical practices in the UK. Don't miss the Grenada 71% bar, which betters other 'fairly traded' products both in terms of quality, and the fact that the factory is attached to the estate, ensuring that the growers benefit from adding value to their beans themselves. Bars such as orange and geranium and coffee and cardamom are available in dark, milk and white chocolate. Beautiful hand-painted eggs made of high-quality couverture are sold at Easter; the likes of crystallised rose petals are sold year round. This branch, the flagship store, is also home to the MaRococo garden café space, a Moorish-style courtyard where you can sip an indulgent hot chocolate. The Chocolate School is also on-site; see the website for details of classes.
Branches 321 King's Road, SW3 5EP (7352 5857); 45 Marylebone High Street, W1U 5HG (7935 7780).

Grocers, delis & health food
Branches of **Whole Foods Market** (www.wholefoodsmarket.com) and **Planet Organic** (www.planetorganic.com) can be found dotted around the more affluent parts of London.

Chegworth Farm Shop
221 Kensington Church Street, W8 7LX (7229 3016, www.chegworthvalley.com). Notting Hill Gate tube. **Open** 8am-8pm Mon-Sat; 9am-6pm Sun.
Stalwarts of many a farmers' market, the producers from this Kent-based organic fruit farm opened their first stand-alone store in 2008. Known especially for the tangy and pure apple and pear juices, as well as special blends using rhubarb, raspberries, strawberries, blackcurrants and blackberries, the shop also stocks organic fruit and veg – including its full range of apple and pear varieties (28 types of apple; four types of pear). Other essentials stocked include Hurdlebrook Farm yoghurts, daily bread from Flourish, Conscious Food products, Cook ready-made dishes and local farm produce (meat, poultry, eggs) from farms in Kent and East Sussex. Best of all, there's a free same-day delivery service (within a five-mile radius).

Daylesford Organic
44B Pimlico Road, SW1W 8LP (7881 8060, www.daylesfordorganic.com). Sloane Square tube. **Open** 8am-7pm Mon-Sat; 10am-4pm Sun.
Everyone shopping at this pristine white marble food hall is likely to be thinner, blonder and richer than you, but pootle about the shelves long enough and you too could take on that serene glow. Daylesford confidently sets its own rules regarding healthfulness, so while you'll find macca powder on the shelves, there are also fat sausages and salamis, cakes and rustic breads. A typical summer veg display includes white and green asparagus, knobbly green tomatoes and bunches of beetroot. Much is from Daylesford's own organic estates (cheddar, soups, meat, quail eggs) but then, a lot is not, like the unusual varieties of rice, posh French and Italian cheeses, and pasta and matching sauces. The attached café sells hot and cold food available for lunchtime takeaway. There is also a concession in Selfridges which – in summer – includes a rooftop café.
Branch 208-212 Westbourne Grove, W11 2RH (7313 8050).

Earth Natural Foods
200 Kentish Town Road, NW5 2AE (7482 2211, www.earthnaturalfoods.co.uk). Kentish Town tube/rail. **Open** 8.30am-7pm Mon-Sat.
Not just organic but vegetarian too, this ordered mini-supermarket offers plenty of mouthwatering foods, from early morning croissants and seeded loaves, to lunchtime takeaway dishes, pasta for supper, gluten- and wheat-free products, loose teas, coffee, local honey, organic wines, artisan cheeses, and tubs of Booja Booja's excellent vegan ice-creams. The range of quality oils, vinegars and condiments is impressive, and there's also a good range of herbal remedies and organic skincare products (with brands including Dr Hauschka), plus an array of Japanese ingredients and organic baby food. It even sells teff flour. Staff are helpful and courteous.

Melrose & Morgan. See p250.

Leila's

15-17 Calvert Avenue, E2 7JP (7729 9789). Old Street tube/rail or Shoreditch High Street rail. **Open** *Shop* 10am-6pm Wed-Sat; 10am-5pm Sun. *Café* 10am-6pm Wed-Sat; 10am-5pm Sun.

Leila McAlister's eclectic store has the nous to distinguish between crusty and gooey brownies and offer customers the choice. There are fresh, seasonal fruit and vegetables, splendid breads and cheeses, French sunflower oil (sold from large plastic bottles), Polish cured meats and sausages, and bags of marcona almonds. Among the packaged groceries are Chegworth Farm juices, teas and coffee, and chutneys and jams from England Preserves. After you've stocked up, head to the café next door for excellent coffee or simple but delicious brunch and lunch fodder.

Melrose & Morgan

42 Gloucester Avenue, NW1 8JD (7722 0011, www.melroseandmorgan.com). Chalk Farm tube. **Open** 8am-7pm Mon-Fri; 8am-6pm Sat; 9am-5pm Sun.

Sophisticated suppers become dreamily low effort when you shop at this ultra-foodie set-up. Made-on-the-premises dishes are put together from organic and free-range products; dishes range from roast aubergine dip to fish cakes, chicken escalopes, lamb and fennel meat-balls, and superior sandwiches. It also offers gourmet picnics, catering packages and a delivery service. The array of cakes, pastries, brownies, pasties, tarts and sausage rolls that covers the large table running down the centre of the store is almost impossible to resist. While there, pick up some Newby teas, Regent's Park honey (in season), artisan cheeses, and M&M's wonderful own-made blueberry and thyme jam. Oh, and Flour Station bread to go with it.

Newington Green Fruit & Vegetables

109 Newington Green Road, N1 4QY (7354 0990). Canonbury rail or bus 73. **Open** 8am-10pm daily.

One of the area's best-loved shops, the family-run Newington Greens, as it's known locally, exemplifies the modern London grocer's shop at its best: not only does it have stacks of beautifully arranged fresh fruit and vegetables, but prices are very reasonable, and the shop is open until 10pm every day, meaning that there's no excuse for not getting your five a day if you live in Newington Green. The popularity of the shop – there are often queues snaking out the door – has meant that the business moved into a larger space at no.109, with the former shop at no.107 now used as a storeroom. As well as the seasonal, local fruit and veg, and a good range of fresh herbs, there are some exotic and novelty items, such as the square melons from Japan.

People's Supermarket

People's Supermarket

72-78 Lamb's Conduit Street, WC1N 3LP (7430 1827, www.peoplessupermarket.org). Holborn tube. **Open** 8am-10pm Mon-Sat; 10am-9pm Sun.
Fighting off Tesco for a site in one of central London's most independently spirited neighbourhoods, the People's Supermarket is a project close to the hearts of celeb chef Arthur Potts-Dawson and ex-Marks & Spencer executive Kate Wickes-Bull. The duo rallied the local community into buying into the scheme – literally. Although anyone can shop at the store, full membership (which scores you a ten per cent discount and a say in how the shop is run) will cost you £25 and four hours per month working in the store. What you get is fresh, locally sourced (where possible) supermarket fare, dirt cheap and airfreight free; new jobs for locals; and all profits going back into the business. The shop also hosts in-store events for the community, such as beer evenings and quiz nights.

Unpackaged

197 Richmond Road, E8 3NJ (www.beunpackaged. com). London Fields rail. **Open** 8am-8pm daily.
Buy only what you need (from local suppliers wherever possible), reduce what you use, reuse old containers and recycle all you can – that's the thinking behind Catherine Conway's impressive enterprise (she also runs a consultancy service to help other businesses reduce waste). Customers bring in their own jars, pots, Tupperware and bags, and fill them with fruit, veg and store cupboard ingredients – all organic, Fairtrade or locally sourced – from the beautifully arranged shop; alternatively, buy a reusable container from the store. Vats of olive oil are on tap for refills, and you can take your fill of the pulses, nuts, pasta, rice, loose teas, Neal's Yard cheeses, herbs and spices, jams, chutney, honey and much more, all arranged in stylish square containers. And there's even an in-house nutritionist. An Amwell Street fixture for many years, the shop moved to new Hackney premises in December 2012 – here there's also room for a café/bar (8am-11pm), allowing Unpackaged to move towards its aim of being a social hub rather than simply a well-realised shop.

International

Al-Abbas

258-262 Uxbridge Road, W12 7JA (8740 1932). Shepherd's Bush tube/rail. **Open** 7am-midnight daily (unable to confirm, no answer).
A short walk from Shepherd's Bush tube, Al-Abbas is one of our favourite Middle Eastern stores in west London, and in fact stocks groceries from all corners of the globe, with Polish, African and Indian essentials, as well as rice, oils, breads and meat. The range of grains and pulses is astonishing and includes the hard-to-find freekeh and moth beans. Spice up your cooking with the jalapeños and other fresh chillies or speciality herbs such as methi. Teetotallers will appreciate exotic cordials of tamarind and mint and the stack of fresh falafel sitting by the till are hard to resist too. Note that, in season, fruit and vegetables are often sold by the crateful at a bargain price.

Giacobazzi's

150 Fleet Road, NW3 2QX (7267 7222, www.giacobazzis.co.uk). Belsize Park tube or Hampstead Heath rail. **Open** 9am-7pm Mon-Fri; 9am-6pm Sat.
Customers queue patiently at this beloved Hampstead Heath deli to get their hands on Giacobazzi's selection of own-made dishes, not to mention the delicious on-the-bone ham. Products, from all over Italy, have helpful labels to explain the difference between, say, the various types of pecorino, or Sicilian and Puglian quince pastes. The antipasti counter has more than the usual suspects, with options such as grilled radicchio and marinated carrot. Filled pastas are made on site, as are truffle butter and desserts. Giacobazzi's can deliver everything you'll need for your meal, from the breadsticks and olives to the seasonal cakes; there's also a catering service. Staff often host in-store seasonal tastings.

Green Valley

36-37 Upper Berkeley Street, W1H 5QF (7402 7385). Marble Arch tube. **Open** 8am-midnight daily.
One of London's best Middle Eastern food halls, Green Valley has a comprehensive meze counter, bursting with colour and offering myriad possibilities for quick, after-work suppers. The fresh produce area includes squat, round Lebanese pears, dainty aubergines, stumpy cucumbers, plus the likes of dragon fruit, guava and young coconuts, as well as freshly prepared juices. The butcher's counter provides fresh cuts of halal meats. In the freezer you'll find molokhia (a high-nutrient green vegetable used in soups and stews) and ready-made kibbeh in chicken, lamb and almond varieties. In addition to the eye-catching display of baklava, the sizeable pâtisserie section includes thickly layered gateaux and tubs of rice pudding and ice-cream. Try one of the speciality coffees, for example, the Lebanese coffee with cardamom. Green Valley also offers a catering service.

I Camisa & Son

61 Old Compton Street, W1D 6HS (7437 7610, www.icamisa.co.uk). Leicester Square or Tottenham Court Road tube. **Open** 8.30am-6pm Mon-Sat.
This long-established rustic Italian deli was opened by the Fratelli Camisi back in 1929. The old Soho stalwart is well worth a visit, if only for its fresh pasta and accompanying sauces (the pesto is particularly good). But that would be to miss out on the fabulous range of cheeses (pecorino, gorgonzola – both sweet and piccante –

Al-Abbas. See p251.

parmesan, mozzarella, ricotta), charcuterie (salamis, mortadella, parma ham), freshly marinated olives, vegetables (artichokes, peppers, aubergines, sun-dried tomatoes, mushrooms) in oil, risotto rices, balsamic vinegars, cakes and biscuits, as well the range of own-label products. Gneerously-filled sandwiches mean substantial queues at lunchtime. A real taste of Italy.

Japan Centre
14-16 Regent Street, SW1Y 4PH (3405 1151, www.japancentre.com). Piccadilly Circus tube.
Open 10am-9pm Mon-Sat; 11am-7pm Sun.
The Japan Centre's basement grocery has taken over next door's premises, allowing for the expansion of the grocery and fresh meat, fish and vegetable ranges, plus the addition of a new trend-setting bakery. Sweet, creamy edamame gateau? It hardly sounds possible but you'll find it here, along with cakes flavoured with red beans and sesame, organic herbs, meats cut specially for shabu-shabu, takeaway sushi, myriad types of tofu, rice, snack foods and Fuji apples, as well as a mind-blowing (and occasionally roof-of-mouth-blowing) range of pastes, sauces, seasonings, pickles and drinks, including an impressive range of green teas, flavoured soy milk and saké. The rest of the store is taken up with cookware, as well as books, gifts and accessories.

Lina Stores
18 Brewer Street, W1R 3FS (7437 6482, www.linastores.co.uk). Piccadilly Circus tube.
Open 8.30am-6.30pm Mon-Fri; 10am-6.30pm Sat; 11am-5pm Sun.

Behind the 1950s green ceramic Soho frontage is Lina Stores, an iconic family-run Italian deli that's been in business for over half a century. Indeed, Jane Grigson used to buy spaghetti in blue wax paper here years before celebrity chefs coasted the streets on scooters. Besides dried pastas (stored in beautiful wooden crates), there's a deli counter chock-full of cured meats, hams, salamis, olives, cheeses, marinated artichokes and fresh pastas. Imported items run from breads to chestnut honey, and Lina is one of the best places to buy truffles in season. Recommended is the fresh pesto and fresh filled pasta. The shop underwent a big refurbishment a year or so ago, adding a new coffee machine and smartening up the space.

Lisboa
54 Golborne Road, W10 5NR (8969 1586). Ladbroke Grove or Westbourne Park tube. **Open** 9.30am-7pm Mon-Sat; 10am-5pm Sun.
Among the packaged groceries at this friendly Portuguese deli are tins of sweet potato and guava paste, beans, pastas and the essential strong coffee. You'll also find white anchovies in vinegar, sardine pâté, Iberian oils, pasteis de bacalhau (salt cod fritters) and pasteis de nata (custard tarts). There's a great range of Portuguese and Spanish sausages and cured meats (merguez, chorizo, morcilla), as well as a large variety of Portuguese cheeses, pickles, herbs and oils. Extend the experience by nipping over the road to the popular, ever busy, Lisboa Pâtisserie for coffee and a cake (orange and coconut, for example); there's usually a queue, but it's worth the wait.

Persepolis

28-30 Peckham High Street, SE15 5DT (7639 8007, www.forataesteofpersia.co.uk). Peckham Rye rail or bus 36. **Open** 10.35am-9pm daily.

Music, handicrafts, tagines, rugs and shisha pipes are stocked alongside edibles at Sally Butcher's colourful Iranian store, an inspiration for food-lovers from the local area and beyond. The Western perspective she brings to proceedings – such as recommending rose petals not just for Persian ice-cream but for pretty party ice cubes – is undoubtedly part of the appeal. And it's a great place to stock up on the likes of fresh Persian dates, sumak, cassia bark, fruit tobacco, dried limes and verjus. There's an enormous range of Persian herbs and spices, books and handicrafts; hampers and gift packages are also available. You'll also find details of a host of Persian literary events.

R García & Sons

248-250 Portobello Road, W11 1LL (7221 6119). Ladbroke Grove or Westbourne Park tube. **Open** 10am-6pm Mon, Sun; 9am-6pm Tue-Fri; 9am-6.30pm Sat.

R Garcia was established back in 1958 and is one of the capital's largest Spanish grocer-delis. The meat counter is a joy to peruse, with a mouthwatering array of cured hams and sausages. There are ready-made dishes, and the store also stocks an excellent range of sherries, along with cava, sangria, red, white and sweet wines. Tins of smoked paprika, marcona almonds, olive oils, rices and pastas, sherry vinegar and slabs of turron line the shelves, while the cheese selection includes manchego, mahon, cabralles and tetilla. Argentinean and Columbian brands are also stocked, as are steel paella pans and terracotta dishes, along with toiletries and even Spanish cologne. There is a café on the premises too.

Turkish Food Centre

89 Ridley Road, E8 2NH (7254 6754, www.tfcsupermarkets.com). Dalston Kingsland rail or bus 30, 56, 149. **Open** 8am-9pm daily.

Now with 14 branches stretching from Catford to Tottenham, this popular supermarket has an excellent range of fresh fruit and veg flown in weekly from Greece, Cyprus and Turkey. Depending on the season, you'll find okra, prickly pears, swiss chard, herbs and *kohngasi* (similar to yam or sweet potato), plus olives in huge vats. An in-house bakery churns out baklava, delicious fresh breads and moreish pastries. There are fresh meats and poultry, savouries and sweets and an enormous range of spices, pulses and nuts, along with apple tea, Turkish delight, and a host of other traditional products, including a selection of rosewater and colognes. **Branches** throughout the city.

Lina Stores

FOOD & DRINK

Drink

Wine

Bedales

5 Bedale Street, SE1 9AL (7403 8853, www.bedales wines.com). London Bridge tube/rail. **Open** 10am-10pm Mon, Tue; 10am-11pm Wed- Fri; 9am-11pm Sat; 10am-7pm Sun.

Wine retailing runs in the bloodstreams of the two families that own Bedales. Their shops offer a globe-trotting list of uniformly high quality, and they sell it with pride and enthusiasm. The attraction is the opportunity to try the wines in combination with simple and immaculately sourced food, from cheese plates to charcuterie. The corkage on every bottle is fixed at £8: the higher you go the better the bargain. While Bedales will admit to favouring Italian and French wines, it stocks and has tastings of wines from around the world, including those harder-to-find wines that you might not be able to source yourself.

Branches 55 Leadenhall Market, EC3V 1LT (7929 3536); 12 Market Street, E1 6DT (7375 1926).

Lea & Sandeman

Berry Bros & Rudd

3 St James's Street, SW1A 1EG (7396 9600, www.bbr.com). Green Park tube. **Open** 9am-6pm Mon-Fri; 10am-4pm Sat.

Visit Berry at least once, just to sniff the history. The company has been selling wine here since William III was king (that's late 17th century, for anyone not up on their history), and the cellars are ancient. Berry's impressive list of discerning patrons includes Lord Byron, William Pitt and Queen Elizabeth II (though probably not personally), all drawn by the heady atmosphere, highly knowledgeable staff and consistently high-quality wines – the shop excels at the traditional favourites of the well heeled, although with prices to match. There's ample choice under £10, however, and its own-label wines (clarets especially) are superb. And despite the shop's heritage (and appealingly creaky floorboards), the brand makes an effort to stay completely up to date with innovations in the wine trade.

Borough Wines

67 Wilton Way, E8 1BG (7923 2001, www.borough wines.com). Hackney Central rail. **Open** 2-10pm Mon-Fri; 10am-10pm Sat; 11am-8pm Sun.

From Borough Market, where it still has a stall (Wed-Sat), to the Borough of Hackney; Borough Wines opened a second London branch in Wilton Way near London Fields in 2011, a third on Dalston Lane (complete with wine bar) and a fourth in Stoke Newington in 2012. At the Wilton Way branch the charming, work-in-progress decor reflects its surroundings well, as does the environmental friendliness: buy an empty 75cl bottle for £2.50 and fill it from barrels of own-label red, white or rosé for £5. Quality takes precedence over economy here – and you'll need to part with a minimum of £10 to get the best value – but the knowledgeable staff ensure it's money well spent. Although France dominates the bins (the owners hail from there), there are a good few New World and Lebanese bottles too.

Branches 163 Church Street, N16 0UL (7923 7722); **L'Entrepot** 230 Dalston Lane, E8 1LA (7249 1176).

Lea & Sandeman

170 Fulham Road, SW10 9PR (7244 0522, www.leaandsandeman.co.uk). Gloucester Road tube. **Open** 10am-8pm Mon-Sat.

Lea & Sandeman – declared 'wine merchant of the year' by the International Wine Challenge every year since 2009 – is so good, you may not know where to start. Founders Charles Lea and the late Patrick Sandeman only bought wines that really excited them, whether a Vin de Pays d'Oc or a £60 red Burgundy. This refreshing emphasis on drinkability, as opposed to prestige, continues. Here, Europe is king, but the coverage is global, and there's always the same attention paid to good buying. What's more, the prices are far lower than you would expect for this part of town, and the modern, airy

FOOD & DRINK

Shop Talk
Corinna at Borough Wines

Tell us about the shop
Borough Wines was originally set up in 2002 at Borough Market by Muriel Chatel to sell wines from her family vineyard. It has since grown to several shops and one bar/restaurant, carrying carefully selected wines from small producers from all over the world, plus we sell our wines wholesale to restaurants, bars and delis.

What's special about it?
We have had great success with our barrel refill system, guaranteeing good wine at £5 per bottle, making good wine accessible for all.

Who are your customers?
We have a wide range of customers, from the wine connoisseur keen to try our latest discoveries to customers trying our refills for the first time.

What are your favourite shops in London?
We have just placed our first Borough Wines corner with our friends at Treacle in Columbia Road, so now you can buy one of their wonderful cakes, a lovely bottle of wine and an interesting art object all under one roof – a fantastic one-stop shop.

What's the best thing about owning/ working in a shop?
Meeting all our lovely customers on a daily basis, working with – such a wonderful Borough Wines team and hearing that familiar clink of a refill bottle coming down the street.

FOOD & DRINK

shop is a highly pleasant space in which to browse. It's no wonder that so many critics regard L&S as the finest wine shop in London.

Branches 167 Chiswick High Road, W4 2DR (8995 7355); 211 Kensington Church Street, W8 7LX (7221 1982); 51 High Street, SW13 9LN (8878 8643).

Roberson

348 Kensington High Street, W14 8NS (7371 2121, www.robersonwinemerchant.co.uk). High Street Kensington tube or Kensington (Olympia) tube/rail. **Open** 10am-8pm Mon-Sat; noon-6pm Sun.
Roberson is a Kensington institution, providing an affluent clientele with a gobsmacking selection, heavily dominated by France, but stretching across the world (the Italian, Spanish and North American sections are especially noteable). Bordeaux and Burgundy account for well over a third of the still wines, with champagne in abundance and smaller offerings from the Loire and the Rhône at similarly exalted levels. The shop prides itself on its friendly, clued-up and passionate staff and its eclectic decor, making it the perfect antidote to the frequently bland experience of buying wine on the high street. If you love France, and you want something special, Roberson is a top choice in west London.

The Sampler

266 Upper Street, N1 2UQ (7226 9500, www.the sampler.co.uk). Highbury & Islington tube/rail. **Open** 11.30am-9pm Mon-Sat; 11.30am-7pm Sun.

The Sampler is unique in London: a shop where you can taste 80 wines out of the 1,500 on offer. You buy a card (minimum £10), then use it to buy 25ml, 50ml and 75ml tastes. Samples cost from 30p to £10-plus for the costliest bottles. The wines are terrific at every level and are sourced from around the globe (France to the USA), including offerings from Greece and India. The wine sampling 'machines' are arranged by grape and the 80 wines are on rotation every two weeks so that, eventually, you'll get to try them all. There are around 100 under £10 and the upper reaches include mature classics. The shop has a list of awards as long as its wine list, including *Harpers'* 'Best Independent Wine Merchant'.

Branch 35 Thurloe Place, SW7 2HP (7225 5091).

Spirits

Gerry's

74 Old Compton Street, W1D 4UW (7734 4215, www.gerrys.uk.com). Leicester Square or Piccadilly Circus tube. **Open** 9am-6.30pm Mon-Thur; 9am-7.30pm Fri; 9am-6.30pm Sat; noon-6pm Sun.

A London institution with a warehouse-worth of spirits packed into its tiny Soho quarters. It has all the names you know, and dozens that you don't, including 200 vodkas, 250 rums, 200 whiskies and 120 tequilas. And its selection of oddities is unrivalled. English elderflower vodka? Armenian brandy? The fun is in the browsing. Pop into Gerry's and chances are it'll be some kind of

Beer Boutique

occasion: there are regular in-store tastings, celebrity bottle signings (Ron Jeremy, for example) and a guest specialist server on Friday evenings to give you top tips on how to make the most of your purchases.

Milroy's of Soho

3 Greek Street, W1D 4NX (7437 2385, www. milroys.co.uk). Tottenham Court Road tube. **Open** 10am-7pm Mon-Sat.
Founded in the 1960s, Milroy's is a whisky-lover's heaven. The range is enormous, with around 400 from Scotland alone. There's a large selection from £14.95, but fine and rare whiskies can cost up to £2,500, including some of Milroy's own bottlings. Other spirits are covered too, with carefully selected Cognac, Armagnac, gins and rums – the brand launched its first own-brand single cask rum (from the Four Square distillery in Barbados) in spring 2010. What's more, staff are knowledgeable and enthusiastic, and the shop runs regular tasting events for those looking to improve their knowledge and appreciation of whisky. Milroy's started life as a wine merchant and wine remains an important part of the operation; the brand is now part of the Jeroboams group of wine merchants.

Tea & coffee

Algerian Coffee Stores

52 Old Compton Street, W1V 6PB (7437 2480, www.algcoffee.co.uk). Leicester Square, Piccadilly Circus or Tottenham Court Road tube. **Open** 9am-7pm Mon-Wed; 9am-9pm Thur, Fri; 9am-8pm Sat.
Unassumingly nestled in the heart of Soho, the Algerian Coffee Stores has traded from its Old Compton Street site for over 120 years and still looks more or less the same. The range of coffees here is improbably large, with a high number of house blends alongside single-origin beans, flavoured beans, rarities and Fairtrade coffees. If you can't decide, opt for the expertly chosen monthly offers, one high roast and one medium roast, a steal at £6/500g. There are also some serious teas and brewing hardware. If you're just passing by, the take-away option is the best coffee deal in London: £1 for an espresso, and not much more for a cappuccino or latte; both delicious, and both available with an extra shot for no extra charge.

Camden Coffee Shop

11 Delancey Street, NW1 7NL (7387 4080). Camden Town or Mornington Crescent tube. **Open** 9.30am-5.30pm Mon-Wed, Fri; 9.30am-2.30pm Thur; 10am-5pm Sat. **No credit cards**.
The Camden Coffee Shop started more than 30 years ago and stepping through the door is like stepping back in time. The roasting and grinding of the beans are done

SIX
Places for beer

Real Ale Shop

371 Richmond Road, Twickenham, Middx TW1 2EF (8892 3710, www.realale.com). St Margarets rail.
This shop sells a compact but outstanding sampling – around 150 beers, ales, ciders and perries – taking in Europe and the USA. Come with a jug (or use one of theirs) and leave with four pints of the daily changing cask beer.

Beer Boutique

134 Upper Richmond Road, SW15 2SP (8780 3168, www.thebeerboutique.co.uk). East Putney tube.
Beer Boutique has a carefully selected range of Trappist, Belgian, fruit and pilsner beers; London ales are well represented too.

City Beverage Company

303 Old Street, EC1V 9IA (7729 2111, www.citybeverage.co.uk). Old Street tube/rail.
Handily placed for all those BYO Vietnamese restaurants is this Hoxton off-licence. All its beer is kept in the fridge, including ales from the Kernal and Redchurch breweries.

Drink of Fulham

349 Fulham Palace Road, SW6 6TB (7610 6795, www.drinkoffulham.com). Fulham Broadway tube.
Visit for an exceptional range of brews (more than 500) from around the world.

Kris Wines

394 York Way, N7 9LW (7607 4871, www.kriswines.com). Caledonian Road tube.
Ales are arranged by country of origin and range from Odell's 90 Shilling Ale (from the States) to bottles from Manchester's Marble Brewery.

Utobeer

Unit 24, Middle Road, SE1 1TL (7378 6617). London Bridge tube/rail.
This stall/shop in Borough Market sells hundreds of different beers from all over the world (Tue-Sat only), including London breweries.

on the premises by owner George Constantinou, who prides himself on making coffee blends for each individual customer according to their taste and constitution. Using his original machines, George sticks to a small range of ten coffees at a time. Prices are low, and the atmosphere is low-key. The shop is a treasure; a lovely little bit of old London and, happily, there are no plans for that to change any time soon.

HR Higgins

79 Duke Street, W1K 5AS (7629 3913, www.hrhiggins.co.uk). Bond Street tube. **Open** 9.30am-6pm Mon-Fri; 10am-6pm Sat.
Established in 1942, HR Higgins is a family-run firm that has a deep commitment to quality in both fine teas and coffee. Teas include some Chinese rarities alongside a full range of both loose tea and teabags. Prices are on the steep side, as you would expect from a holder of a

Postcard Teas

royal warrant (for coffee) operating in Mayfair. A list of the coffees available, from an after-dinner blend to *yirga chefe* produced by the Oromia cooperative in Ethiopia, can be found on the website and ordered online. A range of accessories is also available. Enjoy a cup of fine tea or coffee in the café downstairs (which shuts half an hour before the shop closes).

Monmouth Coffee House

27 Monmouth Street, WC2H 9EU (7379 3516, www.monmouthcoffee.co.uk). Covent Garden or Tottenham Court Road tube. **Open** 8am-6.30pm Mon-Sat.
Founded 30 years ago, Monmouth sets itself daunting standards for quality and ethical trading, and meets them consistently. This is pre-eminently a place for single-estate and co-operative coffees. You'll always be able to find a good Kenyan coffee here, and Central and South America are represented by excellent ranges. Founder Anita Le Roy is an industry leader in the campaign to help growers improve quality and earn higher prices. This original shop-café in Covent Garden is a cosy spot; the Borough space is larger and serves fabulously moreish cakes and savouries to enjoy with your brew, while the training site (Unit 3, Arches Northside, between Dockley Road and Spa Road) is open to the public from 8am to noon on Saturdays as part of a new off-shoot of the foodies' haven that is Maltby Street Market.
Branch 2 Park Street, SE1 9AB (7940 9960).

Postcard Teas

9 Dering Street, W1S 1AG (7629 3654, www.postcardteas.com). Bond Street or Oxford Circus tube. **Open** 10.30am-6.30pm Mon-Sat.
Tim d'Offey lives for tea: he spent a decade travelling to far-flung estates across Asia before opening the diminutive Postcard Teas in an 18th-century Mayfair building. The shop takes pride in its support for high-quality estates in Sri Lanka, India, China, Japan and elsewhere, and the simply furnished tea room is a Zen-like sanctuary from the world outside. You can sit and have a pot at the communal tasting table to help you choose. d'Offey suggests that tea is best enjoyed without milk and sugar, but there are no rigid rules. In the past, we've enjoyed the boldness of 'big smoke' (black tea leaves smoked over cinnamon wood and blended with darjeeling), which is outstanding for its clarity and warm spicy aroma. Equally notable is blossom tea, made with flowers from coffee bushes (which bloom for a day or so twice a year) blended with a variety of silver-needle white tea, for a supremely delicate brew. Chinese oolong teas are a shop speciality. And for those who'd like to learn to be more discerning when it comes to the nation's favourite pick-me-up, there are tea tastings at 10am on Saturday mornings. Teapots are also for sale, tending towards Asian aesthetics rather than traditional English styles.

Babies & Children

EXPLORE FROM THE INSIDE OUT

Time Out Guides written by local experts

Our London city guides are written from a unique insiders' perspective
by teams of local writers covering all you need to know about life in the capital

visit timeout.com/store

'UNSURPASSABLE'
The Times

Babies & Children

It pays to stray from central London for the best children's shops. While the department stores and the chains are certainly worth a gander, the most exciting shops for babies and children are neighbourhood independent ones. Their welcoming community feel, with pinboards and play areas, and a certain sense of 'we're in this child-rearing lark together' make them more sympathetic to the tentative parent.

One the most family-friendly neighbourhood high streets is Northcote Road, between Wandsworth and Clapham Commons. These days, however, its independence is increasingly compromised by chains, and the little locals are being squeezed out.

Stoke Newington would appear to be the new Nappy Valley with, it is averred, more buggies per square mile than anywhere else in London, and home to the excellent **Born** (*see p264*), as well as **Olive Loves Alfie** (*see p266*). Not far away, in Newington Green, is retro-themed children's shop **Three Potato Four** (*see p263*), selling goods that will appeal almost as much to adults as it will their offspring. Another hotspot for classic and old-school toys is **Benjamin Pollock's Toy Shop** (*see p268*), with branches in Covent Garden and Fitzrovia.

Looking to the western side of town, Notting Hill also puts on a good spread. Tucked away in the Portobello Green shopping arcade, a little independent boutique, **Sasti** (*see p267*) has been keeping west London tots looking adorable on a budget since 1995. Don't miss it. Another sweet thing at the business end of Notting Hill is **Honeyjam** (*see p268*), a toyshop run by a pair of women well known in the fashion world and having a lot of fun in the toy one. More expensive, but undoubtedly cool and distinctive, the clothes at **Caramel** (*see p265*) are a big draw.

London's children's shops excel when it comes to eco-friendly, synthetic-free products. For nursery equipment that's all pure and natural, the allergy-free **Natural Mat Company** (*see p264*) ensures quiet nights all round. The baby and toddler clothes at **Aravore** (*see p265*), meanwhile, are all made from organic fabrics. And **Born** (*see p264*) has a big range of green toiletries for both mother and child.

Note that many of the city's bookshops have excellent children's book departments. Of particular note are local bookshops such as the **Big Green Bookshop** (*see p184*), the **Owl Bookshop** (*see p187*), **Tales on Moon Lane** (*see p268*) and **Victoria Park Books** (*see p268*); head to antiquarian bookseller **Marchpane** (*see p193*) for collectible versions of the classics.

For a more extensive selection of London shops for babies and children, get hold of a copy of Time Out's *London for Children* guide.

Babies & Children

All-rounders & gifts

Couverture & the Garb Store (*see p35*) also
carries babies' and children's fashions of pleasing
originality, including hand-knits from the likes of
Lilly Marthe Ebener.

Bob & Blossom
*140 Columbia Road, E2 7RG (7739 4737, www.
bobandblossom.com). Hoxton rail.* **Open** 9am-3pm
Sun.
Bob among the blossoms of Columbia Road flower market on a Sunday to trick out or treat the tot in your life.
Toys are of the retro variety that parents want to leave
around artfully on distressed floorboards: spinning tops,
knitted dogs, vintage cars and wooden bricks. Clothes
are the antidote to supermarket cutie-pie; sturdy hand-
stitched pullovers, romper suits, simple cotton shifts in
nostalgic prints, fine little toddler tees with bold, bright
logos (the skull and crossbones is still a B&B classic).
A perfect shop to visit with proud grandparents and
their wallets.

Buggies & Bikes
*23 Broadway Market, E8 4PH (7241 5382,
www.buggiesandbikes.net). London Fields rail.*
Open 10am-6.30pm Mon-Sat; 11am-5pm Sun.

The most successful children's shops diversify: buying in
to the need for middle-class parents of young children to
congregate and revel in their fecundity. Thus, as well as
stocking a glorious selection of classic toys and tasteful
clothes, this east London landmark runs a rolling programme of toddler play dates, baby massage, mummy
yoga and the rest, so there's never a dull moment, carrying
or bringing up baby. As far as the attractively displayed
stock goes, there are all the classics (Lego, Mary Jane
shoes), plus nostalgic (building bricks, collar button
jumpers) and retro items (pedal cars, print frocks), alongside the must-haves (picture books, fancy dress, coloured
tights and gumboots). There's also a room for hire, which
gives out on to a little garden, perfect for first parties.

Igloo
*300 Upper Street, N1 2TU (7354 7300,
www.iglookids.co.uk). Angel tube or Highbury &
Islington tube/rail.* **Open** 10am-6.30pm Mon-Wed;
9.30am-7pm Thur; 9.30am-6.30pm Fri, Sat; 11am-
5.30pm Sun.
Mother-of-three Karen Bailey's fourth baby has two
London siblings. The shops are all a delight to explore,
and do a fair job of providing everything to wear and
play with under one roof. This, the original branch, has
a hairdressing service for children, as well as a shoe
department, party stuff, dressing up gear and useful
accessories. Little girls can flounce and prance in the very
sticky-outie Angel's Face pettiskirts in a huge range of
colours, or there are more practical sweetie skirts and

Soup Dragon

Three Potato Four

dresses by Tartine et Chocolat and Weekend a la Mer. Shoes include Primigi classics and Hunter wellies or Uggs for a cold snap. Little boys look good enough to eat in tiny cords by Miniature and Petit Bateau. An extensive and imaginative toy collection includes tactile exploratory toys for babies, ride-ons and push-alongs for toddlers, board games, imaginative play kits and garages, farms and forts from distinguished companies such as Le Toy Van.
Branches 80 St John's Wood High Street, NW8 7SH (7483 2332); 227 Kings Road, SW3 5EJ (7352 4572).

Soup Dragon
27 Topsfield Parade, Tottenham Lane, N8 8PT (8348 0224, www.soup-dragon.co.uk). Finsbury Park tube/rail, then bus 41, W7. **Open** 9.30am-6pm Mon-Sat; 11am-5pm Sun.
The name comes from the erstwhile children's programme *The Clangers*, if you're wondering, and establishes this shop as a long runner – over 20 years old now. The East Dulwich branch having closed down, it's up to this handsome Crouch End shop to display the clothes, toys and accessories to their best advantage. It has a play house and a huge range of affordable treasures: dolls houses, games, ride-ons and dressing-up and party accessories. The excellent knitwear by Nikki of Soup Dragon is extremely jolly: fab little crochet-edged cardis for babies, bold striped jumpers and co-ordinates for older children.
Branch 106 Lordship Lane, SE22 8HF (8693 5575).

Three Potato Four
Alliance House, 44-45 Newington Green, N16 9QH (7704 2228, www.threepotatofour.co.uk). Canonbury rail or bus 21, 73, 141, 341, 476. **Open** 10am-5pm Mon-Fri; 9.30am-5pm Sat; 10am-5pm Sun.
Easily the most cheerful shopfront among the little bunch serving the public-spirited Newington Green community, TPF is Genna Sevastio's repository of carefully sourced clothing, homewares, toiletries, toys and books. Unashamedly nostalgic about a childhood in printed cotton and fuelled by picture books and spinning tops, the stock incorporates a healthy proportion of vintage and retro, as well as championing local designers. The premises, which has a children's hairdressing salon lit by a sparkling antique chandelier, is all decked out in reclaimed wood from Sevastio's dad's yard, and looks beautiful. Eye-catching treasures on this visit included colourful Lale Rose suitcases and travel bags, Smafolk baby clothes for small folk, the most adorable sleep suit for babies covered in rodeo cowboys (Hatley) and gorgeous Maileg wooden dolly cots and play kitchen stoves.

Trotters
34 King's Road, SW3 4UD (7259 9620, www.trotters. co.uk). Sloane Square tube. **Open** 9am-7pm Mon-Sat; 10am-6pm Sun.
This is the flagship Trotters. It opened in 1990 and was one of the first to make a Big Occasion out of haircutting for children. The salon, with its fish tank, is still

a draw; if it's your first shearing, you even get a certificate. Like all good all-rounders, it's a pleasure to bring young children to because there's plenty to distract and the staff are well versed in children's little ways when it comes to shoe-fitting, fringe-snipping, clothes-trying and releasing sticky little mits from toys not paid for. Lollipops can be dispensed (with parents' permission, natch). Toys stay on the traditional side: model cars, wooden play things by Le Toy Van, tea sets and really lovely craft equipment (gouache paints, modelling clay by Djeco). The clothes are sturdy and stylish (we like the rather little-manly Thomas Brown label for lads), with reliable quality labels such as Lily Rose and Confiture. Best of all are the accessories and back-to-school essentials. This is a great place to come for your trendy lunch pack, your pencil case and sticker collection, your shiny new shoes and, er, your nit shampoo. There are five other London branches; including one at Westfield London.
Branches throughout the city.

Equipment & accessories

Blue Daisy
13 South End Road, NW3 2PT (7681 4144, www.blue-daisy.com). Hampstead Heath tube/rail. **Open** 9.30am-5.30pm Mon-Fri; 10am-6pm Sat; 11.30am-5pm Sun.
Fab for mewlers and pukers and just-about-to weaners, Blue Daisy has become a bit of a lifeline for first time parents in the area. The stock runs the gamut from super practical (check the £5.99 baby cubes for little puréed portions of lovingly prepared first grub) to just super (Manduco and Ergo carrier backpacks, £99). When it comes to the confusing field of baby and toddler equipment, it's all about knowing what's out there – and what's essential – and the miraculously knowledgeable staff in this shop will tell you. Blue Daisy is also renowned for its skin friendly organic bath-time toiletries and simple, attractive toys. And it's a fun place to be if you're knee high to a grasshopper too: children make straight for the toys alcove to play with the traditional wooden cookers by Tiny Love.
Branch 190 West End Lane, NW6 1SG (7435 3100).

Born
168 Stoke Newington Church Street, N16 0JL (7249 5069, www.borndirect.com). Stoke Newington rail/bus 73, 393, 476. **Open** 9.30am-5pm Tue-Fri; 10am-5.30pm Sat; noon-5pm Sun.
There's nothing like revelling in your Happy Event, and Born is dedicated to those new parents who intend making the most of every aspect of those heady pre-and post-parturition weeks. Whether having your 'baby head' on makes you more profligate with your credit card is of course a moot point, but let's not be cynical, Born

is a delightful place to come with your massive bump, then with your mother's pride snoozing in its ERGO baby sling (available here, of course). Pregnancy products, baby equipment, toys and clothes, mostly with an organic, renewable or Fairtrade bent, are sold and the range is impressive. There are any number of sling and baby-carrying combos; the Moby wraps are perfect for tiny slumberers. Then there are the baby and toddler clothes from the likes of Green Baby, Lille Barn, Imps and Elfs and the wonderful Kidschase. We also rate the silk seamless nursing bra very highly. As well as having a squashy sofa for feeding babies and plenty of space for playing ones, there's a regular roster of pregnancy and parenting get-togethers and courses, held throughout the year (see the website for details).

Dragons of Walton Street
23 Walton Street, SW3 2HX (7589 3795, www.dragonsofwaltonstreet.com). Knightsbridge or South Kensington tube. **Open** 10am-6pm Mon-Sat.
When the late Rosie Fisher started this business 30 years ago she was originally intending to run an antiques shop. The nursery furniture she designed and painted as a sideline grabbed all the passing trade, however, and Dragons became the most fashionable place to deck out the kids' bedrooms. Madonna and Gwyneth Paltrow ordered some furniture in the first flushes of motherhood. Now Fisher's daughter, Lucinda Croft, runs the show and the business booms on. People are commissioning whole houses-worth of stuff. The hand-painted furniture for the nursery comes with all sorts of child favourites: bunnies, boats, soldiers, fairies, pirate mice and vintage roses, and, more recently, the splendid girl and rabbit combo Belle and Boo. Customers are also encouraged to come up with their own ideas for designs. Dragons, on genteel Walton Street amid a host of other posh children's shops, is a pleasant place to visit; staff are friendly, the mood relaxed and personal service is guaranteed.

Natural Mat Company
99 Talbot Road, W11 2AT (7985 0474, www.natural mat.co.uk). Ladbroke Grove or Notting Hill Gate tube. **Open** 10am-6pm Mon-Fri; 11am-5pm Sat.
Layers of organic coconut fibre, lambswool and natural latex are hand-stitched into organic cotton ticking to make mattresses that even the pea princess would slumber on. Parents who invest in cot mattresses and natural lambs' fleeces from this Devonshire company say their children sleep soundly and comfortably. This commitment to a toxin-free nursery environment extends to sleeping bags by Merino Kids and Organics for Kids (the one covered in little green frogs is super), which come in a variety of stripes and patterned designs in lightweight organic cotton or cotton fleece for winter. There are also organic baby clothes, including sweet merino pyjamas and toys, Welsh wool blankets and

West Country willow cribs with leather handles. Adult mattresses and bedding are also sold.

Rub a Dub Dub

15 Park Road, N8 8TE (8342 9898). Archway tube then bus 41 or Finsbury Park tube/rail then bus W7. **Open** 10am-5.30pm Mon-Sat; 11.30am-4.30pm Sun.
Everything for the tub – baby bath, sponges, soft towels – on sale here is eco-friendly if not organic. Then, once baby is bathed and dressed, there are all kinds of modish ways to wheel her about: in a Mountain Buggy or a Phil & Ted buggy or, if you prefer, carry her in a backpack or sling. Little Life Backpacks are the business here. Then there are the accessories and toys: bestsellers when we called were the Melissa & Doug range of wooden educational toys, particularly the wooden bead sets.

Fashion

Many shops listed in the **Maternity** chapter also sell baby togs; **Blossom Mother & Child** is a good bet for baby clothes. *See pp112-113.*

Aravore Babies

31 Park Road, N8 8TE (8347 5752, www.aravore-babies.com). Archway tube then bus 41 or Finsbury Park tube/rail then bus W7. **Open** 10am-5.30pm Mon-Sat; noon-4pm Sun.
The soft, luxurious clothes and accessories for babies and children up to six years old are made from organic, Fairtrade cotton and merino wool and are highly praised by the mumsnet generation. Seasonal collections are always just the chic side of traditional in colours not usu-ally seen on the high street, such as deep plum, navy, cream and grey. Most coveted are the glorious wool coats for wee girls, but the superbly understated dresses and jumpers are lovely too. New parents are delighted by the shawls, blankets and other pieces for stylish baby swaddling. Aravore fashions find their way into many of the best all-rounder shops listed in these pages.

Caramel Baby & Child

77 Ledbury Road, W11 2AG (7727 0906, www.caramel-shop.co.uk). Notting Hill Gate or Westbourne Park tube. **Open** 10am-6pm Mon-Sat; 11am-5pm Sun.
This highly appreciated brand started by former lawyer Eva Karayiannis eschews the cutesie-pie and label-trendy but is instantly recognisable for its tasteful styling and a certain sturdiness. Karayiannis designs her pieces to be functional and fun. Colours are varied and unusual: belted woollen coats for winter in pea green contrast with lambswool jumpers in oatmeal, over the classic Marni print shirt. Accessories include shoes, hats, hair ties and toys, sourced from carefully chosen smaller brands that are constantly changing. Children's haircuts are done on-site on a Tuesday – ring for an appointment – as well as at the Pavilion Road branch. In addition to the branches listed below, there is a Caramel concession in Selfridges. **Branches** 259 Pavilion Road, SW1X 0BP (7730 2564); 291 Brompton Road, SW3 2DY (7589 7001).

Gently Elephant

169 Brockley Road, SE4 2RS (8692 2881, www.gentlyelephant.co.uk). Brockley rail. **Open** 10am-5pm Mon, Tue, Thur, Fri; 9am-5pm Sat; by appointment Wed, Sun.

Rub a Dub Dub

Sasti

It's high time this increasingly yummified area of south-east London had its own children's wear shop. Gently Elephant specialises in 'shoes and stuff' – sizes in footwear go up to adult size six in some cases. The back wall of the big, bright space is dedicated to baby shoes by Bobux and its Step-Up range for when toddlers start toddling, then there are Geox, Pediped, Start-rite, Bloch for ballet shoes and Toughies for gumboots in bright colours (including ones in Elmer elephant checks). There's a pleasantly spacious trying-on area, with reclaimed velvet-topped benches for children to sit on. When feet have been measured and toys and books perused (there's a well-chosen collection of both on sale), the children can have fun making camps in the big wooden tipi while parents unearth the credit card.

Oh Baby London

162 Brick Lane, E1 6RU (7247 4949, www.ohbaby london.com). Shoreditch High Street rail. **Open** 10am-6pm daily.

A Brick Lane destination that's really off the wall. We love the witty legends on the T-shirts and onesies for little kids at Oh Baby. The famous 'been inside for 9 months' stripy playsuit is still a bestseller; other jaunty lines include a sweatshirt bearing the legend 'I'm the man', and a cute leopard-print dress for tiny babes (and girls up to age six). Other lively numbers for children from zero to six include great little leopard-print hats and bibs, cool striped pinafore dresses and welcome baby newborn kits. Take a while to read Oh Baby founder Hannah's blog; it's mostly very jolly but includes some justifiable outrage about the iniquities of marketing aimed at junior fashion victims.

Olive Loves Alfie

84 Stoke Newington Church Street, N16 0AP (7241 4212, www.olivelovesalfie.co.uk). Stoke Newington rail or bus 73, 393, 476. **Open** 10am-6pm Mon-Sat; 10am-5pm Sun.

There are few things more delightful than a chubby baby in a playsuit covered in penguins, which is just one of the many glorious, original designs of tiny apparel on sale here. This 'family lifestyle store' is a very aesthetically pleasing babywear and nursery shop. Bestsellers include Katvig and Mini Rodini in the clothing department, and then there are the imaginative gifty things such as the award-winning range from White Rabbit England; they're large fine white bone china lights in the shape of dogs or rabbits, big enough to stand on the floor and glow comfortably – just gorgeous. The block-printed bedding by Lulu and Nat, with flowers and butterflies, is also appealing. Olive Loves Alfie has a range of toxin-free interior paint in non gender-specific colours (no more pink, blue or primrose nursery misery); it's by the Nursery Paint Company and made to a secret recipe free of Volatile Organic Compounds (VOCs), using colloidal silver to give the paint anti-bacterial qualities.

One Small Step One Giant Leap

3 Blenheim Crescent, W11 2EE (7243 0535, www.onesmallsteponegiantleap.com). Ladbroke Grove or Notting Hill Gate tube. **Open** 10am-6pm Mon-Fri; 9am-6pm Sat; 11am-5pm Sun.

All the major brands, from sensible Start-rite to the latest in slipper cool from Moccis (hand-made moccasin socks from Sweden) are attractively displayed in this, one of the original branches in a pioneering chain of child-centred shoe shops. With space for all the essentials for school, beach, puddles, hiking and a whole catalogue of more frivolous fashion brands (Armani, Juicy Couture, John Galliano, Ralph Lauren), parents are bound to find something that children want and, more importantly, that fits properly. The latter prerequisite is guaranteed courtesy of OSSOGL's unstinting belief in the original Brannock Device®, which was invented in 1927 and is still considered the best for accuracy and functionality. It's good to see that it's not always the computerised bells-and-whistles methods that win out in the end.

Branches throughout the city.

Sasti

6 Portobello Green Arcade, 281 Portobello Road, W10 5TZ (8960 1125, www.sasti.co.uk). Ladbroke Grove tube. **Open** 10am-6pm Mon-Sat; noon-5pm Sun.

Unusual but affordable fashions for babies and children up to eight keep the parents flocking back to find standout gear for their little ones. Much of the stock comprises the designs of two women, Rose Carpenter (label: R.Life) and Julie Taft (label: Ten Fingers Ten Toes), who have been making simply appealing dresses, skirts, trousers and shirts for many years. Bestsellers for girls are the red gingham *Calamity Jane*-style Prairie Girl Blouse and the loose, dreamy, cloud-covered corduroy shift for girls. Boys can have their cords with suedette rabbits and foxes peeking out around the shin, teamed with little waistcoats to complete the understated, but a little bit folk, look.

Toys, games & books

Toys and trinkets can often be found in lifestyle shops and concept stores; *see pp33-41. See also pp184-193* **Books**.

Gently Elephant. See p265.

Benjamin Pollock's Toy Shop

44 The Market, Covent Garden, WC2E 8RF (7379 7866, www.pollocks-coventgarden.co.uk). Covent Garden tube. **Open** 10.30am-6pm Mon-Wed, Fri, Sat; 10.30am-7pm Thur; 11am-4pm Sun.

This independent toyshop is a London institution – it's brilliant that it holds on to its perch in Covent Garden Market while so much around it changes. The shop's stock is mostly devoted to the Pollock's brand of toy theatre ('juvenile drama, a penny plain, twopence coloured'). The cardboard theatres cost a bit more than pennies these days, but they're still extraordinarily good value. Little pieces are about a fiver and the all-new toy theatre based on Charles Dickens's *Great Expectations* is £15. Most covetable is the Praxinoscope, a sort of spinning drum shape first patented by Emile Reynaud in 1877, which reveals animated pictures in the mirrors when you set it going. As well as all these theatricals you have a plethora of traditional toys, including china and tin tea sets, paper planes, finger puppets and music boxes.

Hamleys

188-196 Regent Street, W1B 5BT (0871 704 1977, www.hamleys.com). Oxford Circus tube. **Open** 10am-9pm Mon-Fri; 9.30am-9pm Sat; noon-6pm Sun.

Times are a-changing for humungous Hamleys, the 250-year-old institution and self-proclaimed 'finest toyshop in the world': it has been sold to a French retailer for a rumoured price of about £60 million. The new owners promise that none of its rowdy charm, or as they put it 'magical spirit' will diminish – which may disappoint those parents who find it all a bit much – but that the store will become more of a worldwide brand. Meanwhile the regular school-holiday events for children continue (Hello Kitty was in when we visited) and the five floors bristle with all the must-have toys of the moment, with perky demonstrators showing off certain wares on every one. You'll be lucky if you can spend less than an hour in here if you're accompanied by children. There's much to see – and eat – with a sweet shop, a cupcake store and a milkshake café all thrown into the mix to guarantee a nauseous bus ride home.

Honeyjam

2 Blenheim Crescent , W11 1NN (7243 0449, www.honeyjam.co.uk). Ladbroke Grove tube. **Open** 10am-6pm Mon-Sat; 11am-5pm Sun.

Honeyjam is full of fun, and has a strong line in vintage playthings: seeing the nostalgic box design of the magnetic fishing game (£9.99) sent us right back to the glory days before kids went digital. It's a wonderful, colourful, riotously stocked shop, full of posh young families with their tow-haired chicks. There are some seriously gorgeous role-playing toys, such as le Toy Van's oven and hob set. Most eye-catching are the shelves of pocket-money priced trinkets and sweeties all crowded into jars

and dangling off the wooden dressers. All sorts of playthings from past (space hoppers) to present (make your own lip balm) are ripe to discover, among the more traditional tea sets, tiddlywinks, anatomically correct dolls, forts and dragon castles.

Puppet Planet

787 Wandsworth Road (corner of the Chase), SW8 3JQ (7627 0111, mobile 07900 975276, www.puppetplanet.co.uk). Clapham Common tube. **Open** 8am-8pm daily; also by appointment.

A specialist marionette shop hung with mysterious marionettes, classic Pelham puppets with jointed limbs and easy-to-work strings, glove puppets, puppet-making kits, cardboard puppet theatres and Balinese shadow puppets. The shop is not always open, because sometimes it's the unusual venue for a party, or a puppet making workshop, or sometimes the proprietor is out on a puppet-related mission. Ring, therefore, before you visit.

Tales on Moon Lane

25 Half Moon Lane, SE24 9JU (7274 5759, www.talesonmoonlane.co.uk). Herne Hill rail. **Open** 9am-5.45pm Mon-Fri; 10am-6pm Sat; 10.20am-4.30pm Sun.

Winner of Walker Books' gong for Independent Book Retailer of the Year in 2011 (and the manager scooped Young Bookseller of the year while he was at it), Tales is a fine way to turn your little browsers into bookworms. It's immensely welcoming; small children can sit on cushions and read a story, or they can come to Thursday storytelling sessions. The owner keeps bang up to date with new titles, holds frequent local author events (check the website) and puts together must-have book bundles as brilliant christening gifts for very early readers. New parents receive their child's first book free in a scheme run in conjunction with the National Childbirth Trust and Usborne Books.

Victoria Park Books

174 Victoria Park Road, E9 7HD (8986 1124, www.victoriaparkbooks.co.uk). Cambridge Heath or London Fields rail or bus 277. **Open** 10am-5.30pm daily.

This friendliest of bookshops is the hub of the Victoria Park community and runs plenty of reading-related events, for all the family. Adults and teens are catered for, but the richest variety of stock is reserved for children. The owners have set out to make the store reflect local tastes and interests, with particular strength in catering to the curriculum requirements of nearby schools. Books are categorised by look and feel as well as content – there's a section for interactive titles, and children can get their hands on cloth, bath and buggy books. There are storytelling sessions for parents and pre-schoolers on Fridays at 11am.

BABIES & CHILDREN

Indexes
& Maps

A-Z Index

A-Z INDEX

La Fromagerie p245
2-6 Moxton Street, W1U
4EW (7935 0341, www.
lafromagerie.co.uk). Food

La Fromagerie
30 Highbury Park, N5
2AA (7359 7440).
Branch

F-Troup p116
33 Marshall Street,
W1F 7ET (7494 4566,
www.f-troupe.com). Shoes

Fur Coat No Knickers p108
www.furcoatnoknickers.
co.uk. Weddings

G

Gallery 1930 p174
18 Church Street,
NW8 8EP (7723 1555).
Vintage Furniture &
Homewares

Ganesha p36
3-4 Gabriel's Wharf, 56
Upper Ground, SE1 9PP
(7928 3444, www.ganesha.
co.uk). Lifestyle Boutiques
& Concept Stores

Ganesha
38 King Street, WC2E
8JT (7240 8068). Branch

Gay's the Word p189
66 Marchmont Street,
WC1N 1AB (7278 7654,
www.gaystheword.co.uk).
Books

G Baldwin & Co p144
171-173 Walworth Road,
SE17 1RW (7703 5550,
www.baldwins.co.uk).
Perfumeries & Herbalists

General Eyewear p146
Arch 67 Stables Market,
NW1 8AH (7428 0123,
www.generaleyewear.com).
Eyewear

Gently Elephant p265
169 Brockley Road, SE4
2RS (8692 2881, www.
gentlyelephant.co.uk).
Babies & Children

Geoffrey Drayton p154
85 Hampstead Road,
NW1 2PL (7387 5840,
www.geoffreydrayton.com).
Furniture & Homewares

Gerry's p256
74 Old Compton Street,
W1D 4UW (7734 4215,
www.gerrys.uk.com). Drink

Giacobazzi's p251
150 Fleet Road, NW3
2QX (7267 7222, www.
giacobazzis.co.uk). Food

Gieves & Hawkes p89
1 Savile Row, W1S 3JR
(7434 2001, www.gieves
andhawkes.com). Tailoring
& Bespoke

Gina Foster p108
www.ginafoster.co.uk.
Weddings

Ginger Pig p244
99 Lauriston Road, E9 7HJ
(8986 6911, www.theginger
pig.co.uk). Food

Ginger Pig
Borough Market, SE1 1TL
(7403 4721). Branch

Ginger Pig
8-10 Moxon Street, W1U
4EW (7935 7788). Branch

Ginger Pig
27 Lower Marsh, SE1 7RG
(7921 2975). Branch

Ginger Pig
137-139 Askew Road, W12
9AU (8740 4297). Branch

The Girl Can't Help It p96
Alfie's Antique Market,
13-25 Church Street,
NW8 8DT (7724 8984,
www.thegirlcanthelpit.com).
Vintage & Secondhand

Goldsboro p189
23-25 Cecil Court, WC2N
4EZ (7497 9230, www.
goldsborobooks.com). Books

Goodhood p55
41 Coronet Street,
N1 6HD (7729 3600,
www.goodhoodstore.com).
Boutiques & Indie Labels

Gosh! p189
1 Berwick Street, W1F 0DR
(7636 1011, www.gosh
london.com). Books

Grahams p205
Unit 1, Canonbury Yard,
190A New North Road,
N1 7BS (7226 5500,
www.grahams.co.uk).
Electronics & Photography

Gramex p199
25 Lower Marsh, SE1 7RJ
(7401 3830). Records & CDs

Green & Stone p209
259 King's Road, SW3 5EL
(7352 0837, www.green
andstone.com). Crafts,
Hobbies & Parties

Green Valley p251
36-37 Upper Berkeley Street,
W1H 5QF (7402 7385). Food

Greenwich Market p48
Off College Approach, SE10
(8269 5096, www.greenwich
market.net). Markets

Gucci p80
18 Sloane Street, SW1X
9NE (7235 6707, www.
gucci.com). International
Designer

H

Hamleys p268
188-196 Regent Street,
W1B 5BT (0871 704 1977,
www.hamleys.com).
Babies & Children

H&M p73
261-271 Regent Street,
W1B 2ES 97493 4004,
www.hm.com). High Street

**Harold Moores
Records** p199
2 Great Marlborough Street,
W1F 7HQ (7437 1576,
www.hmrecords.co.uk).
Records & CDs

Harrods p21
87-135 Brompton Road,
SW1X 7XL (7730 1234,
www.harrods.com).
Department Stores

Harvey Nichols p21
109-125 Knightsbridge,
SW1X 7RJ (7235 5000,
www.harveynichols.com).
Department Stores

Hatchards p186
187 Piccadilly, W1J
9LE (7439 9921, www.
hatchards.co.uk). Books

Heal's p155
196 Tottenham Court Road,
W1T 7LQ (7636 1666,
www.heals.co.uk).
Furniture & Homewares

Heal's
234 King's Road, SW3
5UA (7349 8411). Branch

Heal's
49-51 Eden Street, KT1
1BW (8614 5900) Branch

**Health and Beauty at
Wholefoods** p135
20 Glasshouse Street,
W1B 5AR (7406 3100,
www.wholefoodsmarket.
com). Skin Care & Cosmetics

Heidi Klein p103
174 Westbourne Grove,
W11 2RW (7243 5665,
www.heidiklein.com).
Lingerie, Swimwear & Erotica

Heidi Klein
123-124 The Arcade,
Westfield Stratford City, E20
1EJ (8536 5700). Branch

Henry Poole & Co p89
15 Savile Row, W1S 3PJ
(7734 5985, www.henry
poole.com). Tailoring &
Bespoke

Henry Sotheran p192
2-5 Sackville Street,
W1S 3DP (7439 6151,
www.sotherans.co.uk).
Books

Hetty Rose
www.hettyrose.co.uk.
Weddings

Hideout p61
7 Upper James Street,
W1F 9DH (7437 4929,
www.hideoutstore.com).
Boutiques & Indie Labels

High & Mighty p113
145-147 Edgware Road,
W2 2HR (7723 8754,
www.highandmighty.
co.uk). Maternity &
Unusual Sizes

High & Mighty
The Plaza, 120 Oxford Street,
W1N 9DP (7436 4861).
Branch

High & Mighty
81-83 Knightsbridge,
SW1X 7RB (7752 0665).
Branch

HMV Megastore p194
150 Oxford Street, W1D
1DJ (7631 3423, www.
hmv.com). Records & CDs

A-Z INDEX

A-Z INDEX

Pak's p140
25-27 & 31 Stroud Green
Road, N4 3ES (7263 2088,
www.pakcosmetics.com).
Skincare & Cosmetics

Paperchase p220
213-215 Tottenham Court
Road, W1T 7PS (7467 6200,
www.paperchase.co.uk).
Crafts, Hobbies & Parties

Party Party p219
9-13 Ridley Road, E8 2NP
(7254 5168, www.pp
shop.co.uk). Crafts,
Hobbies & Parties

Party Party
206 Kilburn High Road, NW6
4JH (7624 4295). Branch

Paul & Joe p85
134 Sloane Street, SW1X 9AX
(7824 8844, ww.paulandjoe.
com). International Designer

Paul & Joe Homme
33 Floral Street, WC2 E9DJ
(7836 3388). Branch

**Paul A Young Fine
Chocolates** p247
33 Camden Passage,
N1 8EA (7424 5750,
www.payoung.net). Food

Paul A Young Fine Chocolates
20 Royal Exchange, EC3V
3LP (7929 7007). Branch

Paul A Young Fine Chocolates
143 Wardour Street, W1F
8WA (7437 0011). Branch

Paul Smith p83
Westbourne House, 120 &
122 Kensington Park Road,
W11 2EP (7727 3553,
www.paulsmith.co.uk).
International Designer

Paxton & Whitfield p246
93 Jermyn Street, SW1Y 6JE
(7930 0259, www.paxtonand
whitfield.co.uk). Food

Peanut Vendor p174
133 Newington Green Road,
N1 4RA (7226 5727,
www.thepeanutvendor.
co.uk). Vintage Furniture
& Homewares

Peekaboo p99
2 Ganton Street, W1F 7QL
(7328 9191, www.peekaboo
vintage.com). Vintage &
Second-hand

Pelicans & Parrots p40
40 Stoke Newington Road,
N16 7XJ (3215 2083, www.
pelicansandparrots.com).
Concept Stores & Lifestyle
Boutiques

Pennies p99
41A Amwell Street,
EC1R 1UR (7278 3827,
www.penniesvintage.com).
Vintage & Second-hand

People's Supermarket p251
72-78 Lamb's Conduit Street,
WC1N 3LP (www.peoples
supermarket.org). Food

Persephone Books p190
59 Lamb's Conduit Street,
WC1N 3NB (7242 9292,
www.persephonebooks.
co.uk). Books

Persepolis p253
28-30 Peckham High Street,
SE15 5DT (7639 8007,
www.forataseofpersia.
co.uk). Food

Persiflage p95
Alfies Antique Market, 13-25
Church Street, NW8 8DT
(7723 6066, www.alfies
antiques.com). Vintage &
Second-hand

**Peter Jones
(branch of John Lewis)**
Sloane Square, SW1W
8EL (7730 3434). Branch

Petersham Nurseries p177
Church Lane, off Petersham
Road, Petersham, Richmond,
Surrey TW10 7AG (8940
5230, www.petersham
nurseries.com). Gardens
& Flowers

Petit Aimé (branch of Aimé)
34 Ledbury Road, W11 2AB
(7221 3123). Branch

Petticoat Lane Market p43
Middlesex Street, Goulston
Street, New Goulston Street,
Toynbee Street, Wentworth
Street, Bell Lane, Cobb Street,
Leyden Street, Strype Street,
E1 (7364 1717). Markets

Philip Treacy p125
69 Elizabeth Street, SW1W
9PJ (7730 3992, www.
philiptreacy.co.uk).
Accessories Specialists

Phonica p201
51 Poland Street, W1F 7LZ
(7025 6070, www.phonica
records.co.uk). Records
& CDs

Piccadilly Arcade p32
Between Piccadilly & Jermyn
Street, SW1Y 6NH (7647
3000, www.piccadilly-
arcade.com). Shopping
Centres & Arcades

Pistol Panties p104
75 Westbourne Park Road,
W2 5QH (7229 5286, www.
pistolpanties.com). Lingerie,
Swimwear & Erotica

Pitfield London p156
31-35 Pitfield Street,
N1 6HB (7490 6852,
www.pitfieldlondon.com).
Furniture & Homewares

Plain English p165
41 Hoxton Square,
N1 6PB (7613 0022, www.
plainenglishdesign.co.uk).
Furniture & Homewares

Planet Bazaar p176
Arch 86, The Stables
Market, Chalk Farm Road,
NW1 8AH (7485 6000,
www.planetbazaar.co.uk).
Vintage Furniture &
Homewares

Playlounge p218
19 Beak Street,
W1F 9RP (7287 7073,
www.playlounge.co.uk).
Crafts, Hobbies & Parties

The Pocket Library p108
www.thepocketlibrary.co.uk.
Weddings.

Poilâne p242
46 Elizabeth Street,
SW1W 9PA (7808 4910,
www.poilane.fr). Food

**Portobello Green
Arcade** p32
281 Portobello Road,
under the Westway, W10
5TZ (8960 2277, www.
portobellodesigners.com).
Shopping Centres & Arcades

**Portobello Road
Market** p45
Portobello Road, W10
& W11 (www.portobello
road.co.uk). Markets

Postcard Teas p258
9 Dering Street, W1S 1AG
(7629 3654, www.postcard
teas.com). Drink

Poste Mistress p119
61-63 Monmouth street,
WC2H 9EP (7379 4040,
www.office.co.uk/
postemistress). Shoes

Prada p81
16-18 Old Bond Street,
W1X 3DA (7647 5000,
www.prada.com).
International Designer

Preen p58
5 Portobello Green, 281
Portobello Road, W10 5TZ
(8968 1542, www.preen.
eu). Boutiques & Indie Labels

Present p62
140 Shoreditch High Street,
E1 6JE (7033 0500,
www.present-london.com).
Boutiques & Indie Labels

Press p66
3 Erskine Road, NW3 3AJ
(7449 0081, www.press
primrosehill.com). Boutiques
& Indie Labels

Prestat p248
14 Princes Arcade,
SW1Y 6DS (7494 3772,
www.prestat.co.uk). Food

Pretty Pregnant p113
186 King's Road, SW3 5XP
(7349 7450, www.pretty
pregnant.co.uk). Maternity
& Unusual Sizes.

Pretty Pregnant
102 Northcote Road, SW11
6QW (7924 4850). Branch.

Pretty Pregnant
61 North Cross Road, SE22
9ET (8693 9010). Branch.

Pretty Pregnant
271 Upper Street, N1 2UQ
(7226 9822). Branch.

Prick Your Finger p216
260 Globe Road, E2 0JD
(8981 2560, www.prick
yourfinger.com). Crafts,
Hobbies & Parties

Primrose Hill Pets p238
132 Regent's Park Road,
NW1 8XL (7483 2023,
www.primrosehillpets.
co.uk). Pets

A-Z INDEX

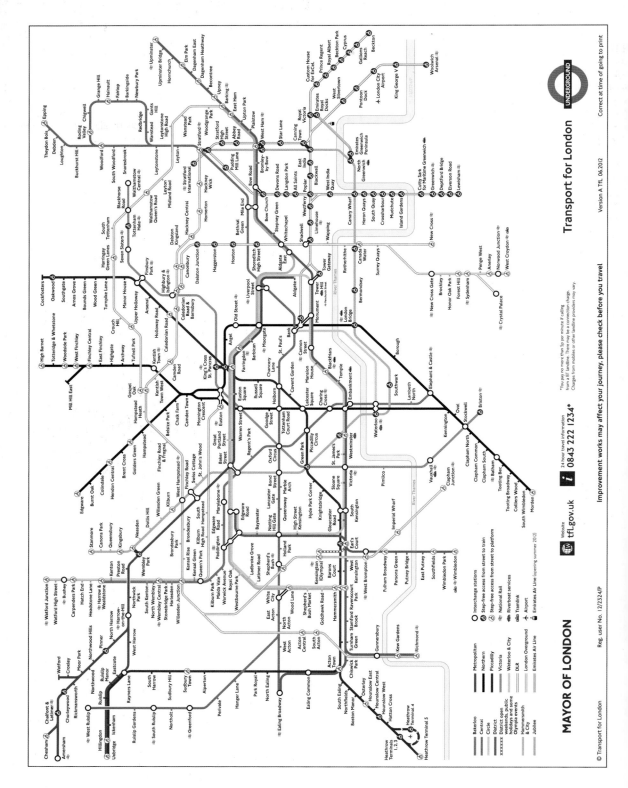

MAYOR OF LONDON

Transport for London